DICTIONARY OF
MUSICAL TERMS

DICTIONARY OF
MUSICAL TERMS

Vincent J. Picerno

HASKELL HOUSE PUBLISHERS Ltd.
Publishers of Scarce Scholarly Books
Brooklyn, NY
1976

HASKELL HOUSE PUBLISHERS LTD.
Publishers of Scarce Scholarly Books
Brooklyn, NY

Library of Congress Cataloging in Publication Data

Picerno, Vincent J
  Dictionary of musical terms.

  1. Music--Terminology.
ML108.P57   780'.3   76-14903
ISBN 0-8383-2119-2

Printed in the United States of America

CONTENTS

PREFACE

This dictionary has been compiled for the college student taking undergraduate courses in music and for the adult or high school student who has a special interest in music. The author was interested not only in a comprehensive dictionary for the music major, but also in providing a quick reference book having an extensive list of musical terms with succinct definitions for the non-music major taking introductory music courses.

One primary difficulty in compiling a dictionary is deciding what to include or exclude. In one volume the problem becomes more acute as space requires that some items be omitted and that definitions be brief. It was decided that names of composers, musicians, and names of musical works be generally excluded as separate entries and that as many musical terms as possible be included which are apt to be used in the undergraduate music courses. These are terms that may be found in readings and in musical scores. The author assumes that the reader comes to any entry with little prior knowledge. The definitions are succinct and the language is simple and easy to read. Not only are the standard musical terms included but also many terms from jazz, contemporary music, electronic music, swing music, etc., which are unusual and unique entries of interest to the high school and college student. However, no dictionary can embrace the whole of music or of any one subject. Therefore, it was decided that a "Selected Annotated Bibliography" be included in order that the reader have access to further information on the subject and to provide him with a source to continue his investigation of an article. The "Selected Annotated Bibliography" is listed, in alphabetical order, under separate categories using the guidelines of the "Library of Congress." The headings are: (1) Analysis, Interpretation, Appreciation; (2) Articles; (3) Bibliography; (4) Church Music; (5) Collections, Music, Addresses, Essays, Lectures, Anthologies, Composers, Musicians; (6) Dictionaries, Encyclopedias, Thematic Catalogs, Analytical Guides;

(7) History and Criticism; (8) Instruction, Study, Manuals; (9) Jazz Music, Folk Music, Popular Music, Musical Revue, Comedy; (10) Musical Instruments, Instrumentation, Orchestration, Conducting; (11) Theory, Composition, Form, Notation. Included are 185 books and articles, most of which are annotated. The separate headings and annotation make it easy for the reader to use this reference list.

The entries are in simple alphabetical order which ignores hyphens and the divisions between separate words. For example, "Abendmusik," "A bene placito," "Abgestossen," follow a strict alphabetical order. Also, the German umlaut is not considered in the alphabetical sequence, for example, the German ä is treated the same as a, not as equivalent to ae.

Most names of languages following foreign terms are given in abbreviation. Fr. for French, Ger. for German, Heb. for Hebrew, It. for Italian, Jap. for Japanese, Lat. for Latin, Sp. for Spanish.

A guide for pronunciation has been provided for foreign words. It is obvious that there are many problems in working out a pronunciation guide. Languages vary according to time in history, from region to region within the same country, etc. It is also obvious that the student who is knowledgeable in languages needs no pronunciation guide and the student who lacks a working knowledge of languages would not accurately pronounce a word even with the most elaborate guide or even with the use of standard phonetic symbols. Therefore, it was decided that a simple pronouncing guide be established for this dictionary, using English consonants and English vowel sounds which provide approximate or near equivalent sounds of the foreign language. The sign (') indicates the stressed syllables. No stress marks are used for French words. Pronunciation for Latin Words is shown only on those used in the Roman Catholic Mass and are in Church Latin. (See the "Guide to Pronunciation" for details.)

GUIDE TO PRONUNCIATION

The object of this guide is to achieve a good pronunciation without the use of complicated phonetic symbols. First say each syllable slowly, then the entire word quickly.

The sign (') indicates the stressed syllables. No stress marks are used for French words. Pronunciation for Latin words is shown only on those used in the Roman Catholic Mass and are in the Church Latin.

ä as in father; ā as in able; ă as in mat; å as in along.

ē as in see; ĕ as in set.

ī as in pine; ĭ as in pin.

ō as in rope; ŏ as in not; ô as in order.

o͞o as in moon; o͝o as in foot.

ŭ as in cub; û as in fir.

ü — shape o͞o with the lips and say ē.

ch as in chair.

g as in go.

j as in just.

aw as in crawl.

oi as in toil.

ow as in towel.

zh as the s in measure.

(m), (n), (r) are not pronounced but thought of with the preceding vowel.

A (1) The note (pitch) to which the orchestra is tuned. It has a frequency of 440 vibrations per second. (2) The first letter used to identify musical tones in the letter system from a — g. (3) The sixth note (submediant) of the scale of C major or the first note of the scale of A minor. (4) On various clefs the note appears as follows:

Treble Clef   Bass Clef   Alto Clef   Tenor Clef

(5) In Italian it means: at, to, by, in, on, for, with. (6) In French (à) it means: to, with, at, or by. (7) In musical form the letter A is used to identify the first section of a piece of music, e.g., A B, B being different from the first section A. (8) The abbreviation for such words as alto or antiphon. (9) Several musical instruments are pitched in the key of A, e.g., clarinet in A. (10) A is used to identify many keys, such as A major, Ab Major, A Minor, A# Minor, Ab Minor. See *Key, *Letter names, *Notation, *Pitch names, *Scale.

A2 (1) Two instruments are to play the same part. (2) A section in two parts is to be played divisi (e.g., in string parts). See *A due, *Divisi.

Ab (Ger.) (äp.) Off, of, from, down.

ABA Letters used to outline ternary form. In three-part structure the first and third sections are very similar or, in fact, repetition. The following is an example of three-part song form (ABA): *Trällerliedchen* (Humming Song) by Robert Schumann (1810—1856).

See *Sonata form, *Ternary form.

Abandon (Fr.) (ä—bä(n)h —dŏ(n)h) Ease, lack of restraint.

A battuta (It.) (ä—bä—too'—tä) (1) A return to strict time after some freedom in the beat or time. (2) A strong beat on the first beat of a measure. (3) A group of measures to be played as a rhythmical unit.

Abbandonarsi (It.) (äb—bän—dō—när'—zē) Without restraint.

Abbellimento (It.) (äb—bĕ l—lē— mĕn '—tō) An embellishment, ornament.

Abbreviations A system of notation and symbols used to eliminate extensive notation in like or repeated patterns. E.g.,.

Abendlied (Ger.) (ä'—bĕ nd—lēt) Evening song.

Abendmusik (Ger.) (ä'—bĕnd—moo—zēk) Evening music. A term used to describe the concerts given by Buxtehude in the late 17th century.

A bene placito (It.) (ä bä'—nā plä—chē '—tō) At your pleasure. The performer may take some liberties with the music. See *Ad libitum, *A piacere.

Abgestossen (Ger.) (äp'—gĕ—shtōs—a n) Detached, short. See *Abstossen.

Abnehmend (Ger.) (äp'—nā—mĕnt) Decreasing, diminishing, softening a tone.

Absatz (Ger.) (äp'—zäts) Pause in music.

Abschwellen (Ger.) (äp'—shvĕl—å n)Diminishing.

Absolute Music Music in its pure form, not associated with extra-musical content. Music for music's sake; the interest being in form and structure. The opposite of program music which associates itself with a poetic idea or pictorial concept. See *Abstract music.

Absolute pitch Identification of a tone or pitch with reference to its relative position within the scale structure. A person is said to have absolute pitch when he has the capacity to identify a pitch by name when it is heard without reference to another note or pitch. See *Pitch.

2

Abstossen (Ger.) (äp'–shtōs–så n) Staccato, detached. See *Abgestossen.

Abstract music Purest form of music. See *Absolute music.

A cappella (It.) (ä käp–pĕ l'–lä) Chapel music, church style. Choral music written and performed without accompaniment.

A capriccio (It.) (ä käp–prēt'–chē–ō)A term indicating that the performer has freedom to play or sing the composition as he fancies with reference to the time and expressive elements of the music.

Accademia (It.) (äk–käd–ā–mē'–ä) Academy. Organizations of professional and amateur musicians who dedicate themselves to the development of musical culture. Activities center on musical research, presentation of concerts, founding schools of music, and other musically related endeavors.

Accelerando (It.) (ät–chā–lä–rän'–dō) **Accelerato** (It.) (ät–chā–lä–rä'–tō) A change to a faster tempo in a passage or composition. To go gradually faster. The abbreviation accel. is often used.

Accent (1) The stress or emphasis on a note or beat within a measure. The natural accent falls on the first beat of a measure. (2) An irregular accent can be indicated by a sign > on a weak beat of a measure. (3) An accent can be placed on a tone or pitch (tonic accent) by moving to a higher pitch. (4) Dynamic accent, from reinforcement, is indicated by signs such as: sf, >, –. (5) Agogic accent is accomplished by making the duration of the note longer. (6) Some signs or words to indicate accent are: >, –, ∧ = strong accent; ♪ = staccato; sfz = forcing (sforzando); fp = loud-soft (sforzando piano); rf = reinforcing (rinforzando); See *Agogic, *Dynamic marks.

Accento (It.) (ät–chĕ n'–tō) Accent. **Accentuare** (It.) (ät–chĕ n–too–ä'–rā) To accentuate.

Accentus (1) The chanting of the priest in liturgical music. (2) A style of plain song using syllabic recitation in a monotone voice. See *Concentus.

3

Acciaccato (It.) (ät–chē–ä–kä'–tō) Applying heavy pressure. Forcibly.

Acciaccatura (It.) (ät–chē–äk–kä–tōō'–rä) To crush. (1) An ornament used in keyboard music during the 17th and 18th centuries. A note which usually lies one half-step below a principal note and is played at the same time as the principal note, but is immediately released while the principal note is held. It is usually used when playing chordal passages. E.g.:

The g# is immediately released after the chord is sounded. (2) An ornament. The term is now applied to a short appoggiatura.

written: and played:

See *Appoggiatura.

Accidental The raising or lowering of the pitch of a note within a composition outside the established key. Notes can be altered by using the sharp (#), which raises the note one half-step; the flat (b), which lowers the note one half-step; the double sharp (x); and the double flat (bb); or the natural (♮), which cancels a sharp or flat. The symbol appears before the note on the staff. See *Modulation.

Accidental chords Altered chords. The notes of the chord are altered by using accidentals.

Accolade (Fr.) (ä–kô–läd) A *brace which connects several staves:

Accompaniment The part·which supports and enhances the melodic line. It is directly related to the melodic line and is important to the purpose of the melody. It is usually instrumental; usually related to the chordal structure; can be a duplication of the melodic line, chords, or even a figured bass as used in the 17th and 18th centuries.

4

Accompanist A person who plays an accompaniment for a soloist or group.

Accopiato (It.) (äk—kō—pē—ä'—tō) Tied, coupled.

Accord (Fr.) (ä—çawr) Chord; harmony.

Accordare (It.) (äk—kôr—dä'—rä) To tune. **Accorder** (Fr.) (äk—kawr—dā) To tune.

Accordatura (It.) (äk—kôr—dä'—tōo'—rä) The tuning of stringed instruments to the regular or usual series of pitches. For example, the usual accordatura for violin would be (from high to low) e'', a', d', g; the viola (from high to low) a', d', g, c; the modern guitar (from high to low) e', b, g, d, A, E.

Accordian A reed instrument related to the concertina and mouth organ. It is portable and was invented by F. Buschmann in Berlin, Germany in 1822. The modern instrument is often called the piano-accordian. The right hand plays on a keyboard while the left hand plays buttons which produce chords or harmonic accompaniment. Bellows supply air which vibrates the reeds. See *Concertina.

Accordo (It.) (äk—kôr'—dō) (1) Chord, consonance. (2) name given to an old Italian double-bass instrument.

Accrescendo (It.) (äh—krĕ—shĕn'—dō) A term indicating an increase in the power of tone. See *Crescendo, *Expression.

Achromatic Diatonic. The opposite of chromatic which requires scalar movement by semitones. See *Chromatic, *Diatonic.

Achtel (Ger.) (äkh'—tä l) Quaver or eighth note (♪).

A cinq (Fr.) (ä sä(n)k) Five parts.

Acoustic bass Resultant bass. The tones produced on a 16 foot organ stop with the simultaneous sounding of the fifth above will produce a resultant tone which is an octave below the 16 foot stop. This gives the effect of the larger 32 foot pipe.

Acoustics (1) The science of sound and sound waves. The physical aspects through which music (vibrations) is transmitted and received. Vibrations set in motion move through air columns, electrical current, gut, wire, metal, reed, brass, etc. Vibrations are set in motion by striking an object, blowing a column of air, setting strings in motion by bowing, plucking a string, or by electronic means. Elements of music affected by a-coustical properties are: pitch, intensity, resonance, and tone quality. (2) The theory of acoustics is applied in making musical instruments, making recordings, building rooms, etc. For example, when the shape of a room is correct and the building materials are properly constructed and applied the result is good resonance. The room is said to have good acoustics.

Act A division or section of an opera or operetta which is required because of scene changes, set changes, mood changes, etc.

Action A term applied to the mechanical elements in keyboard instruments. It relates to the motion and feel of the keys.

Act tune A term used during the 17th and 18th centuries to identify a piece of instrumental music played between the acts of a play or opera. Several examples are to be found in the music of Purcell. See *Entr'acte, *Interlude, *Intermezzo.

Ad (Lat.) At, to. **Ad** (It.) (äd) To, by, in, at.

Adagietto (It.) (ä–dä–jē–ĕ t'–tō) The tempo is a little faster than adagio; moderately slow tempo. See *Tempo, *Adagio.

Adagio (It.) (ä–dä'–jē–ō) (1) A slow, relaxed tempo. A bit slower than andante. (2) The slow movement in a concerto, sonata, symphony, etc. See *Tempo.

Adagio assai (It.) (ä–dä'–jē–ō äs–sä'–ē) Very slow.

Adagissimo (It.) (ä–dä–jĭ ss'–ē–mō) Very, very slow tempo. Slower than adagio.

Adana Music of India. Songs composed to be sung in the very early morning hours. Part of the musical literature of India restricted to specific times of the day.

Added lines Ledger lines added for a specific note or notes above or below the staff. The line is just long enough to hold the note, e.g.

Added sixth (1) Generally, a sixth added to a triad or chord. (2) A term originally used by Jean Philippe Rameau (1683—1764) to describe the addition of a sixth to the IV chord in a plagel cadence which was to be resolved to the dominant or the tonic chord. (3) A chord with an added sixth is common in jazz music.

Additive meter Larger meters are developed by adding together smaller rhythmic units within a specific context. Cumulative.

Addolorato (It.) (ä—dō—lō—rä'—tō) Sorrowful, grieving.

A demi jeu (Fr.) (ä dĕ—mē zhü) To play half. Example, play the instrument at half power.

A demi voix (Fr.) (ä dĕ—mē vwä) At half voice.

A deux mains (Fr.) (ä dü mä(n)) For two hands.

A deux temps (Fr.) (ä dü tä(n)) In double time.

Ad libitum (Lat.) At your pleasure. (1) Freedom to vary the tempo or to be inventive or interpretive in a cadenza. (2) To improvise. (3) In jazz, to play an improvization (to "ride") above a set sequence of chords. (4) A part or voice is optional and may be included or omitted. (5) The composer provides optional notes for the performer. The abbreviation is ad lib. See *Battuta, *A piacere, *A bene placito.

A due (It.) (ä dōō'—ā) (1) A2, both play the one part. (2) Divisi in string parts, e.g., strings to divide parts rather than play double stops. See *A2, *Divisi.

A due corde (It.) (ä dōō'—ā kŏr'—dā) Play the note on two strings rather than one, for extra power.

A dur (Ger.) (ä dōōr) Key of A major.

Aeolian harp An early instrument having six or more strings which varied in thickness and were tuned to the same pitch. Wind blowing across the strings produced various harmonic sounds. Also called wind harp or aeolian lyre.

Aeolian mode An authentic mode. The scale progresses in whole steps and half steps from A to A (consecutive white keys of the piano from A to A) with the final being A and the dominant E. For example:

Medieval Aeolian mode   *Greek Aeolian mode*

1 2 3 4 5 6 7 8   1 2 3 4 5 6 7 8

See *Church modes, *Modality.

Aere Recurvo An ancient Roman horn-type instrument.

Aerophon (Fr.) (ĕr−ō−fō(n)) An early French musical instrument of the reed family. The air is moved by bellows.

Aerophones Any musical wind instrument. Sound is produced by vibrating air.

Aesthetics of music A study of the beautiful in music. The term was first used in its Latin form "aesthetica" by Baumgarten in the mid-eighteenth century to denote the science of sensuous knowledge.

Affabile (It.) (äf−fäb'−ē−lā) Affable, pleasing manner, warm, gentle.

Affettuoso (It.) (äf−fĕt−tōō−ō'−zō) Affectionate, with warm feeling.

Affrettando (It.) (äf−frĕt−tän'−dō) Increase the tempo.

Affrettare (It.) (äf−frĕt−tä'−rä) To hasten.

A flat A♭. A semitone below the note A, e.g.

Clef: Treble Clef   Bass Clef   Alto Clef   Tenor Clef

After beat Coming after the beat, e.g., at the end of a trill.

Agilita (It.) (ä−jēl−ē−tä') Agility.

Agilité (Fr.) (ä−zhē−lē−tā) Nimbleness.

Agitato (It.) (äd−jē−tä'−tō) Agitated, wild.

Agnus Dei (Lat.) (än'−yōōs dā'−ē) "Lamb of God". The last part or section in the musical portion of a Mass composition. The fifth section in the Ordinary of the Mass in the Roman Catholic Mass. It follows the "Sanctus" in the Ordinary. The Latin text is as follows: "Agnus Dei, qui tollis peccata mundi, miserere nobis. Agnus Dei, qui tollis peccata mundi, miserere nobis. Agnus Dei, qui tollis peccata mundi, dona nobis pacem." For centuries the text was sung in Latin. The current practice is to sing the text in the vernacular. The English translation is "Lamb of God, You Who take away the sins of the world, have mercy on us. Lamb of God, You Who take away the sins of the World have mercy on us. Lamb of God, You Who take away the sins of the world, grant us peace." The "Agnus Dei" has also been used by many composers in musical settings. An excellent example is found in the J. S. Bach (1685-1750), *Mass in B Minor*, Section XXII, "Agnus Dei." See *Mass, *Ordinary of the Mass.

Agogic, agogic accent, agoge rhythmica An accent caused by lengthening the note by using a sign or term such as (⌒) (fermata), tempo rubato, etc., rather than by dynamic or pitch changes. Agogics modify strict tempo and rhythm.

Agrémenter (Fr.) (ä—grä—mĕn—tā) To ornament.

Agréments (Fr.) (ä—grä—mä(n)) Ornaments, embellishments in harpsichord music.

Ai (It.) (ä'—ē) At the.

Air Generally, a song or tune. For instance, an air in opera, or a style of song played on an instrument or a group of instruments.

Ais (Ger.) (ä'—i s) A sharp (A#).

Ais-dur (Ger.) (ä'—i s doōr) A# major. .

Aise (Fr.) (āz) Easy, joyful.

Aisis (Ger.) (ä'—i s—is) A double sharp (A× or A##).

Ais-moll (Ger.) (ä'—i s mawl) A# minor.

Akkord (Ger.) (äk—kôrt') Chord.

Al (It.) (äl) To the, as in al fine meaning to the end.

A la (Fr.) (ä lä) In the style of.

Alba (Fr.) (äl—bä) The text of a troubadour song which deals with the parting of lovers at the break of dawn. A dialogue. Literary; a poem.

9

Alberti bass A style of playing broken chords in the left hand accompaniment on a keyboard instrument. It was used a great deal by an 18th century harpsichordist and composer, Domenico Alberti (1710-1740), whose name became identified with the practice. This technique is found in the music of many composers. For example, the style is used in the second movement of the *Sonata No. 4 in A Minor* for Flute and Continuo by George Frideric Handel (1685-1759):
Allegro

Album leaf A short piece of intimate music written in the 19th century. German: Albumblatt

Aleatory (aleatori, Latin) aleator, gambler. Alea, game of dice. Aleatoric, from the word aleatorik (Ger.). Chance music. A form of improvisations. The composer provides an organized musical idea on which the performers improvise. The possibilities of chance music are unlimited. A few examples of how it might work: (1) the musical line provided might be based on a tone row, which will emerge regardless of the order or arrangement of the musical elements; (2) the music is written out entirely and the instrumentation and order of performance is left to chance; (3) the music may be written so that only the intervals are written out while several rhythmic choices are available to the performers and left to chance; (4) any musical element or idea can become the basis while all others are left to improvisation and chance. The central idea of chance music is to unify the composer and performer as one in creating a musical work. The performer is also a composer, as he supplies the improvisation on the composer's idea. A chance piece is not only one piece of music, but an idea which becomes many improvised compositions left to the creative imagination of the performers.

Al fine (It.) (äl fē 'nā) To the end. When repeating a section of music al fine indicates the end of the repeat. For example, da capo al fine means from the beginning to the point marked fine.

Algoja A vertical flute-like instrument of India.

Aliquotflügel (Ger.) (ä–lē–kvōt–flüg'–äl) A German grand piano with a string added over each normal string and tuned an octave higher. The added strings were not struck by the hammer, but picked up the vibrations from the normal string to add richness to the tone.

Aliquot strings Sympathetic strings added by some piano makers. See *Aliquotflügel.

Alla (It.) (äl'–lä) In the manner of, to the, at the.

Alla breve (It.) (äl'–lä brā'–vā) The music is to be played twice as fast as written. A tempo marking (¢) indicating half time. E.g., C is common time ($\frac{4}{4}$) and the quarter note (♩) equals one beat. ¢, or alla breve, indicates "cut time" or ($\frac{2}{2}$) time, and the half note (♩) equals one beat.

Alla camera (It.) (äl'–lä kä'–mě –rä) Chamber music style.

Alla cappella (It.) (äl'–lä käp–pěl'–lä) See *A cappella.

Alla marcia (It.) (äl'–lä mär'–chē–ä) In a marching style.

Allargando (It.) (äl–lär–gän'–dō) Slower tempo and broader style of playing.

Alla zoppa (It.) (äl'–lä dsŏp'–pä) In a limping style which creates an uneven rhythm. Syncopated rhythm. E.g., ♪ ♩.

Alle (Ger.) (äl'–lå) All.

Allegramente (It.) (äl–lě –grä–mě n'–tā) Tempo marking. Lightly or briskly.

Allegretto (It.) (äl–lě –grět'–tō) Tempo marking. It indicates a moderately fast movement which falls between allegro (fast) and andante (moderately slow). The diminutive of allegro. See *Tempo.

Allegro (It.) (äl—lĕ'—grō) (1) Tempo marking. Fast. (2) Title for fast movements or sections of works, such as a movement of a sonata.

Allegro molto (It.) (äl—lĕ '—grō mōl'—tō) Tempo marking. Very fast.

Allein (Ger.) (äl—līn ') Alone.

Alleluia (Lat.) "Praise ye the Lord." Used in music which expresses joy and praise of God, such as Gregorian chant, the Mass, antiphons, and psalmody. See *Hallelujah.

Allemande (Fr., Ger.) (äl—mä(n)d, äl—lĕ —män'—dȧ) A dance, slow, in duple time, which began in Germany, became popular in France in the 16th century and later in England. In the 17th century it was used not as a dance, but as a first movement of a suite. For example, J. S. Bach (1685-1750) "Allemande" from *French Suite, No. 6 in E,* for piano. The tempo was moderate, in ⁴⁄₄ time, and it began with a short upbeat. Later, in the 18th century, it was used as a German dance in fast waltz style in triple time.

All' ottava (It.) (äl ŏt—tä'—vä) Play one octave above or below the written note. 8va = one octave above. 8va bassa = one octave below. See *Ottava.

Alpenhorn (Ger.) (äl'—pĕn—hô rn) Alphorn, Alpine horn. A Swiss horn used by herdsmen. It is made of wood, may be as long as ten feet, is straight or slightly curved, with the end flared in the shape of a bell. The tones produced are of the harmonic series.

Al segno (It.) (äl sĕ n'—yō) From the sign. Repeat not from the beginning but from the sign (𝄋). See *Dal segno.

Alt (1) Notes from g" to f''' are in alt. An octave higher are in altissimo. (2) When naming instruments the second highest in a family is named Alt. For example, alto saxophone.

Alt (Ger.) (ält) Alto.

Alteration (1) Raising or lowering notes by using #, b, ♮. (2) Augmentation or diminution of mensural notation. See *Chromaticism, *Accidentals, *Mensural notation, *Altered chord.

Altered chord Chromatic alteration of one or more tones of a chord. Examples: Neapolitan sixth chord, augmented fifth, diminished fifth, diminished seventh chord.

Alternate fingering A substitute fingering on an instrument used to play a musical passage with greater facility. A false fingering for the same note.

Alternativo (It.) (äl—tĕ r—nä—tē '—vō) A term used in 17th and 18th century compositions to indicate that one section alternates with another in the manner of ABA form. The modern term Trio has the same meaning when it is used in the middle of a movement.

Altflöte (Ger.) (ält '—flĕ (r)—tå) Alto flute. The range extends from g in the bass clef upwards to c '''. Also called bass flute.

Althorn (Ger.) (ält '—hôrn) A German brass instrument belonging to the saxhorn family. In the nature of an upright tuba used in brass bands.

Altissimo (It.) (äl—tēss '—ē—mō) Notes an octave higher than those called alt in the treble clef. See *Alt.

Alto (It.) (äl '—tō) High; loud.

Alto (1) A voice range for men from approximately third line d in the bass clef to fourth line d '' in the treble clef (tenor). (2) The lowest woman's voice, but higher than the male tenor voice. See *Contralto, Voice ranges (3) Alto is used in describing instruments such as the viola, and as a prefix to an instrument the next size larger than soprano. (4) Alto clef.

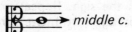 *middle c.*

Alto clef A clef taken from the middle section of the grand staff. Middle c is on the third line of the staff.

grand staff → *middle c*

alto clef

See *Clefs, *Alto (4).

13

Alto flute Bass flute. See *Flute.

Alto Saxophone A woodwind instrument of the modern saxophone family. It is the second highest instrument in this family.

Alto trombone (1) A member of the brass family which is referred to as a tenor trombone. The music is written in tenor or bass clef. (2) A bass trombone, the lowest trombone, which is the second or third lowest brass instrument. The music is written in the bass clef. See *Trombone.

Amabile (It.) (ä—mä'—bē—lä) Love. Play in an amorous style, gently.

Ambitus (Lat.) (1) The range from low to high of the voice or instrument or melody. (2) It is used to describe the range of the melodies of the Gregorian chant from the limited range of the psalms to the wider range of melismatic chants. (3) The normal range of a church mode, e.g., octave. See *Church modes.

Ambrosian chant A style of performing liturgical chants as established by the Bishop of Milan, St. Ambrose, in the 4th century. The melodies are very ornamental and lack methodical organization. They differ from Gregorian chant. See *Gregorian chant.

Amen (Heb.) "So be it." (1) Used in Christian prayer and music, sung or spoken as an answer in prayer. (2) The Amen is used extensively in polyphonic masses in fugal style. (3) The Amen cadence is the plagal cadence which has a chordal sequence of I, IV, I. See *Plagal cadence.

American organ An American keyboard instrument introduced by Mason and Hamlin of Boston in the 19th century. It is similar to the harmonium except that the bellows pull the air in through the reeds. It uses smaller reeds and produces a softer tone with a quality similar to the actual organ tone. A keyboard instrument with two manuals and pedals. See *Harmonium.

A moll (Ger.) (ä mawl) A minor. See *Scales, *Modes, *Minor.

Amore, con (It.) (ä—mōr'—ä kōn) With love.

14

Amoroso (It.) (ä—mō—rō'—zō) Lovingly.

Amorsklang (Ger.) (ä'môrz—kläng) An 18th century German musical instrument much like the French horn. A valve instrument which required the use of the hand in the bell to produce some tones.

Amousikos (Greek) A term to describe a non-musical person.

Amphibrach (Greek) A term from a Greek scheme of poetic meter which is applied to musical rhythms. Trisyllabic foot (short, long, short or unstressed, stressed, unstressed). The Greek poetic meter ˘|– ˘| would be equal to the music rhythm $\frac{3}{4}$ ♩| d ♩|. Note the pick up beat or unaccented start of the meter of rhythm. See *Poetic meter.

Ampollosamente (It.) (äm—pŏl—lō—zä—mĕn'—tā) In a pompous style either for the entire composition or a section.

Ampolloso (It.) (äm—pŏl—lō'—zō) Stilted.

Am Steg (Ger.) (äm shtāk) Play near the bridge. See *Ponticello.

Anacrusis Upbeat. A pick-up or weak beat. A beat or part of a beat other than a downbeat.

E.G.,

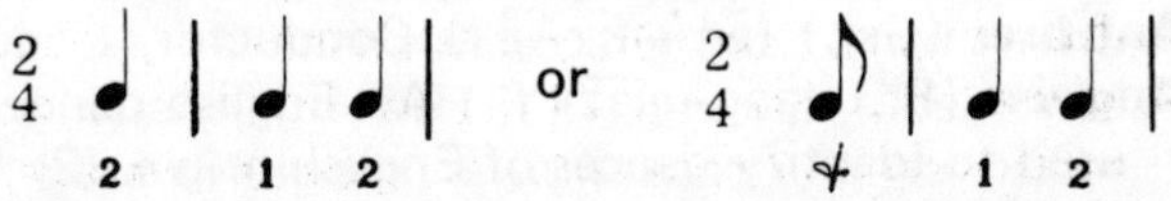

Analysis The study of a composition with reference to all the elements, e.g., melody, harmony, form, style, timbre, dynamics, etc.

Anapaestic A Greek term used in poetic meter which is applied to musical rhythm. The Greek poetic meter, anapest, ˘ ˘|– ˘ ˘|– ˘ ˘, would be equal to the music rhythm

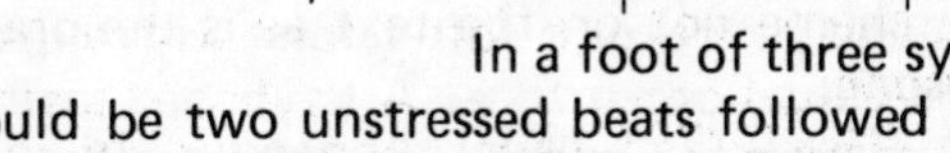

In a foot of three syllables, there would be two unstressed beats followed by one stressed beat. See *Poetic meter.

Anche (Fr.) (ä(n)sh) Reed. Instruments using reeds to produce sound.

Ancora (It.) (än—kaw'—rä) Still or still more; once more.

Andamento (It.) (än–dä–mě n '–tō) (1) In a fugal style or fugue subject. (2) An episode in a fugue. (3) A movement.

Andante (It.) (än–dän '–tā) Tempo marking. (1) A moderate tempo, between allegretto and adagio. (2) A slow movement of a larger work.

Andante Cantabile (It.) (än–dän '–tā ĸän–tä '–bē –lā) In a singing style.

Andante con moto (It.) (än–dän '–tā kōn mō '–tō) Slow, with movement.

Andantino (It.) (än–dän–tē '–nō) Tempo marking. A diminutive of andante. This may be a little slower or a little faster than andante depending on the period, style and the composer's intention.

Andare (It.) (än–dä '–rā) To go on.

Anémocorde (Fr.) (ä–nā–mō–côrd) An instrument invented in Paris in the late 18th century which was in the piano class of instruments. It had bellows which pushed air past the strings to produce sounds. It was similar to the Aeolian harp. Later, as it was developed in the 19th century, it was called the piano éolian.

Anfang (Ger.) (an '–fäng) Beginning.

Anführer (Ger.) (än '–für–å r) Conductor, leader.

Anglaise (Fr.) (äng–glāz) (1) An English dance. A term used to identify dances of English origin. (2) A French dance used in the ballet in the 17th century. It is usually in quick duple time. (3) An optional dance in the Baroque suite.

Anglican chant Music of the Anglican Church. A harmonized setting of psalms and canticles. The technique is based on the principles used in the plainsong. It uses a relationship of two phrases: one three measures and the second four measures. The accents are based on a metrical scheme not on the text as is the practice in the plainsong.

Anhang (Ger.) (än '–häng) Appendix. In music, Coda.

Anima, con (It.) (ä '–nē –mä, kōn) With spirit.

Animato (It.) (än–nē –mä '–tō) Animated. Con animato, with spirit or animation.

Anklang (Ger.) (än '–kläng) Harmony.

Ansatz (Ger.) (än'—zäts)(1) The preparation for the production of a good vocal tone. (2) Setting the proper embouchure to a wind instrument. (3) A proper attack on a stringed instrument. (4) The proper setting of tuning slides in wind instruments. See *Embouchure, *Crook, *Brass instruments.

Answer (1) A general term to denote a response to a musical phrase or a section of a phrase. (2) In strict counterpoint, the repeating of a theme previously proposed, e.g., as in the fugue. In the fugue, the answer follows the exposition of the theme or subject. It is an imitation of the subject usually on the dominant (occasionally on the sub-dominant). The answer in the dominant key retains a close harmonic relationship with the subject. When the answer is in exact imitation, it is called "real" (real fugue). When it is slightly modified (because of harmonic requirements) it is called "tonal" (tonal fugue). A good illustration of a "real" answer is found in the J. S. Bach (1685-1750) *Little Fugue in G Minor.* The subject is in G minor, the answer in in D minor (dominant of G minor):

G minor: Subject

An example of a *"tonal" answer is seen at the beginning of the J. S. Bach *Fugue XVI in G Minor* from "The Well-Tempered Clavier, Book I ". Example:

See *Fugue, *Antecedent and consequent, *Counterfugues, *Counterpoint, *Subject.

Antecedent and consequent The subject and answer in the fugue. Antecedent is the theme of the fugue while consequent is the answer. The relationship is question and answer. See *Answer, *Fugue.

Anthem A short choral work having an English text. It has a solemn or sacred text and is used in the Protestant Church service. It is usually sung with organ accompaniment. There are various forms: (1) full anthem for chorus, with or without accompaniment; (2) anthem for double choir or two choirs in antiphonal style; (3) full anthem including solos; (4) verse anthem where the chorus plays a secondary part while the verses dominate; (5) the solo anthem dominated by solo parts and ending with chorus; (6) instrumental anthem which uses orchestral or other instruments rather than the organ.

Anthologies of Music Books that deal with the History of Music. They may contain musical examples, essays about music, pictures relating to the history of music, etc. For example, Davison and Apel, *Historical Anthology of Music;* Parrish and Ohl, *Masterpieces of Music Before 1750;* Strunk, *Source Readings in Music History.* See *History of Music.

Anticipation A *note of a chord which is played just before the chord of which the note is a member.

See *Nonharmonic tones.

Antiphon (Greek) Musical categories of Gregorian chant, syllabic in style and usually sung before or after a psalm. Narrative types of antiphons are also sung before the Mass, as for example, on Palm Sunday. Others are sung during the various seasons. Some chants of the Mass are called antiphons, e.g., "Introit", "Offertory", and "Communion". These are performed in the same style of antiphonal psalmody. See *Antiphonal.

Antiphonal A volume of choir music used in the Office of the Roman Catholic Church other than the music of the Mass itself which is contained in the Gradual. See *Liturgical books.

Antiphonal singing, Antiphony Alternated singing or playing by two choirs or split choir. A style used in early plainchant and Gregorian chant in which the music alternates between soloist and chorus. In polyphonic music it relates to choruses or half-choruses in alternating pattern.

Anwachsend (Ger.) (än'—väk—sånt) Growing or increasing.

Aperto (It.) (ä—pĕr'—tō) Open. The endings change when sections of music are repeated, e.g., 1st ending and 2nd ending. Also called Ouvert. (Fr.).

A piacere (It.) (ä pē—ä—chä'—rä) At your pleasure. The performer may take a certain amount of freedom in the interpretation of the rhythm and tempo. See *Ad libitum, *A bene placito.

A poco (It.) (ä pō'—cō) A little, gradually, little by little.

Apollonicon A large mechanical organ type instrument having as many as six keyboards and designed to sound like various instruments of the orchestra. It was built by Flight and Robson in 1817, (London).

Appassionata (It.) (äp—päs—sē—ō—nä'—tä) **Appassiona-**
tamente (äp—päs—sē—ō—nä—tä—mĕn'—tä) A term indicating that the work or section is to be played with
passion or with great emotion.

Appoggiatura (It.) (äp—pŏd—jē—ä—tōo'—rä) A non-harmonic note or ornamental note which is related to the
regular notes of the composition. It is now designated
on the score as a smaller note. During the 17th and
18th centuries it was indicated by a stroke

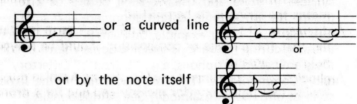

or by the note itself

It is also referred to as an embellishment or grace note. Forms are: long appoggiatura,
short appoggiatura, passing appoggiatura, double appoggiatura. An example of an appoggiatura:

See *Acciaccatura, *Double appoggiatura.

A punto (It.) (ä pŏo n'—tō) Point.

A punto d'arco (It.) (ä pŏo n'—tō där'—kō) Play at the
point of the bow.

Arabesque (Fr.) (ä—rä—bĕ sk) A lyrical, fanciful piece of
music. An ornamented piece of music. Robert Schumann used the term as a title.

Arcata, arcato (It.) (är—kä'—tä, är—kä'—tō) Bowed. The
opposite of pizzicato (plucking the strings).

Arch chanter The prime chanter in religious music.

Archet (Fr.) (är—shä) Bow.

Arch form A form in which sections leading to the middle
section are used in reverse order to the end, e.g.,
ABCBA

Archlute A bass lute having a double neck with two sets of strings. One set of strings on the fingerboard for stopped strings and the other for special bass strings.

Arcicembalo (It.) (är—chē—chĕm—bä'—lō) An instrument of the harpsichord family invented in the 16th century which could play chromatic, diatonic, and enharmonic scales. It had special keys and strings and six keyboards.

Arco (It.) (är'—kō) Bow. Play using the bow of the stringed instrument. The opposite of pizzicato which means the string is to be plucked.

Arditamente (It.) (är—dē—tä—mĕ n Ꞌᵊ—tä) A term indicating that the passage or composition should be played boldly or ardently.

Arghool A wind instrument used in playing Arabian music, having two pipes, one for melody and one for a drone bass or accompaniment.

Aria (It.) (ä'—rē—ä) (1) A solo composition usually performed as a vocal solo with instrumental accompaniment. It is a lyrical melody, air or a piece of symmetrical vocal music. It is used in opera, oratorio, and cantata. (2) The title is used to describe an instrumental piece of music which is song-like or lyrical. See *Da capo aria.

Arietta (It.) (ä—rē—ĕ t'—tä) A short or small aria in binary or two-part form. In the 18th century it was used in the French Opéra Comique as a solo song. See *Arioso, *Aria.

Arioso (It.) (ä—rē—ō'—zō) (1) A short vocal solo which is somewhere between the style of aria (song) and recitativo (declamatory) style. (2) In instrumental music the term indicates a cantabile style of playing. See *Aria.

Armadillo A native tribal instrument in which strings are stretched over an armadillo shell along an attached neck and connected to pegs. It has been adopted by today's "Pop" musicians.

Arpa (It.) (är'—pä) Harp

Arpeggiando (It.) (är—pĕ d—jē—än'—dō) See *Arpeggio.

Arpeggio (It.) (är—pĕd'—jē—ō) (1) Groups of notes to be played in a harp-like fashion. That is, in succession from bottom to top or reversed. Broken chords. Often marked in music with a wavey line, e.g.,

. Harping the notes. The notes are played in (1) free rhythm or (2) in strict time. (2) An excerise for an instrumentalist or vocalist.

Arpicordo (It.) (är—pē—k̂ôr'—dō) Italian name for harpsichord (16th century).

Arpone (It.) (är—pōn'—ä) An Italian harp-like instrument of the 18th century which used horizontal strings.

Arrangement To adapt music for voices or instruments other than those specified in the original score. Some arrangements preserve the original music and format, while others include re-writing for a new media with extensive modifications. The abbreviation is arr.

Ars antiqua (Lat.) (ärz än—tē'—kwä) Old art. Music of the late 12th century and 13th century. Polyphonic music up to the Ars nova (14th century). Ars antiqua includes the School of Notre Dame with the composers Leoninus and Perotinus.

Arsis(Greek) Up-beat.

Ars nova (Lat.) (ärz nō'—vä) New art as opposed to Ars antiqua or old art. Music of the 14th century. The term was introduced by Philippe de Vitry. Machaut was one of the composers.

Articulation The precise interpretation of a musical score in performance. A clear presentation of the form and shape of the music. The organization of the parts into a meaningful whole. One part must have a meaningful relation to the other parts. Attention must be given to every detail of a composition, for example; to the larger units; the phrase, to the articulation of units smaller than the phrase (notes, rests, measures, etc.), to accents, attack, dynamic markings (crescendo, decrescendo, etc.), to bow markings, tonguing, to breathing,

22

expression marks, style considerations, clear and precise treatment of words, to legato, staccato, etc.

Art-song A song written and sung in an artistic manner. The text is recognized as being of good quality and the accompaniment is an integral part of the whole. See *Lied.

As (Ger.) (äs) The note A flat (A♭)

As dur (Ger.) (äs door r) Key of A♭ major.

A sharp A♯ A semitone above the note A.

TREBLE CLEF   BASS CLEF   ALTO CLEF   TENOR CLEF

As moll (Ger.) (äs mawl) Key of A♭ minor.

Assai (It.) (äs–sä'–ē) Very. E.g., molto assai, very much.

Asses (Ger.) (äss'–ĭs) The note A double flat (A♭♭).

Asymmetry Music that has no symmetry for musical reasons.

Atem (Ger.) (ä'–tĕm) A short pause in music which is indicated quite often by an apostrophe. A breath mark.

A tempo (It.) (ä tĕm 'po) In time. Back to the original or normal tempo after a change in tempo. See *Tempo.

A tempo primo (It.) (ä tĕm'–pō prē'–mō) Back to the first or prime tempo given to the piece. See *Tempo.

A tempo rubato (It.) (ä tĕm'–pō roo–bä'–tō) An unsteady or irregular tempo. See *Rubato, *Tempo.

Atonality Music having no tonal center, no key feeling or key center. A rejection of traditional tonal relationships. See *Twelve-tone row.

A tre (It.) (ä trä), **à trois** (Fr.) (ä trwä) Three or trio.

A tre corde (It.) (ä trä kôr'–dä) For three strings or three parts. In piano music the term indicates that the left pedal should be released which allows the three strings, or all the strings, for each note to be struck by the hammers.

Attacca (It.) (ät–täk'–kä) Move on to the next section or movement without a break.

Attacco (It.) (ät—täk '—kō) A short motive used in an episode of a fugue or an imitative figure used in polyphonic music. See *Soggetto.

Attack A precise beginning of a phrase or composition. Instruments or voices beginning together using proper interpretation of dynamic markings, pitch, balance, etc.

Au (Fr.) (ō) To the, at the, in the.

Aubade (Fr.) (ō—bäd) Dawn. A term indicating morning music as opposed to serenade, evening music. It is most often applied to instrumental music.

Audio spectrum The range of oscillations that are heard by man. The range of normal audible sound is a frequency between 20 to 20,000 cycles per second.

Audition To hear. The process of being heard for the purpose of being evaluated by one or more persons.

Aufgeweckt (Ger.) (owf '—gặ —vě kt) Bright, lively.

Aufstrich (Ger.) (owf '—shtr i kh)— Upbow.

Augmentation The process of doubling the value of a note. Diminution requires the halving of a note. Augmentation is a device of lengthening a note and causes the effect of grandioso in music.

Augmented interval Making a major or perfect interval larger by a half-step or more. This can be done by raising the upper note or lowering the lower note of a major or perfect interval by a semitone or more, e.g.;

Augmented: 2nd   3rd   4th

5th   6th

See *Intervals.

Augmented sixth Chords using the augmented sixth. Three traditional forms are: French sixth chord, German sixth chord; and the Italian sixth chord. These chords are built on the flatted submediant of the major scale or on the submediant of the minor scale. Examples in C major:

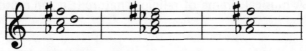

French sixth chord   German sixth chord   Italian sixth chord

See *Sixth chords.

Augmented triad A chord of three notes which include the intervals of a major third and an augmented interval of the fifth (e.g., c e g$^\#$). See *Chord, *Inversion.

Aulos (Greek) A double-reed instrument of the ancient Greeks which sounded like an oboe. It usually consisted of two pipes, the second of which probably provided a drone bass.

Authentic cadence The combination of V - I chords. Also called perfect cadence when the I chord is in root position and the soprano ends on the key tone. See *Cadence.

Authentic modes See *Church modes.

Autoharp A stringed instrument of the zither type having a bar which is depressed, stopping all strings from vibrating except those required to produce the notes of a specific chord. The names of the chords appear on buttons on the bars. The tone is produced by a sweeping motion of the finger or pick across the strings. It is primarily a chordal instrument.

Auxiliary tones Non-chord tones. These tones are outside the basic harmony (e.g., passing tones, embellishments, a grace note, appoggiatura, etc.).

Avant-garde (Fr.) (ä—vä(n)-gärd) The new techniques and ideas. A new movement. Experimental treatment of musical material.

Avec (Fr.) (ä—vĕ k) With.

A vista (It.) (ä vēs'—tä) At sight.

Ayre An English song of the late 16th and early 17th centuries. Like the madrigal, but strophic and less contrapuntal than the madrigal. More like a solo song supported by voices or instruments. Ayre is the English spelling for Air. See *Air.

Azione sacre (It.) (ät—sē—ō'—nä sä'—krā) Sacred action. A musical drama of religious nature (e.g., an oratorio).

B

B (1) The seventh degree (leading tone) of the scale of C major or the second degree of the Scale of A minor. (2) On various clefs the note appears as follows:

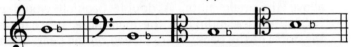

(3) B equals Bb in German. The letter H equals B natural in German. B double flat is B flat in German. (4) The letter B is used in analysis to identify the second section of a piece of music; e.g., AB, B being different from the first section A. (5) The abbreviation for Bass. (6) B is used in the identification of keys, such as B major, Bb major, B minor, Bb minor. (7) Several musical instruments are pitched in the key of Bb (e.g., Trumpet in Bb). (8) Band instruments are tuned to the note B flat. See *Key, *Letter names, *Notation, *Pitch names, *Scale.

Bacchetta (It.) (bäk—kĕ t '—tä) A baton used by the conductor. A wooden wand, drumstick, stick. See *Baton.

Bach choir A group of amateurs organized to study and prepare the Bach *B Minor Mass* in London, 1875. They formed a society to produce choral works. Otto Goldschmidt was the conductor. Since then many other choral groups throughout the world have assumed the name.

Bach-gesellschaft (Ger.) (gä—zĕ l'—shäft) A society in Germany formed in 1850 to publish a complete edition of the works of Johann Sebastian Bach to commemorate the one hundredth anniversary of his death.

Bach trumpet A natural trumpet or clarin, without valves, which was used in the 17th and 18th centuries to play the very high harmonies and fast passages in Bach's music, e.g., *B Minor Mass and Brandenberg Concerto No. 2.* Today there are modern three valved trumpets designed to play the high and flexible parts of the music of Bach and Handel. They are pitched in various keys. See *Trumpet.

Backfall (agré ments, Fr.) An English term used in the 17th century for appoggiatura. An ornament. A single backfall is the appoggiatura or ornament one note above the main note. A double backfall would be two notes descending to the main note. In each case the notes of the backfall are played on the beat. Examples:

SINGLE BACKFALL   DOUBLE BACKFALL

WRITTEN   PLAYED   WRITTEN   PLAYED

Background music Music which supports the action in plays, movies, theatre, etc. It tends to help change moods, pace, etc. It is also incidental music played while working, relaxing, dining, etc.

Badinage (Fr.) (bä—di —näzh) A style of playfulness. A lively composition.

Badinerie (Fr.) (bä—di —ně r—ē) Playful, teasing. A term used in the 18th century to describe a lively fast movement in duple meter. Used as a dance-like section of a suite E.g., the last movement (Badinerie) of *Suite No. 2 in B Minor* for Flute and Strings by J. S. Bach (1685-1750).

Bagatelle (Fr.) (bä—gä—tě l) "Trifle". A short, light, character piece, usually written for the piano. The title was used by many composers including Francois Couperin (1668-1733) in the 18th century and by Beethoven who composed many Bagatelles for pianoforte. For example: Ludwig van Beethoven (1770-1827)Three sets of Bagatelles for Piano: (1) Opus 33 (Seven Bagatelles), (2) Opus 119 (New Bagatelles, easy and agreeable), and (3) Opus 126 (Six Bagatelles).

Bagpipe A group of instruments having several reed pipes and drones. The reeds, either single or double, produce tones when air is moved through reeds from an air bag, while the air moving through larger sound holes produces a tone called a drone. The reeds provide the melody, while the drone sounds provide the accompaniment. The instruments date back to the Greeks and Romans, but the Scottish and Irish varieties are more popularly known today.

Baguette (Fr.) (bäg—ĕ t) Wand or stick. (1) Drumstick. (2) Conductor's baton. (3) The stick part of the bow. See *Bacchetta.

Baile (Sp.) (bä '—ē —lā) A Spanish dance or dancing.

Balada (Sp.) (bä—lä '—dä) Ballad

Balalaika (Russian) A Russian guitar used by the peasant people. A plucked instrument usually with three strings which are tuned in fourths, a triangular body, and the finger board (neck) is fretted in the fashion of the guitar. There are many sizes.

Balancement (Fr.) (bä—lä(n)s—mä(n)) Literally, rocking or swinging. A term used during the 18th century for tremolo in string bowing and playing.

Ballabile (It.) (bäl—lä '—bē —lā) (1) A dance tune; in a dance style. (2) A ballet term used when the entire corps is assembled in a dance number.

Ballad During the 16th century it was a simple verse. Later, a poem or verse accompanied by dancing. Often it dealt with current events and happenings and had a simple accompaniment. During the 19th century it was a narrative and romantic song. Ballads are sung in simple meters, have several stanzas, and are simple in nature and structure. Today we refer to some folk songs and popular tunes as ballads.

Ballade (Fr.) (bäl—läd) Music of the trouvères (12th and 13th centuries) which was both monophonic and polyphonic. Machaut (14th century) developed the polyphonic style of the ballade. In the 19th and 20th centuries it is an instrumental piece of music of lyrical and romantic style. Examples: Guillaume de Machaut (c. 1300-1377), *Je puis trop bien*; Henri Vieuxtemps (1820-1881), *Ballade et Polonaise*, Opus 38 for Violin and Piano.

Ballad meter Common meter. The standard meter used

in hymns. The pattern is iambic and has a four line pattern in which the first line has eight syllables, the second line six syllables, the third line eight syllables, and the fourth line six syllables. See *Common meter, *Poetic meter.

Ballad opera English musical-theater of the 18th century such as John Gay's (1685-1732) *The Beggar's Opera* in 1728. The work included spoken parts and melodies. The melodies were popular, current composed music and ballads, and folk songs. See *Songspiel.

Ballamatia (It.) (bäl—lä—mä'—tē—ä) Dances; in a dance style.

Ballata (It.) (bä—lä'—tä) A 14th century Italian polyphonic vocal form in verse-form. It has a modified ternary design as is found in the French virelai (e.g., a general pattern of refrain, stanza, refrain). Many of the poems called "ballata" were set to music by Brancesco Landino (Landini— (1325-1397).

Ballet (Fr.) (bäl—lä) The performance of a dance group in a theater using costumes and scenery. The dancing is accompanied by an instrumental group. There is no dialogue or singing and the dancing is associated with a program or story. Ballet dates back to ancient ceremonial dances, however, the present form of ballet dates back to the French courts of the 15th century.

Balleti (It.) (bäl—lēt'—tē) A term used to describe music written to support dancing. Dance-songs of the 13th century.

Ballette Related to ballet. Dance-song of medieval time.

Balletto (It.) (bäl—lĕt'—tō) Ballett. Dancing. (1) Name given to a medium fast dance-like piece of music in $\frac{4}{4}$ time, or a movement in music during the 17th century. The term was used by Bach. (2) A 17th century dance-like composition sung in madrigal style which included a fa-la section which might have included dancing.

Ballo (It.) (bäl'—lō) Ball. Dance; dance style; dance tempo.

Ballonchio (It.) (bä—lŏn—kē'—ō) An old Italian dance. See *Passepied.

Band (1) A term once used to describe any group of instrumental performers. (2) It now refers to a large group of wind instrument players which might include any combination of woodwinds, brass, percussion, and sometimes string bass (double bass). See *Brass band, *Military band.

Bandoneon (Sp.) (bän—dōn'—ē—ōn) An accordian of Argentina. See *Accordian.

Bandora A Ibassᵢ size guitar-like instrument of the 16th and 17th centuries. See *Cither, *Pandora.

Bandurria (Sp.) (bän—dōo r—rē'—ä) A Spanish guitar. It has six double strings, an oval body, 12 frets, and a flat head. See *Guitar.

Banjo An American instrument. It has from five to nine strings which are played either with the fingers or a plectrum, a long neck, a circular drum-like body covered on the top by some variety of skin or parchment, and is open in the back. It has frets on the finger board. It is used in playing jazz music and is probably of the guitar family. See *Guitar.

Bar See *Bar line, *Barform, *Measure.

Barbitos A lyre-type instrument of ancient Greece.

Barcarolle (Fr.) (bär—kär—ōl) Barcarole. From barca (It.), boat. A boat song or instrumental composition in keeping with the type of songs sung by the gondoliers of Venice. It has the rhythmic feeling of 2 or 4 ($\frac{6}{8}$ or $\frac{12}{8}$ time.) Examples: Jacques Offenbach (1819-1880) "Barcarolle" from the opera *Tales of Hoffman;* Gabriel Fauré (1845-1924) *Barcarolle, No. 3*; Peter Ilyich Tchaikovsky (1840-1893) *The Seasons*, Piano (Barcarolle, (June), Opus 37, No. 6).

Barform (Ger.) (bär'—fōrm) A German musical form having a scheme of AAB. It originated in the era of the minnesinger and meistersinger. J. S. Bach (1685-1750) used the "bar form" (AAB) in his *Partita No. 4, Chorale Variation: O Gott Du Frommer Gott.*

Bariolage (Fr.) (bär—ē—ō—läzh) A technique used in violin playing by moving from or to open and stopped strings. It is a color change with reference to open and closed strings.

Baritone (1) A voice range of about two octaves from G (1st line on the bass staff) to g ' (second line treble clef). (2) The voice between the male tenor and bass voices. (3) The musical instruments in each family ranging between the tenor and bass instruments. (4) Barytone.

Baritone clef F clef having F below middle C on the third line of the staff. An example of the old F clef:

See *Clefs.

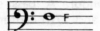

Bartione horn A brass valved instrument built in concert pitch C or Bb. The range is from E to b ' flat. It is primarily used in bands and is a member of the brass section: trumpet (cornet), French Horn, baritone (euphonium), trombone, tuba (sousaphone). In today's bands the baritone is usually played in Bb and reads the notation in the treble clef while the instrument transposes to the bass clef. The euphonium is built in the key of C and the player plays and reads in the bass clef. The baritone, horn and the euphonium are similar in pitch, range, and shape. See *Brass instruments.

Baritone oboe An oboe having a double reed, which plays one octave below the oboe. It was invented by Heckel in 1904. See *Heckelphone.

Baritone saxhorn See *Baritone, *Flügelhorn family.

Baritone saxophone The second lowest instrument in the saxophone family. Pitched in Eb. See *Saxophone.

Baritos A name applied to a number of instruments of the violin class during the 16th and 17th centuries.

Bar line The vertical line on the staff 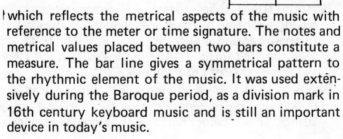 which reflects the metrical aspects of the music with reference to the meter or time signature. The notes and metrical values placed between two bars constitute a measure. The bar line gives a symmetrical pattern to the rhythmic element of the music. It was used extensively during the Baroque period, as a division mark in 16th century keyboard music and is still an important device in today's music.

Barocco (It.) (bär—rŏk '—kō) Baroque; barrócco. A pearl of irregular shape or form. Generally, it means grotesque. See *Baroque music.

Baroque music A style of music from c. 1600-1750 coming between the Renaissance and Classical periods of music. It is a period in which many styles, forms and techniques were developed and defined. For example; ostinato-form, variations, suite, sonata, aria, rondo, concerto, opera, cantata, oratorio, improvization, thorough-bass, concerto grosso, ornamentation, and generally, instrumental music. It is a period of musical growth, exuberance and expressiveness. The music of Bach and Handel seems to sum up this era of tension and drive. Barocco (Sp.); Barock (Ger.).

Barré (Fr.) (bär—rā) A technique of playing chords on a banjo, guitar, etc. by placing a finger across all strings at the same point.

Barrell organ An 18th century English church organ that played a variety of psalms and hymn tunes. This mechanical instrument produced tunes when a revolving barrel, having pins or studs protruding from the surface, would open valves, allowing air to be forced into pipes. These would, in turn, produce a tone or group of tones. The barrels were interchangeable and each represented a different psalm or hymn. Often, the term is applied to the 19th and 20th century street organ which also uses the barrel principle.

Baryton (1) A bass gamba. A viola di bordone, which was a bowed instrument used a great deal in Haydn's time. It was similar to the bass viol with melody strings which vibrated over several added strings. These added strings vibrated from sympathetic vibrations produced by the bowed strings. (2) French and German for baritone.

Barytone See *Baryton, *Baritone.

Bass (1) The lowest range in both vocal and instrumental voices. Generally, the tones below middle C in the bass (F) clef. (2) In instrumental music, some instruments that play in the bass clef are: bass trombone, tuba, bassoon, contrabassoon, cello, and string bass. (3) The voice below the baritone having an approximate range of from E (below bass clef) to c' (middle c) is referred to as the bass voice. See *Treble, *Bass clef.

Bassa (It.) (bäs'–sä), **Bassa Ottava** (It.) (bäs'–sä ŏt–tä'–vä) 8va bassa. Play the note or group of notes one octave lower than written. Con = with, therefore, con 8va bassa means to play the notes written plus doubling the written note one octave lower.

Bassanello A 16th century double reed instrument having a cylindrical-bore in a single tube. They were made in various sizes. A shawm.

Bass bar A strip of wood placed inside and under the belly of instruments of the violin and viol family at the point under the left leg of the bridge. E.g., on the violin it would be glued under the g string side of the bridge.

Bass baritone The voice range encompassing the bass and baritone range. A bass voice and quality, but the ability to sing in the baritone range. Sometimes, a voice having not quite a low bass or a true baritone quality or range.

Bass cither Bijuga cither. A 16th century double neck instrument popular in England. It had bass strings which did not go over the finger board.

Bass clarinet Clarinette basse (Fr.) bassklarinette (Ger.) A single reed woodwind instrument which is built one octave lower than the Bb clarinet. It is built in Bb with a curved metal neck and has a metal bell at the bottom which turns up and outward. The music is written in the treble clef. The compass of the range is an octave lower than the Bb clarinet. With the addition of the low Eb key, the instrument can go an additional half-step lower. It sounds a major ninth lower than the written note. See *Clarinet.

Bass clef The F clef or lower clef of the grand staff. F is designated on the fourth line. The lines are G, B, D, F, A; spaces are A, C, E, G, from lower to upper lines and spaces. See *Clefs.

Bass drum A large cicrular wooden or plastic shell, usually covered on both sides with plastic or skin, called drum heads. It does not have a specific pitch but the drum head is stretched tightly in order to produce a percussive and precise sound when struck with a beater covered with felt or other soft substances. A roll can be played by using two sticks.

Basse (Fr.) (bäs) Bass or fundamental bass.

Basse chiffré (Fr.) (bäs shēf—rā) Figured bass or thorough bass.

Basse continue (Fr.) (bäs kō(n)—tēn—ü) basso continuo (It.) (bäs'—sō kōn—tēn'—ū—ō) Figured bass.

Basse danse (Fr.) (bäs dä(n)s) Low dance. A name given to a French dance popular in the French courts during the 15th and 16th centuries. The dancers kept their feet close to the floor and glided to a moderate tempo in duple or sometimes triple time. It was usually played on a melodic insturment.

Basse fondamentale (Fr.) (bäs fō(n)—dä—mĕn—täl) Foundation. Fundamental bass.

Basset horn An obsolete alto clarinet developed in the late 18th century. It took on several shapes and forms in its development and was used by Mozart, Beethoven and Mendelssohn. Also cor di basset (Fr.); Bassethorn (Ger.); corno de basset (It.) See *Clarinet family.

Basset-oboe Heckelphon in German. A bass oboe which is one octave lower than the regular oboe. See *Oboe.

Bass flute Bassflöte (Ger.) (1) A contrabass flute. A flute built one octave lower than the regular flute. (2) A term sometimes used to identify the alto flute which is built a perfect fourth lower than the regular flute. (3) An organ stop. See *Flute.

Bass horn An 18th century instrument developed from an early instrument called serpent or cornett. It was made of wood or brass with a cup mouthpiece, conical tube, six open finger holes, and some few closed holes. It is also referred to as the Russian bassoon.

Bassist (1) A singer with a bass voice. (2) A player who plays a bass instrument.

35

Bassklarinette (Ger.) (bäs—klär—ĭn—ĕt'—tä) Bass clarinet.

Bass lute A chitarrone. A long archlute. See *Lute.

Basso (It.) (bäs'—sō) Low or bass.

Basso cantante (It.) (bäs'—sō kän—tän—'tä) Singing bass. Lyrical type bass.

Basso concertante (It.) (bäs'—sō cŏn—chĕr—tän'—tä) Concert bass or principal bass. A part played on the cello, for example, of a melodic nature from the bass line.

Basso continuo (It.) (bäs'—sō kŏn—tē'—noō—ō) Continuous bass; figured bass; thorough-bass. In a figured bass the bass line is marked with symbols which indicate what harmony is to be played above on a keyboard instrument. It was used in 17th and 18th century music. It was also used to indicate the accompaniment for one or more instruments or voices. In a ground bass the figure is repeated in the bass throughout the musical work. See *Basso ostinato, *Ground bass, *Figured bass, *Thorough bass.

Basso fundamental The fundamental or root of the chord. The bass and base of the chord.

Basson (Fr.) (bäs—sō(n) Bassoon.

Bassoon Faggott (Ger.) (fä—gŏt'); Fagotto (It.) (fä—gŏt'—tō); Basson (Fr.) (1) A double reed instrument which is the bass of the woodwind section. It has a narrow conical bore. The contrabassoon is made of wood, has a range of three and one-half octaves from B♭b to d'' and plays in the bass and tenor clefs. The total length of the parts (bell, long joint sections, butt, wing, and crook) is about eight feet. The bassoon dates back to the 16th century. The abbreviation is Bsn. (2) An organ stop. See *Instruments, *Woodwinds.

Bassoon quinte A smaller bassoon, a fifth higher than the bassoon. Also called a tenoroon.

Bassoon russe Russian bassoon. A type of 18th century bass horn similar to the serpent or in the style of the bassoon.

Basso ostinato (It.) (bäs'—sō ŏs—tĭn—ä'—tō) Ground bass. Generally, a pattern or single phrase (usually

36

about four measures in length) which is repeated over and over in the bass line while the upper parts change. An early example of the use of ostinato is the two part "pes" or ostinato of *Sumer is icumen* in (c. 1310.) The ostinato technique has been used by many composers since then such as Bach, Brahms, and others. Henry Purcell (1659-1695) used an ostinato in "Dido's Lament" from his opera *Dido and Aeneas*. The ostinato:

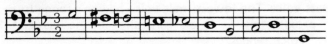

Many contemporary composers such as Bartok and Stravinsky are using the ostinato technique. The "boogie-woogie" piano style popular in the 1930's is a good example of an ostinato bass. An example of one style of "boogie-woogie":

This is repeated over and over.

Basso profundo (It.) (bäs'—sō prō—fŏn'—dō) The lowest male voice. Deep bass or profound bass.

Basso ripieno (It.) (bäs'—sō rē—pē—ā'—nō) A bass part to be played only in the tutti section, not in solo. See *Ripieno, *Tutti.

Bassposaune (Ger.) (bäs—pō—zow'—nå) Bass trombone.

Bass trombone The trombone a fourth lower than the tenor trombone. Built in F. or G. The range is from B' to g'. See *Trombone.

Bass trumpet See *Trumpet.

Bass tuba See *Tuba

Bass viol A short term for double bass or stringed bass. The strings are tuned and sound an octave lower. The range of a four string bass viol is

If a fifth string is added it is tuned to C. During the 17th century it was the viola da gamba. See *Instruments, *Double bass, *Contrabass.

Bass voice The lowest male voice having a range from approximately E. to e', generally in the bass clef. See *Voice ranges.

Batacuda bands (1) Originally percussion ensembles of Africa. (2) In Brazilian folk music, percussion ensembles that play at a club and during carnivals.

Bathyphon A 19th century woodwind instrument of the clarinet family. It had a range from D to b♭ in bass clef. It was much like the serpent. See *Clarinet.

Baton A stick or wand used when directing a group of performers. See *Conducting.

Battaglia (It.) (bät—täl'—yä) Battle. Programmatic music popular during the 16th—18th cenutries in which percussive techniques were used to imitate battle sounds.

Battement (Fr.) (bät—ma(ñ)) A beat. A trill, mordent, or shake which begins a half-tone below the main note. Also, vibrato, ornament. See *Trill, *Mordent.

Batterie (Fr.) (bät—trē) Battery. The percussion section.

Battery (1) An arpeggio. (2) A group of percussion instruments. See *Ornaments.

Battuta (It.) (bät—too'—tä) (1) Beat. An emphasis on the first beat of a measure. (2) A battuta (to the beat) as in tempo, return to strict time.

Bay Psalm Book The first book published in America. A book of psalms published in 1640 in Cambridge, Massachusetts which was the early colonists metrical version of the psalms they had brought from England. The early editions had no music. In 1690 twelve tunes were added. The 1698 edition included thirteen tunes which were harmonized in two parts.

38

BB^b bass Tuba or sousaphone.

B Dur (Ger.) (bā dōor) The key of B^b major in German.

Be (Ger.) (bā) The German sign for the flat (b).

Beat (1) A pulse. Movement in music. Units of time, pace, and accents within the measure. It is related to the time signature and tempo. (2) In acoustics, alternations in intensity are called beats. When two tones are sounded together and vary slightly in pitch "beats" are heard. As the tones come perfectly in tune with each other the "beats" disappear. (3) An old English name for ornaments which resembled a type of trill or appoggiatura. See *Acoustics.

Beats The result of two sound waves of different vibrations conflicting with each other. It is heard as a reoccuring throb at regular intervals. The beats vary depending on the distance between the two frequencies. See *Acoustics.

Be-bop A popular jazz term (slang) for a style of "hot" jazz during the 1940's and 1950's. It was played by a small jazz (instrumental) ensemble. The performers improvised on the basic harmonic structure of a given compostiion without regard to its melody. The rhythm section placed the emphasis on the accents of the music. When this technique of "Bop" music is applied to large bands it is called "Progressive jazz".

Bec (Fr.) (bĕk) A mouthpiece of the type inserted into the mouth by the player of an instrument. E.g., clarinet mouthpiece.

Bécarre (Fr.) (bā—kär) The natural ♮ sign. Return to the natural note after a raised or lowered note as a result of a # or b.

Becken (Ger.) (bĕk'—ản) Cymbals.

Bedeckt (Ger.) (bả—dĕkt') Stopped.

Befiedern (Ger.) (bả—fē'—dĕrn) To feather. A rapid, bouncing, staccato bowing technique.

Begleiten (Ger.) (bả—glī'—tēn) To accompany.

Beitöne (Ger.) (bi'—tĕ(r)—nả) Aliquot tones or scaling. The sympathetic vibrations of strings added above the regular strings.

39

Bel A unit of measurement for intensity or a degree of loudness. Ten decibels equal one bel. See *Acoustics.

Bel canto (It.) (bě l‧ kän'–tō) Beautiful singing. The beautiful, lyric style of singing used in the 18th century Italian vocal music. This style is closely related to the Neapolitan opera.

Bell (1) The larger flared end of a musical instrument, especially on brass instruments. (2) An orchestral percussion instrument. (3) A variety of church bells.

Bell-lyra A glockenspiel. A portable lyre shaped instrument having steel bars pitched in semitones as on the piano keyboard. Portable bells. Used in concert and marching bands.

Bellows The chest where air is collected to be forced out through wind pipes to produce a sound as, for example, in the organ, accordian, etc.

Bells Orchestra bells, orchestral glockenspiel. Metal bars of various sizes and thickness represent chromatic semitones two octaves or more. The tone is sounded by striking the bar or bars with mallets. Sometimes resonators are added.

Belly The upper part (table) of a stringed instrument such as the violin or other bowed instrument. It is a resonator or sound board over which the strings are stretched.

Bé mol (Fr.) (bā–mŏl), **bemolle** (It.) (bā–mŏl'–lā) With a flat. The sign for flat (b).

Ben, bene (It.) (bān, bā'–nā) Good, well.

Benediction (1) The blessing given by a minister at the end of a service. (2) Benediction of the Blessed Sacrament. A special service of the Roman Catholic Church in which the congregation receives a blessing with the Host. It includes prayers, hymn(s), and the blessing.

Benedictus qui venit (Lat.) (bā–nā–dēk'–too s kwē vā'–nit) "Blessed is He Who comes." The Benedictus follows the Sanctus, actually the second part or the conclusion of the Sanctus. It is the fourth part of the Ordinary of the Mass. The Latin test is "Benedictus qui venit in nomine Domini. Hosanna in excelsis."

For centuries the Latin was used. The current practice is to speak or sing the text in the vernacular. The English translation is as follows: "Blessed is He Who comes in the name of the Lord. Hosanna in the highest." The "Benedictus" is also used in musical settings by many composers. A good example is found in the J. S. Bach (1685-1750) *Mass in B Minor,* section XXI, "Benedictus". See *Mass, *Ordinary of the Mass.

Ben marcato (It.) (bān mär—kä '—tō) Well marked.

Bequadro (It.) (bā—kwä '—drō) The natural ♮ sign. See *Bécarre.

Berceuse (Fr.) (bĕr—sûz) Cradle. Cradle song or lullaby. Moderate, quiet and in $\frac{3}{4}$ or $\frac{6}{8}$ time. It may be vocal or instrumental but the title is usually applied to instrumental pieces of this style. Example: Benjamin Godard (1849-1895) "Berceuse" from *Jocelyn*).

Bergerette (Fr.) (bĕr—zhĕr—ĕt) Shepherdess song. (1) A form of 15th century French poetry. (2) Instrumental dances of the 16th century in a lively triple meter. (3) An 18th century French song with a pastoral theme.

Bes (Ger.) (bĕs) Bbb (B double flat).

Betonen (Ger.) (bā—tōn '—å n) Accent or stress.

Bewegt (Ger.) (bā—vāgt ') (mosso (It.) (mōs '—sō)) Motion, moved, fast.

B flat Bb. A semitone below the note B. E.g., Clef:

Treble Clef   Bass Clef   Alto Clef   Tenor Clef

Bible regal A small portable Renaissance reed organ which folded together into the bellows which resembled the shape of a Bible.

Bien (Fr.) (bē—ĕ (n) Good, well, very.

Bijuga cither Bass cither, theorbo cither.

Bimetric Two meters used at the same time. See *Polymetric.

Binary form Two main sections which follow a scheme of AB. Usually a whole which has two halves. A continuous form using similar material throughout. The form may be symmetrical or asymmetrical. The two-part song form is the smallest example of this structure. Many examples are found in folk songs, hymns, and other vocal music. For example, *America* and *Londonderry Air.* The binary structure is also used in instrumental music. For example, Domenico Scarlatti (1685-1757) wrote over 550 single-movement harpsichord sonatas (Esercizi per gravicembalo) most of which are in binary form and have a double bar in the middle. See *Ternary form, *Form.

Binary measure Two beats to a measure.

Bind Tie.

Bis (Lat.) ((Fr.) (bēs)) Twice, encore. Bisser (Fr.) (bēs—sā) To repeat. To play or sing twice, repeat.

Bit (1) An extra piece added to a wind instrument to extend the length of the tubing for lower tones. (2) A tube added to fit special size mouthpieces.

Bitonal Music having two key centers at the same time.

Bitonality The technique of writing in two keys at the same time. The same notes can be related to different keys by being in different positions, or the musical lines can be in separate and unrelated keys. Darius Milhaud (1892-1974) is one exponent of bitonal music. See *Polytonality, *Harmony.

Biwa (Jap.) An ancient Japanese stringed instrument.

Bizzarro (It.) (bet—zä'—rō), bizarre (Fr.) (bē—zär) Bizarre. Whimsical, capricious.

Black keys The black keys of the piano keyboard, which raise or lower the notes of the white keys a semitone, depending on the direction from which the black keys are approached.

Blasmusik (Ger.) (bläz'—moo—zēk) Blasen - to blow. Music for wind or blowing instrument. Blasinstrument (Ger.) Wind instrument.

Blatt (Ger.) (blät) Reed.

Blech (Ger.) (blĕkh) Tin, metal, brass. Blechinstrumente (Ger.) brass instrument.

Blechmusik (Ger.) (blĕ kh '–moo –zēk) Music for brass.

Block chords Chords made up of several voices that are sounded together and move together in parallel motion.

Blockflöte (Ger.) (blŏk '– flĕ (r)–tē) Whistle or flute. Family or recorders or flageolets. Block refers to the blocking of one end (upper end) of the whistle or flute. See *Whistle.

Blue notes In the jazz style of music, a blue note is one that varies from the true pitch. It is usually flatted slightly from the pure intonation. The tones usually involved are those of the 3rd, 5th, and 7th degrees of the scale. Blue notes are used in Jazz and Blues. See *Jazz, *Blues.

Blues A style of folk music of negro origin and related to the negro spiritual of the late 19th century. The blues were introduced between 1900 and 1910. The text consists of three lines, a rhymed couplet in iambic pentameter, with the second line a repetition of the first. The form consists of three, four-measure phrases that equal 12 measures. The tempo is slow and the meter is usually in $\frac{4}{4}$. The chord progression is set in a basic pattern if I, IV, I, V₇, I. The blues scale consists of the major scale with the third and seventh tones often lowered a semitone. Some blues melodies also consist of 8 measures and 16 measures. The blues are both vocal and instrumental and are improvised by the jazz musician. The blues are an expression of what one feels, a type of mood music. See *Jazz, *Blue notes.

B mol (Fr.) (bā mŏl) The B♭.

B moll (Ger.) (bā mawl) Key of B♭ minor

Bocal (Fr.) (bō–käl) Mouthpiece

Bocca aperta (It.) (bŏk '–kä ä–pĕr '–tä) Open mouthed.

Bocca chiusa (It.) (bŏk '–kä kē–oo'–zä) Singing with lips together. See *Bouche fermée.

Body The main part of a stringed instrument which has the resonating section.

Boehm system The system of fingering woodwind instruments invented by Theobald Boehm (1794-1881). The system improved the acoustical position of the finger holes and made the fingering technique easier for the performer. It is used on flutes, oboes, bassoons, and clarinets.

Bogen (Ger.) (bō'—gĕ n) Bow or arch. The bowing of stringed instruments. Arco.

Bolero An early Spanish dance. The music is in a moderate tempo, in triple time, and is rhythmical in nature. Castanets are used in the dance and in some musical compositions. E.g., Maurice Ravel (1875-1937) *Bolero for Orchestra*. An example of bolero rhythm:

repeated over and over in Ravel's *Bolero*.

Bombarda (It.) (bŏ m—bär'—dä) (1) A bass tuba (Bombardon). (2) An organ stop (bombarde). (3) A bass shawm (bombard).

Bombs In jazz, a slang term to describe a technique whereby the drummer plays strong accents off the beat.

Bongos Drums. Small Cuban drums played with the fingers and thumbs.

Bonnang Gong chimes. A Javanese percussion instrument having several gongs suspended on a rectangular frame.

Boogie-woogie A jazz term for swing music which is played on a piano over an ostinato bass that is rhythmical and accented. Primarily a piano style during the 1930's. The left hand plays eight notes to a bar. The chordal structure for several measures is based on a pattern of tonic, subdominant, tonic, dominant tonic. See *Basso ostinato.

Bop A 1940-1950 style of jazz music. The music was performed by small groups with each player having much solo work. There was great freedom of expression and considerable use of extended harmonies, such as the 9th, 11th, 13th chords, etc. It is also called re-bop and be-bop. See *Be-bop.

Bordun (Ger.) (bôr'—dŭn), bordone (It.) (bôr—dō'—nä) (1) The lowest string of the bass. (2) A drone bass. (3) An organ stop having a very low pitch. See *Bourdon.

Bore The size of the opening in a tube of a wind instrument. The width of the tube.

Borre (It.) (bŏr'–rā) See *Bourrée.

Bossa Nova New touch. A development in jazz during the 1960's which was a combination of Brazillan jazz and jazz of the United States. It has a jazz beat, uses South American rhythm, style and instruments. This style is used by the Paul Winter jazz ensemble.

Bouche fermé e (Fr.) (boosh fĕr–mā) With closed mouth. See *Bocca chiusa.

Bourdon (Fr.) (boor–dō (n)) (1) A drone or pedal point. E.g., the bass line of a bagpipe. (2) Name given to pieces of music that have bass lines or accompaniment with repeated notes in the bass or a drone bass. See *Drone.

Bouré e (Fr.) (boo–rā) (1) A French dance which begins on a single upbeat and moves quickly in duple time. (2) A dance movement. (3) One of the dances used in a suite. In the 18th century suite it was often placed between a sarabande and a gigue. For example: J. S. Bach (1685-1750) *English Suite, No. 1 in A,* for piano. (Sarabande, Bourrée, Gigue). Theme I, Bouré e:

Also bore (It.), borry.

Boutade (Fr.) (boo–tād) Whim, caprice. (1) A spectacular dance. (2) An instrumental fantasy.

Bout d'archet (Fr.) (boo d'är–shā) Tip of the bow.

Bow (Archet (Fr.)) A stick, concave, having horsehair attached to each end and pulled taut. It is pulled across the strings to start the strings vibrating.

Bow-clavier An 18th century instrument which had a keyboard and strings. Tones were sounded when small bows rubbed against the strings. Now obsolete.

Bowed string Pulling a bow across the string as opposed to a plucked string.

Bow hair Usually horsehair used in making bows for violins, violas, etc.

45

Bowing The playing of a stringed instrument with a bow. Several techniques are used. Legato(It.), bowing up and down; détaché (Fr.) a broad marked bow; martellato (It.), the hammered stroke; spiccato (It.), rapid, short, bouncing bow; ricochet or jeté (Fr.), the bow bounces as a result of dropping or throwing the bow on the string; staccato (It.), a number of notes played on the same bow in martelé style; tremolo (It.), moving the bow back and forth very quickly; col legno (It.), playing with the stick part of the bow rather than the hair; sul ponticello (It.), playing near the bridge; a punta d'arco (It.), play at the point of the bow; saltando (It.), bow bounces lightly on the string (sautillé (Fr.); flautando (It.), light style, as in flute playing, near the fingerboard; sulla tastiera (It.), play with bow on fingerboard; au talon (Fr.), heel of the bow; arpeggio (It.), broken chords; sur la touche (Fr.), over the fingerboard; am Steg (Ger.) on the bridge; ondule (Fr.) tremolo; arco (It.), bowed. See *Bowing marks.

Bowing Marks ⊓ │down bow; V up bow; ⌒ slur; ♩ detached; ♩♩♩♩ staccato; ♩ hammered stroke; short stroke; ♩♩ slightly separated; tremolo.

Braccio (It.) (brä'– chē–ō) Arm. Instrument of the string family held at arm level.

Brace A bracket and line joining two or more staves. E.g., the treble and bass staves joined to form the Grand Staff.

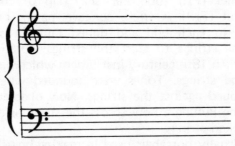

See *Accolade.

Brandenburg Concerti A set of six concerti grossi written by Bach in 1721, commissioned by the Margrave of Brandenburg. *No. 1 in F Major; No. 2 in F Major; No. 3 in G Major; No. 4 in G Major; No. 5 in D Major; No. 6 in Bb Major.* Although these works are considered to be of the concerto grosso style, numbers 1, 3, and 6 do not have a clear and fixed smaller group which contrasts with the larger group as is the case in numbers 2, 4, and 5. See *Concertino, *Ripieno, *Concerto grosso, *Tutti.

Branle (Fr.) (brä(n)l), brando (It.)(brän'–dō) (1) A shaking or tossing motion, jog, brawl, to sway (branler). (2) A French 16th and 17th century dance done with a swaying movement and with singing. Some were in duple meter and some in triple meter.

Brass (1) A reference to the wind instruments of the brass family which are made from brass or other metals or materials (2) The brass band. (3) Brass section. (4) Brass mouthpieces.

Brass band A band consisting of brass and percussion instruments, no woodwinds. It originated in England in the early part of the 19th century. The brass band in England consists of Eb cornet (1), Bb cornets (8), Bb flügelhorn (1), Eb saxhorns (3), Bb baritones (2) Bb euphoniums (2), Bb tenor trombones (2), Bb bass trombone (1), Eb bass tubas (2) called bombardons, and BBb bass tubas (2) The military band includes woodwind instruments. See *Military band.

Brass instruments Instruments made of metal or brass that have cup-shaped or funnel-shaped mouthpieces which are pressed against the lips. When the lips vibrate, they produce vibrations in the brass tubing which produces a tone. The instruments have slides of valves. E.g., trumpet, cornet, flügelhorn, French horn, bugle, baritone, euphonium saxhorn, trombone, tuba, sousaphone. See *Ansatz, *Embouchure, *Crook.

Bratsche (Ger.) (brȧt'–shȧ) Viola.

Braul Round dance. English for branle. Also, brawl. See *Branle.

Bravourarie, bravoure (Fr.) (brä—voo —rä—re, brä—voor) bravura (It.) (brä—voo'—rä) Courage, brave. A florid and brilliant style of playing.

Bravura (It.) (brä—voo'—rä) Skill. Music which demands great virtuosity.

Break (1) In jazz, when a soloist takes a "ride" or plays a short passage ad lib. (2) The break between registers of an instrument, such as is found in the clarinet from Bb to B♮. (3) The point at which the quality of the voice may change when moving form one register to another.

Breit (Ger.) (bri t) Broad, wide.

Breve (1) A short note in its original form. (2) Written |♢|| or ⊨⊣ . It becomes the longest note of the old notation. A semibreve is the equivalent of a whole note. The breve is twice as long as the semibreve.

Bridge (1) The wood piece that holds the strings away from the belly of a string instrument. It is arched and carries the vibrations from the strings to the sound board and body of the instrument. (2) The music that connects two larger sections of music. It may be a modulation from one section to another. (3) In jazz, the third 8 bar section of a 32 measure work. E.g., form: AABA, the B section would be the bridge. See *Bridge passage.

Bridge passage A secondary section or connection between two sections. See *Bridge.

Brillante (It.) (bri l—län '—tä)Brilliant. A style of playing.

Brindisi (It.) (bri n—de '—ze)' Toast, health. A drinking song. Giving a toast as in operatic scenes.

Brio, con (bre '—o, kon) With brilliance, with spirit or verve.

Broken chord Notes of a chord played in succession, not simultaneously. See *Arpeggio.

Broken consort A term used in the 16th and 17th centuries. An ensemble comprised of different kinds of instruments. Whole consort refers to an ensemble comprised of instruments of the same family. See *Consort.

Broken octave (1) During the 19th century an arrangement of the lower octave of the piano in which all the
keys were in a normal poistion except that A ' replaced
C# resulting in a broken octave. Broken octave:

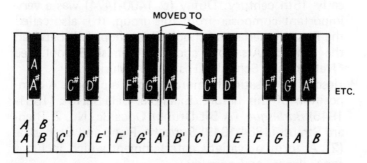

(2) An octave in which the notes are played separately.
Brunette (Fr.) (broo—nĕt) A simple love song of the 17th
and 18th centuries.
Brustwerk (Ger.) (broŏst '–vĕrk) Choir organ. In the early
German organs a manual having stops of a softer tone
than those of the Great organ.
B sharp B#. A semitone above the note B. E.g.
Clef:

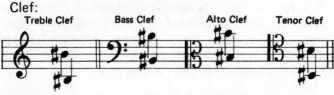

Buccina (Lat.), buccin (Fr.) (bük—să(n)) Name of an instrument of the lower brass used in ancient Rome.
Buffo (It.) (boo'–fō), buffa (It.) (boo'–fä) Comic, buff-
oon, jester. E.g., opera buffa meaning comic opera.
Bugle An instrument used by the military for bugle calls.
A brass instrument, smaller than the trumpet, no valves,
usually in the key of Bb or G. Sometimes a valve is
added to increase the range. Harmonics are used, along
with good lip control to play a melodic line. See *Brass.

Burden (1) A refrain of a song. (2) A drone or bass part. See *Fauxbourdon, *Bourdon, *Drone.

Burgundian School The name given to a school of composers associated with the Duke of Burgandy in the early 15th century. Dufay (c. 1400-1474) was a very important composer from this group. It is also called the First Netherlands School. This school falls between the time of Ars nova and the Flemish School. See *Netherlands School, *History of Music.

Burlesque (1) A satire; humorous work; a parody. A composition of this nature. Example: Bela Bartók (1881-1945) *Burlesque* (A Bit Drunk) Opus 8c, No. 2; Richard Strauss (1864-1949) *Burleske,* Piano and Orchestra. (2) A form of variety entertainment which includes song, dance, and comedy.

Burletta (It.) (boor—lĕt'—tä) Trick or joke. A comic work or one in jest. Also burla or burlesca. See *Burlesque.

Byzantine chant It is modal, monophonic, no accompaniment, basically diatonic, and has no strict or basic meter. The texts were based on free poetry rather than liturgical texts. The music is similar in style to the Gregorian chant. See *Byzantine music.

Byzantine music Church music of the Eastern Roman Empire founded by Constantine during the early 4th century. The term Byzantine is related to Constantinople, later Istanbul. The influence of this Eastern music is shown in the many musical elements which it has in common with the plain song or plain chant of the Western church. See *Byzantine chant.

C

C (1) The first note or tonic of the scale of C major or the third degree of the scale of A minor. (2) On various clefs, the note appears as follows:

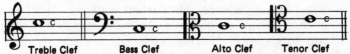

Treble Clef   **Bass Clef**   **Alto Clef**   **Tenor Clef**

(3) An ornamental C is used as a C clef. The line or space identified by the ornamental C is middle C in the grand staff. Two examples of the C clef often seen in orchestral music are;

Alto clef    and tenor clef

(4) C is also used a time signature which equals $\frac{4}{4}$ time, e.g.,

(5) The sign ¢ indicates alla breve. (6) The letter is used as an abbreviation for such words as: con, capo, contralto, etc. (7) Many musical instruments are pitched in the key of C (e.g., trumpet in C). (8) C is used to identify many keys such as C major, Cb major, C# major, C minor, C# minor. See *Alla breve, *Clef, *Grand staff, *Key, *Letter names, *Notation, *Pitch names, *Scale.

C. A. Coll' arco (kŏl är '—kō) A direction in string music. With the bow.

Cabaletta (It.) (kä—bä—lĕt '—tä) (1) The final section of an aria, as in Cavatinetta. (2) A short song in operatic style.

Caccia (It.) (kä '—chē—ä) A chase. (1) A canonic form in two parts used in the 14th century. (2) A form of Italian poetry of the 14th century. The text often dealt with hunting or outdoor activities.

Cachucha (Sp.) (kä—choo'—chä) A Spanish dance, lively and in triple meter. Like bolero.

Cacophony Dissonant sound.

Cadence A feeling of conclusion at the end of a phrase or musical line. There are many varieties such as the final or full cadence which ends on a I chord as well as other cadences which close on a chord other than the tonic. See *Plagal cadence, *Imperfect cadence, *Half cadence, *Deceptive cadence, *Landini cadence, *Interrupted cadence, *Perfect cadence.

Cadence (Fr.) (kä—dä(n) s) Trill, quaver, or ornament.

Cadent Ornamental notes leading away from the main note, whereas appoggiatura means ornamental notes leading to the main note. See *Nachschlag, *Agrément.

Cadenza (It.) (kä—dĕnd'—zä) Cadence, cadenza. This began as improvisation in operatic arias in the 18th century and was later used in instrumental works. In the 19th century the notation for the cadenza was written out for the performer. It is a solo passage without accompaniment, with great freedom for the performer. The technique is used a great deal in the concerto. For example, *Concerto in E Minor for Violin and Orchestra,* Op. 64 by Felix Mendelssohn (1809-1847).

Caesura A sense pause in the movement of the music in sacred music, as in sapphic meter. A pause in the middle of a verse marked by a double vertical line (II).

Caisse (Fr.) (kĕ ss) Acrate or box. A musical drum.

Caisse claire (Fr.) (kĕ ss klĕ r) Side drum, snare drum.

Caisse, grosse (Fr.) (kĕ ss, grōs) Overly large box. Bass drum.

Caisse roulante (Fr.) (kĕ ss rōo —lä(n)t) Rolling drum, tenor drum.

Caisse sourde (Fr.) (kĕss sōord) Hollow drum, tenor drum.

Cake-walk A strut, promenade, or dance to music. This dance was polular with the Negro in the United States during the late 19th century. Cakes were given as prizes for the best dancing. Claude Debussy (1862-1918) wrote a classic example in his *Golliwog's Cakewalk.* The rhythmic pattern is

Calando (It.) (kä—län'—dō) Dying away, becoming softer and slower.

Calata (It.) (kä—lä'—tä) A 16th century Italian dance usually notated in duple time.

Calcando (It.) (käl—kän'—dō) Speed up the tempo. See *Accelerando.

Calliope (1) One of the muses (epic poetry). (2) An American keyboard instrument invented in the late 19th century. The tone is produced through steam whistles. It may be heard at carnivals or on a steam boat.

Calmare, calma, calmato (It.) (käl—mär'—ä, käl'—mä, käl—mät'—ō) Calm or calmer.

Calme (Fr.) (kälm) Tranquil, calm.

Calore, con (It.) (kä—law'—rä, kōn) Heat. With warmth, passion.

Cambiare (It.) (käm—bē—ä'—rä) To change, to shift.

Cambiata (It.) (käm—bē—ä'—tä) nota cambiata. To change or changed note. A non-harmonic note or non-chord note. An accented non-harmonic note. In a scale sequence of notes, the cambiata note would be that note out of sequence whether the sequence is moving up or down. The cambiata note moves (1) an interval of a 3rd down, then up a step or (2) an interval of a 3rd up, then down a step depending on the direction of the scale. E.g., **cambiata note or changing note

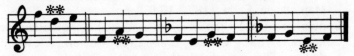

See *Non-harmonic, *Non-chord tones.

Camera (It.) (kä'—mä—rä) Chamber or room. Musica da camera-chamber music. Outside the realm of church music.' Secular.

Camerata (It.) (kä—mä—rä'—tä) Comrade. A group of men (poets, composers, singers, instrumentalists) met in the late 16th century to change the concept of writing music from the polyphonic style to that of the homophonic style. They wanted the text to be more important and to reflect in the new style the old Greek style and relationship of monophonic music and text. This concern led to a revival of the association of music with drama. This new form (opera) is demonstrated in *Eurydice* (about 1600) by Jacopo Peri (1561-1633). See *Nuove musiche

Camminare (It.) (käm—mē—nä'—rā) To walk or step.

Campana (It.) (käm—pä'—nä) Bell.

Campanello (It.) (käm—pä—nḛ l'—lō) A little bell.

Canario (Sp.) (kä—nä'—rē—ō) Canary. A dance named after the people of the Canary Islands. It is somewhat like a gigue. The style can be found in early harpsichord suites.

Cancan A 19th century lively Parisian dance in $\frac{2}{4}$ time which was performed in dance halls. The girls jumped, did acrobatics, and behaved in what was described as a vulgar and scandalous way. The style of music is used in the opera *Orpheus in Hades* by Jacques Offenbach (1819-1880). Also, the can-can (1st theme) in the fifth section of the ballet *La Boutique Fantasque* of Gioacchino Antonio Rossini (1792-1868).

Cancel sign A (♮) natural sign which returns a raised or lowered note to its natural position from a sharp or a flat. It cancels a sharp or a flat.

Cancion (Sp.) (kä—thē—ōn') (1) Song. Words and music. (2) A Spanish dance. For example, "Canción" from *Suite Populaire Espagñole for Violin and Piano* by Manuel de Falla (1876-1946).

Cancionero (Sp.) (kän—thē—ō—nä'—rō) Song collection.

Cancrizans (Lat.) Cancer, crab. Crab motion. A canonic device. The melody is played backwards from end to beginning. See *Retrograde, *Canon.

Canned music Music pre-recorded, taped, records, etc. Not live music. A slang term.

Canon Rule, in Greek. Strict imitation; polyphonic music in which a melodic line is imitated in one or more parts, at the same or different pitch, usually within a measure or so, in pursuit, forming a contrapuntal texture. There are several kinds of canons. For example: (1) Imitation or at the unison - a strict canon, the second voice enters on the same pitch; (2) canon two in one - canon between two parts, the second part imitates the first; (3) canon two in one at the octave - the second voice enters at the octave; (4) canon two in one at the fifth - the second voice enters at the interval of a fifth; (5) canon four in one - four voices, each of which enters in succession on the same melodic line; (6) canon four in two-double canon, four parts in all; (7) accompanied canon - the accompaniment is not a part of the canon; (8) free canon - one modified, not in strict form; (9) perpetual canon, circular canon, or infinite canon - all terms identify a canon that leads back to the beginning to start all over again; (10) the coda is sometimes used to bring a canon to a conclusion; this section deviates from strict canon. Canons are treated by many devices. For example: by augmentation, diminution, inversion or contrary motion, retrograde (crab motion), contrary and retrograde, and combinations of the above. See *Canonic devices.

Canonical hours The time of day or night set aside for "Office hours" of the church by canon rule for devotion and singing. See *Office hours.

Canonic devices Various treatments of musical lines in the canon, as well as other types of music. (1) Augmentation - double the value of each note; (2) diminution - halve the value of each note; (3) retrograde - play backwards (crab motion); (4) inversion - invert the intervals of the musical line; (5) imitation - repeat the line exactly. A combination of these devices can be used in canonic development.

Canonic style A technique or treatment of a section of a large work in the style of canon. The techniques used in development of thematic material.

Canso - Canzo Provencal love song of the troubadour in bar form (a modified two-part song form). See *Bar form.

Cantabile (It.) (kän—tä'—bē—lā) In a singing style. A term used in instrumental music to indicate that the music is to be played in a singing style.

Cantata (It.) (kän—tä'—tä) A work having arias, solos,

55

duets, recitatives, chorus, and accompaniment. Cantata da chiesa is a church cantata having a religious or devotional theme. Cantata da camera is a secular cantata. A Baroque form, originally the term cantata meant vocal, as opposed to sonata which meant instrumental. It is in the nature of the oratorio but less elaborate. J. S. Bach (1685-1750) wrote many church cantatas and secular cantatas. There were also cantatas for solo voice. E.g., Handel (1685-1759) *Nell dolce dell' oblio* (secular).

Cantate (Fr.) (kä(n)—tät) Term for cantata. Cantatille, a short cantata.

Cantatore (kän—tä—tō'—rā) Singer.

Cantatrice (It.) (kän—tä—trē'—chä) Singer, female.

Cante flamenco (Sp.)(kän'—tä flä—mĕn'—kō)cante hondo or deep song of Andalusia. It is emotional in nature.

Canticle — Canticum (Lat.) Hymn. **Cantique** (Fr.) (kä(n)— tēk) (1) A hymn of the church. A song of praise. The text is taken chiefly from the Bible but not from the Book of Psalms. (2) A concert work based on a religious theme.

Cantiga (Sp.) (kän—tē'—gä) A 13th century Portuguese or Spanish popular song, religious in nature and often sung in praise of Holy Mary. It is monophonic.

Cantilena (It.) (kän—tē—lä'—nä) (1) A line of melody that is vocal, lyrical, brief, and popular; a secular song or instrumental piece which is simple and light. There are examples of polyphonic cantilena written by Adam de la Halle (c. 1225-1287) in the *Historical Anthology of Music* ed. Davison and Apel. (2) A smooth and cantabile style of performing instrumental music.

Cantillation The chanting of a liturgical text by the Jews or Christians. The term is particularly used in reference to the style of musical chanting used when reading from the Torah. It is unaccompanied and rhythmically free.

Cantino (It.) (kän—tē'—nō) sangsaite (Ger.) (zäng'—zi — tå), chanterelle (Fr.) (shä(n)—tē—rĕl)The first and highest string of a stringed instrument. See *Sangsaite, *Chanterelle.

Cantionale Often referred to as the hymnal, but it is a complete musical collection for all aspects of the program for worship.

Cantiones sacrae (Lat.) A collection of sacred songs or motets. See *Motet.

Canto (It.) (kän'—tō) Song, singing, melodic line, chant. See *Canto firmo, *Canto primo.

Canto armonica (It.) (kän'—tō är—mōn'—ē+kō) Harmonic singing, part song.

Canto cromatico (It.) (kän'—tō krō—mä'—tē—cō) Singing in half steps (semitones).

Canto fermo (It.) (kän'—tō fe r'—mō) Firm singing or fixed song. The term dates back to the 14th—17th centuries. It identifies the given melody that is the subject for contrapuntal treatment. See *Cantus firmus.

Canto primo (It.) (kän'—tō prē'—mō) First or foremost singer, as in first soprano.

Cantor One who sings. (1) The solo singer or official who sings the liturgy in the Jewish service. (2) The choir director in the Protestant church. (3) The soloist who sings the chanting parts in the Catholic church.

Cantoris (Lat.) The part of the choir that sits on the side of the cantor (precentor). The other half sits on the side of the Dean (decani). The choir is divided for the antiphonal singing and chanting.

Cantus (Lat.) Melody, which is usually the upper part.

Cantus choralis (Lat.) See *Cantus planus.

Cantus firmus (Lat.) Fixed melody or song. A pre-existing melody which is borrowed by a composer and used as a basis for contrapuntal treatment. From the time of early polyphony, the plainsong was an important source. It was used in organa, motets, masses, et. al. Later composers adopted materials from secular songs, chorales, hymns, etc. For example, the organ chorale prelude is an elaboration of a chorale (hymn tune). The chorale is used as a cantus firmus. The art of paraphrasing chorale melodies on organ is established in *Tablatura ·Nova* (1624) by S. Scheidt. It is further developed by J. S. Bach, Buxtehude, Brahms, and many others. Excellent examples are found in Bach's organ works and in Brahms Choral Preludes.

Cantus Gregorianus (Lat.) Gregorian chant.

Cantus lateralis (Lat.) The name given when the parts of a polyphonic work are written side by side on two pages rather than in parts on one page.

Cantus planus (Lat.) Plain chant, Gregorian chant or plainsong.

Canzo A troubadour song. See *Canso, *Chanson.

Canzona (canzone) (It.) (kän—tsō'—nä, kän—tsō'—nā) A lyrical song or instrumental music of a song-like style. (1) A polyphonic vocal setting of a 16th century secular poem. (2) An early instrumental canzona which was a transcription of a vocal work. (3) The Italian name for French chanson. (4) The 16th century French chanson was often transcribed for organ (canzona d'organo) which led to the fugue; others (16th and 17th centuries) were written for instrumental ensembles (canzona de sonare), which later became the 17th century sonata; others were transcribed for lute or keyboard. (5) A 17th century solo song with accompaniment. (6) A 17th and 18th century polyphonic (instrumental) work. (7) A 19th century instrumental piece or movement of a work. (8) An 18th and 19th century song. See *Chanson.

Canzona francese (It.) (kän—tsō'—nä frän—chā'—zā) In Italy the term used to describe the instrumental version of the French chanson. They were arrangements or pieces written for instruments in the style of the chanson.

Canzone a ballo (It.) (kän—tsō'—nä ä bäl'—lō) Dance songs which led to the present form of ballet. They date back to the 13th century.

Canzonetta (canzonet) (It.) (kän—tsō—nĕt'—tä) A shorter form of canzona. A short piece, vocal or instrumental, in the style of the canzona. See *Canzona.

Capella (It.) (kä—pĕl'—lä) See *Cappella.

Capelle (Ger.) (kä—pĕ l'—lå) A chapel orchestra or band. The old spelling for Kapelle. See *Kapelle.

Capo (It.) (kä'—pō) Head, principal. As in da capo, to the head or beginning.

58

Capobanda (It.) (kä—pō—bän'—dä) Bandmaster.

Capotasto (It.) (kä—pō—täs'—tō) A device which can change the length of the strings on a finger board of an instrument, such as the guitar, by moving a bar-like object up or down on the board. The key is charged by shortening or lengthening all strings at the same time. The player can play in a new key by using the same finger pattern from another key. The thumb is used in this way when playing the cello in the upper positions (higher register).

Cappella (It.) (kä—pě l'—lä) Chapel. Singing without accompaniment, as in chapel style. See *A cappella.

Capriccio (It.) (kä—prēt'—chē—ō) (1) A caprice or whimsical piece of music written in a free style such as a fantasia. (2) A term used to indicate a style of playing a piece in a capricious style. (3) 16th and 17th century pieces in fugal style much like the canzona and ricercar. The term is sometimes used in a title, e.g., Frescobaldi (1583-1643) *Capriccio: La Spagnoletta for Harpsichord*. Tchaikovsky (1847-1893) *Capriccio Italien,* Opus 45 for Orchestra.

Caressant (Fr.) (kä—rě s—sä(n)) Tender, caressing.

Carillon Chimes, musical bells. (1) A set of bells played through a keyboard and pedals or sounded by other mechanical means. The music is played from a manual and foot pedals similar to those of an organ. The manual keys of the large standard carillon are played with closed hand. (2) A set of metal plates, a glockenspiel, which is used in the orcehstra. (3) An organ stop.

Carillonneur (Fr.) (kär—ē—yŏ(n)—nûr) Bell-ringer. One who plays the carillon.

Carmagnole (Fr.) (kär—män—yōl) A French revolutionary song and dance.

Carmen (Lat.) (1) A song, upper part. (2) A term used to identify the upper part of an early polyphonic composition. (3) A chanson. (4) A type of instrumental composition. (5) Cantus.

Carmina Burana (Lat.) Songs from Beuren. (1) A collection of Goliard songs. (2) A cantata by Carl Orff (1895-

) with optional movement and dance.

Carnival song A 16th century festival song sung in parts. It was in the style of the frottola and canzonetta.

Carol (Nöel) (Fr.) (nō–ĕl) A song for Christmas. Sometimes sung in church as a song of joy. In general, it applies to songs related to the religious seasons and sung by the people.

Carole A French medieval round dance performed with singing.

Carré e (Fr.) (kär–rā) Square. The breve or double whole note. See *Breve.

Carrure (Fr.) (kä–rür) Square shoulders. The organization of measures into musical phrases, such as four or eight measures.

Cartel (Fr.) (kär–tĕl) Scroll or frame. The first draft of a musical score.

Cartelle (Fr.) (kär–tĕl) The vellum on which music was written.

Cassa (It.) (käs'–sä) Case, box, chest. A drum.

Cassa grande (It.) (käs'–sä grän'–dā) A large box. Bass drum.

Cassa rullante (It.) (käs'–sä rōol–län'–tā) Rolling box. Tenor drum.

Cassation An 18th century suite or serenade for the outdoors. On the order of the diverimento.

Castanets Concave pieces of hard wood clapped together in the hand while performing Spanish dances.

Castrato (It.) (käs–trä'–tō) A high (sporano-like) voice of the adult male as a result of being castrated as a boy. The pure soprano voice quality of the boy remains with the adult.

Catch A round for three or more unaccompanied voices. Each singer comes in at various times and the words are placed in such a way as to produce odd results, often ludicrous. Popular during the 17th and 18th centuries. A device often used was to write rests for one or more measures which caused the various voices and words to alternate, which quite often gave double meaning to the words. A famous example is *Catch*

That Catch Can (1652). A later example is *Of All the Instruments That Are* by Henry Purcell (1659-1695).

Catgut Cords or strings for stringed instruments, usually made of dried intestines of horse or sheep, not of the cat.

Cathedral music Music for the services of the Cathedral, which is the highest church of each diocese, thechurch of the Bishop.

Catholic Church music Music of the Mass, Gregorian chant, etc. for all services and Offices. See *Mass.

Cat's Fugue A fugal piece by Dominico Scarlatti with odd and wide skips. It is as if a cat had walked over the keyboard. Dominico Scalratti (1685-1757) *Longo 499 in G Minor* (Cat's Fugue).

Cauda (Lat.) Tail. The stem or vertical line added to notes.

Cavatina (It.) (kä—vä—tē '—nä) Cavata. A short air or arioso having one section. A short solo song in simple style. Generally, a short composition, including instrumental music. Examples: Charles Francois Gounod (1818-1893) the Cavatinas in his opera *Faust;* Joseph Raff (1822-1882) *Cavatina,* Opus 85, No. 3 for Violin and Piano.

Cavonto A Greek musical instrument of the mandolin type.

C.B. Col. Basso or contrabass.

C clef An elaborate C placed on a staff. The open area identifies middle c on the Grand Staff. E.g.,

Alto clef   Tenor clef

See *Grand Staff.

C Dur (Ger.) (tsä dōor) C major.

Cebell (cibell). A dance form of the 17th and 18th centuries, now called gavotte. See *Gavotte.

Cédez (Fr.) (sä—dä) Yield or hold back. Slow down the tempo.

Celerita (It.) (chä—lä—rē—tä ') Quickness, speed.

Celesta A keyboard instrument of five octaves having graduated steel plates which are struck by hammers. Wooden resonators are under the steel bars.

Céleste (Fr.) (sā—lĕ st) Heavenly, divine, celestial.

Celestina (It.) (chā—lĕ s—tē '—nä) An organ stop which produces a subdued tone. Four foot size.

Cello A short form of the word violoncello. It is the third largest instrument of the violin family. It is played in a vertical position to the floor between the performer's knees. The strings from high to low are a, d, G, C, one octave below the viola. It has a range of over three and one half octaves and plays in the bass clef, tenor clef, and in the higher register, the treble clef. It is bowed or plucked (pizz).

Cellone A large violoncello used as a contrabass for chamber music. It is tuned a fourth lower than the cello. See *Cello.

Cembal d'amour An 18th century keyboard instrument which was a further development of the clavichord.

Cembalist A player of the harpsichord.

Cembalo (chĕ m '—bä—lō) The Italian name for harpsichord. Short for clavicembalo. A dulcimer.

Cent A 100th of a semitone. A measurement of musical intervals.

Cento (Lat.) centone (It.) patchwork. A musical line composed from several musical fragments.

Cercare (It.) (chĕ r—kä '—rā) Look for, as in cercare la note, to anticipate the next note or syllable.

Ces (Ger.) (tsĕ s) C flat.

Ces Dur (Ger.) (tsĕ s dōo r) Key of C flat major.

Ceses (Ger.) (tsĕ s '—ĕ s) C double flat (Cbb).

Cetera (It.) cetra (chā '—tā—rä, chĕ t '—rä) A member of the guitar family. Cittern.

C flat Cb. A semitone below the note C. E.g.,

Clef:

| Treble Clef | Bass Clef | Alto Clef | Tenor Clef |

Chace (Fr.) (shäs) See *Caccia.

Chaconne (Fr.) (shä—kŏn) (1) A Mexican dance imported into Spain at the end of the 16th century. The name is from the Spanish "chacona" meaning "pretty". It became established as a Baroque dance in slow triple meter in the minor mode. (2) A technique of variation, the theme or basis being the succession of chords, usually eight measures in length, which is the basis for the variations. (3) A title for other types of compositions. Examples: T. A. Vitali (c. 1665-1711) *Chaconne for Violin and Piano;* The "Chaconne" from *Patita No. 1* and *Partita No. 2* by J. S. Bach (1685-1750) for solo violin. See *Passacaglia.

Chair organ Another name for a small organ or choir organ.

Chaleur (Fr.) (shä—lûr) Warmth, passion, zeal.

Chalumeau (Fr.) (shäl—ü—mō) (1) Reed-pipe instruments of the woodwind family, such as an oboe, flute, clarinet. (2) The lower register of the clarinet.

Chamber music Kammermusik (Ger.) (käm '—mĕr—moo-zēk) Music played by a small group of people in a room or concert hall. Usually, one person to a part rather than having multiple players on a part as in orchestra music. E.g., trio, quartet, quintet, etc.

Chamber opera An opera on a small scale having an intimate setting, small orchestra, and requiring few performers. For example, operas by Gian-Carlo Menotti (b.1911) and Benjamin Britten (b.1913).

Chamber orchestra A small orchestra having from 20 to 30 players.

Changing note See *Cambiata, *Non-harmonic.

Chanson (Fr.) (shä(n)—sō(n)) A song or ballad of a popular nature written for single voice with accompaniment or as a polyphonic vocal work. Also used to describe certain types of songs, e.g., chanson measurée — putting music to a text and maintaining the accents and rhythm of the text. Several types of chanson were popular during the Middle Ages: 11th century — epic poems; 12th and 13th century chansons — troubadours and trouvères; 14th century — accompanied songs; 15th century — Burgundian School, melodies used in motets; 16th century — polyphonic chanson or French chanson; 17th century — monodic chanson.

Chanson de geste (Fr.) (shä(n)—sō(n) dû zhĕ st) Heroic songs; songs of deeds or achievements from the late Middle Ages.

Chanson de toile (Fr.) (shä(n)—sō(n) dû twäl) Toile meaning cloth or linen. A spinning song or love song from the late Middle Ages in which the central character is a woman.

Chansonnier A collection of songs of the French troubadours and trouveres of the 13th century.

Chant (chant, (Fr.) (shä(n)) meaning singing)) In the style of plainsong. That is, a free rhythmic element which depends on the text. It is vocal with no accompaniment. E.g., Gregorian chant or Ambrosian chant.

Chantant (Fr.) (shä(n)—tä(n)) Easily sung, tuneful. To be performed in a singing style.

Chanter Also, chaunter. The pipes on the bagpipe that play the melodic line or treble part.

Chanterelle (Fr.) (shä(n)—tĕ —rĕ l) The first or highest string of the stringed instruments. For example, the E string of the violin. See *Cantino, *Sangsaite.

Chantey Also, shanty. A song sung by sailors while working the ropes for the sails. It had a rhythm that aided the sailor at his work.

Chanting The singing of the canticles, psalms, etc. of the church (Catholic and Anglican).

Chant sacré (Fr.) (shä(n) sä—crā) A holy chant or sacred song.

Chapelle (Fr.) (shä—pĕ ll) Chapel (1) The choir or the orchestra of a chapel. (2) An orchestra under the patronage of an individual.

Chaque (Fr.) (shäk) Each, every.

Characteristic note The note that leads to the tonic. E.g., the 7th degree (leading tone) in the major scale.

Character piece A piece of music of the 19th century which was descriptive or programmatic. Many pieces for piano fall in this category.

64

Charleston A popular dance to jazz music in the 1920's having a particular type of syncopated rhythm throughout.

Chasse (Fr.) (shäss) Hunt. Music descriptive of hunting sequences or the hunting call.

Chef (Fr.) (shĕf) Head, leader, prinicpal, conductor. Chef de musique, band-master; chef d'orchestre, musical director.

Chef d'attaque (Fr.) (shĕf dä—täk) Concert master; leader.

Chef d'orchestre (Fr.) (shĕ f dôr—kĕ s—tr) Conductor.

Cheng (Sheng) An ancient Chinese reed organ with bamboo reed pipes fitted around an air box. The air moves through the pipe and vibrates a reed. A small finger hole is on each pipe which is closed before a sound is created. It has a mouthpiece. The tone is started by the suction of the air. It may have been the forerunner of thr reed organ.

Chest of viols A set of six viols ranging from the treble to the bass. They were fitted into a chest. Popular during the 17th century.

Chest voice, chest register The lower range of the voice.

Chevalet (Fr.) (shū—vä—lä) Wooden horse. The bridge for stringed instruments that use a bow.

Chevé system During the 19th century Chevé of France invented a system of teaching note reading and singing. It consisted of syllables and numbers using a movable do. The syllables and numbers were related to the tonic. The numbers identified the interval and were sung with syllables. Other syllables were also used to indicate octaves, rests, etc.

Cheville (Fr.) (shū—vē—yū) Peg or pin. This refers to the peg used in holding and tuning string(s) on a stringed instrument.

Chevrotant (Fr.) (shū—vrō—tä(n)) Also, chevrotante, chevrotement. Trembling or quivering. Tremolo. See *Vibrato.

Chiaramente (It.) (kē—ä—rä—mĕ n'—tä) Clearly.

Chiave (It.) (kē—ä'—vä) Key or clef.

Chiavette (It.) (kē—ä—vĕt'—tä) Movable clefs especially used in the late 16th and 17th century vocal music.

The clefs were added to eliminate ledger lines and are considered by some to be a transposing device.

Chiesa (It.) (kē—ā'—zä) Church. Music appropriate for the church as opposed to secular music.

Ch'ih (Chinese) An ancient cross flute of China.

Chimes A chromatic succession of metal tubes suspended from a metal frame and having a range form c' to f''. The tone is produced by striking the hollow tubing with a wooden mallet. The sound is somewhat like a carillon or church bells. Used in orchestra and band.

Ch'in A Chinese instrument of the zither family.

Chinese wood block A hollow block of wood with open slots which is struck with a stick giving a hollow sound. It is often used in playing jazz music.

Chirula A pipe resembling the recorder which is played with a tabor (small drum). Also known as a galoubet.

Chitarra (It.) (kē—tär'—rä) Guitar.

Chitarrone (It.) (kē—tär—rōn'—ä) A long archlute.

Chiuso (It.) (kē—ōo'—zō) Closed, as in playing a stopped horn. The hand is placed in the bell of the horn.

Choeur (Fr.) (kûr) Choir.

Choir (1) A group of singers, usually a church group. Also called chorus. (2) The term choir is used to identify groups of instruments of the orchestra and band. E.g., clarinet choir.

Choir-book A large music book in general use during the 15th century that was placed on a music stand around which the singers stood and read the music. The music was written side by side. Later, part books became popular, that is, a book for each choir member. See *Cantus lateralis.

Choir-organ The lowest manual of the organ or the third manual of the standard organ. Usually the soft stops are used to accompany the choir.

Choke cymbals "Sock" cymbals used in jazz bands. Traps. Two cymbals on a stand operated by a foot pedal.

Chor (Ger.) (kōr) Choir or chorus.

Choral (1) A term used for music being performed by a

chorus (2) A hymn tune or plainsong.

Choral anthem An anthem done in a choral style.

Choral cantata A cantata using a chorus as opposed to the solo cantata.

Chorale A hymn-tune or psalm sung with or without organ accompaniment in the Protestant church. E.g., Lutheran Chorale.

Chorale cantata A cantata using chorale melodies and texts. E.g., Bach's cantatas.

Chorale fantasia A chorale melody used in a free or fantasia style for organ.

Chorale fugue, chorale motet (1) Organ chorale having fugal sections based on the chorale melodies. (2) Vocal motets based on a chorale line.

Chorale partita Variations on a chorale melody. Organ music.

Chorale prelude The organ introduction which comes before the Protestant chorale. The prelude is based on the chorale which follows it. It is a polyphonic elaboration of a chorale (hymn) usually written for organ. A variety of treatments of a chorale can be found in Bach's chorale preludes. See *Cantus firmus.

Chorale variation Also, partita. Variation on a chorale melody. E.g., J. S. Bach (1685-1750) *Chorale Variations, "Vom Himmel hoch"*.

Choral Symphony Many works use the term in a sub-title to describe the use of a chorus in a symphonic work. Others include a chorus but do not use the title. An example of a choral symphony is: Beethoven's *Symphony No. 9 in D Minor*, Op. 125, written in 1823.

Chord A group of tones, organized in some fashion and played simultaneously. The chords are classified: major, minor, diminished, or augmented; consonant or dissonant; have intervals; can be inverted; altered; and are used in many relationships and take on various meanings depending on use. See *Harmony.

Chordal style A matter of texture. The musical composition is written so that the chords or harmonic relationships are of great importance.

Chordophones Instruments that use strings to produce tones. Stringed instruments such as harps, lutes, (plucked, e.g., guitar and bowed, e.g., violin family) zithers, and lyres.

Chord progression A series of chords.

Chorister Generally, a person who sings in a choir or chorus. Now, usually used to identify the boy singer in a church choir.

Chorton (Ger.) (kōr'—tōn) Choir pitch. The pitch to which an organ was tuned. It varied depending on the church and the geographical location.

Chorus (1) A large group of singers. (2) A group singing a work in four parts (SATB), eight parts or a number of combinations. (3) In Greek drama a group speaking parts. (4) In dance music or jazz, the main section of the work. (5) Singers, male or female, or both, singing with more than one on a part in various combinations. (6) A refrain.

Christe eleison (Lat.) (krēs'—tā ā—lā'—ē—sŏn) The text of the "Kyrie" of the Roman Catholic Mass. Now sung in English or the vernacular. "Kyrie eleison" (Lord, have mercy), "Christe eleison" (Christ, have mercy). See *Mass.

Chromatic (1) The raising or lowering of a note in the normal scale by a half step. (2) A succession of semitones. (3) A term of Greek origin related to scale patterns such as diatonic and enharmonic. (4) A term used to describe chromatic instruments, chromatic scales, chromatic chords, and chromatic harmony.

Chromaticism (1) Movement by semitones (2) Notes foreign to the key or chord. When all twelve tones of the scale are used within the octave the chromatic scale results. See *Chromatic, *Chromatic scale.

Chromatic scale A scale moving up or down one octave with all intervals being semitones or half steps. Twelve different tones within the octave. See *Scale.

Chromatic syllables When the degrees of the diatonic scale are designated by syllables instead of letters (i.e., do (doh), re, mi, fa, sol, la, si (ti), do) it is necessary to identify the pitches not present in the diatonic scale with different syllables (i.e., the chromatic notes available when each of the five whole tones of the diatonic scale is divided into two semitones.) The diatonic scale has seven tones to the octave; the chromatic scale twelve tones to the octave. The following chart will illustrate (C major scale):

C SCALE	SYLLABLES	CHROMATIC SCALE	SYLLABLES CHROMATIC SCALE
½ steps ⟩ c / b	⟨ do / ti	Natural ⟨ c / ½ steps b	do ⟩ Natural ti
		b♭ a♯	te li
a	la	a a♭ g♯	la le si
g	sol	g g♭ f♯	sol se fi
½ steps ⟩ f / e	⟨ fa / mi	Natural ⟨ f / ½ steps e	fa ⟩ Natural mi
		e♭ d♯	me ri
d	re	d d♭ c♯	re ra di
c	do	c	do
up c, d, e, etc.		note: going up use sharps, coming down use flats	right side up, left side down

See *Solmization, *Chromatic, *Chromatic scale, *Chromaticism.

Chrotta The Welsh name is crwth. An ancient form of a musical instrument in the shape of a lyre. At first the instrument had no fingerboard and was played like a harp. Later a bow was used. A later development was the addition of a finger board suggesting it might be an early member of the violin family. See *Crowd.

Church modes Ecclesiatical modes. The tonal system used in music prior to the 17th century as in Gregorian chant. The modes were diatonic, one octave, and were identified by the ambitus (range) and finalis (center-tone). There are six authentic modes and six plagal modes. The authentic mode starts with the finalis and ends one octave higher. The plagal mode begins with

the fourth below the finalis and has a range a fifth a-
bove the finalis.

Mode		finalis	ambitus
Dorian	authentic	d	d — d'
Hypodorian	plagal	d	A — a
Phrygian	authentic	e	e — e'
Hypophrygian	plagal	e	B — b
Lydian	authentic	f	f — f'
Hypolydian	plagal	f	c — c'
Mixolydian	authentic	g	g — g'
Hypomixolydian	plagal	g	d — d'
Aeolian	authentic	a	a — a'
Hypoaeolian	plagal	a	e — e'
Ionian	authentic	c'	c' — c''
Hypoionian	plagal	c'	g — g'

Church music Music of the Christian church. Examples;
chant, pslams, canticles, hymns, tropes, liturgical dramas, motets, mass, anthem, Protestant chorale, and chorale
cantata.

Chute (Fr.) (shüt) Fall, tumble. An ornament (nachschlag).

Chyn A classic Chinese zither.

Ciaccona (It.) (chē—ä—kō '—nä) Chaconne.

Cialamello (It.) (chē—äl—ä—mĕl '—lō) Shawm. In Europe
the instruments of the double reeds are called shawm.

Cimbalo (Sp.) (thĕm '—bä—lō) Cymbal.

Cimbalon (Hungarian) A large dulcimer. See *Dulcimer.

Cinelli (It.) (chē—nĕ l '—lē) Cymbals. They are usually
used in pairs.

Cinfonia (Sp.) (thĕn—fō '—nē—ä) The Spanish name for
the medieval hurdy-gurdy.

Cinq (Fr.) (sä n(n)k) Five.

Circle canon A canon which goes back to the beginning
several times, as in the round.

Circle, cycle of fifths A system of showing the progression of keys, from key to key and moving by intervals of a fifth. C, G, D, A, E, B, (Cb), F#, (Gb), C#,
(Db), Ab, Eb, Bb, F, C. The keys of B and Cb, F#,
and Gb, C#, and Db are enharmonic keys. Note that it
becomes necessary to change from sharp keys to flat

keys at the key of C# (Db).

Cis (Ger.) (tsi s) C sharp (C#).

Cis Dur (Ger.) (tsi s door) C sharp major.

Cisis (Ger.) (tsis'—is) C double sharp (Cx) (C##).

Cis Moll (Ger.) (tsi s mawl) C sharp minor.

Cister A member of the guitar family. Generally related to the lute family.

Cither A member of the guitar family. Not a spelling for zither. See *Cister.

Cittern See *Cither.

Cl. The abbreviation for the reed instrument, clarinet.

Claire, caisse (Fr.) (cle r, ke ss) Side drum.

Clairon (Fr.) (kle —ro(n)) Clarion, bugle.

Claquebois (Fr.) (kläk—bwä) Xylophone.

Clarinet (clarinette (Fr.) (klär—e—ne t), clarinetto (It.) (klär—e—ne t'—to) A single reed instrument of the woodwind family. The Bb clarinet range sounds from d to b'''b. The Bb clarinet sounds a tone lower than the written concert (piano) pitch. The register above the break is called clarion, below the break chalumeau. The clarinets are built in several keys and sizes, for example: C, Bb, and A. The Bb and A clarinets are used extensively in the orchestra of today. Many smaller and larger sizes are made to be used in military and concert bands. The abbreviation is Cl. See *Clarinet family.

Clarinet family Single reed instruments related to the clarinet. Instruments: clarinet, alto clarinet, bass clarinet, contrabass clarinet; saxophones of various sizes (soprano, alto, tenor, baritone, and bass). Some examples of obsolete forms of the clarinet are: basset horn, chalumeau, clarinet d'amour and Heckel-clarina.

Clarinette d'amour (Fr.) (klär—e—ne t dä—moo r) An old clarinet of larger size pitched in G or Ab. It follows the general pattern of building instruments in various sizes and pitches. E.g., oboe d'amour, flute d'amour, etc.

Clarino (It.) (klä—re '—no) (1) High register (clarion) of the clarinet. (2) The high register of the Baroque trumpet. (3) Clarinetto.

71

Clarion (1) A clear sound as heard in the trumpet. (2) An ancient trumpet. (3) Generally, a trumpet. (4) An organ stop.

Clarone (It.) (klä—rō'—nā) Bass clarinet.

Classicism (1) An era in music from the 18th century and the early part of the 19th century. The emphasis is on form and structure. A period of absolute music. Generally, a period of homophonic music. Composers representative of this Viennese classic school are Haydn and Mozart. Some forms used in this period are: symphony; opera; sonata; song cycle; lieder; divertimento; and chamber music. (2) Any period which upholds classical traditions such as, balance, objectivity, emphasis on form and structure, etc.

Clausula (Lat.) Close or ending. The clausula during medieval times was the term used to define a cadence used in polyphonic music. During the Ars antiqua a clausula was the short melismatic section of a chant which was placed in the cantus firmus. Many times it amounted to just a word or two which covered many tones in the musical line.

Clavecin (Fr.) (kläv—sā (n)) Harpsichord.

Claves (Lat.) (1) Keys on a keyboard. (2) Clef signs.

Claves (Sp.) Cuban rhythm instruments. Two round sticks, about eight inches long, which are struck one against the other. One is held in each hand.

Clavicembalo (It.) (klä—vē—chĕm'—bä—lō) Harpsichord.

Clavicembalum A small harpsichord.

Clavichord A keyboard instrument (16th to the 18th centuries) having strings. The tone is produced by metal tangents which set the strings in motion as the tangent rests at a given point on the string. It divides the string into parts. One part of the string vibrates while the other section is damped by a piece of cloth. One string could be used for several tones by placing tangents at various points. The clavichord was developed from the monochord. The clavichord is shaped as an oblong box, has a keyboard, tangents, and produces a soft sound. Later, more strings were added. See *Monochord.

72

Clavicitherium A vertical harpsichord.

Clavier (Fr.) (klä—vē—ā) Keyboard of piano, organ and like instruments. In German, klavier menas keyboard instruments of the stringed variety.

Clavierübung (Ger.) (klä—fēr'—ü—boöng) Keyboard study or practice. A collection of four keyboard works by J. S. Bach published from 1731-1742.

Clef (clé or clef, (Fr.) (klā, or klĕ f) Key. A symbol placed at the beginning of a staff which identifies the names of the lines and spaces of the staff. It also shows the range of the staff in relationship to the grand staff. There are several symbols:

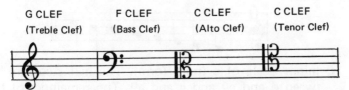

| G CLEF | F CLEF | C CLEF | C CLEF |
| (Treble Clef) | (Bass Clef) | (Alto Clef) | (Tenor Clef) |

The G clef indicates the g' is on the second line; F clef indicates the f is on the 4th line; C clef is used in the alto clef where middle c is the third line; C clef is also used in the tenor clef where middle c is the fourth line. C clefs are also moveable: middle c can be placed on any line or space in order to eliminate ledger lines.

( ) G clef resembles the letter G; ( ) F clef resembles the letter F; C clef resembles an old and fancy letter C.

Climax An ancient or rise in emotional feeling in a line of music. A high point in the development or resolution of a piece of music.

Cloche (Fr.) (klōsh) Bell. E.g., cloches would be orchestra bells.

Clocking Also, clappering. The clapper of the bell moves to produce a sound.

Clos (Fr.) (klō) Closed and completed. A final cadence.

Close See *Cadence, *Perfect cadence or full close, *Authentic cadence, *Imperfect cadence or half close.

Closed key In wind instruments the key that covers an open hole.

Close harmony In harmony a chord is said to be in close position when the notes of the chord are within an octave and a half. This is as opposed to open harmony or open position where notes are spread beyond the interval of an octave and a half. The upper three notes of a four note chord are close together in close position.

C major Scale of C, one octave. The half steps are between e and f and b and c. The remainder of the intervals are whole steps. No flats or sharps are in the C scale.

C minor Scale of c (pure form). The half steps are between d and e♭ and g and a♭. The remainder of the intervals are whole steps. One octave:

C moll (Ger.) (tsā mawl) Key of c minor.

Coda (It.) (kō'—dä) Tail. A short or long section added at the end of a musical composition. The idea or material used comes from the composition itself. The coda brings the composition to a complete ending. The coda is often added to the compoistion beyond the basic form or structure. E.g., sonata allegro form, coda is added. In a fugue it may be a conclusion of the work by ending with the theme or pedal point.

Codetta (kō—dě t'—tä) Small coda. See *Coda.

Colla (It.) (kôl'—lä) Also, coll' meaning with the.

Colla parte (It.) (kôl'—lä pär'—tä) With the part. Instructions for the accompanist to follow the soloist. The soloist may take some freedom.

Colla punta dell' arco (It.) (kôl'—lä pōo n'—tä dě l— lär'—cō) Play with (at) the point of the bow.

Coll' arco (It.) (kôl–lär'–cō) Playing a stringed instrument, such as the violin, with the bow rather than pizzacato or plucking the strings.

Colla voce (It.) (kôl'–lä vō'–chā) With the voice. The accompanist is instructed to follow the (voice) vocal soloist.

Collegium Musicum (Lat.) A group or society usually associated with a university whose purpose is to study and play music of early times and little known music not often performed in public. It was introduced in Germany during the 17th century. Such societies are in existence today. Many older instruments are used to perform the music as it might have been performed at the time it was written.

Col legno (It.) (kôl lĕn'–yō) The string player bounces the wood part of the bow on the string rather than using the hair of the bow.

Coll' ottava (It.) (kôl–lŏ t–tä'–vä) Eighth or octave. Play with the octave; doubled at the octave above or below the note given. See *Ottava.

Color (Lat.) (1) The timbre or other elements of music related to a composition. E.g., rhythm, melody, harmony, etc. Color is also related to sound and acoustics, as well as to the psychological approach to musical sound. Mood music is often related to color. (2) In early music color was used to identify some elements related to composition. It was used in the structure and relationship of rhythm and melody in the 14th century motets. The melody was often identified by color.

Coloratura (It.) (kō–lō–rä–too'–rä) (1) Florid passages, trills, elaborate ornamentation, and generally rapid running passages in a musical line. (2) The coloratura soprano, a very high female voice, specializing in virtuoso operatic arias of the Classical and Romantic periods of music. See *Voice ranges.

Color organ Color and music. Projection units having several colors are connected in a mecahnical way to a keyboard. The purpose is to associate the visual (color) with a particular sound called color music or lumia.

Sometimes a keyboard is used to project a color without sound. Many 20th century composers have experimented with tone and color as an aesthetic experience.

Colpo (It.) (kôl'–pō) Hit, strike, rap. Colpo d'arco (kôl'–pō där'–kō) stroke of the bow on a stringed instrument.

Combination tone The resultant tone (a third tone) which is heard when two tones of different pitch are sounded simultaneously. A phonemenon of acoustics. Different tones result from the difference between frequencies while summation tones result from the sum of the frequencies.

Come (It.) (kō'–mā) Like, as, or how.

Comédie (Fr.) (kô–mā–dē) Comedy; to make people laugh. An opera in a light vein such as comic opera.

Come prima (It.) (kō'–mā prē'–mä) As the first or prime. Play as in the beginning or first presentation.

Comes (Lat.) The part that enters second in the fugue or round. The companion part to the first part. See *Canon, *Fugue.

Come sopra (It.) (kō'–mā sŏp'–rä) As above.

Come sta (It.) (kō'–mā stä) As it stands, play as is.

Comic opera An opera on a light subject which has a happy ending. Earlier, comic operas had spoken dialogue and music, but later the spoken parts diminished. The music is lighter and of a more popular style than that of other types of operas. Some types of comic opera are: opéra bouffe, opera buffa, and operetta. The opéra comique is a more serious type of opera.

Comique (Fr.) (kô–mēk) Comic, ludicrous, funny.

Commedia dell'arte (kôm–mā'–dē–ä dĕl–lär'–tā) Comic opera leading to the opera buffa. A comedy of the Renaissance and Baroque periods. The art of comedy.

Commodo (It.) (kôm'–mō–dō) Comodo (It.) (kō'–mō–do) Ease, leisure, moderate, or convenient. Easy tempo. Often used with allegro.

Common chord (1) A pivot chord. One which has· a shared relationship with more than one tonal center. The term is used with reference to modulation. (2) An old term meaning a triad that consists of a fundamental note played with its third and fifth. See *Harmony, *Modulation, *Pivot.

Common metre Ballad meter. The metrical structure in hymns. A four line verse in iambic measure having the syllables of each line following in order — 8, 6, 8, 6.

Common of the Mass The Ordinary of the Mass. The part which is always the same. See *Ordinary of the Mass, *Mass.

Common time C at the beginning of the composition is equal to the time signature of $\frac{4}{4}$. That is, four beats or crotchets to a measure. Double or quadruple time.

Communion The part of the Mass which is sung after the "Agnus Dei" (Lamb of God. An antiphon sung after the Host is given out. Communion is part of the Proper of the Mass. See *Mass.

Compass The complete range possible of an instrument or voice.

Compiacevolmente (It.) (kôm—pē—ä—chä—vŏl—mĕn'—tä) Pleasingly.

Complement The interval needed to complete an octave when added to a given interval. When used in determining inversions, for example, the major second inverted becomes a minor seventh, etc. See *Inversions.

Composition The development, putting together, and the organization of many elements in an artful and skilled way. The end product, an aesthetic experience reflecting the creator's ideas.

Compound interval Intervals larger than the octave. For example; intervals of a ninth, tenth, etc. See *Interval.

Compound time or meter Simple meters are duple, triple, and quadruple. The unit of beat in a simple meter divides into two. For example: $\frac{2}{4}$ simple meter, the quarter note unit of beat divides into two;

The unit of beat in a compound meter divides into three. For example: $\frac{6}{8}$ compound meter, the dotted quarter note divides into three. In $\frac{6}{8}$ time there are two units of dotted quarter notes:

Some examples of simple duple meter: $\frac{2}{4}$, $\frac{2}{2}$, $\frac{2}{8}$, etc; compound duple meter: $\frac{6}{4}$, $\frac{6}{2}$, $\frac{6}{8}$, etc.; simple triple meter: $\frac{3}{4}$, $\frac{3}{2}$, $\frac{3}{8}$, etc.; compound triple meter: $\frac{9}{4}$, $\frac{9}{2}$, $\frac{9}{8}$, etc.; simple quadruple meter: $\frac{4}{4}$, $\frac{4}{2}$, $\frac{4}{8}$, etc.; compound quadruple meter: $\frac{12}{4}$, $\frac{12}{8}$, etc. See *Meter, *Time.

Con (It.) (kōn) With. For example: con amore (with love); con 8va (with octave doubling), etc.

Con abbandono (It.) (kōn ä—bän—dō'—nō) With abandon, passionately.

Con affetto (It.) (kōn äf—fĕ t'—tō) With emotion.

Con amore (It.) (kōn ä—mōr'—ä) With love.

Con anima (It.) (kōn än'—ē—mä) With animation or spirit.

Con brio (It.) (kōn brē'—ō) With vigor or brilliance.

Concento (It.) (kôn—chĕ n'—tō) Concord.

Concentus (1) In the performance of litrugical music, the chanting of the choir or soloist. (2) A term for melodic chants such as hymns, antiphons, etc. See *Accentus.

Concert A performance for the public by singers, instrumentalists, or both. When a soloist gives a concert it is called a recital.

Concertante (It.) (kôn—chĕ r—tän'—tä) An orchestral piece of music having solo parts. This was prevalent in the 18th century symphonic works that had solo instruments. Concertato also referred to the style of 17th century choral music in which a group of soloists sang in contrast to the full choir. This style was used in the Baroque instrumental form called concerto grosso.

Concertato (It.) (kôn—chĕ r—tä'—tō) Concerted. See *Concertante.

Concertgebouw (Dutch) Concert building. The name of the concert orchestra and the musical society in Amsterdam.

Concert grand The largest grand pianoforte.

Concertina A popular, portable, and small accordian-like instrument having button keys played by the fingers (not a keyboard). It is hexagonal in shape, has bellows, and metallic reeds through which the air is forced to produce a tone. It has a range of about three and one-half octaves.

Concertino (1) A shorter concerto. (2) The group of soloists in the Baroque concerto grosso. (3) The solo instrument or instruments playing with orchestra in a concerto-type composition which has a free form and is often in one movement.

Concert master (Konzertmeister (Ger.)) The principal violinist of the orchestra. The first violinist of the first violin section.

Concerto An orchestral composition for solo and orchestra, usually in sonata form, having three movements (fast, slow, fast). The form of the first movement is in concerto-sonata form, which is a modified sonata-allegro-form that is used in the symphony. The second movement is usually slow and demonstrates slow melodic playing. The third movement is usually in rondo form and shows off the virtuosity and technical ability of the player. The concerto has a cadenza, usually in the first movement, which is a solo part, usually without accompaniment and demonstrating the virtuoso style of playing. Other meanings are applied to the word concerto. For example: concerto for orchestra, in which solo parts are played by members of the orchestra; the Baroque style of concerto grosso, in which a group of solo instruments play against an accompaniment group; concerti ecclesiastici, a type of church concerto of the late 16th and early 17th centuries for voices with instrumental accompaniment and with figured bass; concertino, a diminutive form of concerto; concerto spirituale, a sacred piece performed in concerto style. See examples of concerti by: J. S. Bach (1685-1750); J. Brahms (1833-1897); F. Mendelssohn (1809-1847). See *Concerto grosso, *Concertino.

Concerto di chiesa (It.) (kôn—chĕ r'—tō dē kē—ā'—zä)

79

A church concerto, including voice and instrumental accompaniment.

Concerto grosso (It.) (kôn—chĕr'—tō grō'—sō) A Baroque instrumental form consisting of a small orchestral group divided into two groups. The smaller solo group is called the concertino section and the larger accompaniment group the ripieno or tutti section. The solo instruments often consist of two violins, cello and harpsichord. The cello and harpsichord play the thorough bass. The concerto grosso is a several movement work. It is an example of an early type of concerto. Examples: J. S. Bach (1685-1750) *Six Brandenberg Concerti* See *Concerto.

Concert overture A one movement concert piece for orchestra of the 19th century Romantic era. It is a variety of program music which is based on an idea which is literary, dramatic, patriotic, etc. The structure is based on sonata-allegro-form which is the same form used in the first and often the last movement of the symphony. It is related to the idea of an operatic overture and is developed as an absolute form in the manner of a movement of the symphony. Examples: J. Brahms (1833-1897), *Academic Festival Overture,* Opus 80; Peter Ilyich Tchaikovsky (1840-1893), *Romeo and Juliet,* "Fantasy Overture".

Concert pitch The pitch to which instruments are tuned. The tone a' vibrates at 440 cycles per second and is used as a standard.

Concertstück (Ger.) (kôn—tsĕrt'—shtēk) Concert piece.

Concord A consonant sound when tones are sounded together. A pleasing aesthetic experience. A pleasant sounding chord. A generally stable group of tones.

Conducting To lead or to guide. The directing of a musical group. It is the art of interpreting and conveying the printed page to the performers. To coordinate all the performers. It involves time, the beat, the balance, and interpretation of the music, the preparation of the score, the dynamics, understanding the form, etc. It is essential to good performance. Some basic conducting patterns are used for various meters. For example: beats to a measure: (One) — used for fast $\frac{3}{4}$ time (Two - $\frac{2}{4}$ $\frac{2}{8}$ $\frac{2}{16}$, etc. (also used to conduct a fast tempo in six.)

LEFT HAND   RIGHT HAND

ONE BEAT TO MEASURE

(Same direction)

X—Rebound   X—Rebound

TWO BEATS TO THE MEASURE

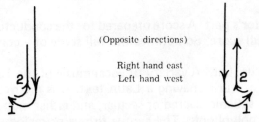

(Opposite directions)

Right hand east
Left hand west

THREE BEATS TO THE MEASURE

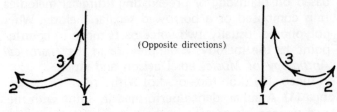

(Opposite directions)

FOUR BEATS TO THE MEASURE

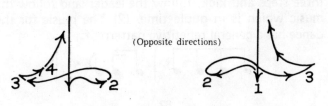

(Opposite directions)

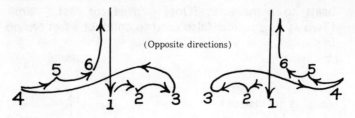

(Opposite directions)

Note: The first beat of each measure is a downstroke, the last beat in each measure an upstroke.

Conductor A leader, director, or one who conducts a musical group by means of a baton, instrument, or with his hands. He communicates his interpretation of the musical score to the performers. His goal is to prepare the group for a performance or to study a musical work.

Conductor's part A score prepared for the conductor from the full score. Sometimes the full score of a composition.

Conductus (Lat.) A variety of vocal music of the 12th and 13th centuries having a Latin text. It is metrical, generally syllabic, sacred or secular, and either monophonic or polyphonic. The cantus firmus or melody is not based on plainsong or pre-existing liturgical melodies. It is composed or a borrowed secular melody. When polyphonic, usually two voice parts move in counterpoint to the melody. Examples are in the *Historical Anthology of Music,* ed. Davison and Apel.

Con fuoco (It.) (kōn foo—ō '—kō) With fire.

Conga (1) A cuban dance performed in a line with men and women alternating in the line. The dancers move three steps and kick, follow the leader, and follow the music which is in duple time. (2) The music for the dance has a general repetitive pattern of:

Conjunct Close association. A conjunct scale would move in each successive degree of a scale. Intervals moving by a distance of a second or less are called conjunct. An interval moving a greater degree than a second is called disjunct.

Con ottava (It.) (kōn ôt–tä '–vä) With octaves. Usually indicated, con 8va (i.e., with octave doubling). See *Octave.

Consecutive intervals Harmonic intervals of the same size moving in succession. E.g., consecutive thirds, fourths, etc.

Consequent A relationship of question and answer. The consequent is the answer. The question is the antecedent. In a fugue, it is the answer to the subject.

Console The console of the organ. That case or part which includes the controls such as keyboards, pedals, etc. The desk-like section of the organ.

Consonance Sounds which are said to be in a state of repose. The subjective evaluation of sounds said to be pleasant, agreeable, or in accord. The opposite, unrest or disagreeable, is said to be dissonance. An important factor in the whole of harmonic writing and analysis.

Con sordino (It.) (kōn sôr–dē '–nō) Play with the mute attached.

Consort A group performing music. A chamber group of the 17th century. A group of like instruments of one family (such as: viols playing in ensemble – a whole consort). See *Broken consort.

Con spirito (It.) (kōn spēr '–ē–tō) With spirit.

Continuo (It.) (kōn–tē '–noo –ō) Continued bass. See *Basso continuo.

Contra (It.) (kôn '–trä) Against or opposite. E.g., contrapuntal or contratenor. Also contra, meaning the octave below.

Contrabass (1) The instrument below the bass instrument in each instrumental family. (2) The double bass in the violin family.

Contrabass clarinet The clarinet one octave below the bass clarinet.

Contra basso (It.) (kôn'—trä bäs'—sō) Double bass.

Contra-bassoon A double bassoon. It is one octave lower than the bassoon and is larger in size. It has about sixteen feet of tubing. See *Bassoon.

Contrafactum (Lat.) During the medieval period of music, a practice of changing a text from sacred to secular, or from secular to sacred using the original music.

Contralto (It.) (kôn—träl'—tō) (1) The lowest female voice or part. The vocal range is approximately from f to f". (2) The highest male voice or part. See *Voice ranges.

Contra-octave The third octave below middle c.

Contrapuntal, Contrapuntus (Lat.) The technique of using counterpoint. The word counterpoint is derived from the latin "punctus contra punctum" which means "point against point" or "note against note". The basic devices used in counterpoint are: imitation, sequence, repetition, augmentation, diminution, retrograde, contrary motion, inverted counterpoint, pedal point, transposition, change of mode, and stretto. See *Counterpoint.

Contrary motion Musical lines or notes of chords, moving in opposite directions.

Contrast The juxtaposition or contrasting of two or more musical elements to develop or evoke immediate or long range effects, tension, or musical ideas.

Contratenor An additional voice range used in the 14th century which was in the tenor range. It later developed into two voice ranges, one a high tenor and the other a low tenor. Finally, two terms evolved: contratenor altus, meaning alto and contratenor bassus, meaning bass.

Contrebasse (Fr.) (kō(n)—trä—bäs) Double bass.

Contrebasson (Fr.) (kō(n)—trä—bäs—sō(n)) Contrabassoon or double bassoon.

Cool jazz A jazz movement during the 1950's in which an attempt was made to cool off or calm down the earlier style of hot jazz. It was a more abstract type of jazz which used polyrythms, various meters, such as $\frac{5}{4}$, fugal techniques, and contrapuntal writing. It was a type of chamber jazz, that is, music for listening. Symphonic instruments are often used (e.g., oboe, French horn, etc.). Dave Brubeck (b. 1920) and his Quartet play "cool" jazz.

Coperta, coperto (It.) (kō—pĕr'—tä, kō—pĕr'—tō) Cover or blanket. To mute a percussion instrument with a cloth or cover.

Copla (Sp.) (kōp'—lä) Popular song. A couplet. A stanza of four lines of eight or eleven syllables, the second and fourth lines rhyming. See *Cantiga.

Cor (Fr.) (kôr) Horn or hunting horn. French horn.

Cor Anglais (Fr.) (kôr ä(n)—glä) English horn. The alto of the oboe, having a range a fifth lower than the oboe and a darker quality of tone. It has a slight bend in the neck to which the double reed is attached and a bulb-like bell at the bottom end of the horn. The general range sounds from e (below middle c') to a" (above the treble clef).

Corda (It.) (kôr'—dä) String. When una corda is indicated in piano music, the player uses the soft (left) pedal on the piano. This pedal moves the action and hammers a little to the left so that the hammer(s) hits only one string for a softer sound. The term tre corde indicates that the player should release the pedal so that the hammer can hit all the strings in the normal position. Corda vuoto (It.), would mean open string on the cello, viola, violin, etc.

Corde (Fr.) (kôrd) String.

Cor de basset (Fr.) (kôr dû bäs—sä) Basset horn.

Cor de chasse (Fr.) (kôr dû shäss) Hunting horn. French name for French horn.

Cornet (Cornetta, (It.) (kôr—nĕt'—tä)) A Bb instrument (also in A) like the trumpet. It is used in brass bands and concert bands and has a more mellow sound than that of the trumpet. It has a wider bore than the trumpet and a range from f# to c''' as does the trumpet. Like the trumpet, it has three vlaves, tuning slides, and is a member of the brass family.

Cornet à bouquin (Fr.) (kôr—nä ä boo—kä(n)) An obsolete woodwind instrument used during the Renaissance.

It was made of wood or sometimes of ivory, had a cupped mouthpiece, and six finger holes. It was also called: Cornett; Cornetto (It.); and Zink (Ger.). The range extended from a to a".

Cornet à pistons (Fr.) (kôr—nā ä pēs—tō(n)) Concert.

Cornetta (It.)(kôr—ně t'—tä) Cornet.

Cornetta a chiavi (It.) (kôr—ně t'—tä ä kē—ä'—vē) Key bugle.

Cornetto (It.) (kôr—ně t'—tō) The cornett which is now obsolete.

Corno (It.) (kôr'—nō) Italian for horn. The abbreviation is Cor.

Corno cromatico (It.) (kôr'—nō krō—mä'—tē—cō) Chromatic horn or valved horn.

Corno da caccia (It.) (kôr'—nō dä kä'—chē—ä) Hunting horn. Also, French horn.

Corno da tirarsi (It.) (kôr'—nō dä tē—rär'—sē) Sliding horn or slide trumpet.

Corno di bassetto (It.) (kôr'—nō dē bäs—sět'—tō) Bassett horn.

Corno Inglese (It.) (kôr'—nō ēng—glä'—zā) English horn.

Corno sordo (It.) (kôr'—nō sôr'—dǒ) Deaf. Horn mutes. A cone-shaped object made of fiber, metal, card-board, etc. which is put into the bell of a brass instrument of the horn class to mute the sound.

Coro primo (It.) (kō'—rō prē'—mō) The first chorus or choir.

Corrente (It.) (kôr—rě n'—tä) (1) A 17th century dance in fast triple time to which dancers glided or seemed to run. (2) A movement or section in the Baroque and Classical suite. Examples are found in the "suites" of J. S. Bach (1685-1750). See *Courante.

Cortège (Fr.) (kôr—tězh) Train; attendants. Music played at a ceremonial procession.

Coulé (Fr.) (koō —lā) Slur or slide. A passing note. A double appoggiatura or slide. An agrément of the Baroque and Classical periods of music.

Counter fugue The answer to the subject is inverted on the tonic of the subject.

Countermelody A second melody which moves along with another melody.

Counterpoint The technique of combining several melodies. It is a polyphonic texture and is considered from the vertical as well as the horizontal aspect in harmony. The texture is such that the melodies interweave. The melodic lines and the rhythmic elements are independent of each other but are combined in counterpoint. The term counterpoint is a matter of organization rather than form. There are several types and species of counterpoint. Examples of some types of counterpoint in history are: organum — two parts; motet — 13th century, three parts and later four parts; imitation in counterpoint — 15th century; the organization of the theory of counterpoint — 17th century; the species of counterpoint by Fux — 18th century; and the twelve-tone technique applied to counterpoint during the 20th century. The five species of counterpoint are: (1) note against note — one note in the counter-melody for each note in the canto fermo; (2) counter-melody — two notes against each note in the canto fermo; (3) four notes against each note in the canto fermo; (4) syncopated rhythms; and (5) free- or combinations of the other four species. Double counterpoint or invertible counterpoint means that the parts are written so that they may be interchanged. Triple or quadruple counterpoint would indicate that three or four melodies would change positions. See *Canon, *Contrapuntal, *Fugue, *Polyphony, *Double counterpoint, *Triple counterpoint.

Countersubject A fugue has a subject in one voice and an answer in another voice. The subject continues in counterpoint with the answer. The countersubject is the part which moves in counterpoint with the answer and is a continuation of the subject. This relationship and development continues throughout the exposition of the fugue. Sometimes, the countersubject supplies material for the episodes that follow the exposition. The countersubject may be used above or below the subject. An example: J. S. Bach (1685-1750)"Fugue

87

No.IV" from Volume I, *The Well-Tempered Clavier.*

See *Fugue.

Counter tenor The highest adult male voice. It is higher than the tenor and is sometimes called alto or head voice.

Country dance A simple, lively English country dance. Popular ballads would accompany the dancing. People would form a square or circle to dance. Movements changed with each eight measure phrase. Some of the dances were similar to the Virginia reel. Examples of these dances and songs are found in a series called *The English Dancing Master* by Playford, 1651.

Coup d'archet (Fr.) (ko͞o där—shā) Blow or stroke of the bow. Attack with the bow.

Courante (Fr.) (ko͞o —rä(n)t) (1) A 16th century lively dance in triple meter. (2) Music for a dance which alternated between three and two accents. (3) A dance style used in suites and partitas and popular during the 17th and 18th centuries. Examples: "Courante" from J. S. Bach (1685-1750) *Suite No. 1 in C for Orchestra;* J. S. Bach, *English Suite No. 2 in A Minor for Piano.* See *Courrente.

Course Strings tuned in the octave or in unison and played at the same time in order to produce more volume or sound. Primarily used on the lute-type instruments. see *Lute.

Cow bells A cow bell without a clapper which is used primarily in dance bands. It is mounted and struck by a drum stick or by brushes. It is sometimes used by the percussion player in symphonic works.

Crab motion Moving backwards. A melody which is read

from the last note to the first note. J. S. Bach (1685-1750) used this technique in the canon of his *Musik-alische Opfer*. See *Retrograde, *Cancrizans.

Credo (Lat.) (krā '—dō) "I believe". In the ordinary of the Mass, it is sung after the "Gloria" and before the "Sanctus". The "Credo" is the third part of the Ordinare in the Roman Catholic Mass. The priest sings, "Credo in unum Deum", (see theme below) which means "I believe in one God". The choir continues with the Nicene Creed "Patrem omnipotentem, factorem coeli et terrae, visibilium omnium et invisibilium. Et in unum Dominum Jesum Christum, Filium Dei unigenitum. Et ex Patre natum ante omnia saecula. Deum de Deo, lumen de lumine, Deum verum de Deo vero. Genitum, non factum, consubstantialem Patri: per quem omnia facta sunt. Qui propter nos homines, et propter nostram saluten descendit de coelis. Et incarnatus est de Spiritu Sancto ex Maria Virgine: Et Homo Factus Est. Crucifixus etiam pro nobis; sub Pontio Pilato passus, et sepultus est. Et resurrexit tertia die, secundum Scripturas. Et ascendit in coelum: sedet ad dexteram Patris. Et iterum venturus est cum gloria judicare vivos, et mortuos: cujus regni non erit finis. Et in Spiritum Sanctum, Dominum et vivificantem: qui ex Patre Filioque procedit. Qui cum Patre, et Filio simul adoratur, et conglorificatur: qui locutus est per Prophetas. Et unam, sanctam, catholicam et apostolicam Ecclesiam. Confietor unum baptisma in remissionem peccatorum. Et exspecto resurrectionem mortuorum. Et vitam venturi saeculi. Amen." In English it means, "The Father Almighty, Maker of heaven and earth, and of all things visible and invisible. And in one Lord Jesus Christ, the Only-begotten Son of God. Born of the Father before all ages. God of God; Light of Light; true God of true God. Begotten not made; of one being with the Father; by Whom all things were made. Who for us men, and for our salvation, came down from heaven. And was made Flesh by the Holy Spirit of the Virgin Mary: And Was Made Man. He was also crucified for us, suffered under Pontius Pilate and was buried. And on the third day He rose again according to the Scriptures. And ascending into heaven, He sits at the right hand of the Father. And He shall come again in glory to judge the living and the dead; and of His kingdom there shall be no end. And I believe in the Holy Spirit, Lord and Giver of Life, Who proceeds from the Father and the Son. Who together with the Father and Son is no less adored, and glorified: Who spoke by the Prophets. And I believe in One, Holy, Catholic and Apostolic Church. I confess one Baptism for the remission of sins. And I look for the resurrection of the dead. And the life of the world to come. Amen". The Nicene Creed is of considerable length. Therefore, when it was put in a polyphonic setting it was treated in several ways, e.g.: in elaborate polyphonic style with the full text; in an abbreviated form (i.e., omitting some of the words); and in a combination of polyphonic and simple homophonic style. Today, the polyphonic Mass is sung in the vernacular. Originally, and for centuries, it was sung in Latin. The Latin test has been used by many great composers. An example of an excellent setting of the "Credo" is found in the J. S. Bach (1685-1750) *Mass in B Minor.* The traditional plainsong treatment used by the priest in the opening of the "Credo" section, is also used by Bach in his "Credo". Example from section XI, "Credo" No. 1:

See *Mass, *Ordinary of the Mass.

Crescendo (It.) (krĕ–shĕn'–dō) A term indicating an increase in intensity, i.e., becoming louder. It is indicated by either an abbreviation of the term (cres.) or the symbol ———————— placed above or below a note or a group of notes.

Croche (Fr.) (krôsh) Crooked or bent. A quaver which is equal to an eighth-note. A demisoupir is a quaver rest.

Croma (It.) (krō'–mä) A quaver which is equal to an eighth-note.

Cromatico (It.) (krō—mä'—tē—kō) Chromatics as used in scales, chords, and instruments. In the 16th century the term referred to compositions which made considerable use of balck notes, i.e., shorter notes. See *Chromatic.

Cromorne An obsolete instrument that had the reed encased in a wooden cap. The reed was vibrated by indirect wind. A Krummhorn.

Crook A piece of tubing added between the brass instrument and the mouthpiece. It lengthens the tubing which in turn lowers the pitch. Various lengths and sized tubings could be used to vary the pitch. Before valves were added to the brass instruments, an instrument could sound only a limited number of tones within the harmonic series. The crook made it possible to change the harmonic series and thereby add notes. The same instrument with different crooks played in many keys.

Cross relation or false relation Two successive tones that normally occur in one voice are placed in different voices. Generally, the notes that are normally used in a melodic or horizontal pattern are used in a vertical pattern. For example, a given note g moves normally up to a g# in a melodic line. A cross relation would have the g in the soprano or some other upper voice and have the g# appear as the sequential note of the next chord in the bass line.

Cross-rhythms Two or more different rhythmic patterns used to create a counter-rhythm of accents.

Crotchet A quarter note (♩). One-quarter of a semibreve.

Crowd A bowed lyre. An ancient Celtic bowed stringed instrument which had a rectangular frame. Early instruments had no fingerboard, so it is thought to be in the harp family. Later, finger boards were added and the instrument had four strings over the fingerboard and two free strings along the side. The Welsh name is Crwth. See Chrotta.

Crwth (Welsh) See *Crowd, *Chrotta.

C sharp C#. A semitone above the note C. E.g.;

Clef:

Treble Clef   Bass Clef   Alto Clef   Tenor Clef

Cue To come in. (1) Small notes in a musical score that serve as a guide to which instrument(s) or group is playing. (2) A conductor cues a player or group to enter.

Cuivres (Fr.) (cwēvr) Copper instruments. Cuivre jaune (Fr.) means brass instrument. The French name for brass instruments.

Curtain tune Music performed between the acts of a play. Also known as act-tunes, or entr'acte which means interlude. See *Entr'acte.

Cycle of songs Liederkreis in German. A group of songs, considered a whole unit, which are related in thought or ideas. Example: Franz Schubert (1792-1828), *Die Winterreise,* Opus 89 (song cycle). See *Song cycle.

Cyclic A cycle or cycles. (1) The unity among sections of a work. Thematic material used in all or some movements of a work is said to be of cyclic form. (2) The term is sometimes used when a work opens and closes with the same thematic material. (3) A reference to forms having several sections or movements. Examples: César Franck (1822-1890), *Symphony in D Minor;* Hector Berlioz (1803-1869), *Symphonie Fantastique,* Op. 14 (e.g., the recurrent idée fixe).

Cymbals Two metal discs in the shape of a plate which are clashed together to produce a ringing sound. It can also be struck by a stick or by steel brushes as is the case in dance music or jazz. There are several types of cymbals: choke cymbals, sizzle cymbals, sock cymbals, etc. An instrument classed as an idiophone. See *Idiophones.

D

D (1) The supertonic (2nd) note of the scale of C major
or the fourth degree of the scale of A minor. (2) On
various clefs the note appears as follows:

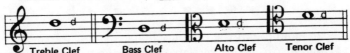

Treble Clef   Bass Clef   Alto Clef   Tenor Clef

(3) The letter is used as an abbreviation for such words
as dominant and da capo (D. C.) (4) Some musical instruments are pitched in the key of D (e.g., Trumpet in
D). (5) D is used to identify many keys such as: D
major, Db major, D minor, D# major. (6) D or doh is
the tonic of the major scale in the sol-fa system. See
*Key, *Letter names, *Notation, *Pitch names, *Scale.

Da (It.) (dä) Of; from; for; by.

Da ballo (It.) (dä bäl '–lō) Dance, ballet. To play in the
style of a dance.

Da camera (It.) (dä käm '–ā–rä) Chamber or room. In
chamber music style.

Da Capo (It.) (dä kä '–pō) Head, chief. Italian for from
the head. Repeat from the beginning of the composition. The abbreviation is D.C.

Da capo al fine (It.) (dä kä '–pō äl fē '–nä) Go back to
the beginning of the composition and end at the term
"fine". Usually abbreviated D.C. al Fine.

Da capo al segno (It.) (dä kä '–pō äl sĕn '–yō) From the
beginning to the sign (𝄋).

Da capo aria (It.) (dä kä '–pō ä '–rē–ä) The first section
of a song is repeated after the second section. Often
used in 17th and 18th century opera and oratorio. A
— first section, B — middle section, usually in a different key and having different material, A — return of
the first section. The scheme is ABA. It was used by
many Baroque composers, e.g., J. S. Bach (1685-1750)
and George Frideric Handel (1685-1759).

Da capo sin' al segno (It.) (dä kä '–pō sēn äl sĕn '–yō)
Go back to the beginning, play until the sign (⊕) is
reached, then jump to the coda or the section indicated.

93

Dactyl, dactylic A scheme of accented and unaccented notes which is related to the Greek poetic meter. The patterns are called feet; dactyl having a long note followed by two short notes. An example in notation:

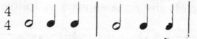

an example of the poetic scheme: | _ ◡ ◡ | _ ◡ ◡ |

Dahareh An early Persian tambourine-type instrument.

Daily hours The hours at which particular services are held in the Roman Catholic Church. See *Office hours.

Dairi A tambourine-type musical instrument of Turkey.

Dal segno (It.) (däl se̊ n '–yō) Return to the sign. Used when indicating a repeat of a section. The sign is (𝄋). The abbreviation is D.S.

Dal segno al fine (It.) (däl se̊n '–yō äl fē '–nä) A repeat designation. Go back to the sign and then to the end. Usually abbreviated D.S. al Fine.

Damenisation Another system of solmization used during the 18th century in Europe. See *Solmization.

Damp Dull or deaden a sound. To reduce the amplitude of a string, percussion head, etc.

Damper pedal Sometimes called loud pedal or open pedal on the piano. The pedal that raises the dampers away from the strings allowing them to vibrate. The damper pedal is the one to the right. The soft pedal is the one on the left and the sostenuto pedal is in the middle. The pedals are depressed with the feet. See *Piano.

Dampers (1) The felt pads on the piano and other stringed keyboard instruments. They are located above the strings and stop the string from vibrating just after the release of the key. (2) A mute on a brass instrument.

Dämpfer (Ger.) (de̊ mp '–fûr) Mute.

Dance Movement to music. Music rhythmically suited for dancing.

Dance band A term generally used to identify the large instrumental groups that played "swing" music during the 1930's and 40's. It is an era of development in jazz in which the large bands played written arrangements with some opportunity for solo improvisation. The dance band included the following sections: (1) saxophone section — 1st alto, 2nd alto, 1st tenor, 2nd tenor, and Barionte saxophone (sometimes soprano saxophone and B♭ clarinet were added), (2) Trumpet section — 1st, 2nd, 3rd, and 4th trumpet, (3) trombone section — 1st, 2nd, 3rd, and 4th trombone, (4) rhythm section — string bass (arco and Pizz.), guitar, drums, and piano. Some examples of dance bands of this era are the bands of: Benny Goodman, Glen Miller, Lionel Hampton, et al. The swing band or dance band is still with us, but since the 1950's we have bands (smaller combos — pop groups) playing improvised music on amplified instruments. The music is called Bop (1940-50), cool jazz (1949-55), Funky, or hard bop (1955-60), Third Stream Music (1960's), Soul jazz (1960's), and Rock (1970's).

Dance form Instrumental pieces, sections of suites, or movements used in the 18th century which were influenced by various types of dances.

Dance music (1) Music related to specific dances and used as musical accompaniment. (2) Music reflecting dance pieces but written for the purpose of being played as concert pieces. For example; movements of symphonies, suites, Chopin piano pieces, etc.

Dance rhythm Those rhythmic phrases related to the many styles and types of dancing that have influenced musical compositions. The dance has played an important part in the development of musical style and form.

Dance songs Musical style related to the dance such as ballerti, conzone, a ballo, etc.

Danse (Fr.) (dä(n)s) Dance or dancing.

Danse Macabre (Fr.) (dä(n)s mä—kä̀br) Dance of death; gruesome. Several composers have used this theme to portray the dance of the skeletons or death. It is an old legend. The name for a work by Camille Saint-Saens (1835-1921), *Danse Macabre,* Op. 40.

Danza (It.) (dän'—tsä) Italian and Spanish for dance.

Danza española (Sp.) (dän'—tsä ĕs—pän—yōl'—ä) Spanish dance.

Danza tedesca (It.) (dän'–tsä tä–dĕ s'–kä) Italian for German dance.

Dargason An English country dance and folk tune dating back to the 15th and 16th centuries.

Das (Ger.) (däs) The or thus. Used in German titles.

Daseian notation A system of notation used during the 9th and 10th centuries.

Das Selbe (Ger.) (däs zĕl'–bå), der Selbe (dĕr zĕl'–bå), die Selbe (dē zĕl'–bå) The same.

Dauer (Ger.) (dow'–å r) Length; dauernd (Ger.) (dow'–årnt) Enduring, lasting, or continual.

Davul A large drum used in Turkish folk music.

D.C. The abbreviation for Da capo.

D Dur (Ger.) (dā do͞or) Key of D major.

De (Fr.) (dû) French for: of, out of; from.

Deaconing An English term for lining out the music. The Deacon or leader would read the line before the congregation sang the phrase. A rote technique for singing.

Dead march A slow, stately march which is solemn and is usually used as a funeral march.

Debole (It.) (dā'–bō—lā) Weak or frail.

Début (Fr.) (dā–bü) First cast. The first appearance; to open.

Dec. The abbreviation for decani.

Decani (Lat.) Of the dean. The choir in an English cathedral, when divided into two sections, has one section sit on the side of the precentor (the half called cantoris) while the other half sits on the dean's side (called the decani); usually the south side of the church chancel.

Decelerando (It.) (dā–chä—lā—rän'–dō) The tempo becomes slower.

Deceptive cadence Interrupted cadence. When the resolution of a chord within a cadence moves to some harmony other than that which is expected. For example: when a V chord moves to a VI chord rather than to the I chord.

Déchant (Fr.) (dā–shä(n)) French for discant or descant. See *Discant.

Decibel A unit of measurement for intensity. One-tenth

of a bel. Decibel (db.) is the smallest unit used in measuring intensity or loudness.

Décidé (Fr.) (dā–sē–dā) (decisione, (It.) (dā–chē–zē–ō'–nā)) Decided, resolute, resolved, or decision.

Declamando; declamato (It.) (dĕ–klä–män'–dō, dĕ–klä–mä'–tō) In a declamatory style.

Declamation Declamatory style. Half-sung or half-spoken. The emphasis is on the enunciation of words.

Décoration (Fr.) (dā–kôr–ä–sē–ō(n)) (1) Embellishment or ornamentation. (2) The term denotes the signature of a piece of music.

Decorative notes "Non-harmony" notes in a musical line in the form of (common examples): an embellishment, appoggiatura, passing note, auxiliary note, anticipation, or suspension.

Decrescendo (It.) (dā–krĕ–shĕn'–dō) (decrescituo, It.) (dā–krĕ–shē–ōo'–tō)) A term indicating a decrease in intensity, i.e., growing softer. It is indicated by either an abbreviation of the term (decresc.) or by the symbol ⊐══════ placed above or below a note or a group of notes.

Degree A tone, note, or step of a scale. An interval between two tones. The relative position of a note on a staff.

Dehnen (Ger.) (dā'–nån) To prolong, expand.

Dehors (Fr.) (dû–awr) Without; outside. To stress or make prominent.

Delà (Fr.) (dû–lä) French for beyond or past; of the or from the.

Delicato (It.) (dā–lē–kä'–tō) Delicate.

Delirante (It.) (dā–lē–rän'–tā) Delirious or frenzied.

Delirio (It.) (dā–lēr'–ē–ō) Frenzy or delirium.

Delivery The manner in which one performs a piece of music. The style, articulation, tone, expression, interpretation, etc.

Delizioso (It.) (dā–lē–tsē–ō'–zō) Delicious or sweet.

Démanchement (Fr.) (dā–mä(n)sh–mä(n)) From manché (Fr.). (1) The fingerboard of a violin, etc., the neck of an instrument. (2) Shifting the left hand position in string playing, for example, from the first to the fourth position on the violin.

Demi (Fr.) (dĕ —mē) Half. The Italian is mezza.

Demi-cadence Half cadence. See *Cadence.

Demi-jeu (Fr.) (dĕ —mē—zhû) Half-play. Jeu means play in French and stop in organ music. Play at half power or half stop.

Demisemiquaver The thirty-second note (♪) or half a semiquaver which is a sixteenth note. Also, a triple croche (Fr.) or a biscroma (It.)

Demisoupir (Fr.) (dĕ —mē sōo—pir) Quaver rest. Eighth rest.

Demiton (Fr.) (dĕ —mē—tō(n)) Half-tone, semitone, or half-step. See *Semitone, *Half-step.

Demi-voix (Fr.) (dĕ—mē—vwä) In a low voice or half-voice.

Demütig (Ger.) (dā'—mü—tĭk) Humble.

Denkmäler der Tonkunst in Bayern (Ger.) (dĕngk'—mē—lår dĕr tōn'—kōonst i n Bī'—ĕrn) [DTB] (Monuments of Music in Bavaria). The series has 36 volumes, 1900-1931. A series which is supplementary to *Denkmäler deutscher Tonkunst*. The Bavarian series is called Zweite Folge (second series). A new revised edition is now in progress. See *Denkmäler der Tonkunst in Oesterreich, *Denkmäler deutscher Tonkunst.*

Denkmäler der Tonkunst in Oesterreich (Ger.) (dĕngk'—mē—lår dĕr tōn'—kōonst i n ĕ(r)s'—tĕr—ri kh) [DTO] (Monuments of Music in Austria). The series has 115 volumes to date, the first volume published in 1894. A series of publications (reprints) of old Austrian music which includes works by foreign composers written in Austria or works found in Austrian libraries. See *Denkmäler der Tonkunst in Bayern, *Denkmäler deutscher Tonkunst.*

Denkmäler deutscher Tonkunst (Ger.) (dĕngk'—mē —lår doit'—chår tōn'—kōonst) [DdT] (Monuments of German Music). The series has 65 volumes, 1892-1931. A new revised edition was published from 1957-1961. A series of publications of old music by German com-

98

posers and works by foreign composers who lived in Germany. The series started in 1892. After the first two volumes were published, a long period elapsed during which time the Austrian musicians started their own series. The German series resumed in 1900 and was divided into two sections, one for Germany, the other for Bavaria (Zweite Folge — second series). See *Denkmäler der Tonkunst in Bayern, *Denkmäler der Tonkunst in Oesterreich.

Der (Ger.) (dĕr) This, the, that, he, who, etc.

Dès (Fr.) (dĕs) Since, from.

Des (Ger.) (dĕs) D flat (Db).

Descant To sing. (1) The soprano. (2) A melodic line which is usually written above the musical theme either in counterpoint or as an accompaniment. (3) The highest instruments, for example, the descant recorder. (4) The florid melody in a hymn added above the normal melody and sung by a soloist or a small group. (5) A 17th century variation.

Descant viol The highest pitched instrument of the viol family.

Descriptive music Music that is associated with programmatic ideas or extra-musical ideas. An association with a place, person, etc.

Des dur (Ger.) (dĕs dōor) D flat major (Db major).

Deses (Ger.) (dĕs'–ĕs) D double flat (Dbb).

Desiderio (It.) (dā–zē–dā'–rē–ō) Desire. The music is to be played with emotion.

Design The form or structure of the musical composition. The style and nature of the composition. The structure of the elements of music. For example: form, melody, harmony, etc. See *Form.

Desk (1) The music rack on a keyboard instrument. (2) The console of the organ. (3) The controls of the organ. (4) A music stand.

Des moll (Ger.) (dĕs mawl) D flat minor (Db minor).

Dessous (Fr.) (dĕ s–sōo) Below, underneath, under. En dessous (Fr.) means in the lower part.

Dessus (Fr.) (dĕ s–sü) Above, upper part, over. En dessus

(Fr.) means in the upper part, also treble clef.

Desto (It.) (dĕs'–tō) Brisk.

De suite (Fr.) (dû swēt) Succession, one after another, to follow in order.

Détaché (Fr.) (dā–tä–shā) Detached. A style of bowing a stringed instrument. Play a strong and broad single bow on each note. See *Bowing.

Determinato (It.) (dā–tĕ r –mē–nä'–tō) Determined. Perform in a determined style.

Deuteros (Ger.) (doi'–tĕr–ōs) One of the church modes, examples of which are found in Gregorian chant. See *Modes.

Deutlich (Ger.) (doit'–lĭkh) Distinct.

Deux (Fr.) (dû) Two or both. Used to indicate two instruments or voices on a part or a part is to be divided for two performers.

Deuxieme (Fr.) (dû–zē–ĕm) Second. The indication of a voicing or second part.

Development The process of pulling-through or the development of an idea, theme, subject, etc. in a composition. See *Development section.

Development section That part of a composition where fragments of thematic material are developed. An example of this technique occurs in the sonata form in the middle part of the movement. This is done by expanding and modifying thematic material, by key changes, by using climaxes, through the use of the canonic devices (e.g., imitation, augmentation, inversion, diminution, and retrograde), texture treatment, by a change of instrumentation, through harmonic changes, etc. Many forms of music make use of this development technique, such as: fugues, symphonies, overtures, etc. See *Sonata-allegro-form.

Devoto (It.) (dā–vō'–tō) Devout, devoted.

Dezime (Ger.) (dā–tsē'–må); zehnt, (Ger.) (tsānt). A tenth in music.

D flat Db. A semitone below the note D. E.g.;

| Treble Clef | Bass Clef | Alto Clef | Tenor Clef |

Di (It.) (dē) Of; than.

Diabolism In a literary sense, a theme of horror, sin, or the theme concerned with the devil. Diabolus in Musica (Lat.) means the devil in music. It referred to the use of the tritone (the type of interval which uses three whole tones). The tritone was avoided, as a general rule, by medieval theorists in writing counterpoint and also avoided in early polyphonic writing. See *Tritone.

Dialogo (It.) (dē—ä—lō '—gō); dialog, (Ger.) (dē—ä—lōk '). Dialogue. Generally, a musical work in which two groups or parts are used in response to one another (question and answer). Alternating parts. It was often used in 17th and 18th century vocal and instrumental music as well as in earlier vocal works, such as caccia, lauda, madrigal, etc. The dialogue technique is often used in 19th and 20th century music.

Diapason (Diapason (Fr.) (dyä—pä—sō(n)). (1) A tuning fork or pitch. (2) The diapason normal pitch (A = 435 vps) known as French pitch or concert pitch. (3) A family of flue-pipes of the organ. The diapason is the foundation of the organ tone. The pipes may be open or stopped. The manual stop of 8 foot pitch is called stopped diapason. The manual stop of 16 foot pitch is called double diapason. (4) Originally, in Greek and medieval theory, it meant octave.

Diapente (Greek) Greek name for the interval of a fifth.

Diaphone A type of organ stop with a tone having great power and which may sound as a diapason.

Diaphony (Greek) (1) Dissonance. (2) A style of medieval polyphonic writing called organum. (3) A technique of writing harmony to a cantus firmus or writing a descant.

Diaphragm A muscular wall which the singer or wind player uses to support the breathing mechanism when producing a tone in a proper manner.

Diatessaron Greek name for the interval of a fourth.

Diatonic An interval, triad, chord, or note (tone) belonging to a given major or minor scale.

Diatonic melody A melodic line having only those notes belonging to the key signature. No altered tones are used except those indicated by the key signature. See *Diatonic, *Diatonic scale.

Diatonic scale Seven different tones within the octave arranged in whole steps and half-steps. For example: the major scale; a succession of tones having half-steps between the 3rd and 4th degrees and the 7th and 8th degrees of the scale. All other intervals are whole steps. Also, the minor scale: a succession of tones having half-steps between the 2nd and 3rd degrees and the 5th and 6th degrees of the scale (pure form of the minor scale). All others being whole steps. See *Scale, *Major scale, *Minor scale.

Dichtung (Ger.) (dihkh '–tŏong). Poetry.

Di colto (It.) (dē kôl '–tō) Cultivated. At once.

Diction Generally, the selection of words, verbal phrasing accents, intonation, quality, etc. of speech. Voice instructors relate the term to the enuncuation and articulation of the words and syllables while singing.

Dictionaries of Music Books that give information on the particular subject, music. Some of the several types are: (1) those that give definitions; (2) those containing articles on musical subjects; (3) biographies; (4) writings on special periods or styles of music; (5) on musical instruments. Many examples are listed at the end of this dictionary. See *"A Selected Annotated Bibliography".

Die (Ger.) (dē) The.

Dièse (Fr.) (dē–ĕz) Sharp (#).

Die Selbe See *Das Selbe.

Dies irae (Lat.) (dē '–ās ē '–rā) Day of wrath or day of judgment. A sequence of words used in the Mass for the dead (Requiem Mass) of the Roman Catholic Church. The text was also used in a plainsong melodic line, the first part of which was used by such composers as Berlioz in his *Symphony Fantastique.* The text was also used in new musical settings. The "Dies Irae" is usually the second section of a Requiem. Examples of Requiem settings; Hector Berlioz (1803-1869) and Giuseppe Verdi (1813-1901).

Diesis (Greek) Division. A quarter tone. In modern acoustics it is related to the acoustics of intervals.

Diesis (It.) (dē—ās'—is) Sharp (#).

Dietro (It.) (dē—ĕt'—rō) Behind; following.

Diferencia (Sp.) (dē—fā—rĕn'—thē—ä) Difference. A term for variation.

Difference tone or differential tone The sound heard, which is the difference between the frequencies of the two tones sounded at the same time. See *Combination tone, *Resultant tone.

Differential tones See *Difference tone, *Resultant tone.

Digital One of the keys on the keyboard. Any one finger lever of a keyboard instrument.

Digitorium An exercise box used by keyboard players to strengthen the fingers. It has five keys attached to heavy springs which resist the depression of the keys.

Dillettant (Ger.) (di—lä—tänt') One who dabbles in an art. A superficial approach or attitude toward an art. An amateur.

Diluendo (It.) (dē—loō—ĕn'—dō) Dying away.

Dilungando (dē—loōn—gän'—dō) Lengthening.

Dimeter Poetic meter. Two feet in a line of poetry.

Diminished Made smaller. The abbreviation is dim.

Diminished chord A chord having an interval of a minor third and a diminished fifth above the root of the chord. The octave when added, is perfect. Example:

DIM. CHORD ON C

Diminished intervals Those intervals which are smaller than a perfect interval or a minor interval. They are smaller by a half-step. Examples:

103

Diminished seventh chord A chord having a root, minor third, a diminished 5th, and a diminished 7th. It is often used when changing the key center and is usually built on the seventh degree of a major or minor scale. The resolution is to the dominant or to the tonic chord. E.g., in C major:

DIM. ∇II₇° V₇₆   I

Diminished triad Three tones is a vertical sequence having the intervals of a minor 3rd and a diminished 5th above a root. E.g.,

DIM. CHORD ON C

Diminuendo (It.) (dē—mē—noo̅—ĕn'—dō). Also, decrescendo (It.) A term indicating a decrease in the intensity, i.e., becoming softer. It is indicated by either an abbreviation of the term (dim. or dimin.) or by the symbol ⟩ placed above or below a note or a group of notes.

Diminution A theme presented again with the note values shortened. Each note is often cut by half its value. A canonic device.

Di molto (dè mȏl'—tō) Very much.

Di nuovo (It.) (dē noo̅—ō'—vō) Anew, again.

Dip The key-fall or the amount of pressure response of a key on a keyboard instrument.

Diphona (Greek) Two parts in music.

Direct A sign (w) placed at the end of a page or staff to indicate the next note to be performed. It was placed where the next note would appear, i.e., on a line or space. Used in older music.

Directaneus Singing a psalm without modification, also direct psalmody.

Direct psalmody Psalms which did not require a response. The verses were sung without the use of a refrain or antiphon.

Dirge A musical composition performed at the funeral service. An experssion of lament or mourning.

Dirigent (Ger.) (di–ri–gĕnt ') Conductor.

Dis (Ger.) (dis) D sharp (D#).

Discant See *Descant.

Discant bassoon A member of the bassoon family during the 17th century. The soprano had a range from a — c''; alto, from g — c''.

Discantus supra librum (Lat.) Descant from the book. Improvisation from the melodic line given in the book. A term used during the Middle Ages.

Discord Dissonance. A group of notes sounded together or a chord that is not harmonious.

Discreto (It.) (dēs–krā '–tō) Discreet; moderate.

Disinvolto (It.) (dē–zĕn–vôl '–tō) In an easy going style.

Disis (It.) (dis '–is) D double sharp. (D##) (Dx).

Disjunct A melodic line moving in intervals larger than a second. See *Conjunct.

Disjunct interval A melodic interval larger than a second.

Diskant (Ger.) (dis–kănt ') Soprano; treble.

Dis moll (Ger.) (dis mawl) D sharp minor (D# minor).

Disperazione (It.) (dēs–pĕ r–ä–tsē–ō '–nä) Desperation. Perform in a despairing manner.

Disque (Fr.) (dēsk) Recording disk, record.

Dissonance A discord or harsh sound. A group of tones played together having an incomplete feeling or a need to be resolved.

Distance An interval between two notes, horizontal or vertical.

Dital On the lute-harp, a finger key which pushes a string upon a fret on the finger board. It causes the string to become shorter, and therefore, changes the pitch.

Dital harp A 19th century lute-harp or harp-guitar, shaped like a guitar, and employing a finger key called a dital. See *Dital.

Div. The abbreviation for divisi. See *Divisi.

Diva (It.) (dē '–vä) A famous female singer.

Divertimento (It.) (dē–vĕr–tē–mĕ n '–tō) An 18th cen-

105

tury instrumental work having several movements like those in the symphony or suite. Such movements as dances, variations, sonata form, etc. It is performed in small ensemble on orchestral instruments. It was considered to be in the class of chamber music and was designed to be played for entertainment or for a specific purpose. Examples: Wolfgang Amadeus Mozart (1756-1791) *Divertimento in F,* K 138 for 2 violins, viola, and bass; *Divertimento in C,* K188 for 2 flutes, trumpets, and drums. See *Divertissement, *Serenade.

Divertissement (Fr.) (di—vĕ r—ti s—mä(n)) (1) A light musical composition. A divertimento. (2) A piece of music having several musical lines from opera, ballet, etc. A medley. (3) Music that is played between the acts of an opera, etc. (4) A suite of dances. See *Divertimento, *Entr'acte.

Divided stops A device which divides the whole rank of organ pipes into an upper half and lower half with each having its own stop.

Divisi (It.) (dē—vē '—sē) The term is used in string parts to indicate that the two or more notes or parts are not to be played as double stops but are to be divided between or among the players. See *A due, *A2.

Division In the style of variations on a theme or ornamentation of a simple melodic line which appears in the bass. The ground bass is written out. The soloist, often a viol or flute, improvises above the bass line which was usually played by a harpsichord.

Division viol A smaller bass viol used to play divisions. See *Division.

D moll (Ger.) (dā mawl) (Key of D major.

Do (Fr.) (dō) Do or ut. The syllable for the first note in a diatonic scale when using the system of movable do. In the system of fixed do it is always the note C.

Dodecaphony, dodecaphonic Equivalent to twelve-tone music or music employing a twelve-tone set. The term usually applies to twelve-tone serial composition. However, dodecaphonic music may also include a tonal feeling in the sense that elements related to the major-minor system are sometimes used, such as the use of triads in twelve-tone music or the existence of tonal centers in certain types of twelve-tone compositions. This is a matter of interpretation in the analysis of a particular work or a section of a work. See *Twelve-tone system, *Serial technique.

Doglia (It.) (dôl'–yä) Sorrow.

Doh Anglicized do (It.) The first syllable of the major scale. See *Tonic, *Do.

Doight (Fr.) (dwä) Digit or finger. Doigté (Fr.) (dwä–tā) Fingering, as in a fingering pattern used in playing piano or other instruments.

Dolce (It.) (dôl'–chā) Candy. Sweetly.

Dolcian, dolcino, dulcian An obsolete type of bassoon having a soft tone.

Dolcissimo (It.) (dôl–chĭs'–sē–mō) Very sweetly.

Dolendo (It.) (dō–lĕn'–dō) Lamenting. Dolentemente, (It.) (dō–lĕn–tā–mĕn–tā) dolefully, mournfully.

Doloroso (It.) (dō–lō–rō'–zō) Sorrowfully.

Domchor (Ger.) (dōm'–kôr) German cathedral choir or chorus.

Dominant (1) The fifth degree of a major or minor scale. (2) The chord and triad built on the fifth degree of the scale. (3) The secondary dominant which is the dominant of any note of the scale excluding the tonic.

Dominant cadence The authentic cadence from the dominant (V) to the tonic (I). The use of the dominant in a cadential sequence. See *Cadence.

Dominant key The key which is a fifth higher from the established key.

Dominant seventh chord The chord built on the fifth degree of a scale of a given key having a root, third, fifth, plus a minor seventh added above the root of the chord. It is usually indicated by the small Arabic number 7 next to the Roman number V (V7). E.g., Dom. 7th, Key of C:

$$V_7 (G_7)$$

Domra A Russian lute.

Dopo (It.) (dō'–pō) After; afterwards.

Doppel (Ger.) (dŏp'–păl) Double or dual.

Doppel-Be (Ger.) (dŏp'–păl̄–bā) Double flat.

Doppel-Fagott (Ger.) (dôp'–păl–fä–gôt') Double bassoon. The sub-bass of the bassoon family during the 17th century. It had a range form F' to g.

Doppelfugue (Ger.) (dôp'–păl–foo–gä) Double fugue.

Dopplegriff (Ger.) (dôp'–păl–grif) Double stop (thirds, octaves, etc.

Doppelzunge (Ger.) (dôp'–păl–tsoong–ä) Double tonguing.

Doppio (It.) (dôp'–ē–ō) Double.

Doppio bemolle (It.) (dôp'–ē–ō bā–môl'–lā) Double flat (bb).

Doppio diesis (It.))dôp'–ē–ō dē–äs'–ĭs) Double sharp (x) (##).

Doppio movimento (It.) (dôp'–ē–ō mō–vē–měn'–tō) Double time. Move twice as fast.

Doppio pedale (It.) (dôp'–ē–ō pā–dä'–lā) Double pedal. A term in organ playing to indicate that both feet play simultaneously.

Doppio tempo (It.) (dôp'–ē–ō těm'–pō) Double the time. Twice as fast.

Dorian mode An ecclesiastical mode which is represented by playing all white keys on a keyboard instrument from D to D in an ascending scale. The final is D and the dominant is A. See *Church Modes.

Dot (1) A dot used in music above or below a note and indicates that the note is to be played shorter. (2) A dot plus a slur indicates a detached note. (3) A series of dots above or below the note head would indicate a repetition of the note related to the number of dots used. (4) When a dot appears after a note it indicates that additional length is added. For example, a dotted half note (♩.) in $\frac{4}{4}$ time would require an additional beat added to the half note. The dot after a note or rest adds half the value of the note or rest.

Dotted notes The dot after a note or rest adds half the

value of that note or rest. The dot adds half the value of whatever immediately precedes it. For example: $\frac{4}{4}$ time ♩ = 2 beats; ♩. = 3 beats; double dot ♩.. = 3½ beats; double dot ♪.. = 1¾ beats, etc.

Double (1) A classical term used to indicate variation or embellishment. (2) To double a part using another instrument. (3) The word double is used to indicate an instrument within a family which plays an octave lower, e.g., the bassoon and the double bassoon. (4) To double or play a second instrument.

Doublé (Fr.) (dōo̅ —blā̅) A musical turn or ornament.

Double appoggiatura Examples: (1) Two appoggiaturas played at the same time (e.g., in thirds);

(2) two consecutive notes moving to the main note, in either direction, within an interval of a third. ;

(3) A double appoggiautra having two notes moving to the main note, one from below and one from above the main note

See *Appoggiatura.

Double bar The vertical lines on a staff
A double bar is used to mark off sections or sub-divisions of music or to end a composition. It may appear at any point in a measure or at the end of a measure.

Double bass (1) The largest instrument of the orchestra string section (violin family), called bass viol. (2) The term used to describe any instrument one octave below the bass instrument. See *Contrabass, *Bass viol.

Double bass clarinet A single reed clarinet pitched one octave below the bass clarinet. It is used in concert bands and, on occasion, in the orchestra for special works. See *Bass clarinet.

Double bassoon The largest and lowest pitched double reed instrument of the oboe family. It is one octave lower than the regular bassoon and sounds an octave lower than the written note. See *Bassoon, *Contrabassoon.

Double bass viol Double bass, bass fiddle. See *String bass, *Double bass.

Double bémol (Fr.) (dōo bl bā—mŏl) Double flat (bb).

Double C The C that is two octaves below middle c', two ledger lines below the bass staff. See *Pitch names.

Double cadence (Fr.) (dōobl kä—dĕ(n)s) A double turn, agrément, or ornament.

Double canon Two canons, of two voices each, proceeding at the same time. Example: W. A. Mozart (1756-1791), "Menuetto" from *String Quartet K. 406*. See *Canon.

Double chant Two verses of a chant adapted ot a psalm or canticle.

Double choir (1) Two equal and full choirs that respond to one another. (2) A large choir divided into eight parts.

Double chorus See *Double choir.

Double concerto A concerto having two solo instruments with orchestra. E.g., J. S. Bach (1685-1750) *Concerto in D Minor for Two violins and Orchestra.* See *Concerto.

Double corde (Fr.) (dōobl kôrd) Chord. String instrument playing double stops.

Double counterpoint A contrapuntal melody structured so as to sound equally good above or below the first melody. Also called invertible counterpoint. It is often used in fugues. Double counterpoint involves the octave, tenth and twelfth as well as other intervals. When this concept of inversion is used in two melodies, it is called double counterpoint or invertible counterpoint. See *Counterpoint, *Fugue, *Invertible counterpoint.

Double croche (Fr.) (dōobl krôsh) Semiquaver or sixteenth note (♪).

Double diapason A sixteen foot pitch on the organ. See *Diapason, *Organ.

Double-dièse (Fr.) (dōobl dē—ĕz) Double sharp (x) (##).

Double dot A double dot after a note or rest increases the value by three-quarters of the value of the note or rest.

Double flat The sign bb. It lowers a natural note two half-steps. See *Flat, *Accidental.

Double fugue A fugue having two subjects. There are several types of double fugues. For example: (1) the two subjects may be presented at the same time in different voices at the beginning; (2) the first subject is presented after which the second subject enters as a counter-subject to the answer of the first subject; (3) subject one is treated separately in all voices and subject two is treated separately in all voices, later they may be treated together; (4) Subject two may be combined with subject one. Many examples of the double fugue in its various types may be found in *The Well-Tempered Clavier* by J. S. Bach (1685-1750) (e.g., Vol. 1, Fugue XII; Vol. II, Fugues IV and XVI): and in *The Art of the Fugue* by J. S. Bach (e.g., No. IX, et al.). See *Fugue, *Subject, *Countersubject.

Double note Twice the length of a whole note (♢ = semi-breve). Also called breve, which is notated (⊨⊣) and is equal to two semibreves (♢♢).

Double pedal In organ music, two parts (intervals) being played simultaneously by the feet. See *Organ.

Double period A period is a section of music of 8 or 16 measures consisting of two or more contrasting or complementary phrases which end in a cadence. The double period is composed of two periods which can form a complete unit. It is used in folk songs or other short forms.

Double reed The mouthpiece of the oboe, bassoon, etc. It is made of two thin pieces of cane bound together by string or wire around a small metal tube.

Double sharp The sign (x) or (##). The note is to be raised by two half-steps from the natural. See *accidentals, *Sharp.

Double stop Two or more notes played at the same time on a stringed instrument. Open and/or closed strings and more than one string is used. E.g., J. S. Bach (1685-1750) *Sonata No. 1 in G Minor* for Violin Alone.

Double tonguing Rapid tonguing on a brass instrument, piccolo, or flute. It is used in rapid passages, especially on the same note. The player continues the air stream and pressure but interrupts the flow by articulating the letters T and K in rapid succession. See *Tonguing.

Double touch On some organs, two different registrations can be played on the same keys without changing stops, by applying two different degrees of pressure while playing.

Double whole note The breve. Equal to two whole notes (two semibreves tied together (○‿○).

Douloureusement (Fr.) (dōō —lōō —rûz—mä(n)). Grievously, sadly.

Doux (Fr.) (dōō) Soft, sweet, easy, smooth.

Downbeat (1) The conductor's downward motion of the baton at the beginning of each measure. (2) The first beat of each measure. See *Conducting.

Downbow The downward motion of a bow when bowing a stringed instrument. The bow moves from the frog of the bow to the tip of the bow. It is the strongest bow action. It is often designated by (⊓) When the bow moves from the tip to the frog it is called an upbow. See *Bowing.

Doxology Praise to God sung in a hymn or psalm. In the Roman Catholic Mass, the greater doxology is the "Gloria" which is found in the Ordinary of the Mass. The lesser doxology is the "Gloria patri" which is found in the "Introit". The text can be found in many canticles and pslams. See *Ordinary of the Mass, *Mass, *Gloria in excelsis Deo, *Gloria patri et filio.

Dramatic music Music of a dramatic nature. Music pertaining to or relating to a play. Music associated with or incidental to a drama.

Dramma per musica (It.) (drä'—mä pĕr mōō'—zē—kä) The early name given to Italian operas of a serious nature. They were later called opera seria.

Drammatico (It.) (drä—mä'—tē—kō) Dramatic.

112

Drängen (Ger.) (drĕng'—ån) Press, urge. To move forward or to press on with the music.

Drehleier (Ger.) (drā'—li̅—å r) Hurdy-gurdy.

Dreiklang (dri̅—kläng) A triad in music.

Dreistimmig (Ger.) (dri̅—shtim—mikh) Three parts.

Dringend (Ger.) (drig'—ĕnt) Urgent.

Drone (1) A low and continuous sound of the bass instruments. (2) The low tone produced by the bagpipe. The pipe of the bagpipe that sounds the one continuous tone is called the drone pipe. (3) A drone bass is the low continuous tone on the same note.

Drum A percussion instrument of several types and sizes. It has a hollow center, usually a cylindrical shape, and is covered on both ends or one end by a skin, plastic, etc. The tone is produced by striking the head with a stick, brush, the hand, etc. Types: snare drum, field drum, side drum, tenor drum, bass drum, timpani, bongos, and others.

Drumstick The stick used to strike a drum head. There are several sizes, lengths, weights, and types. Different types of sticks are used to produce a variety of sounds and for varied styles of music. Some sticks have felt or rubber pads attached to the head to produce muffled sounds.

D. S. The abbreviation for dal segno (It.) meaning to the sign.

D sharp D#. A semitone above the note D. E.g.:

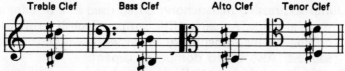

Treble Clef   Bass Clef   Alto Clef   Tenor Clef

Dudelsack (Ger.) (do̅o̅dl'—zäk) Bagpipe.

Due (It.) (do̅o̅'—ā) Two.

Due corde (It.) (do̅o̅'—ā kôr'—dā) (1) In string playing, the direction to double the note by playing the note on two strings to increase the sound. (2) On piano, the soft pedal is depressed in order that the hammers on the piano strike only two strings rather than the normal three strings. In the lower register, the term una chorda (It.) indicates that one string is to be struck instead of the normal two. See *Corda, *Una Cora, *Tre Corde.

Duet A composition for two performers having equal parts.

Dugazon A French term used to describe operatic sopranos having a light quality and often playing light hearted characters.

Dulcet Pleasant, melodious. A term used to describe the melodious or dulcet tones of the cello.

Dulciana An organ stop having a soft, string-like quality.

Dulcimer An instrument constructed like the psaltery, of trapezoidal shape, having metal strings over a soundboard which are struck with small hammers. Today, a guitar-like modern version is used which is plucked with the fingers.

Dulcitone A keyboard instrument having steel tuning forks which are struck by hammers to produce the sound.

Dulzian (Ger.) (dŏŏl'–tsē—än) The German name for a 16th and 17th century bassoon. Also called dolcino.

Dumka A Slavic dance, folk song, or ballad which alternated between a slow-sad mood and a fast-lively section. Excellent examples are found in Antonin Dvořvak (1841-1904) *Trio* for Violin, Piano and Cello, Opus 90.

Dump Expressing melancholy. Often used as a title for a musical work. An early 16th century English term describing an instrumental or vocal work which evoked sadness. Also called dompe or lament.

Dumpf (Ger.) (dŏŏmpf) Dull,-muted.

Duo (Fr.) (dü—ō) **Duett,** (Ger.) (dŏŏ—ĕt') **Duetto,** (It.) (dŏŏ—ĕt'—tō) Duet.

Duodecuple scale The twelve tones of the chromatic scale, not regarded as altered tones moving in half-steps of the chromatic scale ar altered tones of the diatonic scale, but as separate and equal tones as they are considered when used in the twelve-tone row. From duodecim (Lat.) meaning twelve.

114

Duple Double or having two parts.

Duplet Two notes played in the time normally allowed for the time of three of the same notes. E.g.; $\frac{3}{4}$ ♩♩♩

Duplet $\frac{3}{4}$ ♩♩

Duple time Two beats to a measure. Simple duple meter: $\frac{2}{4}$, $\frac{2}{8}$, etc; compound duple meter: $\frac{6}{4}$, $\frac{6}{8}$, etc.

Duplex instruments Instruments that play in two different keys and have two ranges as a result of a minor adjustment. The French horn is a good example. It is called double horn as it has both the key of F and Bb. The key of Bb is established by using the thumb rotary valve. The double baritone or double euphonium is another examples. A valve can change the air from moving through one bell to the second bell, changing the tone quality.

Duplum (Lat.) The part above the tenor part in organum during the period of music called Ars antiqua (13th century). The motetus was also called duplum in the 13th century motet.

Dur (Ger.) (door) Major. Dur, (Fr.) (dür) Hard.

Duramente (It.) (doo—rä—měn'—tā) Harshly. Play the music in a harsh manner.

Durchführung (Ger.) (doorkh'—füh—roong) Carry out. (1) The development of a theme. (2) The exposition of a theme in the fugue.

Durchgangsnote (Ger.) (doorkh'—gängz—nō—tå) Passage-note. Passing-tone or note.

Durchkomponiert (Ger.) (doorkh'—kŏm—pō—nērt) Through-composed vocal music (songs). A song having new music for each verse as opposed to a song which has the same music repeated for each verse (strophic).

Durezza (It.) (door—ĕt'—tsä) Hardness. Play with resolution. Earlier, it was related to dissonance.

Dux (Lat.) Leader, first. The subject of the fugue is called the dux. It is also the first part of the canon.

Dynamic curve The technique of creating climaxes in music by the use of dynamic changes. It was often used in the music of the Romantic period.

Dynamic marks The intensity or volume marks, signs, or

terms. Examples: Pianissimo (very soft — pp), piano
(soft — p), mezzo-piano (medium soft — mp), mezzo-
forte (medium loud — mf), forte (loud — f), fortissimo
(very loud — ff), sforzando (sudden accent — sfz),
⟨──── crescendo (grow louder), ────⟩
decrescendo (grow softer), forte-piano (loud-soft — fp),
────────⟩diminuendo (grow softer), accent marks
(> , — , ∧). See *Dynamics,

Dynamics Intensity or volume. The terms or signs that
indicate the degree of loudness and softness required
in the music. See *Dynamic marks.

E (1) E is the mediant (3rd) note of the scale of C major or the fifth degree of the scale of A minor. (2) On various clefs the note appears as follows:

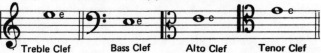

Treble Clef   Bass Clef   Alto Clef   Tenor Clef

(3) Musical instruments are pitched in the key of Eᵇ (e.g., alto saxophone in Eᵇ). (4) E is used to identify many keys, such as: E major, Eᵇ major, E minor, Eᵇ minor. See *Key, *Letter names, *Notation, *Pitch names, *Scale.

E (It.) (ā) And.

Ear training The study of intervals and rhythm through musical sound. Often, the syllable system, letter system or number system is used in connection with the development of a perceptive ear for music.

Ebenfalls (Ger.) (ā'—bå n—fäls) Likewise. Music to be played in the same manner.

Ebenso (Ger.) (ā'—bå n—zō) Just as or likewise.

Ecclesiastical modes Pertaining to a system used in church modes. See *Church modes.

Échappée (Fr.) (ā—shäp—pā) Runaway. A nonharmonic tone. A note which is not within the harmonic pattern. The échappée is a *note which moves in the opposite direction from the movement to the next harmonic note. E.g.,

Échappement (Fr.) (ā—shäp—mä(n)) See *Escapement.

Échelle (Fr.) (ā—shĕl) Ladder. Scale. Échelle chromatique, (Fr.) (ā—shĕl krō—mä—tēk) Chromatic scale. Échelle diatonique, (Fr.) (ā—shĕl dyä—tō(n)—nēk) diatonic scale.

Échelon (Fr.) (āsh—lō(n)) Step of a ladder. The degree of a scale.

Échiquier (Fr.) (ā—shē—kyā) A 14th century keyboard instrument having strings.

Echo (Écho, (Fr.) (ā—kō). To imitate or resound. (1) An organ stop which produces echo like sounds. (2) A sound which is reflected. A phenomenon in acoustics.

Echo chamber A broadcasting or recording sound studio which embellishes the original sound by picking up the echoes. A sound effect which is used in many of today's recordings.

Echo organ (1) One division of the organ keyboard. (2) Pipes of the organ which give an echo effect. They may be placed a distance away from the main body of the organ.

Eclat (Fr.) (ā—klä) Crash, bright. (Brio, (It.)).

Éclatante (Fr.) (ā—klä—tä(n)t) Brilliant, piercing, loud or shrill.

Eco (It.) (ā '—kō) Echo.

Ecole (Fr.) (ā—kôl) School or college.

Écossaise (Fr.) (ā—kô—sĕz) Scottish. (1) A country dance in duple meter in quick tempo. It was popular in Europe during the 18th and 19th centuries. (2) Music in the spirit of this type of dance. For example, *Ecossaises for Piano,* Ludwig van Beethoven (1770-1827); *Écossaise, No. 1,* Opus 72, No. 3, Frédéric Chopin (1810-1849).

Ed (It.) (ād) And.

Ed. The abbreviation for edited or edition.

E dur (Ger.) (ā dōor) E major

Effleurer (Fr.) (ĕf —flûr—ā) To touch lightly; to graze or glide over.

E flat Eb. A semitone below the note E. E.g.; Clef:

Treble Clef   Bass Clef   Alto Clef   Tenor Clef

Égal (Fr.) (ā—gäl) Even; equal; smooth.

Eifer (Ger.) (ī —fȧr) Fervour, passion.

Eighth Octave. An interval of an eighth is an octave. The symbol is 8 or VIII.

Eighth note The quaver. The symbol for the eighth note is ♪. See *Note.

Eighth rest The rest or pause in music having the same value as the quaver or eighth note. The symbol is ⅞ See * Rests.

Eile (Ger.) (ī '–lå) Haste. Eilen, (Ger.) (ī '–lå n) Hurry.

Eilend (Ger.) (ī '–lĕnt) Hurrying.

Ein, eine (Ger.) (ī n, ī n–å) One, an.

Einfach (Ger.) (ī n '–fäkh) Simple.

Eingang (Ger.) (ī n '–gäng) Introduction; entrance.

Eingestrichen (Ger.) (ī n '–gå –shtrik–å n) One stroke, one line.

Einhalten (Ger.) (ī n '–häl–tå n) Pause, stop.

Einklang (Ger.) (ī n '–kläng) One tone, unison.

Einleitung (Ger.) (ī n '–lī –tŏong) Introduction or prelude.

Einmal (Ger.) (ī n '–mäl) Once. Noch einmal (nŏkh ī n '–mäl) Once again; auf enimal (owf ī n '–mäl) All of a sudden.

Eins (Ger.) (ī nts) The number one.

Einsang (Ger.) (ī n '–zang) Solo.

Einschlafen (Ger.) (ī n '–shlä–få n) To sleep. Die away.

Einschnitt (Ger.) (ī n–shnĭt) A phrase or segment.

Einstimmig (Ger.) (ī n '–shtim–mik) Unanimous. One voice or line. Monophonic.

Eintracht (Ger.) (ī n '–träkht) Harmony.

Eintragen (Ger.) (ī n '–trä–gå n) To bring in, to enter.

Eintritt (Ger.) (ī n '–trĭt) Beginning; to make an entrance as in, for example, the canon or fugue.

Eis (Ger.) (ā '–is) E sharp (E#).

Eisis (Ger.) (ā–is '–is) E double sharp (Eˣ) (E##).

El (Sp.) (ĕl) The one; the.

Élan (Fr.) (ā–lä(n)) Rush, start or flight.

Elargir (Fr.) (ā–lär–zhēr) To widen, to broaden.

Electric guitar A guitar having an electrical attachment which amplifies the sound through a speaker system. See *Guitar.

Electric organ An organ which has the action mechanism

controlled by electrical impulses. It generates frequencies which are converted into sound.

Electronic music Musical sounds which are produced, modified and recorded electronically. Oscillations produce sounds unlike conventional musical sounds both in pitch and quality. These sounds may also be combined with standard musical sounds. The composer arranges these sounds into a meaningful organization. The sounds are usually recorded on tape. Examples: Milton Babbitt (b.1916), *Composition for Synthesizer* (1964); *Switched on Bach,* J. S. Bach (1685-1750), *Brandenburg Concerto No. 3, Jesu, Joy of Man's Desiring,* etc., Walter Carlos, Moog Synthesizer; Luciano Berio (b. 1925), *Momenti* (1960), *Visage* (1961); Jacob Durckman, *Animus I for Trombone and Tape* (1966). See *Musique concrète.

Electronic musical instruments (1) The sound is produced by electrical circuits. On some instruments the sound is produced entirely by electronic means, for example, the electronic organ. (2) On other instruments the sound is produced on a standard instrument and amplified electronically, for example, the electric guitar.

Electrosonics The term used in electronic music which includes the whole area of electronically produced sounds.

Elegante (It.) (ā—lā—gän—tā) Elegant.

Elegiac meter A hymn-meter. Elegiac, to express sorrow.

Elegy, Elegia (It.) A composition expressing lament. A poem of lamentation. A dirge.

Elements of music The parts of music and the relationship of those parts. For example: melody, harmony, rhythm, phrase, texture, dynamics, form, style, timbre, meter, time, expression, scale, mode, etc.

Elevatio (Lat.) The elevation. Vocal or organ music performed during the elevation of the sacred Host during the Mass of the Roman Catholic Church. The Host is lifted immediately after the consecration.

Elevazione (It.) (ā—lā—vä—tsē—ō'—nā) Elevation.

Eleventh The compound interval of two tones having a distance which is equal to eleven notes of the diatonic scale.

Embellishment An ornament, grace note, decoration, or auxiliary tone. In general, a florid passage or addition to the music.

Embouchure (1) The mouthpiece of a wind instrument. (2) The manner in which the mouth is applied to the instrument or the position of the lips when placed to the mouthpiece.

Émerillonné (Fr.) (ā—měr—ē—yōn—nā) Lively, brisk.

E moll (Ger.) (ā mawl) E minor.

Emotivo (It.) (ā—mō—tē'—vō) emozionabile, (It.) (ā—mō—tsē—ō—nä'—bē—lā) Emotional.

Empfindsamer Stil (Ger.) (ĕmp—fĭnd'—zäm—å r shtēl) Empfindsam, (Ger.) (ĕ mp—fĭnd'—zäm) Sentimental style, sentimental. A style of music in Germany during the second half of the 18th century in which the composer emphasized subtle nuances and sentimentality. This was a movement away from the Baroque style. Examples which represent this view may be found in compositions by Wilhelm Friedemann Bach (1710-1784), and Carl Philipp Emanuel Bach (1714-1788), as well as by other composers of that period.

Empfindung (Ger.) (ĕ mp—fĭn'—dooong) Sensation or feeling.

Emphase (Fr.) (ă(m)—fäs) Stress or emphasis.

Emportée (Fr.) (ă (m)—pôr—tā) Fiery or passionate.

Empressée (Fr.) (ă (m)—prē s—sā) Gushing or earnest.

Ému (Fr.) (ā—mü) Affected or moved.

En (Fr.) (ä(n)) In; at; to.

Enchainez (Fr.) (ä(n)—shěn—ā) Link or connect. Go on to the next movement without a break.

Enclumeau (Fr.) (ä(n)—clü—mō) Hand-anvil.

Encore (Fr.) (ä(n)—kôr) Once again. To repeat a musical work at a concert or to add a piece of music at the end of a concert.

Encyclopedia of Music A book or set of books containing articles that cover all aspects of music. See *"A Selected Annotated Bibliography" for examples.

En dehors (Fr.) (ä(n)—dû—ôr) This indicates that a given part on a musical score must be heard.

Enden (Ger.) (ĕn'–dån) End.

Endless canon A continuous canon that leads back to the beginning and repeats without a break. See *Circle canon, *Canon.

Energico (It.) (ā–nĕr–jē'–ko) Energetic.

Enfasi (It.) (ĕn'–fä–zē) Emphasis.

Engführung (Ger.) (ĕng–fü'–roŏng) The stretto in a fugue.

Englisches Horn (Ger.) (ĕng'–lĭsh–ås hôrn) German for English horn.

English discant A 14th and 15th century style of three part writing. The cantus firmus, the lowest voice, is notated while the other two voices are improvised above and move in parallel motion. The result is the sixth-chord harmony (first inversion chords) except for the first and last note. See *Fauxbourdon.

English flute Instruments of the flute family in which the air is blown through the end of the instrument as is done when playing the recorder. Our standard orchestra flute or German flute is a cross-blown instrument. See *Flute, *Recorder.

English guitar A name used for the cittern in England during the 18th century.

English horn A double-reed instrument of the oboe family which is built a fifth lower than the oboe and has a bulb-shaped end. It produces a soft, dark tone. The range sounds from e to a″. See *Cor anglais.

English opera See *Ballad opera.

Enharmonic (1) One of the genera of Greek music. A scale or tetrachord which included quarter-tones. Other Greek genera were diatonic and chromatic. (2) Notes of the same pitch but identified by different names and written differently on the staff, e.g.

(3) Two scales of the same pitch but identified by different names (e.g., F# and Gb) and written differently on the staff. (4) Two intervals of the same pitch but identified by different names (e.g., an augmented 2nd and a minor 3rd) and written differently. There are en-

harmonic notes, enharmonic instruments and enharmonic chords.

Enigmatic canon Mysterious canon. Also called riddle canon and enigma canon. A canon which is not completely written out in notation. Clues are given by the composer. He might, for example, indicate that crab motion be used, a given note should be omitted, a section should be augmented, and so on. There may also be many other clues given, such as for entrances, pitches, certain treatment of succeeding parts, etc. J. S. Bach (1685-1750) offers some "puzzle" canons in his "Musikalische Opfer". For example: the Latin phrase "Quaerendo invenietis" ("Seek and ye shall find") is given at the beginning of this canon from the "Musikalische Opfer".

Enigma Variations Sir Edward Elgar's (1857-1934) *Theme with Variations for Orchestra,* Opus 36. The enigma: the initials given for each variation identify a relative or friend. The music for that variation is descriptive of that person. See *Variation.

Enjoué (Fr.) (ä(n)—zhoō—ā) Lively.

Enlever (Fr.) (ä(n)—lĕ—vā) To remove. To remove the mute from an instrument.

Ensalada (Sp.) (ĕn—sä—lä'—dä) Salad. A group of humorous songs. A mixture of different texts seems to be the more important characteristic of these 16th century Spanish songs.

Ensemble (Fr.) (ä(n)—sä(m)bl) Together (1) A group playing or singing in consort. (2) A united performance. The balance of a group. (3) In opera, a group of singers within the whole. In ensemble music the emphasis in on the whole while in the solo piece the focus is on the individual.

Entr'acte (Fr.) (ä(n)—tr'ă kt) Interlude, between the acts. Instrumental music performed between the acts of an opera or play. The term is also used as a title for some works. See *Interlude, *Intermezzo.

Entrada (Sp.) (ĕ n—trä'—dä) Entrance pieces. Opening pieces of a festive nature. Also, intrada.

Entrain (Fr.) (ä(n)—tră(n)) Spirit; animation.

Entrata (It.) (ĕn—trä'—tä) Beginning pieces. See *Entrada.

Entrée (Fr.) (ä(n)—trā) Entering. (1) The entrance of the dancers in ballet. (2) The introductory piece of music in opera, ballet, etc. in a scene, act, etc. (3) A name applied to a piece in this style.

Entremés (Sp.) (ën—trā—mĕs') Side dish. (1) A brief musical section, of a comic nature, in a play. (2) An intermezzo.

Entremets (Fr.) (ä(n)—trĕ—mā) Side-dish, sweets. An interlude. Short musical selections and dances that were performed between the dinner courses. They were popular in the Burgundian courts.

Entschieden (Ger.) (ĕnt—shē'—då n) Resolute or definite.

Entschlafen (Ger.) (ĕnt—shlä'—få n) Diminish. Diminuendo in Italian.

Entusiasmo (It.) (ĕ n—tōō—zē—äz'—mō) Enthusiasm. Entusiasta, (It.) enthusiastic.

Epidiapente The fifth above.

Epinette (Fr.) (ā—pē—nĕt) Spinet.

Episode The intermediate or secondary sections of a fugue or rondo. It can also be found in other musical forms. In the fugue, the episode serves to bring about a contrast to the subject. It often involves modulations, can use fragmented thematic material from the subject or countersubject, or present new material. The episode does not present the principal subject in its complete form. It follows the exposition of the fugue. In rondo form, the contrasting material to the re-entries of the main theme is called the episode. Examples of episodes in fugues are available in *The Well-Tempered*

124

Clavier by J. S. Bach (1685-1750). See *Exposition, *Fugue, *Rondo.

Episodical form Rondo form. See *Rondo.

Epitasis (Greek) (1) An increase in intensity. (2) To tighten a string, causing the pitch to rise.

Equale (It.) (ĕ —kwä '—lā) Equal. Music for like instruments or like voices. For example, for all male voices or all trombones. The name for three pieces written by Beethoven (1770-1827) for four trombones to be played in a solemn manner.

Equal-interval scale All the intervals of the scale are equal. For example, the twelve semitones within the octave on the piano keyboard. See *Equal temperament.

Equal temperament The piano is tuned in equal temperament. The octave is tuned into twelve equal half-steps. All half-steps are related to one another by ratio. The semitones form chromatic scales which can be played by starting on any tone of the keyboard and playing a succession of twelve semitones within the octave.

Equal voices (1) Voices of equal range. For example, tenors or voices in the tenor range. (2) Voices of the same kind, i.e., men's voices or women's voices. (3) The term is sometimes used to describe works for like voices such as male voices or women's voices.

Equilibrare (It.) (ĕ—kwēl—lē—brä '—rā) Balance. Equilibrato, (It.) (ĕ—kwē—lē—brä '—tō) Balanced.

Erfreulich (Ger.)(ĕr—froi '—lĭkh) Enjoyable.

Ergriffen (Ger.)(ĕr—gri f '—fĕn) Deeply stirred.

Erlöschend (Ger.)(ĕr—lĕ(r)sh '—å nt) Dying away.

Ermattend (Ger.)(ĕr—mät '—tå nt) Weakening.

Eroica (It.)(ĕ—rō '—ē—kä) Heroic. Name used as a title or to describe some musical compositions. E.g., Beethoven's *Symphony No. 3 in E♭ Major*, Op. 55 (1804).

Erotik (Ger.)(ā—rō '—tēk) Eroticism. Erotiken or eroticon. A love song, an amorous poem, an amorous composition.

Erst (Ger.) (ĕrst) First; only.

Erste mal (Ger.)(ĕrs '—tå mäl) First time.

Ersterbend (Ger.)(ĕr—shtĕr '—bĕnt) Dying away.

Erwägen (Ger.)(ĕr–vĕ'–gå n) Deliberate.

Erzlaute (Ger.)(ĕrts'–low–tå)Archlute.

Es (Ger.) (ĕs) E flat (Eᵇ).

Esaltare (It.) (ā–zäl–tä'–rā) Exalt. Esaltato (It.)(ā–zäl–tä'–tō)Excited or elated.

Esattamente (It.)(ā–zät–tä–mĕn'–tā)Exactly.

Escapement That part of the mechnaism of the piano which enables the hammer to escape or pull back from the string after striking the string. This allows the string to vibrate.

Es dur (Ger.) (ĕs dōor) Key of E flat (Eᵇ) major.

Esercitare (It.) (ā–zĕr–chē–tä'–rā) Drill or exercise.

Esercizio (It.)(ā–zĕr–chē'–tsē–ō)Exercise, as in Etude.

Eses (Ger.(ĕs'–ĕs) E double flat (Eᵇᵇ).

E sharp E#. A semitone above the note E. E.g.:

Treble Clef   Bass Clef   Alto Clef   Tenor Clef

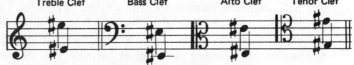

Esotico (It.)(ā–zō'–tē–cō) Exotic.

Espressione (It.)(ĕs–prĕs–sē–ō'–nā)Expression. Espressivo, (It.)(ĕs–prĕs–sē'–vō)Expressively.

Estampie (Fr.) (ĕs–tä(m)–pē) A 13th and 14th century instrumental form and medieval monophonic dance. It has from four to seven puncti or sections, each of which is repeated with first and second endings. Estampie is derived from the sequence form. Examples can be seen in Davison and Apel, ed., *Historical Anthology of Music.*

Estinguendo (It.)(ĕs–tēn–gōoĕn'–dō) Music dying away as in morendo. Estinguere, (It.)(ĕs–tēn–gōoā'–rā) Extinguish.

Estinto (It.) (ĕs–tēn'–tō) Extinct; very, very soft.

Estomper (Fr.) (ĕs–tŏ(m)–pā) To tone down.

Ęt (Fr.) (ā), Lat. (ĕt) And.

Étiendre (Fr.) (ā–tä(n)–dr) To put out or to smother. Very soft.

Ethnomusicology The study of music as it relates to

people and their culture. The study of folk and primitive music.

Et incarnatus est (Lat.) (ĕt ĭn—kär—nä'—tōos ĕst) "And was incarnate." See *Mass, *Credo.

Et in Spiritum Sanctum (Lat.)(ĕt ĭn spi r'—ē—tōom sänk' tōom) "And in the Holy Spirit." See *Mass, *Credo.

Et in terra pax (Lat.) (ĕt ĭn tĕr'—rä päks) "And peace on earth." See *Mass, *Gloria.

Et in unum Dominum (Lat.) (ĕt ĭn ōo'—nōom Dō'—mē—nōom) "And in one Lord." See *Mass, *Credo.

Étouffer (Fr.) (ā—tōo—fä) To deaden; to mute.

Et resurrexit (Lat.) (ĕt rĕ—zōor—rĕks'—ĭt) "And rose again." See *Mass, *Credo.

Étude (Fr.) (ā—tüd) (1) A study or exercise. An instrumental piece used to develop a specific technique related to the playing of the instrument. For example: finger patterns, scales, etc. (2) The name étude is also used as a title to musical compositions. Many of these "studies" are of great artistic quality. Examples: the many Études of Frédéric Chopin (1810-1849).

Etwas (Ger.) (ĕt'—väs) Somewhat.

Euphonium Sometimes called the tenor tuba (Baryton in German). A brass instrument in Bᵇ (four valves) and it has a range from Bᵇ' to bᵇ'. It is held in an upright position. It has an upright bell or one that is adjustable. It is similar to the baritone, but has four valves, a larger bore and a more mellow tone. See *Baritone.

Eurhythmics Using body motions to react to and interpret the element of rhythm in musical works. A term used in the Jacques—Dalcroze rhythmic method.

Éveiller (Fr.) (ā—vû—yā) To awaken. Play more briskly; animated.

Evening song A term often applied to a serenade. A nocturne.

Evensong Vespers or evening prayer in the Anglican Church. It is spoken or sung during the evening service.

Even temperament See *Equal temperament.

Exaltée (Fr.) (āg—zäl—tā) Exalted; very excited.

127

Excerpt A passage or section taken from the whole work.

Execution A matter of technical skill in preformance.

Exercice (Fr.) (āg—zĕr—sēs) Exercise; practice.

Exotic music (1) Music of foreign origin, not native. (2) Music that is unusual. (3) It is often used with reference to music not of the European culture.

Exposition (1) The section or musical statement which forms the basic idea of the composition. (2) The first statement or the subject of the fugue which is presented in turn in all parts. (3) The presentation of the first theme or themes in the sonata form that come before the development section.

Expressif (Fr.) (ĕk—sprĕs—ēf) Expressive.

Expression That element of music which includes the interpretation and presentation of the other elements of music. It is the personal quality in performance and goes beyond the printed page. Artistic execution, emotion, attitude, understanding, etc. as related to the music.

Expressionism In music, a term which identifies a 20th century movement in composition which was concerned with objectivity and the expression of the inner self. It was a reaction against the Impressionistic movement. The music of the Expressionists is abstract. Some characteristics of the style are: dissonances, atonality, complex and irregular rhythms, discordant harmony, etc. Some techniques used are: twleve tone row, quarter tones, tone clusters, etc. Some of the composers are: Schönberg, Berg, et al. See *Impressionism.

Expressive organ The orgue expressif (Fr.). A 19th century keyed instrument. A forerunner of the harmonium. See *Harmonium.

Extemporization To improvise on a theme or a succession of chords. To compose and play at the same time. See *Improvisation.

Extended cadence A chordal cadence. It is extended one or more measures beyond the cadence measure through the use of arpeggios or by holding the chord.

Extended compass or range To go beyond the standard

128

upper or lower limits of a voice or instrument.

Extended phrase To add to the normal or original phrase.

Extension organ Unit organ. A modern device to allow pipes to do multiple duty. A rank of pipes can produce tones an octave from the regular pitch when regulated by a couple device. A device used in theater type organs and small organs. See *Unit organ.

Extension pedal The foot pedal on the piano which allows the dampers to raise or stand away from the vibrating strings. The tone is sustained. Also called loud pedal. See *Damper pedal.

Extravaganza A musical production having a frivolous or light theme and one which requires elaborate staging. The term is most often identified with theatrical productions but can apply to musical compositions reflecting the same spirit. A musical satire or farce.

Extrême (Fr.) (ĕk–strêm) Extreme. Extrêmement,(Fr.) (ĕk–strĕm–û–mä(n)) Extremely.

Exubérance (Fr.) (āg–zü–bā–rä(n)s) To abound or exuberate.

F (1) F is the subdominant (4th) note of the scale of C major or the sixth degree of the scale of A minor (pure form). (2) On various clefs the note appears as follows:

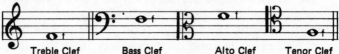

| Treble Clef | Bass Clef | Alto Clef | Tenor Clef |

(3) f is used as an abbreviation for forte, fortissimo (ff), mezzo forte (mf), fah (f), etc. (4) Some musical instruments are pitched in the key of F (e.g., French horn in F). Instruments pitched in F play a written note C which sounds F. (5) F identifies several keys, such as: F major, F# major, F minor, F# minor. (6) The bass clef ⟨image⟩ is also called the F clef.

The sign for the bass clef is an ornamental F. F is on the fourth line. (7) The sound holes in stringed instruments resemble the letter f and are called f holes. (8) F or Fah is the subdominant of the major scale in the tonic sol-fa system. See *Key, *Letter names, *Notation, *Pitch names, *Scale.

Fa (1) The fourth syllable in the hexachord as designated by Guido d'Arezzo. The syllables used are ut, re, mi, fa, sol, la. (2) In the movable do system (do, re, mi, fa, sol, la, ti, do) The syllable fa is the fourth degree of the major scale. (3) The note F in the system of fixed do.

Fa bemol (Fr.) (fä bā—mǒl) F Flat (F♭).

Fa bemolle (It. (fä bā—mǒl '—lā) F flat (F♭).

Faburden See *Fauxbourdon.

Facile (Fr.) (fä—sēl) and (It.)(fä—chē '—lā). Easy, flowing or complying. Style facile — fluent style. An easier version of a difficult piece of music.

Facilement (Fr.) (fä—sēl—mä(n)) and facilmente (It.)(fä—chēl—měn '—tā)Easily.

Fa dièse (Fr.) (fä dē—ěz) F sharp (F#)

Fa diesis (It.)(fä dē—ās '—i s)F sharp (F#).

Fading (1) A 16th and 17th century Irish dance. (2) A

refrain of a song.

Fado A popular song or dance of Portugal with guitar accompaniment.

Fa doppio bemolle (It.) (fä dôp '–ē–ō bā–mŏl '–lā) F double flat (Fbb).

Fa doppio diesis (It.)(fä dôp '–ē–ō dē–ās '–ĭ s)F double sharp (Fˣ) (F##).

Fa double bémol (Fr.) (fä dōobl bā–mŏl) F double flat (Fbb).

Fagott (Ger.) (fä–gŏt '). Fagotto, (It.) (fä–gŏt '–tō). Bassoon. The range is from Bᵇ' to d''.

Fagottino (It.)(fä–gŏt–tē '–no) A small bassoon or tenor oboe. It is a 19th century instrument and is tuned a fifth higher than the bassoon.

Fagotto (It.) (fä–gŏt '–tō) Bassoon. The abbreviation is Fg.

Fagottone (It.) (fä–gŏt–tō '–nā) Contrabassoon. Also, fagotto contra (It.) The sound is one octave lower than the written note. See *Bassoon, *Contrabassoon.

Fah Fa. The fourth syllable of the major scale in the tonic sol-fa system.

Fahren (Ger.)(fä '–rĕn) Drive; to go.

Faire (Fr.) (fĕr) To compose; to perform; to create.

Fa–la Ballett (Eng); balletto (It.)(bäl–lĕt '–tō). Songs of the 16th and 17th centuries in which the refrain was sung on the syllables fa-la-la.

Fall Old English term for cadence.

False accent The accent is placed on the second or fourth beat of the measure.

False bass See *Fauxbourdon.

False cadence Deceptive cadence. In a plagal or authentic cadence a tonic is replaced by another chord, often the VI chord. See *Deceptive cadence.

False fifth A term used to identify an imperfect or diminished fifth (old usage).

False modulation A modulation is said to be "false" when the music moves to a new key, but quickly modulates back to the first key.

False music (falsa musica) See *Musica ficta.

False relation See *Cross relation.

Falsetto (It.) (fäl–sĕt'–tō) A high, artificial voice of the male singer. The tones are above the normal voice range. It is sometimes known as a head voice as opposed to the so-called chest voice. In earlier times the falsetto voice was cultivated and widely used.

Falsobordone (It.) (fäl–sō bôr–dō'–nā) See *Fauxbourdon.

Familiar style In chordal music, the four voices move in strict chordal style singing uniform note values and syllables.

Family of instruments Those instruments having like tone quality. E.g., brass family, woodwind family, violin family.

Fancy (16th century Fantasia (It.)) Sixteenth and 17th century English works for stringed instruments or keyboard instruments.

Fandango (Sp.) (fän–dän'–gō) A lively Spanish dance in triple time which is performed by a man and woman. The dance is accompanied by guitar and castanets. Also, the music used to accompany the dancers or a piece of music having the rhythmic characteristics and style of the dance itself.

Fandanguillo (Sp.) (fän–dän–gēl'–yō) Andaluz folk songs.

Fanfare (1) A short musical passage played by a trumpet as an introduction. An announcement that a ceremony is beginning, such as at coronations, etc. Fanfares were originally designed for natural horns which favor the tones of the triad. Fanfares are also played on other brass instruments imitating the trumpet style. (2) French for brass band or flourish. (3) In England, known as Flourishes.

Fantasia (Eng.) (It.) (fän–tä'–zē–ä) Generally, a piece of music of a fanciful style and in free form. The composer writes according to his own whim or fancy. There are several styles of fantasia: (1) improvisatory style, as in Bach's harpsichord music, e.g., Chromatic Fantasia; (2) the free fantasia in the development section of a movement; (3) a mood piece of the 19th century Romantic era; (4) an arrangement of tunes or a pot-pourri of airs; (5) a fantasia on an established theme; (6) a

132

short work such as a capriccio; (7) 16th and 17th century pieces written in contrapuntal style; (8) a formal treatment of fantasia in contemporary music. Examples: Henry Purcell (c.1659-1695), *Fantasias;* Ralph Vaughan Williams (1872-1958) *Fantasia on a Theme by Tallis;* Wolfgang Amadeus Mozart (1756-1791), *Fantasia in D Minor,* K 397, for Piano.

Fantasia section The development section of a movement. For example, in sonata-allegro form, the development section (middle section) is sometimes called the free fantasia section.

Fantastico (It.) (fän—täs'—tē—kō) Fantastic.

Fantasy See *Fantasia.

Farandole A lively dance, the music of which is usually in $\frac{6}{8}$ meter. The dance is done with the dancers joining hands and forming a long line. They follow the leader through many movements and patterns. The music is played on the pipe and tabor. It is a very early dance and is still popular in southern France. Georges Bizet (1838-1875) used the "Farandole" in his music to Daudet's *L'Arlésienne.*

Farza (It.) (fär'—sä) (1) A light and humorous opera in which situations are exploited. Italian comic opera. A farce refers to light plays or operas in which outside elements are introduced to produce a humorous effect. (2) Farse or farce also refers to the addition of words between two words of the actual text. For example, early interpolations of liturgical tropes.

Fast (Ger.) (fäst) Almost.

Fasto (It.) (fäs'—tō) Pomp. Fastoso, (It.) (fäs—tō'—zō) Pompous.

Fausset (Fr.) (fō—sä) Falsetto.

Fauxbourdon (Fr.) (fō—boor—dō(n)) (1) The cantus firmus is in the upper voice. Two parts are noted and move in parallel sixths. The improvised part is an interval of a 4th below the cantus firmus which results in a succession of parallel first inversion chords (sixth chords). It is an early 15th century technique. See *Cantus firmus. (2) Present day harmony using sixth chord style. (3) The descant in English hymnody. (4) The Italian falso bordone. A simple four part harmonization of a plainsong, etc., i.e., the top three voices moving in sixth chord harmony with an added bass part.

F clef Bass clef. F is located on the fourth line of the bass clef which is a fifth below middle c (c').

F clef:

F double flat (Fbb). The note F is lowered by two half-steps.

F double sharp (F##) (Fˣ). The note F is raised by two half-steps.

F dur (Ger.) (ĕf do͞or) F major.

Feathering The delicate use of the bow when playing rapid passages on the violin or other stringed instruments. Rapid separate bow strokes are used as well as a bouncing bow. Befiedern (Ger.).

Feeders Small bellows of an organ that supply large bellows with forced air.

Feet Metrical units of verse that are also applied to certain styles of music of the Medieval period.

Feierlich (Ger.)(fī '–ĕr–lĭ kh) Solemn; festive, ceremonious.

Feldpartita (Ger.)(fĕld '–pär–tē '–tä)A composition for a military band of wind instruments. Fanfares in harmony. A field suite.

Feldton (Ger.) (fĕld '–tōn) The tone of the trumpet.

Feldtrompete (Ger.) (fĕld '–trôm–pā–tå) Field trumpet or military trumpet. Bugle.

Felicemente (It.)(fā–lē–chā–mĕn '–tä)Happily.

Feminine The conotation of being weak. In a feminine cadence the final chord of the cadence comes on a weak beat. A masculine cadence has the final chord on the strong beat. An example of the last measure ending in a feminine cadence:

134

See *Feminine ending.

Feminine ending An unaccented syllable at the end. In music, a hymn that ends on an unaccented syllable or weak beat is said to have a feminine ending. See *Feminine.

Feria The original meaning was a religious holiday or feast day. Now, within the Roman Catholic Church, it is a weekday which is not a feast day.

Ferma (It.) (fĕr'–mä) Firm, steady. Fermamente, (It.) (fĕr–mä–mĕn'–tä)Firmly; fast.

Fermata (It.) (fĕr–mä'–tä) Stop, pause; to hold. The sign (⌒) is used over a note or rest which prolongs the note or rest. When used alone it indicates an interruption.

Fermer (Fr.) (fĕr–mā) To close or put an end to.

Fermeté (Fr.) (fĕr–mĕ–tā) Firm or steady.

Fermo (It.) (fĕr'–mō) Firm or steady.

Fernflöte (Ger.) (fĕrn'–flĕ(r)–tå) Distant flute. An organ stop.

Fernwerk (Ger.)(fĕrn'–vĕrk) Echo organ or echo manual.

Ferocemente (It.) (fā–rō–chä–mĕn'–tä) Ferociously, wildly.

Fervente (It.) (fĕr–vĕn'–tä) Fervent; warmly; feeling.

Fes (Ger.) (fĕs) F flat (F♭).

Feses (Ger.) (fĕs'–ĕss) F double flat (F♭♭).

Fest (Ger.) (fĕst) Festival, celebration.

Festa (It.) (fĕs'–tä) Festival.

Festal Days of the feast. See *Feria.

Feuer (Ger.) (foi '–ĕr) Fire; verve. **Feurig,** (Ger.)(foi '–rĭ k) Fiery.

ff The abbreviation for fortissimo. Very loud.

F flat F♭. A semitone below the note F. E.g.,

Treble Clef   Bass Clef   Alto Clef   Tenor Clef

F holes The sound-holes of stringed instruments. The openings on the upper part (table) of the body (e.g., violin) that resemble the letter f.

Fiacco (It.)(fē–äk '–kō) Weak or limp.

Fiato (It.)(fē–ät '–tō) Breath, as it applies to wind blown instruments.

Fiddle (fiedel, (Ger.)). The informal name for the violin. It also applies to other bowed stringed instruments. An instrument of the viol family. See * Violin.

Fides (Lat.) (1) A fiddle or stringed instrument. (2) A string of a stringed instrument.

Fidicen (Lat.) A fiddler. One who plays a stringed instrument.

Fidicula A small stringed instrument.

Field hollers or cries Sung in the fields by Negro slaves. A forerunner of the blues. Also called a shout. It was often a secret system of communication among the slaves.

Fierezza (It.) (fē–ā–rĕt '–tsä) Fierceness.

Fife A high pitched (small) transverse flute. The very early fifes had several finger holes and no keys. Later, one or more keys were added along with the finger holes. It was used in military bands, marching bands and fife and drum corps. Generally, the fife has been replaced by the piccolo.

Fifre (Fr.) (fēfr) Fife.

Fifteenth (1) The interval of two octaves. (2) A two-foot stop of the organ. An organ stop that sounds fifteen notes above the normal pitch.

Fifth The fifth degree above the first tone. The distance between the first and fifth degrees of the diatonic scale. The interval formed by counting up four steps in a diatonic scale above the root. E.g., from F to C. The size of the interval is determined by counting the lower note as one and ascending the diatonic scale until reaching five. The interval of a perfect fifth consists of three whole steps and a half-step. Intervals of the fifth can be: perfect fifth (e.g., G–D); diminished fifth (e.g., G–D♭) which is a semitone smaller than the perfect fifth; augmented fifth (e.g., G–D♯) which is a semitone larger than the perfect fifth. E.g.:

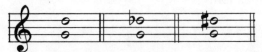

PERFECT 5th   DIMINISHED 5th   AUGMENTED 5th

See *Intervals, *Triads, *Chords.

Figural Figures. The use of musical figuration or motive.

Figurate Florid style. Music making great use of embellishments and florid figures.

Figuration The use of a figure, melody, motive, etc. over and over in a piece of music.

Figure A short motive or phrase. The figure is often used as a basis for the development of a larger division of a musical idea.

Figured Use of figures (numbers).

Figured bass A continuo bass which was used during the 17th and 18th centuries. The notated bass line was given along with the numbers (figures) which indicated what harmonization was to be used above the given bass line. The system was used primarily in keyboard music and allowed freedom of performance but required that the harmony indicated by the figures be used. For example: the number (figure) given indicates what interval is required above the note in the particular key. Chromatics are indicated by a (#) or flat (b), placed next to the number or by a stroke through the figure (7). The figure (o) indicates that there is to be no chord added. The intervals of a third, fifth, or octave are usually not indicated by a number. A dash (—)

137

requires that the upper notes be held or continued; a slash (/) indicates a sequence of a figure above each successive bass note. A note without a figure indicates automatic use of the third and fifth above. An accidental given without a figure indicates that the third of the chord is to be altered. Some examples:

Figured Bass written:

Realization:

Recommended for further study: Franck Thomas Arnold, *The Art of Accompaniment From a Thoroughbass as Practiced in the XVIIth and XVIIIth Centuries.* See *"A Selected Anotated Bibliography", *Continuo, *Thorough-bass, *Basso Continuo.

Figured chorale An organ chorale in which a figural passage is used over and over throughout the composition.

Film music Music written for motion pictures. Background music, related mood music, incidental music, etc. That music which associates with the story of the film.

Fin (Fr.) (fã(n)) End, close, conclusion.

Final Also, finalis. (1) It is the "tonic" or note on which the melody ends when using church modes. The finalis is the center tone. That is, analogous with the key center of a major or minor scale. E.g., as G is related to the key and scale of G major. In the plagal modes the position of the finalis is the fourth degree of the scale; in the authentic modes it is the first degree of the scale. See *Church modes, *Modes. (2) Also, final (Fr.), finale; Final (Sp.), meaning end.

Final close Last cadence or final cadence. A perfect or full cadence that can be used to close a composition.

138

Finale (It.)(fē–nä'–lā) (1) The close of an act or section of a larger work, e.g., Finale to Act 1. (2) The last movement of a work having several movements, e.g., symphony. (3) The final section or ensemble ending of an opera, musical play, ballet, etc. (4) The grouping of the players toward the end of a performance in a musical variety show, etc.

Finalis Mode final. See *Final, *Church modes.

Fin'al segno (It.)(fēn äl sĕn'–yō) Play to the sign. A repeat mark used when the player goes back to the beginning and play until the sign (𝄋).

Fine (It.)(fē'–nā) The end. Usually used when the piece of music ends at a point which is not the last written measure, but at a point designated within the piece after a repeat. See *Dal segno, *Da capo.

Finger board The strip of wood on the neck of stringed instruments over which the strings are stretched. When the finger forces the string to touch the board the pitch is altered. Some finger boards have frets, e.g., guitar, lute, etc.

Finger holes Tone holes. A series of holes on wind and reed instruments which can be closed or left open in order to change the pitch of the instrument. Pitches change when individual holes are open or closed or when combinations of holes are open or closed.

Fingering An organized way in which fingers are used in playing musical instruments. The way in which the fingers are used and the order in which they are used in a given passage. For example, piano fingering; thumb is one on either hand while the small finger is five; stringed instruments the index finger is one; for trumpet, the index finger of the right hand is one, etc.

Finite canon One that does not go in a perpetual motion. One not repeated.

Fino (It.)(fē'–nō) As far as, up to, till, until.

Fioritura (It.) (fē–ō–rē–too'–rä) Flourish or decorations. (1) Embellishments or ornamentation on a melody, improvised or written out. (2) Improvisation on a melody.

First-Movement form Sonata form. A form used in the

first movement of a symphony. The form is also used in other movements. See *Sonata form.

First subject See *Sonata-allegro form, *Exposition, *Fugue, *Subject.

First violins A term used to identify the players of the orchestra violin section that play the first parts, usually the upper parts.

Fis (Ger.) (fiss) F sharp (F$^\#$).

Fisarmonica (It.)(fēs—är—mōn '—ē—kä) Accordian.

Fis dur (Ger.) (fiss dōor) F sharp (F$^\#$) major.

Fisis (Ger.) (fiss '—iss) F double sharp (F$^\times$) (F##).

Fistel (Ger.) (fis '—tål) Falsetto.

Five, The The Russian Five. A group of 19th century Russian composers who worked to develop the national music of Russia. Balakirev, Borodin, Cui, Mussorgski, and Rimsky-Korsakov. See *Russian Five.

Five-three chord The triad having the third and fifth above the root of the chord. It is marked $\frac{5}{3}$ in figured bass.

Fixed do The syllables are used on fixed notes. For example, C is do in the scale of C major as well as in any other key.

Flageolet tones Harmonics produced on stringed instruments. The harmonic is produced by lightly touching the string at a given point. The string is not pressed all the way down to the finger board. See *Harmonics.

Flageolet (Fr.) (flä—zhĕ—ō—lā) and (Ger.)(flä—zhō—lĕt ')) A fipple flute which is end blown and has a tone similar to that of the piccolo. It is a small instrument with four finger holes on top and two thumb holes on the lower side. The double flageolet has two pipes side by side which use one mouthpiece and produce two part music. See *Recorder.

Flam The flam is a two note figure (♪♪) usually played in quick succession on the snare drum. When the emphasis is placed on the first note it is called open flam. When the second note is accented, the flam is referred to as a closed flam.

Flamenco (Sp.) (flä—mĕn '—kō) (1) An Andalusian dance of a bold and rhythmic style, performed to the accompaniment of a guitar and castanets. (2) A type of guitar music played in this bold style. Example: *The Tango Flamenco in Eb* by Issac Albéniz (1860-1909).

Flat (1) The symbol for a flat is (b). The note is to be lowered by a half-step (semitone). (2) A key signature having one or more flats is identified as a flat key. (3) Playing or singing below the correct pitch is referred to as singing or playing flat. See *Accidentals.

Flatter (Fr.) (flä—tā) To stroke or caress; as in delicate bowing.

Flatterzunge (Ger.) (flä'—tĕr—tsŏong—å) Flutter tongue. A style of tonguing used in playing such wind instruments as the flute and trumpet. The flutter tone is produced by fluttering the tongue on the letter R.

Flautando (It.)(flä—ōo—tän'—dō) Fluted or flute-like. (1) A style of string playing in which the bowing is done very gently near the end of the finger board. (2) Similar bowing is used when harmonics are played on bowed instruments.

Flautato (It.)(flä—ōo—tä'—tō) See *Flautando.

Flautina (It.) (flä—ōo—tē'—nä) A small flute or piccolo.

Flauto (It.) (flä'—ōo—tō) The flute, recorder, or transverse flute. The meaning depends on the period of music in which the term is used.

Flautone (It.)(flä—ōo—tō'—nä) Bass flute.

Flauto piccolo (It.)(flä'—ōo—tō pē'—kō—lō) Little flute or piccolo.

Flauto traverso (It.) (flä'—ōo—tō trä—vĕr'—sō) (1) Transverse flute. (2) A 4 foot organ stop.

Flehentlich (Ger.)(flā'—ĕnt—lĭkh) Beseeching.

Flemish school An important Renaissance school which followed the Burgundian school. Generally, the Flemish school covers the second half of the 15th century and the 16th century. The composers of this period contributed a great deal to the development of polyphonic music. For example, Ockeghem (c. 1430-1495) and Obrecht (c. 1452-1505) contributed to the development of the principles of imitative counterpoint and Josquin des Prés (c. 1440-1521) contributed to the art of writing polyphonic music. The period is also characterized by the development of four-part writing. The term Flemish pertains to Flanders, a northern part of France, Belgium, and surrounding areas.

Flessibilita (It.) (flĕs—ē—bē—lē—tä') Flexibility.

Flicorno (It.) (flē—kôr'—nō) Italian make of saxhorn or flügelhorn. See *Flügelhorn.

Fliessend (Ger.) (flē'—sĕnt) Flowing.

Florid Passages that are ornamented, embellished, or have runs or grace notes.

Florid melody An ornamented or figured melody.

Flöte (Ger.) (flĕ(r)'—tå) German for flute or whistle.

Flott (Ger.) (flôt) Dashing or quick.

Flourish See *Fanfare.

Flüchtig (Ger.) (flükh'—tĭk) Lightly; fleeting.

Flue pipe A type of organ pipe in which the air passes through a narrow opening similar to the opening in a whistle or recorder. Not a reed-pipe.

Flügel (Ger.) (flü'—gå l) Wing. A wing shaped keyboard instrument such as the grand piano.

Flügelhorn (Ger.) (flü'—gå l—hôrn) A brass instrument that has the shape of a bugle, a bore like the French horn, three piston valves like the trumpet, and a cup-shaped mouthpiece. It is usually pitched in the key of Bb and has the range of the cornet sounding from e to bb". The tone is fuller than that of the cornet but less mellow than that of the French horn. It is used in bands. See *Bugle, *Saxhorn, *Cornet.

Fluido (It.) (floo'—ē—dō) Fluid.

Flüssig (Ger.) (flüs'—ĭk) Fluid.

Flüstern (Ger.) (flüs'—tĕrn) Whisper.

Flute (Flöte, (Ger.(flĕ(r)'—tå); Flauto, (It.) (flow'—tō), Flûte (Fr.) (flüt)) (1) Generally a recorder, a beaked instrument, a transverse instrument, a member of the woodwind family. (2) The modern flute is a wood or metal instrument having a cylindrical tube, a closed end, and a mouthpiece with an opening in the side (top) across which air is blown to produce a tone. It has fifteen holes and twenty-three levers and keys, a range of about three octaves from middle c' to c'''', with a tone ranging from mellow to brilliant. The two upper octaves are produced by overblowing the notes of the first octave. The abbreviation is Fl. See *Piccolo, *Alto flute.

Flûte a bec (Fr.) (flüt ä běk) A beak flute; a recorder.

Flûte allemande (Fr.) (flüt äl—lě—mä(n)d) The cross flute or standard orchestra flute.

Flûte d'amour (Fr.) (flüt dä—moor) An obsolete flute built a minor third lower than the standard flute. It had a mellow tone.

Flûte douce (Fr.) (flüt doos) Recorder.

Flûte eunuque (Fr.) (flüt ûn—yŭk) A 17th century eunuch flute. A mirliton or onion flute. A vibrating instrument on which a tone is produced by humming into a tube which has one end covered by a membrane. The same principle is employed when humming through a comb covered with paper or playing the kazoo.

Flûte harmonique (flüt är—mōn—ēk) A 19th century vertical flute containing a number of pipes or recorders.

Flute tone An organ tone of flute-like quality.

Flutter tonguing A style of tonguing an instrument of the brass family or flutes. The player flutters his tonque as in rolling an R. See *Flatterzunge.

Fluttuazione (It.) (floo—too—ä—tsē—ō'—nä) Fluctuation, alternating variation.

F moll (Ger.) (ěf mawl) F minor.

Focoso (It.) (fō—kō'—zō) Fiery.

Fois (Fr.) (fwä) Time.

Folâtre (Fr.) (fō—lä—tr) Playful.

Folia (Sp.) (fō—lē'—ä) (1) Originally, an ancient Portuguese dance of a noisy character, accompanied by tambourines. (2) The melody used for the dance. It was sung as a solo and had a ground bass. (3) The tune was often used during the Renaissance as a theme, or basis for variations. It was treated in several ways by such composers as Vivaldi and others. For example: Arcangelo Corelli (1653-1713), *Sonata in D Minor, Opus 5, Number 12* "La Folia".

Folk music Music handed down by oral tradition. It is usually of a simple variety and not identified with a composer.

Folk song A song of the country people which is passed from generation to generation and place to place orally. It usually has many versions as a result of the oral transmission. These songs are simple and are usually in ballad form and range in length from a phrase to a three-part song form. They reflect characteristics of a race, region, etc. They have simple harmony, are popular, are metric and have simple accompaniment. A folk song may be anonymous, a collective work, or a composed song by one person, which is accepted by a large (ethnic, regional, social, etc.) group.

Folksong hymn A hymn based on a folk song or popular melody.

Follia (It.) (fōl—yē '—ä) Folly. See *Folia.

Foot Length. (1) Organ pipes are of various lengths and are measured in feet. An 8 foot stop would sound a note one octave higher than a 16 foot pipe. (2) A metrical unit in poetry.

Forlana (It.) (fōr—län '—ä) Also, furlano, furlana. An Italian dance in duple time, usually in fast $\frac{6}{8}$ time. An example of a forlana in $\frac{6}{4}$ time: J. S. Bach (1685-1750), *Suite No. 1 in C for Orchestra.*

Form The organization and structure of music. The relationship of some basic techniques used in music such as imitation, repetition, contrast, and variation. These techniques are applied to such basic elements of music as melody, harmony, rhythm, and tone-color. Various treatment of these elements of music takes place as the music is developed. Keys change, harmony changes, melodies are developed and are fragmented, rhythm is developed, canonic devices are used (such as, imitation, augmentation, diminution, retrograde, and inversion), texture changes, etc. Generally, this aspect of form refers to the emergence or development of ideas. Musical form is usually identified with the overall organization or pattern of the piece. For example, binary

144

form, ternary form, variations, rondo, sonata-allegro form, or multiple larger forms such as symphony, concerto, oratorio, opera, overture, etc. See the specific entries listed above.

Formant It is related to timbre or tone color. The range, number, and dominance of partials in a tone spectrum determines the timbre. The formants allow us to distinguish the difference between instruments, voices, etc.

Fort (Ger.) (fôrt) Forward; away. For example, the term might be used in organ music to indicate that an organ stop is to be silenced.

Forte (It.) (fôr'–tā) A term meaning loud or strong. It indicates that the music is to be played at a loud dynamic level. The abbreviation for the term is the letter f. A double f (ff) means very loud; an mf, medium loud; fp, loud then soft; piu forte, louder; etc. See *Dynamics.

Fortepiano (It.) (fôr'–tā–pē–än'–ō)(1) A term indicating that the music is to be played loud and immediately soft again. The abbreviation for the term is fp. (2) A name applied to the early form of the pianoforte (popularly known as the piano). See *Dynamics.

Fortissimo (It.) (fôr–tēs'–sē–mō) A term meaning very loud. The abbreviation of the term is ff. See *Dynamics.

Forza (It.)(fôr'–tsä) Force, strength, vigor.

Forzando (It.)(fôr–tsän'–dō) Play with force. The term indicates that the note, chord, or passage should be played with accent or strength. The abbreviation for the term is fz.

Forzare (It.)(fôr–tsä'–rä) To strengthen or force.

Fougue (Fr.) (foog) Passion, spirit, impetuosity.

Fournitures (Fr.)(foor–ni–tyû r) Supplies, furnishings. Organ stops, mixture stops.

Fourth The fourth degree above a given tone which is identified as one. The interval between the first and fourth degree. The interval of a fourth is figured by taking four steps above the root in the major or minor scale counting 1–4 inclusive. The interval of a perfect fourth consists of two whole steps and a half step (e.g., G to C). The interval of an augmented fourth would be one semitone larger than the perfect fourth (e.g., G to C#). The diminished fourth would be a semitone smaller than the perfect fourth (e.g., G to Cb). E.g.,

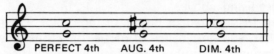

PERFECT 4th   AUG. 4th   DIM. 4th

See *Intervals.

Foxtrot An American ballroom dance in duple or quadruple meter which was popular beginning in the early quarter of the 20th century. It was a part of the jazz movement in America. The early dances were performed in a trot-like manner. Some were fast, others slow.

fp The abbreviation for forte piano.

Frappé (Fr.) (frä–pā) Fall; downbeat. Frapper, (fr.) (frä–pā) strike, beat, mark. To beat time.

Frauenchor (Ger.) (frow'–ĕn–kôr) Women's choir or or women's chorus.

Freddo (It.) (frĕd'–dō) In a cold manner.

Free counterpoint Counterpoint not bound by the strict rules of contrapuntal writing. See *Counterpoint, *Canon, *Fugue.

Free imitation Musical lines used in imitation are not repeated in strict or exact imitation.

Free organum (Later 11th and early 12th centuries) The duplum or added voices do not move in parallel motion alone but do move in the same rhythm or note against note. Parts cross and often move in contrary motion.

Example: Style of free organum in the 11th century; lower part is called the "vox principalis". See *Organum.

French chanson See *Chanson.

French discant A composition technique used on the continent in the Burgundian School (first half of the 15th century). See *Fauxbourdon.

French horn A brass instrument having a nine to twelve foot coiled tube with a conical bore, a large flared bell,

146

a range over three and one half octaves which sounds from B' to f" for the F horn. The mouthpiece is funnel shaped. It has three rotary valves which enables it to play chromatics. Changeable crooks in the single horn also enable the player to change the horn from the key of F to the key of E^b. The double horn can be played in F or B^b by engaging the thumb rotary key. The pitch can also be altered by varying the hand position in the bell of the horn. Earlier instruments had no valves and played within the harmonic series. Slides and crooks were changed to vary the series of tones. About mid-19th century the valved horn was developed. The horn is a transposing instrument and sounds a fifth lower than the written note.

French overture An overture that precedes a large work such as an opera or ballet. It was used in France during the 17th and 18th centuries. It was structured as follows: slow beginning and incorporated dotted rhtyms and was played in a grand style; the second section was fast and in imitative style. Sometimes the second section ended in a slow tempo which was sometimes identified as a third section. Example of the French overture: Christoph Gluck (1714-1787), *Iphigenia in Aulis, Overture.* The French overture was also extended into a suite. For example, George Frideric Handel (1685-1759) Overture to *Rinaldo.*

French sixth An augmented sixth chord. The French sixth consists of a bass, a major third, an augmented 4th, and an augmented 6th. It often occurs on the flatted submediant of the major scale or the submediant of the minor scale. It includes an augmented sixth. For example, in the key of G major:

See *Augmented, *Sixth chords.

French Suites The name applied to J. S. Bach's (1685-1750) six suites for keyboard. *French Suites: No. 1 in D Minor; No. 2 in C Minor; No. 3 in B minor; No. 4 in E^b; No. 5 in G; No. 6 in E.*

147

Frenesia (It.)(frā—nā—zē '—ä)Frenzy.

Frenetico (It.)(frā—nā '—tē—kō)Frantic.

Frequency The number of complete vibrations per second. Pitch is related to the frequency of a signal.

Frequency modulation Variance of frequency affecting pitch.

Fresco (It.)(frĕs '—kō) Vigorous, fresh, lively.

Fret The finger board of the guitar and like instruments have strips of metal or wood placed across the finger board at regular intervals. The finger presses the string against the fret making the string shorter and thereby raising the pitch.

Fretta (It.) (frĕt '—tä) Haste. The music moves faster.

Frettolosamente (It.) (frĕt—tō—lō—zä—mĕn '—tä) Hastily.

Fricassée (Fr.) (frē—käs—sā) An 18th century French dance.

Frog A part of the bow for the violin, cello, etc. The end of the bow having the nut.

Frölich (Ger.)(frĕ(r) '—li kh)Happy, cheerful.

Froid (Fr.) (frwä) Also, froide (Fr.) (frwäd). Cool, cold, lifeless.

Frôlement (Fr.) (frōl—mä(n)) To touch lightly.

Frosch (Ger.) (frōsh) Frog or nut of the bow of the violin, viola, cello, etc.

Frottola (It.) (frōt '—tō—lä) A popular Italian secular song around the turn of the 16th century which was strophic, for several voices (usually in three or four parts), had simple harmony and rhythm and was sung with or without accompaniment. The melody was usually in the upper voice and the lower parts were often played on instruments. Some frottola were sung as solo melodies with choral accompaniment. It was in ternary form, the scheme being: A (ripresa), B (piedi), A' (volta). The frottola influenced the madrigal of Flemish composers of the late 15th century. Examples are found in the *Historical Anthology of Music* — Davison and Apel, ed.

Frühling (Ger.)(frü '—ling) The season of Spring. Frühlingslied, (Ger.) (frü '—lĭngz—lēt) Spring song. Frühlingssonate,(Ger.)(frü '—lingz—zō—nä '—tå)Spring sonata. Frühlingssymphonie, (Ger.)(frü'–lĭngz–zĭm '–fōn–ē)Spring symphony.

F sharp F#. A semitone above the note F. E.g.;

Clef: Treble Clef   Bass Clef   Alto Clef   Tenor Clef

Fuga (It.) (foo'–gä) Fugue; flight. Fuga originally meant canon. See *Fugue.

Fugato (It.) (foo–gä'–tō) A section of music which is treated in fugal style. Not necessarily part of a fugue.

Fuge (Ger.) (foo'–gå) Fugue.

Fughetta (It.)(foo–gĕt '–tä) A little fugue or one that is of shorter length than the normal fugue.

Fugue A polyphonic composition based on one or more themes. The fugue is based on imitative counterpoint. The subject is presented in the home key by one voice and imitated in the dominant by a second voice (called answer), while the first voice continues in counterpoint (see *Countersubject). If other voices enter they alternate in the same manner presenting the subject and the answer. The sections of the fugue are: exposition – the first section just described in which the complete subject is used in all voices; episodes – follow the exposition. In the episodes, fragments of the subject are presented or material related to the subject. Many fugues end with a coda. A fugue is a technique rather than a strict form. Devices commonly used in the fugue are imitation, stretto, canonic devices (augmentation, diminution, inversion). (See these individual entries). Extensive treatment of the fugue is given in the two volume *Well-Tempered Clavier* by J. S. Bach (1685-1750) and in his *Die Kunst der Fuge* ("The Art of Fugue"). See *Answer, *Antecedent and consequence, *Countersubject, *Counterfugues, *Subject.

Fuguing tune An American hymn tune used during the 18th century which includes a homophonic and a polyphonic style of writing. The polyphonic style is often referred to as being in the style of a fugue. The style of American fuguing tune is an extension of the earlier English form. Examples are in William Billings' (1746-1800) book, *The Singing Master's Assistant* (1778).

Full anthem An anthem which is sung by the full choir as opposed to the verse anthem in which sections are sung by solo voices with accompaniment. See *Anthem.

Full close Perfect cadence.

Full orchestra The complete orchestra with each section of strings, woodwinds, brass, and percussion at full strength.

Full organ The organ playing at full power.

Full score All parts are written out in full on separate staves, as opposed to a condensed score in which the parts are arranged on the grand staff as in piano keyboard music.

Full tone Full step. The equivalent of two half-steps or semitones.

Fundamental (1) The root of the chord. The first or lowest note of an interval or chord, the others being the upper tones. The bass note of the chord. (2) The lowest note of a harmonic series.

Fundamental bass (1) The root of a chord upon which a chord is built. Applied to the theory of chord inversion. The root of the chord may not be the lowest note as in the case in inversion. See *Inversion. (2) A bass line consisting of the root notes of a progression of chords.

Fundamental tone The base upon which the chord is built. In root position, the bass of the chord or lowest note.

Funky jazz music A movement in jazz during the 1950's which was a reaction against the cool jazz movement. It used some of the melodic and rhythmic innovations of the be-bop era, but employed a more traditional harmonic (vertical) structure. It was emotional music with a happy sound, a rhythmic melody, and used special accents on the 2nd and 4th beats. See *Jazz, *Bop.

Fuoco (It.) (foo–ō'–kō) Fire. Usually the word is used

150

with "con", as in con fuoco, which indicates that the
music is to be played "with fire".

Für (Ger.) (für) For.

Furia (It.) (foo'—re̅—ä) Fury, passion.

Furiant A Czech folk dance in fast triple time with changing accents and rhythms.

Furlana See *Forlana.

Fusa (Lat.) Equal in value to a quaver or eighth note.

Fusée (Fr.) (fü—za̅) Rocket. Agrément; grace note; cou-
lade.

Futurism An Italian school of thought in the arts during
the first part of the 20th century which attempted to
express the arts in a most radical way. They rejected
the traditional. Music was expressed through noise instruments and mechanical devices.

fz The abbreviation for forzando. Also, sforzando, (sfz,
sf).

G

G (1) G is the dominant (5th) Note of the scale of C major or the seventh degree of the scale of A minor (pure form). (2) On various clefs, the note appears as follows:

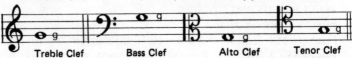

Treble Clef   Bass Clef   Alto Clef   Tenor Clef

(3) G is used as an abbreviation for Generalpause (G.P.).
(4) A string or instrument may be tuned to the key of G.
(5) G identifies several keys such as: G major, Gb major, G minor, G# minor. (6) The treble clef

is also called G clef. The sign for the treble clef is an ornamental G. G is on the second line. See *Key, *Letter names, *Notation, *Pitch names, *Scale.

G (Fr.) (zhā) (1) Letter number seven in the alphabet. (2) The G in French has a hard sound before the vowels a, u, and o and a soft sound before the vowels e and i. (3) G is used as an abbreviation for the French word gauche which means left.

Gabelgriff (Ger.)(gä'—bĕl—gri f)Fork-handle. German term referring to cross fingering on musical instruments.

Gagliarda (It.)(gäl—yärd'—dä) Galliard.

Gagliardamente (It.)(gäl—yärd—dä—mĕn'—tā)Briskly, gay-ly. See *Galliard.

Gaillarde (Fr.) (gä—yärd) Merry, lively. See *Galliard.

Gaio (It.) (gä'—ē—ō) Gay, cheerful.

Gaita (Sp.) (gä'—ē—tä) Bagpipe.

Galamment (Fr.) (gä—lä—mĕ(n)) (galant (Ger.) (gä—länt') galante (It.)(gä—län'—tā)) Gallantly; gallant.

Galantemente (It.)(gä—län—tā—mĕn'—tā) Boldly.

Galanterien (Ger.) (gä—län—tĕr—ēn') Those dances or sections of the 18th century suite which were added, or included by option, to the standard group of dances which were the allemande, courante, sarabande and gigue. Optional parts were dances such as the minuet, gavotte, bourée, etc. Examples: Suites of J. S. Bach (1685-1750) and G. F. Handel (1685-1759).

Galanter Stil (Ger.) (gä—län'—tå r shtēl) Gallant style A German term used to describe an elegant homophonic style of music during the middle of the 18th century. The style is identified with a period of music called Rococo. The Rococo style overlaps the late Baroque style, which is serious and elaborate, and the early classical style.

Galanteries (Fr.) (gä—lä(n)—tĕr—rē) French term to describe those extra dances added to the 18th century suites. See *Galanterien.

Galliard A lively dance in triple time popular during the 16th century. Later, the Galliard was used to contrast the slow pavane which was in duple time. The dance featured running, jumps, and kicks. Example: William Byrd (1543-1623), *Galliard for Harpsichord,* Fitzwilliam Virginal Book Number 92.

Galop (Gallopade) A gay, springing round dance which employed a hop and glide. The music is fast and in $\frac{2}{4}$ time. It was popular during the middle of the 19th century.

Galoubet (Fr.) (gä—loo—bā) Pipe, A whistle flute having three finger holes. It was held in the left hand and played as the right hand played the tabor (drum) which formed the accompaniment. See *Tabor.

Gamba (1) Abbreviation of viola da gamba. (2) An organ stop.

Gamba bass A 16 foot organ stop.

Gambang Javanese xylophone.

Gamelan An instrumental ensemble of southeast Asia which includes various wind, percussion, and primitive stringed instruments. E.g., marimba, gongs, flutes, etc.

Gamma (Greek) (1) The third of any series. (2) In the Greek alphabet, the third letter. Greek name for the letter G. Gamma ut would be the G eleven notes below middle c'.

Gamme (Fr.) (gäm) Scale or gamut.

Gamut (1) A term referring to the range of a voice or instrument. (2) A scale. (3) The key of G. Gamma ut refers to the first line G of the bass clef (gamma meaning G and ut meaning the lowest note of the hexacord).

Ganascione (It.) (gä—nä—shē—ō'—nä) Italian lute.

Gang (Ger.) (gäng) Motion; walk.

Ganibry An African lute-type instrument.

Ganz (Ger.) (gänts) Whole. To use a whole bow or entire bow. Ganze Note (Ger.) (gänt'—så nō'—tå) Whole note or semibreve note. Ganze Pause (Ger.)(gänt'—så pow'—zå) Whole rest or semibreve rest. Ganze Taktnote (Ger.) (gänt'—så täkt'—nō—tå) Whole note or semibreve. Ganzschluss (Ger.) (gänts'—shlōōs) Full cadence. Ganzton (Ger.) (gänts'—tōn) Whole tone. Ganztonleiter (Ger.) (gänts'—tōn—lī—tå r)Whole tone scale.

Gapped scale A scale developed by omitting specific tones from a more complete scale. E.g., the pentatonic scale is a gapped scale from the diatonic scale.

Garbato (It.) (gär—bä'—tō) Graceful.

Garder (Fr.) (gär—dä) To keep or hold.

Gariglione (It.) (gä—rēl—yō'—nä) Chimes or bells. Chiming of bells.

Gathering note The note played by the organist for the congregation as the pitch from which they will sing a hymn or psalm.

Gauche (Fr.) (gōsh) Left. (1) Use left hand. (2) A movement to the left in dance.

Gaudioso (It.) (gä—ōo—dē—ō'—zō) Merry.

Gavotte A French peasant dance popular during the 17th century. It was danced to music which was in quadruple meter, of fast tempo, began on the third beat and the dancers moved in small jump steps. The instrumental form is played in $\frac{4}{4}$ time, quite fast but stately, usually starting on the third beat (third and fourth beats were usually on quarter notes.) It was used in the instrumental suite as an optional dance, as in some of Bach's suites. Sometimes it was used between the sarabande and gigue. It was often followed by the musette. Examples: J. S. Bach (1685-1750), *English Suite No. 6 in D Minor for Piano;* Courante, Sarabande, Gavotte 1, Gavotte 2, Gigue: *English Suite No. 3 in G minor for Piano;* Prelude, Allemande, Sarabande, Gavotte, Musette, Gigue.

G clef Treble clef.

G dur (Ger.) (gā dōor) Key of G Major.

Gebrauchmusik (Ger.)(gå —browkh '—mōo—zēk)Gebrauch meaning use or useage. Music written to be played by amateurs. Hindemith (1895-1963) devoted much effort to this type of functional music. It was written in simple style, was limited in difficulty, for small groups, and had parts which were interchangable in order that each part could be played on whatever instruments were available. This music was generally for practical use and not for concerts or professional use.

Gebrochen (Ger.)(gå —brôkh '—å n)Broken; arpeggio.

Gebrochener Akkord (Ger.)(gå —brôkh '—å n—åräk—kôrt ') An arpeggiated chord or broken chord.

Gebunden (Ger.) (gå —bŏon '—då n) Connected; slurred; legato.

Gedackt (Ger.) (gå —däkt ') Covered or stopped. A class of end-stopped organ pipes as opposed to the open pipe. The modern term for stopped or covered is gedeckt (Ger.)

Gedämpft (Ger.) (gå —dēmpft ') Damped; muted.

Gedehnt (Ger.) (gå —dänt ') Lengthened or held.

Gefallen (Ger.)(gå —fäl '—å n) Please, favor.

Gefällig (Ger.)(gå —fěl '—i k) Pleasing.

Gefühl (Ger.) (gå —fül ') Feeling or sentiment.

Gefühlvoll (Ger.) (gå —fül '—fōl) Sentimental.

Gegen (Ger.) (gā '—gå n) Toward; against.

Gegenbewegung (Ger.)(gā—gå n—bå —vā '—gŏong)Contrary motion.

Gegengesang Ger.)(gā '—gå n—gå —zäng)Voice against voice as in the antiphonal technique of performing.

Gegensatz (Ger.) (gā '—gå n—zäts) Opposite or contrast.

Gehalten (Ger.) (gå —hält '—å n) Held out or sustained.

Gehaucht (Ger.)(gå —howkht ')Whispered.

Geheimnisvoll (Ger.)(gå —hïm '—nïs—fōll)Secretive.

Gehend (Ger.)(gā '—hěnt) Walking or going. A moderately moving tempo.

Geige (Ger.)(gī '—gå)Bowed instrument, violin.
Geist (Ger.) (gist) Spirit.
Geistlich (Ger.) (gist '—likh)Ecclesiastical, sacred, religious.
Gekneipt (Ger.)(gå —knipt ')Plucked.
Gelassen (Ger.)(gå —läss '—å n)Calm, composed.
Geläufigkeit (Ger.)(gå —loi '—fik—kit)Skill, facility.
Gellenflöte (Ger.) (gĕl '—lĕn—flĕ(r)—tå) Shriek flute, e.g., clarinet.
Gemächlich (Ger.)(gå —mĕkh '—likh) Moving in a leisurely manner.
Gemässigt (Ger.) (gå —mĕss '—ikt) Moderate speed.
Gemere (It.)(jā '—mā—rā)Groan.
Gemessen (Ger.) (gå —mĕss '—ĕn) Moderate speed; measured or held back.
Gemischte (Ger.)(gå —mish '—tå) Mixed.
Gemshorn A 4 foot open organ stop. Soft tone.
Gemütlich (Ger.) (gå —müt '—likh) Comfortable, cheerful.
Genau (Ger.)(gå —now ') Accurate, exact, strict.
Generalbass (Ger.)(gĕn—å r—äl '—bäss)General bass; figured bass, thorough-bass.

Generalpause (Ger.)(gĕn—å r—äl'—pow '—zå)The abbreviation is G.P. The group stops. There is a general silence.
Genre (Fr.) (zhä(n)r) Style or genus. A particular content, technique, form, etc.
Gentile (It.)(jĕn—tē '—lā)Graceful, gentile.
German flute Orchestra flute. The side-blown or transverse flute, as opposed to the end-blown flute or recorder.
German scale In German, the letter B is used to identify the pitch B flat. Therefore, the C scale would use the letter H (for B natural) in place of the letter B. E.g., CDEFGAHC.
German sixth An augmented sixth chord. It often occurs on the flatted submediant of a major scale or the submediant of the minor scale. It includes an augmented sixth. The intervals, figured from the lowest note upwards would be, major third, perfect fifth, and an augmented sixth. Example of German sixth in the Key of G major:

156

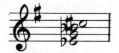

See *Augmented sixth, *Sixth chords.

Ges (Ger.) (gĕss) The note G flat. (Gᵇ).

Gesamtausgabe (Ger.)(gå –zäm '–tows–gä–bå) Complete edition.

Gesamtkunstwerk (Ger.) (gå –zämt '–kŏonst–vĕrk) Complete art works. A collated study which includes all types of art.

Gesang (Ger.) (gå –zäng ') Chant or song.

Gesangbuch (Ger.) (gå –zäng '–bōokh) Hymnal.

Geschick (Ger.)(gå –shi k ') Dexterity, skill.

Geschwind (Ger.)(gå –shvi nt ') Quick, rapid, swift.

Ges dur (Ger.) (gĕss dōor) Key of G flat major.

Geses (Ger.) (gĕss '–ĕss) G double flat (Gᵇᵇ).

Gesprochen (Ger.) (gå –shprŏkh '–å n) Spoken.

Gestopft (Ger.)(gå –shtŏpft ') The stopped notes played on the French horn.

Gestossen (Ger.)(gå –shtŏs '–å n)Staccato.

Geteilt (Ger.)(gå –ti͞ lt ') ; Getheilt (Ger.) (gå –ti͞ lt ') Divided or divisi.

Getragen (Ger.)(gå –träg '–å n)Carried or sustained.

G flat Gᵇ. A semitone below the note G.

E.g., Clef:

Treble Clef   Bass Clef   Alto Clef   Tenor Clef

Giga (It.)(jē '–gä) Jig, gigue.

Gigelira (It.)(jē–jä–lē '–rä)Xylophone.

Gighardo (It.)(jē–gär '–dō) An Italian jig.

Gigue (Fr.) (jēg) Jig, dance. It is of English or Irish origin. The 17th and 18th century suites included the gigue as one of the four sections (allemande, courante, sarabande, and gigue). The gigue is fast, in compound triple time (⁶⁄₈ or ⁶⁄₄), in binary form, in fugal style, and uses rhythmic patterns (dotted rhythm and wide skips). Optional dances used in the suite usually came just before the gigue. For example: G. F. Handel (1685-1759) *Suite Number 4 in E Minor.* It includes Allemande, Courante, Sarabande, and the Gigue. A suite which includes optional dances is by J. S. Bach (1685-1750) *English Suite No. 3 in G Minor* for Piano (Prelude, Allemande, Sarabande, Gavotte, Musette, Gigue).

Giochevole (It.) (jē—ō—kā'—vō—lā) Playfully.

Giocoso (It.) (jē—ō—kō'—zō) Joyous, playful.

Gioioso (It.) (jē—ō—ē—ō'—zō) Happy, gleeful.

Giro (It.) (jē'—rō) Turn; round.

Gis (Ger.) (gĭss) G sharp (G#).

Gisis (Ger.) (gĭss'—ĭss) G double sharp (G##), (Gx).

Gis moll (Ger.) (gĭss mawl) Key of G# minor.

Gittern A guitar-like instrument of the Middle ages. See *Cittern.

Giustamente (It.)(jē—ōos—tä—mĕn'—tä)Justly; precisely.

Giusto (It.) (jē—ōos'—tō) Just, strict, or suitable. E.g., strict time.

Given bass The bass line is given and the harmonization is to be added.

Glänzend (Ger.)(glĕn'—tsĕnt)Brilliant.

Glass harmonica Bowls of various sizes were turned on a spindle by a foot pedal, set to vibrating (thereby producing a pitch) by rubbing the revolving rims with moist fingers. Benjamin Franklin is credited with the invention of the glass harmonica (armonica).

Glassichord A musical instrument that had tiers of glass plates of various sizes which were struck by hammers which were apparently activated by a keyboard. See *Harmonica.

Glatt (Ger.) (glät) Smooth.

Glee (from the Anglo-Saxon word "gleo", fun, music, play, etc.) A harmonic choral piece written in three or more parts and usually performed by male voices. It is simple and short, harmonic in texture, and is unaccompanied. It was popular in England during the 18th and early 19th centuries.

Glee club Originally a group formed to sing glees. Until lately a group organized to sing choral music of a popular type, lighter variety, and glees. Now serious music may be included in the repertoire. Usually the term is used to identify men's glee clubs but it is often used by women's groups and mixed groups.

Gleich (Ger.) (glīkh) Same, equal, even. Gleichmässig (Ger.) (glikh '—mĕss—ik) Regular or even.

Glide Moving from one note to another without a break.

Glissando (It.) (glēs—sän '—dō) Sliding or gliding, from note to note in rapid succession. On piano, the finger nail is drawn rapidly over a series of notes in either direction. On trombone, the slide moves up and down sliding through several tones in rapid succession. On harp, the fingers glide across the strings. On violin, the finger slides up and down the string. On wind instruments, the tone is "lipped" from one note to the next. The abbreviation is gliss., or a straight or wavy stroke between notes is used as follows:

Glocke (Ger.) (glŏk '—ả) A bell.

Glockenspiel (Ger.)(glŏk '—ả n—shpēl)Carillon, set of bells, chimes. (1) A keyboard instrument of the 18th century which had a bell sound. (2) A percussion instrument having graduated steel bars which sound in half steps and are mounted on a metal lyre-shaped frame. The sound is produced by striking the bars with a hammer or mallet. It can be mounted on a stand or is portable. (3) An organ stop which produces this type of bell sound.

Gloria in excelsis Deo (Lat.)(glō '—rē—ä in ĕg—shĕl '—sēs Dā '—ō) "Glory to God in the highest." The Gloria follows the "Kyrie" in the Ordinary of the Roman Catholic Mass. It is the second part in the Ordinary of the Mass. The complete text in Latin is as follows: "Gloria in excelsis Deo. Et in terra pax hominibus bonae voluntatis. Laudamus te. Benedicimus te. Adoramus te. Glorificamus te. Gratias agimus tibi propter magnam gloriam tuam. Domine Deus, Rex coelestis, Deus Pater omnipotens. Domine Fili unigenite, Jesu Christe. Domine Deus, Agnus Dei, Filius Patris. Qui tollis peccata mundi, miserere nobis. Qui tollis peccata mundi suscipe deprecationem nostram. Qui sedes ad dexteram Patris, miserere nobis. Quoniam tu solus Sanctus.Tu solus Dominus. Tu solus Altissimus, Jesu Christe. Cum Sancto Spiritu in gloria Dei Patris. Amen." The Latin text was used in the Roman Catholic Church for centuries. However, the Ordinary of the Mass is now done in the vernacular. The English translation follows: "Glory to God in the highest. And on earth peace to men of good will. We praise You. We bless You. We adore You. We glorify You. We give You thanks for Your great glory. O Lord God, heavenly King, God the Father Almighty. O Lord Jesus Christ, the Only begotten Son. O Lord God, Lamb of God, Son of the Father: You Who take away the sins of the world, have mercy on us. You Who take away the sins of the world, receive our prayer. You Who sit at the right hand of the Father, have mercy on us. For You alone are holy. You alone are the Lord. You Alone, O Jesus Christ, are most high. Together with the Holy Spirit in the glory of God the Father. Amen." The "Gloria" is used in musical settings by many composers. A good example is found in the J. S. Bach (1685-1750) *Mass in B Minor,* section IV, "Gloria". See *Mass, *Ordinary of the Mass.

Gloria patri et filio (Lat.) (glō̄—rē̄—ä pä'—trē ̄ĕt fē'—lē̄—ō)
The lesser doxology which is sung at the end of canticles or psalms. "Glory be to the Father, and to the Son, and to the Holy Spirit. As it was in the beginning, is now, and ever shall be, world without end. Amen."

Glosa (Sp.) (glō̄'—sä) Gloss; diminution; a type of variation.

Glühen (Ger.) (glü'—å n) To glow; **Glühend** (Ger.) (glü'—ĕnt) glowing.

G moll (Ger.) (gā̄ mawl) Key of G minor.

Goat's trill An exaggerated shake or trill.

Goblet drums Footed drums that are portable.

Goliard songs Satirical Latin ·verse written by goliards or wandering poets. Many were written during the 12th and 13th centuries in England, France, and Germany. Example: the collection "Carmina Burana".

Gondoliera (It.) (gŏn—dō—lē—ā'—rä) A gondola song.

Gong A large bronze or metal disc, of oriental origin, which is sounded by striking it with a padded hammer. Also called Tam-tam.

Gopak A lively Ukrainian folk dance in duple time. Used by some Russian composers, e.g., Moussorgsky: Also, Hopak.

Gorgia (It.) (gôr'—jē—ä) Embellishments or ornaments used by singers of the 16th and 17th centuries.

Gourd The dried shell of a furit. Some instruments are made of gourd because of its resonance.

G.P. The abbreviation for General Pause.

Grace An ornament.

Grace note A note (usually in small type) that borrows time from the note to which it is attached, e.g., An ornament; a short auxiliary note; an embellishment.

Gracieusement (Fr.) (grä—sē—ûz—mä(n)) Graciously or gracefully.

Gradation A succession of chords moving diatonically.

Gradevolmente (It.) (grä—dā—vōl—mĕn'—tä) Pleasingly.

Gradino (It.) (grä—dē'—nō) Step, e.g., the steps of a scale.

Grado (It.) (grä'—dō) A degree, e.g., a step or degree of a scale.

Gradual (1) In the Proper of the Roman Catholic Mass, the "Gradual" is the second part which is sung between the Epistle and the Gospel. It is a responsorial chant. (2) The book that contains the words and music which are sung by the choir.

Gradualmente (It.)(grä—dōō—äl—mĕn'—tä) Gradually.

Gramophone A phonograph.

Gran (It.) (grän) Great, big.

Gran cassa (It.) (grän kä'—sä) Big drum, bass drum.

Grand (Fr.) (grä(n)) Great, large.

Grand bourdon A double bourdon. A 32 foot organ stop.

Grand choeur (Fr.) (grä(n) kŭr) Full choir or full chorus. Full organ.

Grandezza (It.) (grän—dĕt'—tsä) Magnitude, grandeur.

Grandioso (It.) (grän—dē—ō'—zō) Majestically, broadly.

Grandisonante (It.) (grän—dē—sō—nän'—tä) Sonorous.

Grand opera A dramatic or tragic opera which is sung throughout. It usually includes a large orchestra, large chorus, elaborate sets, dance or ballet, and a large cast. The term is sometimes used to distinquish the larger type opera from the comic opera, light opera or operetta. It is also used to distinquish between grand operas, which are sung throughout, and the opera comique, which has spoken dialogue. Example of grand opera: Giuseppe Verdi (1813-1901), *Aida.*

Grand orchestra (Fr.) (grä(n) dôr—kĕs—tr) Large or full orchestra.

Grand orgue (Fr.) (grä(n) dôrg) Full organ or great organ.

Grand piano A piano which has a harp shape and rests on three legs in a horizontal position. It is built in several sizes.

Grandsire A style of ringing changes on a set of bells.

Grand staff (great staff) The staff used for piano, organ, etc. It is comprised of the treble clef (G clef) above the bass clef (F clef). The system of lines and spaces upon which musical notes are placed.

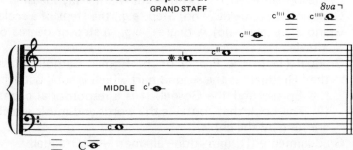

*a' vibrates at 440 v.p.s. The tones of the piano vibrate (low to high) from approximately 30 v.p.s. to 4,000 v.p.s.

Grave (It.) (grä'—vä) Grave, heavy. A very slow tempo.

Grazioso (It.) (grä—tse̅—o̅ '—zo̅) Gracious.

Great organ The principal organ manual (keyboard) and controls. It is situated between the Choir Organ and the Swell Organ.

Grecian lyre A small Greek lyre used to accompany singing and recitation.

Greek modes See *Modes, *Church modes.

Gregorian chant A type of plainchant or liturgical chant named after Pope Gregory I (590-604) and used in the Roman Catholic Church. The Gregorian chant reflects Jewish traditions, some influence from Greek music and a similarity to the Eastern chants. It is in free rhythm, monodic, modal and set to a Latin text. The melodies are melismatic, neumatic, and syllabic. The chants are also strophic, psalmodic, and through-composed. Examples of plainchant are found in: the *Liber Usualis* (includes music of the Mass and Office) and in the *Paléographie Musicale.* Music (chants) for the Mass is found in the collection "Graduale Romanum"; music (chants) for the daily Office is found in the collection "Antiphonale Romanum".

Gregorian modes See *Church modes, *Modes.

Griffbrett (Ger.) (grif '—bret̆) Play on the finger board; above the finger board.

Grimm (Ger.) (grim) Anger.

Grob (Ger.) (gro̅p) Coarse, clumsy.

Gros (Fr.) (grosse (Fr.)) (gro̅, gro̅s) Great, large.

Grosse caisse (Fr.) (gro̅s kĕss) Bass drum.

Grosse flöte (Ger.) (gro̅ '—så flĕ(r) '—tå)(1) Large flute; regular orchestra flute. (2) An organ stop.

Grosse oktave (Ger.)(gro̅ '—så ŏk—tä '—vå) Great octave.

Grosses orchester (Ger.)(gro̅ '—sĕs ôr—kĕs '—tå r) Full orchestra.

Grosse trommel (Ger.) (gro̅ '—så trŏ'—mĕl) Bass drum.

Grosso (It.) (gro̅s '—so̅) Full, large.

Grotesk (Ger.) (gro̅—tĕsk ') Grotesque.

Ground bass A bass line or phrase which is repeated over and over throughout a composition as the upper parts variate. The ground was used extensively during the

163

17th and early 18th centuries. Improvisation above a ground bass was a common practice in England during the 17th Century (called DIVISION.) The ground forms a basis for such forms as chaconne, passacaglia, folia, and variation. See *Division, *Chaconne, *Passacaglia, *Folia, *Variation, *Ostinato, *Basso ostinato.

Growl In jazz playing it is the flutter tonguing, gutteral or raspy sound produced on wind instruments. The growl is often employed when certain types of mutes are used, such as a plunger mute or cup mute.

Grundton (Ger.) (grōond '–tōn) The root or fundamental tone in a chord.

Grundtonart (Ger.) (grōond '–tōn–ärt) The key center of a composition.

Gruppo (It.) (grōo'–pō) Group. A group of ornamental notes such as a turn, trill, or shake.

G sharp G#. A semitone above the note G.

E.g. Clef:

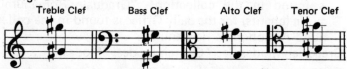

Treble Clef Bass Clef Alto Clef Tenor Clef

G string A string tuned to the pitch of G, such as the lowest string of the violin, the 3rd lowest string of the cello, etc.

Guaracha (Sp.) (gōo–ä–rä'–chä) A lively Cuban dance in triple meter. It also incorporates sections which move in duple meter.

Guida (It.) (gōo–ē'–dä) Guide, leadership. (1) A guide or direct. See *Direct. (2) A subject.

Guidonian hand A drawing of the hand and fingers used to understand the hexachord, solmisation, and mutation. The various tips and joints of the fingers were associated with specific syllables and notes. Although the name is associated with Guido d'Arezzo(c.995-c.1049) the Guidonian hand appears in writings of a much later time. See *Guidonian syllables.

Guidonian syllables Used by Guido d'Arezzo. Each note of the hexachord was identified with a specific syllable.

The syllables are: ut, re, mi, fa, sol, la. The system of syllables is called solmization.

Guimbarde (Fr.) (gă(m)—bärd) A Jew's harp.

Guitar A stringed instrument which is played by plucking the strings and is used for melody and harmony. It is of Oriental origin and similar to the lute. It has a long, fretted neck, flat back, curved sides, and is made in several sizes. The modern guitar normally has six strings tuned to the pitches E, A, d, g, b, e'. It sounds an octave lower than the written note. Other modern versions: folk guitar, Hawaiian guitar, steel guitar, electric guitar, bass guitar. An example of the "tablature" used in guitar music to designate chords: The guitar is tuned:

The tablature: (designating — F chord)

F CHORD

See *Gittern, *Cittern, *Bandurria, *Tablature.

Guitare (Fr.) (gē—tär) Guitar.
Guitarra (Sp.)(gē—tär '—rä) Guitar.
Gustare (It.)(goos—tä '—rä)Taste.
Gut (Ger.) (goot) Good.
Gut Gut or catgut. A type of string used on musical instruments. See *Catgut.
Gutbucket An early jazz style often referred to as low down music. It was played in a raucous manner as was common in barrel-house music of New Orleans during the early part of the 20th Century.

Gymel (Lat.) (gemellus) Twin or two parts. (1) Two part music of the Middle Ages which was sung primarily in intervals of the third or sixth. Gymel is a two-part version of the Fauxbourdon. The gymel is said to be the earliest form of English polyphony. It was also used on the continent. A later form of gymel is in three parts the two upper parts being gymel. (2) The term is used in 15th and 16th Century polyphony in the modern sense of divisi. See *Fauxbourdon.

H

H (Ger.) B natural (B♮). B in German is a B flat (B♭).

Habanera (Sp.) (hä–bä–nā'–rä) A dance from Havana, Cuba which was introduced in Spain during the mid-Romantic period (19th century). A dance in slow duple time using various rhythms such as

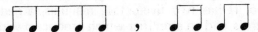

Examples: Georges Bizet (1838-1875) from the opera *Carmen*, the "Habanera" from Act I; Louis Aubert (b. 1877), *Habanera for Orchestra* (1919).

Hackbrett (Ger.)(häk'–brět) Dulcimer.

Hai-lo (Chinese) An ancient Chinese shell flute.

Halb (Ger.) (hälp) also halbe(häl'–bå). Halbe Note, (Ger.) (häl'–bå nō'–tå) half note. Halbe Pause (Ger.)(häl'–bå pow'–zà) half rest. Halbschluss, (Ger.) (hälb'–shloǒs) half-cadence. Halbsopran, (Ger.) (hälb'–zō–prän) mezzo-soprano.. Halbton, (Ger.)(hälb'–tōn) Half-tone, half-step.

Half-cadence A cadence ending on the dominant.

Half-close Imperfect cadence.

Half-note A minim (♩).

Half rest A pause (▬) equal to the value of a half note.

Half step The smallest interval used in the standard music of the Western culture. A semitone. The distance between a black key and a white key, or between B and C or E and F on the piano keyboard.

Hälfte, die (Ger.)(hělf'–tå, dē)Half. A German term used to indicate that only half of the section should play the passage.

Hallelujah ((Heb.) Hallelujah, Praise Jehovah) "Praise ye the Lord" Praise or joy. Musical works sometimes use the word throughout the composition, e.g., "Hallelujah Chorus" from Handel's *Messiah.*

Halling An athletic Norwegian folk dance for men in duple time. Grieg used the dance style in his nationalistic works.

Halten (Ger.)(häl '–tå n) To hold or stop.

Hammer (1) The felt hammer that strikes the strings of the piano. (2) The clapper on a bell. (3) A mallet or like instrument used to start a tone.

Hammerklavier (Ger.) (häm '–må r–klä–vēr) Hammer piano. A German term for piano used during the 1800's.

Hammond organ An electric organ shaped like an upright piano. It has two five-octave manuals, a pedal board, controls, and an amplifier which produce a wide variety of tone colors. Made by the Hammond Organ Company. It was invented by L. Hammond in 1934.

Hand bells Small bells which are held by leather handles and are sounded by swinging the bell up or down allowing the clappers to strike the bell. They are used for playing melodies or in change ringing.

Hand horn A 17th century horn which resembled the modern horn but had no valves and was called a natural horn. The performer could produce only the tones of the harmonic series with a few additional tones produced by placing the hand in the bell. It preceded the modern French horn.

Hand organ (1) A mechanical barrel organ which is portable and operated by a crank turned by hand. (2) The barrel organ. See *Barrel organ.

Handtrommel (Ger.)(händ '–trŏm–å l) Tambourine.

Hardanger fiddle A Norwegian fiddle which has four sympathetic strings below the four regualr strings. This instrument provides the accompaniment for the Halling. See *Halling.

Hard bop A type of modern jazz which followed the cool jazz of the 1950's and moved toward a more basic and emotional type of music. It had the characteristics of the folk-rooted jazz, such as the hot-gospel style, and that of the blues. See *Funky jazz music.

Hardiment (Fr.) (är–dē–mä(n)) Boldly or daringly.

Harfe (Ger.) (här '–få) Harp.

Harmonic An overtone. Relating to the harmony. See *Harmonics.

Harmonica (1) The mouth organ. A small, flat, rectangular shaped instrument which has a series of square holes that hold metal reeds, each of which represents a pitch. The instrument is played by blowing air into the holes. Pitch is changed by pulling or pushing the instrument across the lips in either direction. Sound is produced by inhaling or exhaling. They vary in size and range. (2) The glass harmonica (armonica) invented by Benjamin Franklin.

Harmonica de bois (Fr.) (är—mō—nē—kä dü bwä) Xylophone.

Harmonic analysis The stydy of the chordal structure and chordal relationships within a piece of music. The relationship of the total piece to the chordal construction.

Harmonic Bass An organ stop which produces a resultant tone. An acoustic bass. See *Resultant tone, *Acoustic bass.

Harmonic division The geometric division of a string which produces harmonics.

Harmonic figuration The use of a harmonic figure or broken chord.

Harmonic flute An organ stop. An opening is made in an 8 foot pipe at the mid-point, which also makes possible the production of the 4 foot pitch or octave.

Harmonic inversion The process by which an interval is inverted by placing the lower note an octave higher or the upper note an octave lower. E.g., an interval of a major third, (c'—e') becomes an interval of a minor sixth (e'—c''); an interval of a perfect fourth (f' to bb') inverted becomes a perfect fifth (bb' to f'', or bb to f'). The intervals are within the compass of an octave and the numbers of both intervals will total nine. A major interval inverted becomes a minor; a minor becomes a major; a diminished inverted becomes augmented; an augmented becomes diminished; a perfect interval remains a perfect interval. A chord is inverted when a note other than the root is in the lowest part. See *Inversions.

Harmonic mark A mark (○) or a diamond (◊) in string music (e.g., violin music) to indicate that a note or passage is to be played on the part of the open string which will produce harmonic tones.

Harmonic minor scale The harmonic minor scale is one form of the minor scale. The three forms of minor scales are: pure, harmonic, and melodic. The harmonic minor scale is formed from the pure form by raising the seventh degree of the scale by one half-step ascending and descending. E.g.:

Key of a minor

Harmonic minor

See *Minor scales, *Major scales, *Scales.

Harmonic modulation A key change within the composition using harmonic or chordal progressions from one key to another. When a pivot chord is used (a chord common to the old and the new key) it is called diatonic modulation. Another type of modulation involves an abrupt move from a chord in the old key to a quite different chord in the new key. This usually requires the use of chromatics. Another method of modulation is called enharmonic modulation, where one or several notes of the chord are changed enharmonically resulting in a chord of a different key. See *Modulation.

Harmonicon Mouth organ. Harmonica.

Harmonic piccolo An organ stop of 2 foot pitch that sounds an octave higher than the harmonic flute. See *Harmonic flute.

Harmonics The overtones or partials of the fundamental tone. The science of musical tones. A harmonic is produced on a string by lightly pressing a string at a given point. Different tones are produced by touching the string at various points on the string. E.g., a tone an octave higher will result when an open string is touched at the mid-point. Harmonics produced on the open strings are called natural harmonics. Those produced on closed strings are called artificial harmonics. See *Flageolet tones.

Harmonic series When a fundamental tone is sounded, other notes sound above as a result of sympathetic vibrations. For each note there are these upper partials or overtones that vibrate within a given ratio relative to the fundamental. These harmonics are important to the system of playing harmonies, to our harmonic structure, timbre and to the acoustical aspects of musical instruments. Following is an example of the harmonic series based on the fundamental note C. Note the sequence of intervals above the fundamental.

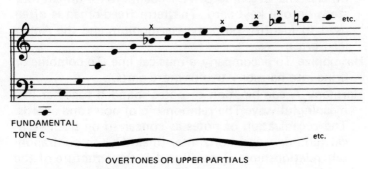

FUNDAMENTAL
TONE C ‿‿‿‿‿‿‿‿‿‿ etc.

OVERTONES OR UPPER PARTIALS

X—NOT IN TUNE WITH NORMAL SCALE

Harmonic stops The flue-pipes of the organ, each of which has a hole at the mid-point of the pipe which causes it to sound a harmonic tone.

Harmonic tone A prominent overtone.

Harmonie (Ger. and Fr.) (här'—mōn'—ē, är—mŏ—nē) (1) The French term which identifies the group of wind instruments of the orchestra. (2) A wind band. (3) Harmony.

Harmoniemusik (Ger.) (här—mōn'—ē—moo—sēk) Music for the wind band including woodwinds, brasses, and percussion instruments.

Harmoniflute A 19th century portable reed instrument having a keyboard with a compass of three octaves.

Harmonika (Ger.) (här—mōn'—ē—kä) Harmonica or mouthorgan.

171

Harmonium A metal-reed organ. It has a keyboard (five octaves) and a pair of foot pedals or treadles. The treadles feed the bellows which forces air into the wind-chest and reservoir. The air moves through the feeders past the metal tongues causing them to vibrate, which in turn causes the compressed air within the channels to vibrate. The vibrating air in each chamber produces different timbres. A variety of timbre results when using different stops. There were many types during the early 19th century, such as the orgue expressif of Grenié, the organo-violine, the Aeoline, and others. The Organino of A. Debain (1840) united four stops on one keyboard. The term Reed-organ is often used to identify both the Harmonium and the American organ.

Harmonize To accompany a musical line. To combine or bring into harmony two or more parts.

Harmony A combination of notes sounded together in a meaningful way. The relationship of notes and chords. The organization of notes as conceived on both vertical (chordal) and horizontal (melodic and contrapuntal) relationships. Generally, it is the structure of the music and the function of the vertical relationship. Many aspects of the musical score are affected by the harmony. The rhythmic movement of the chords is directly related to the harmony; the sequence of chords relates to the key center; chordal sequences relate to modulation; and the harmonic element is very important to the development of form or the design of a composition.

Harp A double action harp is a stringed instrument which is plucked. It has a triangular shape, which includes a pillar, a back, a curved neck, a sound board and forty-six strings which are stretched between the sound box and the neck. The strings are tuned to the key of C^b major. There are seven pedals and each string can be raised a half-step or a whole step by using a specific pedal. E.g., the C^b string can be raised to C or $C^\#$. All major and minor keys can be played. The range is from Çᵇ′ upwards to six octaves and a fifth. The chromatic harp has no pedals and one string is available for each semitone within the octave.

Harp, dital Harp lute.

Harpe (Fr.) (ärp) Harp.

Harpège (Fr.) (är—pĕzh) Arpeggio. Broken chord.

Harp-Guitar Features of the harp and those of the guitar are combined. An attempt to replace the guitar. It had eight strings. See *Dital harp.

Harp lute Features of the harp and those of the guitar are combined. An elegant form of the earlier Harp-Guitar, it has eleven or more strings. See *Dital harp.

Harpsichord A keyboard instrument which was popular during the 16th to 18th centuries and is gaining in popularity today. It has one or two manuals (in which case it would have two sets of strings) and looks, in shape, rather like our present day smaller grand piano. The strings are plucked by a plectrum made of leather or quill. When the key is pressed, a strip of wood with a plectrum attached moves up and plucks the string. The tone is sustained only as long as the keys are depressed. The player has little control over the tone quality by touch, however, stops and couplers are available to the player.

Hart (Ger.) (härt) Hard. Sometimes used to describe the major mode.

Hastig (Ger.)(häs '—ti k) Hasty.

Hasur A dechordon.

Haupt (Ger.) (howpt) Head, leader, chief. Hauptsatz, (Ger.) (howpt '—zäts) Principal theme or first theme. Hauptstimme, (Ger.) (howpt '—shtim—må) Principal voice. Hauptwerk, (Ger.)(howpt '—vĕrk)Great organ or chief work.

Haut (Fr.) (ō) High, raised, upper or chief.

Hautbois (Fr.) (ō—bwä) Hautboy, oboe. The abbreviation is Hb.

'**Haut-dessus** (Fr.) (ō—dĕş—sü) Soprano.

Haute-contre (Fr.) (ōt—cŏn—tr) Counter-tenor; alto.

Haute-taille (Fr.) (ōt—tä—yå) Tenor.

173

H dur (Ger.) (hä dōōr) Key of B major.

Head (1) Drum head. (2) Point of the bow, top. (3) The head of a note.

Head register The high register of the voice. Other registers may be referred to as throat register and chest register. See *Head voice.

Head voice Used with reference to the highest voice register.

Heckel-clarina A single-reed instrument which looks like the straight soprano saxophone and has somewhat the same range. It is in B♭ and was named after the Heckel firm by which it was developed.

Heckelphone A double reed instrument which is pitched one octave lower than the oboe. A baritone oboe.

Heel The nut end of the bow; the part by which the bow is held.

Heftig (Ger.)(hĕf'–tĭ k)Vehement.

Heilig Ger.(hī'–lĭ k) Sacred, holy.

Heiss (Ger.) (hī s) Ardent, passionate.

Heiter (Ger.)(hī'–tå r)Clear, happy.

Heldentenor (Ger.) (hĕl'–dĕn–tĕn–ōr) Heroic tenor. A tenor voice of considerable power. A voice of the type suited for heavy operatic parts such as those in the operas of Wagner.

Helicon The tuba which circles the body of the player and rests on his shoulder. The sousaphone which is used in marching bands.

Hell (Ger.) (hĕl) Bright.

Hemidemisemiquaver An obsolete term for the sixty-fourth note (♪). The rest ( ).

Hemiola (Greek) The term refers to the ratio of three to two. (1) The relationship of playing a group of three equal notes in the time value of the first two notes. (2) Playing three notes against two. (3) The rhythmic change from a feeling of two to three or three to two within the same meter. (4) A relationship of 3:2 in the number of vibrations of two notes.

Heptachord (Greek) (1) The seven different notes of the

major or minor scale. (2) The interval of a seventh.
(3) A musical instrument having seven strings.
Herabstrich (Ger.)(hĕr—äb '—shtri kḥ) Down-bow.
Heraufstrich (Ger.) (hĕr—owf '—shtrikh) Up-bow.
Hertz (Ger.) (hĕrts) The abbreviation is Hz. Heinrich
  Rudolph Hertz was first to detect and measure elector-
  magnetic waves. The term Hertz is used in place of
  cycles per second.
Herunterstrich (Ger.)(hĕr—o̐on '—tĕr—shtrĭkh) Down-bow.
Hervortretend (Ger.)(hĕr—fô r '—trä—tĕnt) Prominent. Em-
  phasized.
Herzhaft (Ger.)(hĕrts '—häft) Hearty, bold.
Herzig (Ger.)(hĕr '—tsi k) Tender, lovable.
Herzlich (Ger.) (hĕrts '—likh) Affectionate; tenderly.
Hesitation step A ballroom dance during the 1920's in
  which the music and dance paused within each alternate measure.
Hesitation waltz A waltz popular after World War I, having a step alternating between a pause and glide.
Heterometric Individual parts have metric and rhythmic
  independence.
Heterophony (Greek) Variations or ornamentations in the
  melody which are introduced by the performers. Performance of the same melody by two or more performers simultaneously with the addition of their variations. Also, the harmonic and rhythmic independence
  of individual parts.
Hexachord (Greek) (1) A diatonic scale system in medieval theory of Guido d'Arezzo in which the scale of
  six tones has the intervals: whole step, whole step, half
  step, whole step, whole step. E.g., hard hexachord, G, A,
  B, C, D, E; natural hexachord, C, D, E, F, G, A; soft
  hexachord, F, G, A, Bb, C, D. Hexa means six. (2) An
  instrument having six strings. See *Diatonic, *Scale.
Hidden fifths Fifths reached by similar motion rather than
  by parallel motion. See *Parallel fifths.
Hidden octaves Octaves reached by similar motion rather
  than by parallel motion. See *Parallel octaves.
High Mass The Roman Catholic service (Mass) in which

175

the choir and priest sing the liturgy, as opposed to the Low Mass which is spoken. Also called Solemn Mass.

Hi-hat cymbals The jazz drummer used this type of cymbal. Two cymbals are mounted on a stand and operated by a foot pedal which crashes the two together.

Hilfslinie (Ger.)(hĭlfs'—lē—nå) An added line. A ledger line.

Hilfsnote (Ger.)(hĭlfs'—nō—tå) An added note. An auxiliary note.

Hilfstimme (hĭlf'—shtĭm—må)A mutation stop.

Hillbilly music Country and Western music. A combination of elements from folk music and popular music. Music of the mountain areas and southern area of the United States.

Hinsterbend (Ger.)(hĭn'—shtĕr—bĕnt)Dying away. Softer and slower.

Hinstrich (Ger.)(hĭn'—shtrĭkh)Up-bow.

His (Ger.) (hĭss) B sharp (B#).

Hisis (Ger.) (hiss'—ĭss) B double sharp (B×) (B##).

History, General Musical Periods Middle Ages (c. 500-1450) Early Middle Ages (c. 600-850), Gregorian chant c. 600, monophony, plainsong, chant. Romanesque (c. 850-1150). Gothic (c. 1150-1450), polyphony; School St. Martial 1150, School Notre Dame 1175. Ars antiqua, 13th century. Ars nova, 14th century. Renaissance (c. 1430-1600), Burgundian School, early 15th century, Flemish School, late 15th century. Baroque (1575-1750), Nuove Musiche (1600). Rococo, gallant style (1700). Classical (1725-1800), Mannheim School (1750), Emfindsamkeit (1750-1800), Berlin School (1750-1800), Viennese School, 18th century. Romantic (1800-1910), Nationalism. Impressionism, late 19th and early 20th centuries. Twentieth century, new music. These periods overlapped.

H moll (Ger.) (hä mawl) Key of B minor.

Hoboe (Ger.)(hō—bō'—å) (Also, hoboy, hautbois (Fr.) (ō—bwä), hautboy (English)) Oboe.

Hoboy English name for oboe. Another spelling for hautboy.

Hosanna in excelsis Benedictus qui venit in nomine Domini. Hosanna in excelsis." In English: "Holy, Holy, Holy, Lord God of Hosts. Heaven and earth are filled with Your glory. Hosanna in the highest. Blessed is He Who comes in the name of the Lord. Hosanna in the highest." Examples: Hector Berlioz (1803-1869), *Requiem* (Sanctus); Charles Francois Gounod (1818-1893), oratorio *Mors et Vita* (Hosanna); Giovanni Palestrina (1524-1594) a Mass, *Assumpta est Maria* (Hosanna). See *Mass.

Hot jazz (1) A complex and fiery type of jazz. For example, bop, bebop or rebop. (2) A period of jazz (1940-1950). See *Jazz.

Humoresque (Fr.) (ü—mōr—ĕsk) A piece of music which is of a light or humorous character. Example: Antonin Dvořák (1841-1904) *Humoresque for Piano,* Opus 101, No. 7.

Hunting horn An early type horn which had a conical bore, a bell and a cup mouthpiece. It was coiled and rested on the shoulder. Used for hunting calls.

Hüpfend (Ger.) (hüp '—fĕnt) Hopping. Jumping bow or hopping bow, as in spiccato bowing.

Hurdy-gurdy (vielle, (Fr.)) A stringed instrument of medieval times. The body resembled that of the lute. It had keys and a wooden wheel rather than a bow. Some strings were used to play the melody while others played a drone bass. The tone was produced by cranking a rosined wheel which touched the strings. The pitches were changed by pressing a key attached to a rod which stopped a string.

Hurtig (Ger.)(hŏor '—tĭ k) Quick. Allegro.

Hymn A song or ode in praise of God, Holy Mary, saints, etc. A short lyric song of a religious nature. The hymn is designed to be sung by a congregation or choir in churches. Some important types of hymns are (1) translations of psalms, (2) English hymns, (3) Lutheran chorales, (4) Latin hymns.

Hyper (Greek) Above or upper.

Hypo (Greek) Below or lower. A prefix used in identifying certain modes such as Hypoaeolian, Hypodorian, Hypoionian, Hypolydian, Hypomixolydian, Hypophrygian. See *Church modes, *Modes.

Hz The abbreviation for Hertz. See *Hertz.

I

I (1) (It.) (ē) The. (2) The Roman numeral for one, e.g., used to identify a tonic or I chord.

Iamb (iambic, iambus) A metrical foot of two syllables, a short syllable followed by a long syllable. See *Iambic meter, *Meter.

Iambic meter Musical meter in which the rhythm begins on an uanccented beat or syllable at the beginning of each line of music: ‿ — ‿ —

Ictus A rhythmis stress or metrical accent. It is used to group notes or sections when chanting.

Idée fixe (Fr.) (ē—dā fēks) Fixed idea. A term used to identify the reoccuring motto theme in the *Symphonie Fantastique* by Berlioz (1803-1869).

Idiophone Instruments of the percussion family which do not use a vibrating membrane to produce sound. E.g., rattles, cymbals etc.

Idyl A composition having a pastoral quality, usually an instrumental work.

Il (It.) (ēl) The.

Ilarita (It.)(ē—lär—ē—tä ') Hiliarity.

Il piu (It.) (ēl pē—ōo') The more. The most.

Im (Ger.) (im) A contraction of in dem meaning in the or within the.

Image (Fr.) (ē—mäzh) Picture.

Imbrogliare (It.)(ēm—brŏl—yä '—rā) Embroil or entangle. As in inbroglio (It.). The art of confusion as heard and seen in certain operatic scenes.

Imitando (It.)(ē—mē—tän '—dō) Imitating.

Imitation A technique used in part writing where a melodic line, phrase or figure is restated in various voices one after another forming counterpoint. If the complete line is repeated in all parts, exactly in imitative counterpoint, it would form a canon. This complete imitation of a line is also used in the fugue. The imitative technique is often used with fragments of a line in developing an idea or as accompaniment. See *Canon,

181

*Fugue, *Motet.

Imitativo (It.)(ē—mē—tä—tē '—vō) Imitative.

Immer (Ger.)(ī'—må r) Always.

Impaziente (It.) (ĭm—pä—tsē—ĕn '—tā) Impatient. Impazientemente, (It.)(i m—pä—tsē—ĕn—tē—mĕn'—tā) Eagerly.

Imperfect cadence A half-close, a progression which ends on the five chord. Also, a cadence is said to be imperfect when the top note or bottom note of the last chord in either the plagal or authentic cadence is not the tonic note of the chord. The tonic chord at the end is in a position other than the root position. A perfect cadence (full close) requires that the final chord be a tonic chord and that the tonic be in the soprano voice. See *Cadence, *Plagal, *Authentic.

Imperfect intervals Intervals of the major or minor third or sixth.

Imperfect time A time division in mensural notation. A note in imperfect time which equalled two of the next lower note values. For example, in imperfect time the breve equalled two semibreves. See *Prolation, *Perfect time.

Impetuoso (It.) (ĭ m—pĕ—tōo—ō '—zō) Impetuous or dashing.

Imporre (It.) (ĭ m—pŏ'—rā) Impose.

Imposant (Fr.) (ä(m)—pō—zä(n)) Imposing.

Impresario (It.)(i m—prā—zä '—rē—ō)A director or manager of an opera company, ballet company, concert group, theater, etc.

Impressionism A period of music of the late 19th century and early 20th century which is represented by such composers as Ravel, Debussy, Delius, de Falla, etc. The term is borrowed from the painting movement represented by such artists as Renoir, Degas, Monet, Manet, who painted first Impressions and left vague lines. These artists were concerned with the outer world rather than the inner self. The symbolists writers (Mallarmé, Verlaine, and Baudelaire) also represented this period in their use of words and phrases. New meanings and sounds were developed. The entire movement was a reaction against the German movement which relied so heavily on form and structure. The impressionists rejected form, moved toward subjectivity and vagueness. Techniques in music: use of the whole tone scale, new harmonies, new chordal progressions, new instrumentation and use of instruments, a moving away from strict tonal centers and strict measured music to subtle rhythms. Generally, a movement away from the German Romantic school of the 19th century toward a new 20th century concept.

Impromptu (Fr.) (ă(m)—prō(m)—tü) A 19th century term that conveyed the impression that a composition was being played extemporaneously or being improvised. Actually, the piece is structured and has form. Example: Frédéric Chopin (1810-1849) *Impromptu for Piano,* Opus 29.

Improperia (Lat.) The reproaches. The antiphons or chants sung on Good Friday in the Roman Catholic Church. From the 16th century on some were set in choral style.

Improvisation To create music as one plays. To extemporize. For example: when using counterpoint; figured bass; when using fauxbourdon; a descant; variations; and in jazz improvisation.

Im takt (Ger.) (ĭm täkt) In rhythm; in time.

In (It. and Lat.) (ĕn) In, into.

In alt (It.) (ēn ält) The notes above the treble clef (g″ to f‴) are said to be in alt.

Incalzando (It.)(ĭ n—käl—tsän '—dō) Hastening.

Incarnatus (Lat.)(ĭn—kär—nä '—tōos) In the "Credo" of the Mass, the middle section reads: "Et incarnatus est de Spiritu Sancto ex Maria Virgine: Et Homo Factus Est." Translated it reads: "and was made Flesh by the Holy Spirit of the Virgin Mary: And Was Made Man." This is sung by the choir during the High Mass of the Roman Catholic Church. See *Mass.

Incidental music (1) Music written to be played as a parallel or to accompany a play. It associates with the play in mood and style. E.g., Felix Mendelssohn (1809-

1847) Music for a *Midsummer Night's Dream*. (2) Music between acts, overtures, interludes, etc.

Incisivo (It.) (ĭn–chē–sě '–vō)Incisive.

Incominciare (It.)(ĭn–kō–min–chē–ä'–rā)Start, begin.

Incordare (It.) (in–kōr–dä'–rā) To string; as in putting a string on an instrument.

Indeciso (It.)(ĭn–dä–chē '–zō)Undecided.

Indicare (It.)(in–dē–kä'–rā) Indicate. Point out.

Inégales See *Notes inégalis.

Inferiore (It.)(ĭn–fā–rē–ō '–rā)Lower; under.

Infinite canon Circle canon or perpetual canon. One that leads back to the beginning and is repeated over and over again, e.g., a round. See *Canon, *Circle canon, *Perpetual canon.

Inflection The inflection is the slight variation in pitch up or down during the singing of a chant or the recitation of a liturgical text. It relieves the monotonous tone and style of recitative.

Ingannevole (It.) (ĭn–gän–nā '–vō–lä) Deceptive; as in a deceptive cadence.

Inglese (It.)(ĭn–glä'–zā) English.

Innig (Ger.) (in '–nik)Intimate; warm feeling.

Inno (It.)(in '–nō)Hymn.

In Nomine Patris (Lat.) (ĭn nō '–mē–nā pä '–trēs) (1) Said at the beginning of the Mass: "In Nomine Patris, et Filii, et Spiritus Sancti. Amen." Translated: "In the name of the Father, and the Son, and the Holy Spirit. Amen." Also, following the "Sanctus" and the "Benediction": "Benedictus qui venit in nomine Domini." Translated: "Blessed is He Who comes in the name of the Lord." (2) Sixteenth and 17th century compositions using an antiphon as a cantus firmus are called In Nomine.

Input language In electronic music the code used to give instructions when programming an electronic instrument.

Inquiet (Fr.) (ǎ(n)–kē–ā) Uneasy, restless.

Insieme (It.) (ĭn–sē–ā '–mä) Ensemble; together.

Inständig (Ger.) (in '–shtěn–dǐ k) Earnest; urgent.

Instantemente (It.) (ĭn–stän–tā–mĕn'–tā)Urgently. Instantly.

Instrument à cordes (Fr.) (ă(n)–strü–mä(n) tä kôrd) An instrument having strings.

Instrumental music Music designed to be played on instruments.

Instrumentation Orchestrating for orchestra, band or ensemble. The writing and arranging of parts for instruments. The listing of instrumental parts on a score.

Instrument à vent (Fr.) (ă(n)–strü–mă(n) tä vĕ(n)) Instruments of the wind family.

Instrumento da fiato (It.)(ĭn–strōō–mĕn'–tō dä fē–ä'–tō) Instruments of the breath (wind instruments).

Instrumento da percotimento (It.)(ĭn–strōō–mĕn'–tō dä pĕr–kō–tē–mĕn'–tō)An instrument to strike. Percussion.

Instrumento da tastiera (It.)(ĭn–strōō–mĕn'–tō dä täs–tē–ä'–rä)Keyboard instrument.

Instruments Some examples by family. Stringed instruments: piano (also percussion and keyboard), violin, viola, violoncello, string bass (bass viol), viol instruments, guitar family, lute family, zithers, lyres, harps, etc. Woodwind family: flute, piccolo, clarinet, alto clarinet, bass clarinet, contra-bass clarinet, basset horn, oboe, English horn, bassoon, contra-bassoon, recorders. Brass instruments: cornet, trumpet, French horn, flügelhorn, trombone, baritone (euphonium) tuba, saxhorns, helicon, horn family, etc. Percussion instruments: kettle drum, xylophone, glockenspiel, bells, celesta, snare drum, bass-drum, military drum, cymbals, gong, marimba, tambourine, bongos, castanets, chimes, triangle, etc. Keyboard instruments: celesta, piano, organ, harpsichord, clavichord, etc.

Interlude (1) A piece of music played between other musical pieces. (2) Music played between acts or within an act between stage action. (3) Interludes (often improvised) played between verses of a hymn. (4) A title of a work or an incidental piece. (5) Interludes are also used in the accompanied vocal fugue. A sec-

185

tion, different from the theme, which appears between a theme and its repetition, within a song, is called an interlude. See *Entr'acte, *Intermezzo.

Interludio (It.) (ĭn—tĕr—lōō'—dē—ō) Interlude.

Intermède (Fr.) (ă(n)—tĕr—mĕd) Interlude.

Intermezzo (1) A piece played between the acts of an opera or drama. For example: Pietro Mascagni (1863-1945), "Intermezzo" from the opera *Cavalleria Rusticana*. (2) A separate musical composition. (3) Part of an extended work. An example of a comic intermezzo is "La serva padrona" which was performed in 1733 between the acts of the opera *Il prigionero superbo* by Giovanni Pergolesi (1710-1736). See *Entr'acte.

Interpretation To bring forth the meaning of a work. A personal factor in the performance of a work which exhibits an understanding of the score with reference to the style, period, form, technique, etc, as well as a personal involvement with the music. A personal translation of the printed score which forms a bridge from the composer, through the score, to the listener.

Interrupted cadence A deceptive cadence. The dominant chord moves to a chord other than the tonic. For example, usually from the V chord to VI:

Interval The space between two tones on a scale. The difference in pitch. Two separate tones sounded in succession form a melodic interval. The harmonic interval from c' to e' above is an interval of a third, from c' to f' above is a fourth, from c' to g' above is a fifth, etc, The interval is counted from the root (one) and every line

186

and space inclusively to the top note. The number identifies the size of the interval while major, minor, diminished, augmented and perfect identify the kind or type of interval. Intervals of a 4th, 5th or octave may be perfect, augmented or diminished, while intervals of a 2nd, 3rd, 6th, or 7th may be major, minor, augmented or diminished. The intervals of a unison or octave use the same note or the octave. Compound intervals are those beyond the octave and are identified in the same manner as the simple intervals which are within the octave. E.g., an interval of a major 9th from c' to d" is treated as the major 2nd from c' to d', etc. Examples of some intervals:

Maj 3ʳᵈ Min 3ʳᵈ Dim 3ʳᵈ Aug 3ʳᵈ   Perfect 5ᵗʰ Dim 5ᵗʰ Aug 5ᵗʰ

For a further discussion see *Essentials of Music* (1969) by V. J. Picerno. See *Major, *Minor, *Augmented, *Diminished, *Perfect.

Intimo (It. and Sp.) (i n '–tē–mō) Intimate.

Intona A mechanical hand-cranked instrument having a circular and perforated disc, bellows, valves, and an air chamber. The levers and bellows were activated by the cranks as the disc turned.

Intonation (1) The production of a tone with reference to pitch and tone quality. (2) The opening tones by the cantor, or a few strings, in Gregorian chant just before the rest join singing. Also known as Incipit, which in Latin means, "it begins".

Intoning To produce a series of tones. To chant on one tone. Sing in a monotone style.

Intrada (It.) (in–trä '–dä) An introduction, entrance, prelude or overture. In the 17th century the first movement of a suite or overture. See *Entrada.

Intrepidamente (It.)(i n–trā–pē–dä–měn '–tä)Fearlessly; boldly.

Introduction Generally, a preliminary or opening strain in a piece of music. E.g., introduction to a movement. It can be a single chord or group of chords or as elaborate as a complete movement.

Introit The first part of the Proper of the Roman Catholic Mass which is one of the changeable parts of the Mass. It consists of an antiphon and psalm followed by the "Gloria Patri". The anitphon is repeated after the "Gloria".

Invention A short musical piece in contrapuntal style. E.g., J. S. Bach (1685-1750) clavier pieces written in two-part counterpoint (inventions) and his three-part inventions.

Inversion An interval is inverted when the lower note is placed an octave above or the upper note is placed an octave below. E.g.,

Maj 6th   min 3rd   inversion

See *Harmonic inversion. A chord is inverted when the notes are placed in a position other than the normal root position.

root position   1st inversion   2nd inversion
F chord   F6 chord   F6 chord
                      3   4

A chord consisting of root, 3rd, 5th, and 7th could have its inversions marked as follows using the V7 in F Major as an example:

root postion   1st inversion   2nd inversion   3rd inversion
V7   V6   V4   V2
                 5   3

A melody is inverted when the size of the interval from note to note moves in the opposite direction.

188

Eg.

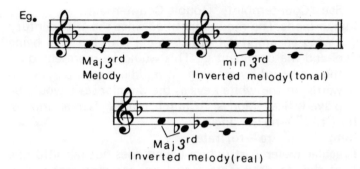

Maj 3rd
Melody

min 3rd
Inverted melody(tonal)

Maj 3rd
Inverted melody(real)

The inversion would be identified as real if the exact intervals were used.

Inversion canon The melody is used in its inversion when imitated. A canon may be inverted by retrograde motion.

Inverted mordent A Baroque ornament which turns on the upper note. It was called Schneller until about 1800, after that the German name Pralltriller is used. The turn is usually played on the upper two notes in a descending second. An example:

WRITTEN   PLAYED(on beat)

OR

See *Mordent.

Invertible counterpoint Counterpoint, double counterpoint, triple counterpoint, etc., so designed that an upper part can be played in the lower voice and the lower part can be played in the upper voice. An example of invertible counterpoint at the octave can be seen in the "Prelude XX in A Minor" by J. S. Bach (1685-1750) from *The Well-Tempered Clavier*, Book II.

See *Counterpoint, *Double Counterpoint.

Ionian mode The mode identified since the 16th century having an ambitus from c' to c'', with the final being c' and the dominant g'. This would be represented on the keyboard by starting on middle c and playing upwards on the white keys as the C major scale would be played. See *Modes, *Church modes, *Greek modes.

Ira (It.) (ē'–rä) Ire, anger.

Irato (It.) (ē–rä'–tō) Irate.

Irregular meter A structure which does not fall into one of the standard meters, such as: common meter; dactylic meter; etc. See *Meter.

Isometric All voices move in the same rhythm.

Isorhythmic The repetition of the same rhythmic phrase, usually in the tenor part. Often used in the 14th century motets.

Istesso tempo, L' (It.) (lēs tĕs'–sō tĕm'–pō) The same time. A marking used when the meter changes, but the music is to move at the same speed. E.g., if the tempo was moving at M.M. ♩ = 120 in $\frac{2}{4}$ time, a march tempo, and the music changed to $\frac{6}{8}$ time, the term l'istesso tempo would require that the music continue to move in two at the same speed. The M.M. would be ♩. = 120.

Italian sixth chord An augmented sixth chord. It often occurs on the flatted submediant of a major scale or the submediant of the minor scale. It consists of an interval of a major third and an augmented sixth. A first inversion. An example of the Italian sixth chord in the key of G major:

See *Sixth chord, *Augmented.

It cum spiritu tuo. Ite, Missa est (Lat.) (it kŏom spǐr'–ē– tōo tōo'–ō. ē'–tä, mis'–sä ĕst) A part of the conclusion or final prayers of the Ordinary of the Roman Catholic Mass. Following is the Final Prayer which is sung at High Mass or spoken at Low Mass (now in English or the vernacular).

Latin	English
Priest — Dominus vobiscum	The Lord be with you.
Response — Et cum spiritu tuo.	And with your spirit.
Priest — Ite, Missa est.	Go, you are dismissed.
Response — Deo gratias.	Thanks be to God.

See *Mass.

Jack The vertical piece of wood to which a plectrum is attached. The jack rises causing the quill to pluck the string of the harpsichord when the key is depressed. See *Harpsichord.

Jagd (Ger.) (yäkt) Hunt; chase.

Jagdhorn (Ger.) (yägd'—hôrn) Hunting horn.

Jagdstück (Ger.) (yägd'—shtük) Hunting piece or chase music.

Jäger (Ger.) (yĕ'—gä̊ r) Hunter.

Jaleo (Sp.) (hä—lä'—ō) A national dance of Spain in a moderately slow $\frac{3}{8}$ time. It is performed by one dancer with castanets or hand clapping as accompaniment.

Jämmerlich (Ger.) (yĕm'—mår—lĭ kh) Miserable or lamenting style.

Jam session An impromptu or informal gathering of jazz musicians who improvise on jazz tunes. See *Jazz.

Janko keyboard One of the many attempts to improve the keyboard. A late 19th century keyboard on which the keys were set in a series of six rows. See *Keyboard.

Jarabe (Sp.) (hä—rä'—bä) A Spanish dance of the 19th century.

Jargon The peculiar language used by jazz musicians to communicate musical ideas.

Jaw's harp Probably a corruption of Jew's harp. See *Jew's harp.

Jazz A term used to identify a type of popular music introduced during the early 20th century. It was both vocal and instrumental and was often associated with dancing. It was both written music and improvised music. Some characteristics or elements of jazz are: syncopation; jazz interpretation; often improvised specific types of rhythms; definite forms and structure; certain types of musical instruments; certain combinations of instruments; special ways of playing instruments (vibrato, mutes, etc.); and the blues scales and notes. Several styles of jazz have contributed to the whole of American jazz: Dixieland—New Orleans style at the turn of the century; Ragtime—at the end of the 19th century and into the 20th century (a piano style of playing jazz); the 1920 Chicago style; Boogie-Woogie (piano style of the 1930's); the swing bands of the 1930's and 1940's; the bebop style of the 1940's: the cool jazz of the 1950's; the hard bop around 1960; and the newer third stream jazz, soul jazz, and avant-garde jazz. See *Blue notes, *Symphonic jazz, *Blues, *"A Selected Annotated Bibliography", as well as separate entries listed above.

Jazz band The various combinations of instruments needed to play certain styles and types of jazz music. Often, it included a rhythm section, stringed bass, guitar, and a number of solo instruments of the saxophone family, clarinet, trumpet, trombone, piano, etc. The size of the group varied. See *Jazz.

Jedoch (Ger.) (yā—dŏ kh ') However. Nevertheless.

Jeter (Fr.) (zhě—tā) Throw. Also, jeté (Fr.) A bowing mark meaning to throw the bow on the string and allow it to bounce and produce a series of notes, usually on the down bow. Also called ricochet bow.

Jeu (Fr.) (zhû) Play, game. A stop of rank of organ pipes.

Jeu d'anche (Fr.) (zhû dä(n)sh) Reed stop of the organ.

Jeu de clochettes (Fr.) (zhû dû klōsh—ě t) Glockenspiel.

Jew de fonds (Fr.) (zhû dû fō(n)) Foundation stops.

Jeu de timbres (Fr.) (zhû dû tǎ (m)br) Glockenspiel.

Jew's harp A lyre-shaped instrument made of metal with a spring-like metal tongue. The instrument is held in the mouth while the finger vibrates the metal strip running through the center of the instrument. Pitches change as the tongue, lips, and cheeks change position.

Jig A lively piece of music and dance. It is fast, light, and usually found in meters of $\frac{6}{8}$ or $\frac{12}{8}$ as well as others. See *Gigue.

Jive talk Jazz talk. The language or jargon relative to popular music introduced around the 1940's. Jive. Swing music.

Jodel See *Yodel.

Jodeln (Ger.) (yō'—då ln) Yodel.

Joint The detachable section of a woodwind instrument.

Jongleur (Fr.) (zhō(n)—glŏor) Juggler. During the medieval period (c. 11th and 12th centuries) the traveling minstrels of France who spread news, joy, music, etc. were called Jongleurs.

Joropo (Sp.) (hō—rō'—pō) A ballroom dance of Venezuela.

Jota (Sp.) (hō'—tä) A popular dance of northern Spain performed with castanets by one or more couples. It has elaborate rhythms and is in rapid triple time. Example: the "Jota" from the *Suite Populaire Espagñole for Violin and Piano* by Manuel de Falla (1876-1946).

Jouer (Fr.) (zhōo—ā) To play.

Jovialisch (Ger.) (yō—vi ä'—li sh) Jovial, joyous.

Joyeux (Fr.) (zhwä—yû) Joyful.

Jubilate (Lat.) (yōo—bē—lä'—tä) Rejoice (1) Jubilate Sunday. The third Sunday after Easter. (2) A musical setting. Psalm.

Jubilee In Negro folk music a folk song concerned with the future and possible happiness.

Just A term used to describe consonant intervals.

Just intonation A system of tuning which would require that the intervals of a scale be tuned in true ratios. Equal temperament allows a given piano key or tone to be used in several scales and tonal relationships. A just scale would require many more keys on a piano as each key would be in exact ratio, or tuned perfectly, and would apply in one situation and for one scale. See *Temperament.

K

K For Ludwig Köchel (1800-1877), who listed the works of Mozart in chronological order. The letter K is used before the number. Also, K.V. for Köchel—Verzeichnis.

Kadenz (Ger.) (kä—dĕnts') Cadence.

Kalt (Ger.) (kält) Cold.

Kammer (Ger.) (käm'—mȧr) Chamber or room.

Kammerkantate (Ger.) (käm—mȧr—kän—tä'—tȧ) Chamber cantata.

Kammermusik (Ger.) (käm'—mȧr—mōō—sēk') Chamber music.

Kammerton (Ger.) (käm'—mȧr—tōn) Chamber pitch. Standard pitch. E.g., 440 double vibrations for a'.

Kanon (Ger.) (kä'—nŏn) Canon.

Kanonisch (Ger.) (kä—nŏn'—i sh) Canonical.

Kantate (Ger.) (kän—tä'—tȧ) Cantata.

Kapell (Ger.) (kä—pĕl'—lȧ) Chapel. A musical group, e.g., band, orchestra. A private group. See *Kapelle-meister.

Kapellmeister (Ger.) (kä—pĕl'—mīs—tȧr) Director of music, conductor. Originally, a director of music in the chapel of a nobleman, for an establishment or a court.

Karnal An old trumpet of Persia.

Kastagnetten (Ger.) (käs—tän—yĕt'—ĕ n) Castanets.

Kazoo Also called mirliton. A toy instrument shaped like a tube with a membrane stretched inside. The performer hums into the instrument which produces a sound similar to that produced by humming into a comb and tissue.

K. B. The German abbreviation of Kontrabass.

Keck (Ger.) (kĕk) Bold, saucy or fearless.

Keirnine A small Irish harp.

Kent bugle A keyed bugle, or Kenthorn. An instrument. the pitch, size, and shape of a bugle but with side holes which were opened and closed by means of keys similar to those of the saxophone. It was invented about 1810 and used during the first half of the 19th century.

Kenthorn (Ger.) (kĕnt'—hôrn) See *Kent bugle.

Kesseltrommel (Ger.) (kĕs'–så l–trŏm–må l) Kettledrum or timpani.

Kettledrum A large brass or copper pot-like instrument over which a skin or plastic head is stretched. The pitch is true and can be changed by adjusting the tension either by hand or by using pedals. The tone is produced by striking the head with a stick covered with a soft material. See *Timpani.

Key (1) A piano key. (2) The lever or action part of various types of keyboard instruments. (3) A lever on a wind instrument. (4) A key signature identifies a key or tonal center. (5) The tonal center of a series of notes. (6) A mode, such as major or minor. Tonality. Tone or pitch. See *Tonality, *Scale.

Keyboard The row of keys (played with the fingers) on piano, organ, harmonium, etc. The manuals on organ or harpsichord. The pedal keyboard of the organ played with the feet. The following is an example of the piano keyboard with 88 black and white keys from A'' to c'''''. Example – see next page ⟶

Keyboard instruments Any instrument having a keyboard. Examples: organ, harpsichord, clavichord, piano, accordian.

Key bugle See *Kent bugle.

Key center Tonal center. Key. See *Tonic.

Keyed guitar An instrument used during the 18th century. A mechanical piece, which had a series of buttons to which plectra were attached, was added over the bridge of the English guitar. The player pressed the buttons to vibrate the strings. See *Guitar.

Keynote Tonic or key center. The note that identifies the name of the key or scale. The tonic of the scale. See *Tonic.

Key relationship The relationship between keys, especially: (1) relative; the relative minor and major key share the same signature (e.g., F major and D minor); (2) parallel; the tonic minor begins on the same note as its tonic or parallel major (e.g., F major and F minor; (3) related; the more similar the key signature the closer the relationship, i.e., the key of F is more

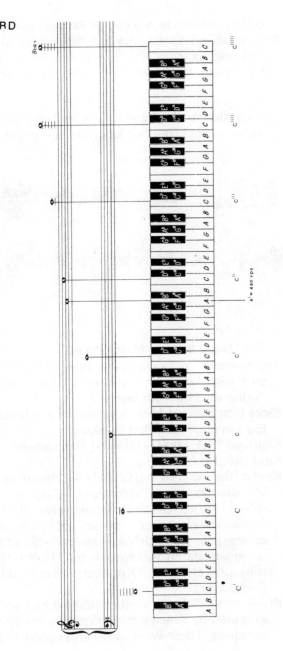

197

closely related to the key of B♭ than to the key of C♭.

Key signatures The sharps and flats placed after the clef and used to identify a key. Following are the key signatures of the major and minor (treble clef 𝄞).

Note that each signature serves both the major and minor mode. Tonic or key note, x = major, o = minor.

C Major G Maj. D Maj. A Maj. E Maj. B Maj. F♯ Maj. C♯ Maj.
a Minor e Min. b Min. f♯ Min. c♯ Min. g♯ Min. d♯ Min. a♯ Min.

F Maj. B♭ Maj. E♭ Maj. A♭ Maj. D♭ Maj. G♭ Maj. C♭ Maj.
d Min. g Min. C Min. f Min. b♭ Min. e♭ Min. a♭ Min.

See *Major scales, *Minor scales.

Key trumpet Trumpets having side holes which were covered with keys. An instrument which was developed during the late 18th century.

Kicks (Ger.) (ki ks) Miss. A reference to a break in a tone. E.g., an oboe tone that breaks.

Kielflügel (Ger.) (kēl '–flü–gå l) Harpsichord.

Kind (Ger.) (ki ṇt) Child.

Kirche (Ger.) (ki rkh '–a) Church. Kirchen (Ger.) (ki rkh '–ån) Church-like. Kirchkantate, (Ger.) (ki rkh '–kän–tä '–tå) Church cantata. Kirchenmusik, (Ger.) (ki rkh '–å n–mōō –zēk ') Sacred music, church music. Kirchensonate, (Ger.) (ki rkh '–å n–zō–nä '–tå) Church sonata or sonata da chiesa. Kirchenton, (Ger.) (ki rkh '–å n–tōn) Church mode. Kirchlich, (Ger.) (ki rkh '–li kh) Ecclesiastical.

Kit A small violin or pocket fiddle about sixteen inches long used by dancing masters during the 18th and 19th centuries. There were also earlier models shaped like a rebec. The kit was also used in the 16th and 17th centuries and probably earlier. Also known as pochette.

Kithara An ancient Greek musical instrument which looked like the lyre and was plucked by the fingers. It had a soundbox of wood which had two parallel and lateral arm-like sections across which a bar was extend-en and upon which were attached the upper ends of the strings. It looked rather like an elaborate horseshoe with strings. Also, cithara.

Kitsch (Ger.) (kǐ tsh) Also, kitschig, (Ger.) (kǐ tsh '–ǐ k) Gaudy. Art, music, or literature of little aesthetic value and produced to satisfy popular taste.

Klagend (Ger.) (klä '–gȧ nt) Plaintive, lamenting.

Klang (Ger.) (kläng) Ring or sound. Klangboden, (Ger.) (kläng '–bō—dȧ n) Soundboard. Klangfarbe, (Ger.) (kläng '–fär—bȧ) Timbre or tone colour.

Klangfarbenmelodie (Ger.) (kläng '–fär—bȧ n—mā—lō—dē ') Klangfarbe in German means tone color. The term Klangfarbenmelodie is a term used by Schoenberg (1874-1951) and Webern (1883-1945) to identify a method of composing on a melodic line using various tone colors on a single pitch and on varying pitches. The note values and dynamic levels would also vary with individual notes of the melodic line. This method requires that timbre be a most important element in the composition and that timbre be used thematically. The importance placed on tone color is noted in *Five Pieces for Orchestra (Fünf Orchestücke),* Opus 16 by Schoenberg, new version (reduced to normal sized orchestra by the composer) especially, in the piece called *Summer Mornings by a Lake* (colors). The color is so important in this piece, that in the Peters Edition (#6061), they find it necessary (pg. 31) to give the conductor specific directions; "The change of chords in this piece has to be executed with the greatest subtlety, avoiding accentuation of entering instruments, so that only the difference in color becomes noticeable." They also direct the conductor to see that the dynamics are played accurately.

Klappe (Ger.) (kläp'–å̊) Key, flap, lid or valve. E.g., a key of a wind instrument.

Klappenhorn (Ger.) (kläp'–å̊n–hôrn) Key bugle or Kent bugle.

Klar (Ger.) (klär) Clear.

Klarinette (Ger.) (klär–ē̆–nĕt'–å̊) Clarinet.

Klausel (Ger.) (klow'–zå̊l) Clause or cadence.

Klavarskribo An early 20th century system of musical notation. The system centered around the use of vertical staff lines upon which the black and white keys of the keyboard were shown by dark and light printing.

Klaviatur (Ger.) (klä–vē–ä–toor') Keyboard.

Klavier (Ger.) (klä–vēr') (1) Pianoforte. (2) Keyboard instruments employing strings, such as piano, harpsichord, clavichord. Also, clavier.

Klavierauszug (Ger.) (klä–vēr–ows'–tsook) A piano score or reduction from a larger score to be played on piano.

Klavierstück (Ger.) (klä–vēr'–shtükh) A piece of music for piano.

Klein (Ger.) (klīn) Small or little. It may also refer to minor when compared with the larger interval of the major.

Kleinbassgeige (Ger.) (klīn–bäs'–gī–gå̊) Small bass violin or violoncello.

Kleine Flöte (Ger.) (klīn'–å̊ flĕ(r)'–tå̊) Piccolo.

Kleine Oktave (Ger.) (klīn'–å̊ ŏk–tä'–vå̊) Little octave from c to c'.

Kleine Trommel (Ger.) (klīn'–å̊ trŏm'–å̊l) Side drum or little drum.

Kleinzink (Ger.) (klīn'–tsĭngk) The Renaissance cornettino. A small obsolete wood cornet.

Klingel (Ger.) (kli ng'–å̊l) Small bell.

Klingen (Ger.) (kling'–å̊n) Ring or sound.

Knarren (Ger.) (knär'–rå̊n) Creak or rattle.

Kneifend (Ger.) (knīf–å̊nt) Pinch, pluck, squeeze. E.g., pizzacato on stringed instruments.

Köchel-Verzeichnis (Ger.) (kĕk'–å̊l–fĕr–tsĭkh'–nĭs) See *K, *K.V.

Koloratur (Ger.) (kō–lō–rä–toor') Grace; Coloratura.

200

Koloraturen, (Ger.) (kō—lō—rä—tōor '—å n) Grace notes.
Koloratursängerin, (Ger.) (kō—lō—rä—tōo r '—zĕ ng '—ĕ r—i n) Florid singer.
Komponieren (Ger.) (kŏ m—pō—nē '—rå n) To compose.
Komponiert, (Ger.) (kŏm—pō—nē rt ') Composed. Komponist, (Ger.) (kŏm—pō—ni st ') Composer.
Kontra (Ger.) (kŏn '—trä) Counter or contra. Kontrabass (Ger.) (kŏ n '—trä—bäs) Double-bass. Kontrabassklarinette (Ger.) (kŏn '—trä—bäs—klär—ē—nĕ t '—å) Contrabass clarinet. Kontrafagott, (Ger.) (kŏ n '—trä—fä—gŏ t ') Contrabassoon or double-basson. Also, organ stop.
Kontrapunkt (Ger.) (kŏ n—trä—pŏongkt) Counterpoint.
Konzert (Ger.) (kŏ n—tsĕ rt ') Concert or concerto. Konzertmeister (Ger.) (kŏn—tsert '—mi s—tå r) Concert-meister; concert-master. The principal violinist of the orchestra. Also, The leader of an orchestra. Konzertmusik, (Ger.) (kŏ n—tsert '—mōo —zēk ') Concert music. Konzertstück, (Ger.) (kŏn—tsert '—shtükh) Concerted piece or concertino.
Kopf (Ger.) (kŏ pf) Head. Kofpstimme, (Ger.) (kŏpf '—shti m—å) Falsetto or head voice.
Kornett (Ger.) (kŏr—nĕ t ') Cornet.
Koto (Jap.) A national instrument of Japan. A large plucked stringed instrument that looks like a long dulcimer.
Kräftig (Ger.) (krĕf '—ti k) Powerful or robust.
Kreis (Ger.) (kri s) Circle, ring, or cycle.
Kreuz (Ger.) (kroits) Sharp (#).
Kreux-doppelt (Ger.) (kroits-dŏp '—å lt) Double sharp (x or ##).
Krummhorn (Ger.) (krōo m '—hô rn) An obsolete Renaissance double reed woodwind instrument which had a narrow cylindrical tube which curved at the end. The double reed was enclosed in a cover or pierced cap. The player would blow air into the cap to start the reed vibrating. Also called Cromorne.
Kunst (Ger.) (kōonst) Art.
Kunst der Fuge, Die (Ger.) (dē kŏonst dĕr fōo'—gå) (The art of Fugue) Written by J. S. Bach in 1749 and

published after his death in 1750. The work demonstrates (by example) almost every possible contrapuntal technique of writing based on the following theme:

Various devices of imitative counterpoint are found in this work, such as: augmentation, diminution, canon, inversion, double fugue, triple fugue, etc. The work includes fourteen fugues (counterpoints), four canons, and two fugues for two claviers based on the theme shown above. It also includes a fugue on three new subjects, the third subject which is based on the German notation B, A, C, H

B   A   C   H

The choral *Wenn wir in höchsten Nöten sein* was added when published by Marpurg in 1752. The choral has no connection with the work. The score does not give instrumentation. Most of the work, except for "Contrapunctus XII". "Contrapunctus XIII", and part of "Contrapuctus VI" could be played on the keyboard. An orchestral transcription was done by W. Graeser and a transcription for string quartet was done by R. Harris.

Künstlerisch (Ger.) (künst'–lå r–i sh) Artistic.

Kunstlied (Ger.) (ko͝onst'–lēt) Art song.

Kurz (Ger.) (ko͝orts) Short. Staccato. Kurz oktave — short octave.

K.V. Chronological list of all the works of Mozart made by Ludwig von Köchel.

Kyriale The book which contains the music and text for each part of the Ordinary of the Mass.

Kyrie eleison (Greek) (ki'–rē–ā ā–lā'–ē–so͝n) "Lord, have mercy". In the Roman Catholic Mass, the first part or section of the Ordinary of the Mass. It follows the "Introit". The full text of the "Kyrie" is: "Kyrie eleison; Kyrie eleison; Kyrie eleison; Christe eleison; Christe eleison; Christe eleison; Kyrie eleison; Kyrie eleison; Kyrie eleison." It is the only section of the Mass in which the Greek words still exist. Currently the text is sung in the vernacular. The English translation is: "Lord, have mercy; Lord, have mercy; Lord, have mercy; Christ, have mercy; Christ, have mercy; Christ, have mercy; Lord, have mercy; Lord, have mercy; Lord, have mercy." The "Kyrie" is found in music settings ranging from types of Gregorian chant to more elaborate settings in which the "Kyrie" is interpolated (called "farced" Kyrie) into the polyphonic settings. For example: Giovanni Palestrina (1524-1594) *Missa Papae Marcelli* (Kyrie Eleison); "Kyrie" from the *Requiem* by Guiseppi Verdi (1813-1901); the "Kyrie" from the *Mass in B Minor* by J. S. Bach (1685-1750). See *Mass, *Ordinary of the Mass.

L

L (Links, (Ger.) (lĭnks))' An abbreviation of left.
L' (Fr. and It.) The.
La (1) The note A in the fixed system of solmization. (2) The sixth tone of a major scale in the sol-fa system.
La (1) (Fr.) (lä) The. Pron.; her. Là, adv.; there. (2) (It.) (lä) The. Pron.; her. Adv.; there. (3) (Sp.) (lä) The.
La bémol (Fr.) (lä bā—mŏ l) The note A flat (Ab).
Labial Flue pipe. A pipe having a lip rather than a reed.
Labialpfeifen (Ger.) (lä—bē—äl'—pfi —få n) Labial pipes.
Labialstimme, (Ger.) (lä—bē—äl'—shtim—å) Flue stop.
Lacrimosa (Lat.) (lä—krē—mō'—sä) Mournful. A portion of the Requiem Mass. Example: "Lacrimosa" in the Verdi *Requiem* II "Dies Irae".
Lacrimoso (It.) (lä—krē—mō'—zō) Mournful or tearful.
La destra (It.) (lä dĕs'—trä) Right hand. A term used in keyboard music to indicate which hand is to play a section.
Lage (Ger.) (lä'—gå) Location or position. (1) The open or closed position of a chord, root position or inversion. (2) The hand position on a stringed instrument. (3) The range of instruments or voices.
Lagnoso (It.) (län—yō'—zō) Sorrowful.
Lagrimoso (It.) (lä—grē—mō'—zō) Tearful or mournful style of performance.
Lah Form of the Italian la. See *La.
Lai (Fr.) (lā) Poem or song. A medieval love poem or, more rarely, a religious poem, having great metrical variety and irregular stanzas sung to popular tunes. A form (rather irregular) developed by the trouvères in the 13th century which is somewhat like the sequence. However, the lai can be either more elaborate or simpler in that some melodies may be repeated three or four times and others may be presented only once. Early forms were monodic and some later examples had several voices. Examples: the eighteen lais of Machaut (c. 1300-1377) which are in a less irregular form. The

204

German equivalent is the 14th century Leich which adhered more closely to the form of the sequence.

Laisser vibrer (Fr.) (lĕ s—sā vē—brā) To allow to vibrate. Undamped. E.g., let the cymbal ring or the string vibrate.

Lali A large drum used by the poeple of the Fiji Islands.

Lamb of God The English translation of "Agnus Dei". That part of the Ordinary of the Roman Catholic Mass which comes between the "Sanctus" and the "Ite, Missa est". Also used in musical settings. Examples: Giovanni Palestrina (1524-1594), *Missa Papae Marcelli* (Agnus Dei); Giuseppe Verdi (1813-1901), *Requiem* (Agnus Dei). See *Mass, *Agnus Dei.

Lament An expression of sorrow in verse or song. Among Scottish and Irish clans, mournful melodies played on the bagpipe or airs performed at the funeral of a member clansman. Each clan had its own tune or lament.

Lamentando (It.) (lä—mĕ n—tän '—dō) Mourning or lamenting.

Lamentations The three First Lessons from the Lamentations of Jeremiah traditionally sung in the Roman Catholic Church of the Office of Matins on Thursday, Firday, and Saturday of Holy Week. There are several settings of the text. One example, which continues to be used in the Sistine Chapel, is the setting by Palestrina (1588). The first setting was by Okeghem (1474). See *Tenebrae.

Lamento (It.) (lä—mĕn—tō) (1) Music of a sorrowful nature. (2) The sorrowful aria or scene that came before the climax or "Happy ending" of the 17th century opera.

Lamentoso (It.) (lä—mĕ n—tō '—zō) In a lamentable or mournful style of performance.

La mineur (Fr.) (lä mē—nû r) The minor (key or scale) of A.

Lampons (Fr.) (lä(m)—pō(n)) From lamper meaning to drink or gulp. Lampons are drinking songs.

Lancers (1) A sequence of quadrilles. (2) The music for the set of dances.

Lanciare (It.) (län–chē–ä'–rā) To hurl or throw. To move.

Landini cadence A type of cadence called the Landini sixth in which the cadence moves from the leading tone to the submediant to the tonic. The resolution moves in the soprano voice 7 – 6 – 8. Named for Francesco Landini (1325-1397) and used by many composers of the Ars Nova and of the Burgundian School.

See *Cadence.

Ländler (Ger.) (lĕnd'–lå r) A dance of southern Germany or Austria popular during the early 19th century. It was in slow triple time and similar to the slow waltz. Examples are found in the music of Beethoven and Schubert.

Landlied (Ger.) (länd'–lēt) Country song or rustic song.

Lang (Ger.) (läng) Long.

Langsam (Ger.) (läng'–zäm) Slow; in slow tempo, as in adagio or lento.

Langsamer (Ger.) (läng'–zäm–å r) Slower.

Larga (It.) (lär'–gä) See *Large.

Largamente (It.) (lär–gä–mĕ n'–tä) Broadly. The music is to be performed in a full and deliberate style or manner.

Largando (It.) (lär–gän'–dō) See *Allargando.

Large (Fr.) (lärzh) Broad, large, extensive. The longest note or largest value as applied to the medieval system of mensural notation.

Larghetto (It.) (lär–gĕt'–tō) A diminutive of Largo (slow), but the tempo is not as slow as Largo. In a broad style.

Larghissimo (It.) (lär–gĭss'–ē–mō) Very slow.

Largo (It.) (lär'–gō) Wide. Slow, stately, broad. A tempo and style marking.

Largiot (Fr.) (lä–rē–gō) (1) Flageolet or an old small flute. (2) An Organ stop sounding at the nineteenth.

Laud (Sp.) (lä—ōōd´) Lute or type of cittern. See *Ban-durria.

Lauda (It.) (low´—dä) (Laude, plural) Hymn of praise. Italian songs of devotion which date back to the time of St. Francis (c.1182-1226). The 13th century Italian laùde were monophonic hymns, some in varied ternary patterns as appear in the French virelai. The 16th century laude were chordal works having three or four parts and in binary form.

Laudamus te (Lat.) (low—dä´—mōōs tä) "We praise Thee." Part of the "Gloria" in the Ordinary of the Roman Catholic Mass. See *Mass.

Lauda Sion (Lat.) (low´—dä sē´—än) "Praise, O Zion". The Latin name for a sequence sung at the Roman Catholic Mass celebrating the feast of Corpus Christi. It is sung in plainchant style or in one of the many polyphonic settings. Palestrina did a complex setting for eight voices. The text was written by St. Thomas Aquinas.

Laudes (Lat.) One of the Office hours or canonical hours of the Roman Catholic Church. Laudes follows the Matins and is at sunrise. See *Office hours.

Lauds (Lat.) Laudes. The second of the Office hours. See *Laudes.

Läufer (Ger.) (loif´—år) Running passages.

Laune (Ger.) (low´—nå) Whim.

Launig (Ger.) (low´—nik) Humorous.

Launisch (Ger.) (low´—nish) Moody.

Laut (Ger.) (lowt) Loud or aloud. Forte.

Laute (Ger.) (low´—tå) Lute.

Läuten (Ger.) (loit´—å n) Ring, sound.

Lautenclavicymble (Ger.) (lowt´—å n—klä—vē—sim—bl) Lute-harpsichord. Gut strings were used instead of metal strings which produced a tone similar to that of the lute.

Lay A short poem to be sung. A tune.

Le (1) (Fr.) (lü) The. (2) (It. plural) (lä) The.

Leader In America, the leader is the conductor of the group. In Great Britain, the leader is the American equivalent of concert-master.

Leading melody The main melody of a composition.

Leading motive Leading theme. (Leitmotiv, (Ger.)) A recurring theme used to identify a person, place, event, thing, etc.

Leading note The seventh degree of the major scale. The seventh degree of the ascending minor scale in the Harmonic and Melodic forms of minor. A half-step or semitone below the tonic of the scale. The seventh note leads upwards a half-step to the tonic. See *Scales, *Major scales, *Minor scales.

Leading seventh chord A leading note chord. A chord built on the seventh degree of a scale having a minor third and diminished fifth. It is usually resolved to the tonic chord.

Leading tone The note one half-step below the tonic in the major and minor modes. Generally, a tone that tends to lean towards another. See *Leading note.

Lead man In jazz, one who plays the top part, such as the first trumpet player.

Lebendig (Ger.) (lā—bĕn'—dĭk) Alive, lively. Lebendigkeit, (Ger.) (lā—bĕn'—dĭk—kĭt) Vivacity.

Lebhaft (Ger.) (lāb'—häft) Lively, vivacious.

Lecon (Fr.) (lĕ—sō(n)) Study; a lesson; an exercise.

Ledger line A short line placed above or below the staff used to identify notes which are beyond the limits of the staff. E.g.

Also spelled leger line.

Leere Saiten (Ger.) (lā'—rặ zā'—tặn) Open strings.

Legatissimo (It.) (lā—gä—tĭs'—ē—mō) Very smooth.

Legato (It.) (lā—gä'—tō) Bound together. Smooth succession of notes. The opposite of staccato which calls for detached notes.

Legatura (It.) (lā—gä—tōo'—rä) Slur.

Légende (Fr.) (lā—zhă(n)d) Legend or story. Music written in a narrative, romantic style.

Léger (Fr.) (lā—zhā) Light, bouyant.

Leger lines See *Ledger line.

Leggero (It.) (lĕd—jā'—rō) Light.

Leggiadro (It.) (lĕd—jē—ä'—drō) Lovely, graceful.

Leggiero (It.) (lĕd—jē—ä'—rō) Light.

Legno, col (It.) (kōl lĕn'—yō) With the wood. A direction to string players to bounce the wood of the bow on the strings, rather than playing with the hair side of the bow.

Leich (Ger.) (līkh) See *Lai.

Leicht (Ger.) (līkht) Light, easy.

Leid (Ger.) (līt) Sorrow. Leiden, (Ger.) (lī'—dån) Suffering.

Leidenschaftlich, (Ger.) (lī'—dån—shäft—līkh) Impassioned.

Leier (Ger.) (lī'—år) (1) Hurdy-gurdy. (2) Lyre.

Leierkasten (Ger.) (lī'—år—käst—ån) Lyre-box or street organ.

Leise (Ger.) (lī'—zå) Soft, quiet.

Leistung (Ger.) (lī—shtoong) Performance.

Leiten (Ger.) (lī'—tån) Conduct, lead.

Leiter (Ger.) (lī'—tår) Ladder. Scale.

Leitmotiv (Ger.) (līt—mōt—ēf') Leitmotif. Leading motive. A short recurring theme which identifies with a place, person, event, character, etc. The idea of recurring themes is used in earlier and later operas, but the term leitmotiv is particularly applied to the motifs in Wagner's operas. For example, the "Ring". See *Leading motive.

Leitton (Ger.) (līt'—tōn) Leading note or tone.

Lent (Fr.) (lĕ(n)) Slow. Lentement, (Fr.) (lĕ(n)t—ma(n)) Slowly.

Lentamente (It.) (lĕn—tä—mĕn'—tä) Slowly. Lentando, (It.) (lĕn—tän'—dō) To slow down the tempo by degrees.

Lento (It.) (lĕn'—tō) Slow.

Les (Fr.) (lä) The. The plural form of the French articles la and le.

Lesser Doxology The "Gloria Patri" which concludes the psalmns and is part of the Introitus. The text is: "Gloria patri et filio et Spiritui Sancto, sicut erat in principio, et nunc, et semper: et in saeculum saeculorm. Amen". See *Doxology.

209

Lesson (1) A term used to identify primarily keyboard pieces during the 17th and 18th centuries. A group of these pieces formed a suite. (2) Study pieces or pieces used for lessons. E.g., *Forty-two Lessons for the Harpsichord* by Domenico Scarlatti (1685-1757).

Lesto (It.) (lĕs'–tō) Nimbly, lively.

Levare (It.) (lā–vä'–rā) Raise. To lift off.

Levezza (It.) (lā–vĕt'–tsä) Lightness.

Levigare (It.) (lā–vē–gä'–rā) Smooth.

L.H. The abbreviation for left hand.

Liason (Fr.) (lĭ–ĕ–zō(n)) Slur, tie, bind.

Libero (It.) (lē'–bā–rō) Free. Not restrained.

Libre (Fr.) (lēbr) Free; at liberty. Librement. (Fr.) (lē–brå–ma(n)) Without restraint, boldly.

Libretto (It.) (lĭ–brĕt'–tō) (1) The words of an opera or other extended piece of music. (2) A booklet containing the text.

Licenza (It.) (lē–chĕn'–tsä) License or freedom. Liberty in performance.

Lick In jazz, a quick or short jazz phrase. An improvised jazz figure.

Lié (Fr.) (lē–ā) Bound, connected, slurred or tied.

Liebe (Ger.) (lē'–bå) Love.

Liebesflöte (Ger.) (lē'–bås–flĕ (r)–tå) A small flute, now obsolete.

Liebeseige (Ger.) (lē'–bås–gī–gå) Love-violin. The viola d'amore.

Liebeslied (Ger.) (lē'–bås–lēt) Love song.

Liebesoboe (Ger.) (lē'–bås–ō–bō'–å) Love oboe. Oboe d'amore.

Lieblich (Ger.) (lēb'–lĭkh) Lovely.

Lieblich gedackt (Ger.) (lēb'–lĭkh gå–däkt') Organ stops having a lovely or sweet tone.

Lied (Ger.) (lēt) Song. A term used to describe a type of Romantic song with artistic piano accompaniment, especially those composed by Schubert and Brahms. The accompaniment played an important role in interpreting the mood and meaning of the text. Franz Schubert (1797–1828) wrote over 600 such songs.

Example; *Schwanengesang, Fourteen Lieder* by Franz Schubert. Some other composers of lieder are Robert Schumann (1810-1856), Hugo Wolf (1860-1903), Gustav Mahler (1860-1911), Richard Strauss (1864-1949).

Lieder (Ger.) (lēd'—år) Songs.

Liederbuch (Ger.) (lēd'—år—boōkh) Song book. Collections of German songs (15th and 16th centuries). E.g., *Lachamer Liederbuch.*

Liederkreis (Ger.) (lēd'—år—krīs) Song cycle. Several songs relative to the same subject forming a group. E.g., Robert Schumann (1810-1856), *Liederkreis,* Op. 39; Franz Schubert (1797-1828), Die *Winterreise,* Op. 89. See *Song cycle.

Liedersammlung (Ger.) (lēd'—år—zäm—loŏng) A collection of songs.

Liederspiel (Ger.) (led'—år—shpēl) A song-play. Ballad opera. Vaudeville.

Liedertanz (Ger.) (lēd'—år—tänts) Songs and dance.

Liedform (Ger.) (lēd'—fôrm) Song form. Usually identified with what is called ternary form (ABA), but it is also used for binary form, (AB). See *Song form.

Lieto (It.) (lē—ā'—tō) Happy.

Lieve (It.) (lē—ā'—vā) Light.

Ligature, A slur. (1) In vocal music an indication that a group of notes are to be sung on one syllable. (2) A group of notes to be played in one phrase. (3) On an instrument, a group of notes played on one bow or in one breath. (4) A metal band which holds a single reed on a mouthpiece. (5) In mensural notation a notational sign which combined two or more notes. For example: using longa-longa: ascending and descending .

Light opera An operetta. A non-technical term sometimes used to distinguish between an opera which is of a light character and the so-called grand opera.

Lilt A rhythmic and happy tune to be played, piped, or danced in a lively manner. The term is of Scottish origin.

Linear counterpoint The term is used to emphasize the horizontal movement and organization of independent contrapuntal lines of music rather than the harmonic (vertical) relationships preferred by the early 20th century composers. Hindemith and Stravinsky used the term. See *Counterpoint, *Double counterpoint, *Invertible counterpoint.

Liniensystem (Ger.) (lēn'—ĕn—zis—tām) Line-system. A staff or staves.

Lining out A practice used in psalm and hymn singing whereby an individual would present a line of music and text which would then be repeated by the congregation. A form of rote learning. Used in England and America.

Linke Hande (Ger.) (link'—ȧ hän'—dȧ) Left hand.

Lip The embouchure. (1) The manner in which the lips are applied to the mouthpiece of a wind instrument. (2) The lips of a flue pipe.

Lira (It.) (lē'—rä) A bowed-stringed instrument. An instrument of the violin variety used during the 15th and 16th centuries.

Lira da braccio (It.) (lē'—rä dä brät'—chē—ō) A 15th and 16th century bowed stringed instrument (like a fiddle) which had five stopped strings and two open (drone or bourdon) strings which were placed to the side of the finger board. These two side strings could be bowed or plucked. The body was rather flat and the pegs were upright. See *Lira.

Lira da gamba (It.) (lē'—rä dä gäm'—bä) A larger instrument than the lira da braccio. It was held between the knees. The number of strings varied from nine to fourteen plus the two open or drone strings placed to the side of the finger board. See *Lira da braccio.

Lira organizzata (It.) (lē'—rä ôr—gän—ēt—tsä'—tä) An 18th century form of hurdy-gurdy.

Lirico (It.) (lē'—rē—kō) Lyric. Operatic.

Lisciare (It.) (lē—shē—ä'—rä) Smooth.

Liscio (It.) (lē'—shē—ō) Smooth, sleek.

L'istesso tempo (It.) (lis—tĕss'—sō tĕm'—pō) The same tempo is to be continued. See *Istesso tempo, I'.

Litany A luturgical form of prayer. A prayer for help which is often set to music. In the Roman Catholic Church a series of short prayers in which the priest leads and the congregation responds with short phrases, such as "Lord, have mercy" (Kyrie eleison) or "Christ, have mercy" (Christe eleison). The responses are given in a chant on a monotonous tone. It is also used in the Anglican Church. Musical settings are in several styles, such as the plainsong, polyphonic settings by Palestrina and others.

Little Organ Book (Orgelbüchlein, (Ger.)) Forty-six chorale preludes for organ by J. S. Bach (1685-1750).

Liturgical books (1) Books of the Roman Catholic Church. Some examples are: the "Missal" (the Mass); the "Breviary" (service of the Office); the "Gradual" (Mass chants); the "Antiphonal" (Office chants); the "Liber usualis" (a combination of the above), etc. Books which include modern changes in the many services, older books which include chants in various church modes, and special music for processions, functions, etc. (2) The official book issued by individual Protestant churches.

Liturgical dramas (plays). Medieval plays which were centered on Biblical stories. These religious plays included music and acting. The liturgical drama developed from the 11th century tropes and were followed by the 15th and 16th century mysteries. See *Trope, *Mysteries.

Liturgical hours The Office hours of the Roman Catholic Church. See *Office hours.

Liturgical Jazz Jazz music and instruments used to accompany or in association with a sacred service. Many Catholic Churches now have adopted the use of the Folk Mass or liturgical jazz.

Liturgical Mass The setting to music of the text of the Ordinary of the Roman Catholic Mass. See *Mass.

Liturgy A ritual. The official service of a church.

Lituus (Lat.) Crooked staff. (1) A long cavalry trumpet used by the Romans. It had a cup mouthpiece, cylindrical bore, a long tube which curved upwards at the bell, and was pitched in G one octave above the Buscina. (2) The 17th century Krummhorn.

Liuto (It.) (lē—oo'—tō) Lute.

Livre (Fr.) (lēvr) Book. Livre d'heures, (Fr.) prayer-book.

Livret (Fr.) (lē—vrā) Book; libretto.

Lo (1) (It.) (lō). The (pronoun) it, you, him. (2) A Chinese gong. (3) The abbreviation for loco.

Loco (It.) (lō'—kō) Place. An indication to return to the normal or written pitch or range after playing 8va bassa, 8va sopra, or all'ottava. The abbreviation is lo.

Locrian mode A system of twelve modes appeared in Glareanus-Dodekachordon in 1547. Two additional modes, the Locrian and Hypolocrian are sometimes added to the twelve in later writings. The Locrian mode has a range from B to B, a final of B, the dominant is G, and the mediant is D. Modes which have B as the final are rejected as the interval between the first and fifth is diminished, whereas all other modes have a perfect fifth. The Hypolocrian mode has a range from F to F, a final of B, a dominant of E, and a mediant of D. See *Modes, *Church modes.

Long (longa, Lat.) In medieval mensural notation a longa is the second longest note, the largest being the perfect large or maxima (Lat.) and the smaller being the breve. Perfect long = three breves; imperfect long = two breves; perfect large = three longs; imperfect large = two longs. See *Mensural notation.

Long dance Dances performed in a straight line or a curved line in a style similar to that used in the performance of the dance-song. The participants move in line or face each other in place. Other type dances are square, round, rock, modern, etc.

Long drum Usually identified as the tenor drum.

Longeur (Fr.) (lŏ(n)—gûr) Vibrato.

Longue (Fr.) lŏ (n)g Long syllable.

Lontano (It.) (lŏn—tä'—nō) Distant. Far off.

Los (Fr.) (lō) Praise.

Los (Ger.) (lōs) Loose, lax.

Loud pedal The damper pedal on the piano. The right ·

pedal which removes the dampers and allows the strings to continue to vibrate thus sustaining the tone.

Lourdement (Fr.) (lōord—mä(n)) Heavily.

Loure (Fr.) (lōor) (1) A type of 16th century French bagpipe. (2) A dance of the 17th century in a moderate tempo using $\frac{6}{4}$ time.

Louré (Fr.) (lōo —rā) A type of slurred bowing. In a group of slurred notes each note is slightly detached on a given bow stroke.

Lourer (Fr.) (lōo—rā) To tie the notes. See *Louré.

Luftpause (Ger.) (lōoft'—pow—zà) A pause for breath which is indicated by a comma. It is a pause (rest) which is not part of the regular rhythmic scheme.

Lullaby A cradlesong. A gentle or lulling song.

Lunga pausa (It.) (lōon'—gä pä'—ōo —zä) Long pause.

Lungo (It.) (lōon'—gō) Long.

Lur A prehistoric bronze musical horn. Several examples have been found in Sweden and Denmark.

Lusinghevole (It.) (lōo —zēn—gä'—vō—lā) Also, lusinghiero. Flattering, persuading, or in a soothing manner.

Lustig (Ger.) (lōos'—ti k) Merry.

Lute (Luth, Fr.) A stringed instrument which was plucked with the right hand and fingered with the left hand. It had a fretted finger board, a hollow, pear-shaped body and a peg-area which was bent backwards away from the finger board. It was used for solo work or accompaniment. It had eleven strings, ten of which were tuned in pairs called courses. Many sizes were made and the number and function of the strings varied. For example, some lutes had strings added to the side which did not alter in pitch. Some lutes had long necks, others short necks. The instrument was popular during the 16th and 17th centuries, although the lute goes well back into ancient history. See *Frets.

Lutto (It.) (lōot'—tō) Mourning.

Luttuoso (It.) (lōot—tōo—ō'—zō) Sorrowful or mournful.

215

Lydian mode An authentic church mode. It can be demonstrated by playing all the white keys on the piano keyboard in succession from F to F, one octave. The range is from F — F, the final is F, the dominant is C and the mediant is A. See *Modes.

Lyra (1) An ancient Greek instrument. (2) A medieval rebec. (3) Chimes or glockenspiel. See *Glockenspiel, *Libra, *Rebec.

Lyraflügel (Ger.) (lē '—rä—flü—gå l) A 19th century German upright piano made in the shape of a lyre.

Lyra viol The viol bastarda. It was sized between the bass viol and the tenor viol. It was tuned in fourths and fifths which made chords easier to play. Chords were read from a letter tablature.

Lyre An ancient Greek plucked instrument. It had a sound-box of turtle shell, two parallel vertical curved arms, a yoke across the top with the strings extended from the yoke to the body of the instrument. See *Harp.

Lyre aeolian Aeolian harp.

Lyre guitar An 18th century instrument shaped in the fashion of the lyre but having six strings stretched over a fretted finger board which extended from the body of the lyre to the cross-bar above. The finger board and strings were located in the middle of the instrument in a vertical position. See *Lyre.

Lyric (1) Pertaining to the lyre. Sung to the lyre. (2) A musical song-like quality. A cantabile style. (3) A voice category, e.g., Lyric Soprano, Lyric Tenor.

Lyrichord An 18th century harpsichord that had several devices which would give tones sustaining power.

Lyric opera Opera, in which the empahsis is on the expressive and subjective aspects of the work and is lyric or song-like in nature.

Lyrics The words of a song.

Lyrisch (Ger.) (lēr '—ish) Lyric.

M Abbreviation for: mediant; medius (middle voice); mezzo; manual; the third syllable mi in the sol-fa system; medieval; meter; metronome.

Ma (It.) (mä) But.

Machete A four stringed Portuguese guitar. A forerunner of the ukulele. See *Guitar.

Machicotage (Fr.) (mä–shē–kō–täzh) A technique of adding ornamental notes between the basic notes of a plainsong musical line. See *Plainsong.

Machine-head A tuning device used in place of a standard tuning peg. E.g., the metal mechanical tuning gears used on a string bass.

Mächtig (Ger.) (mĕkh'–tik) Powerful.

Machtlos (Ger.) (mäkt'–lōs) Powerless.

Madriale See *Matricale, *Madrigal.

Madrigal Generally, an unaccompanied polyphonic vocal work. It is contrapuntal in style and employs a great deal of imitation among voices. One or more voices may sing each part. It was a very important new form of the Italian Ars nova. The madrigals of Italy during the 14th century had two or three parts. They developed from the conductus. The madrigal was again popular during the 16th and 17th centuries and usually had five or six voices. The 16th century form of madrigal was developed from the frottola. It is suggested that some parts of the madrigals were often performed on instruments. Later madrigals were written with accompaniment by continuo. Examples of composers of madrigals: 14th century composers, Landini and Giovanni da Cascia; early 16th century composers Willaert and Arcadelt; later 16th century composers, A. Gabrieli, Orlando di Lassus and Palestrina; early 17th century composers, Gesualdo and Monteverdi. Many Italian madrigals with a translation into English may be found in *Musica Transalpina* (1588). Composers of English madrigals: Bryd, Morley, and Weelkes. See *Frottola, *Conductus.

Madrigal comedy A play which is set to a succession of madrigals and other polyphonic vocal music. A form of the late sixteenth century.

Maestoso (It.) (mä–ĕ s–tō'–zō) Majestic style. Stately.

Maestro (It.) (mä–ĕ s'–trō) Master, teacher, or artist.

Maestro del coro (It.) (mä–ĕs'–trō dĕl kō'–rō) Master of the chorus or choir.

Maestor di cappella (It.) (mä–ĕ s'–trō dē kä–pĕ l'–lä) Master of the chapel. See *Kapellmeister.

Maggiore (It.) (mäd–jē–ō'–rä) Major or greater. E.g., major key or mode.

Maggot A fancy or whim. A piece of music in that style.

Magnificat (Lat.) It magnifies. Hymn of the Virgin Mary. The text is from Luke 1: 46–55 which begins "My soul doth magnify the Lord," (Latin: "Magnificat anima mea Dominum"). In the Roman Catholic Church it is sung during the office of Vespers. When it is performed in plainsong style it is sung to one of the eight tones (toni) in an antiphonal pattern (alternating choruses). The text is often used in polyphonic settings. Settings throughout the Renaissance usually had odd-numbered verses sung in plainsong and even-numbered verses set polyphonically by the composer. Later settings used the complete text in polyphonic style. Baroque settings were very elaborate. For example: J. S. Bach (1685-1750) *Magnificat in D.* The text translated into English is sung at Evening Service in the Anglican Church. The text has been set as a part of the Evening Service since the Reformation. The text has also been set by contemporary composers. For example, Ralph Vaughan Williams (1872-1958), used the text in his concert piece, *Magnificat.*

Magno (Sp.) (mäg'–nō) Grand, great.

Mahambi An African marimba.

Main (Fr.) (mă (n)) Hand or fist.

Main droite (Fr.) (mă (n) drwät) Right hand.

Main gauche (Fr.) (mă (n) gōsh) Left hand.

Maintenir (Fr.) (mă(n)–tĕ–nē r) To sustain, to keep together.

Mais (Fr.) (mĕ) But; why.

Maître (Fr.) (mĕtr) Master; instructor, teacher, tutor; director.

Maître de chapelle (Fr.) (mĕtr dū shă –pĕll) Precentor. Director of a chapel or church choir.

Maîtrise (Fr.) (mĕ–trēz) Mastership. A choir school or church choir in France.

Majesté (Fr.) (mä–zhĕs–tā) Majesty or stateliness.

Majeur (Fr.) (mä–zhûr) Major.

Major Main; greater. A major scale, interval, chord, triad, mode, etc. See *Major chord, *Major interval, *Major key, *Major scale, *Major triad, *Minor.

Major bob Change ringing. A full peal upon eight bells using a short jerky motion.

Major chord A chord having an interval of a major third and perfect fifth above the root or fundamental of the chord. E.g., F, A, C, F. See *Intervals, *Perfect.

Major flute An organ stop of 8 or 16 foot length.

Major intervals The intervals of a 2nd, 3rd, 6th and 7th may be major, minor, augmented or diminished intervals. Intervals of the 4th and 5th may be perfect, augmented or diminished. A major interval is a half-step smaller than an augmented interval and is one-half step larger than the minor interval. Examples:

See *Intervals, *Major.

Major key Major mode. The key and harmony are based on the major scale. For example, the fundamental or tonic of a C major scale is the note C, the tonic is the anchor tone and the key center. All notes in the key are related to that tonic note C and the major key is C. Example of major key signatures and keys:

Major Mode See *Major key, *Major scale.

Major scale A diatonic scale. A succession of tones moving in whole and half-steps within an octave. The half-steps appear between the 3rd and 4th and the 7th and 8th degrees of the scale with the remaining intervals being whole steps. There are seven different notes within the octave of the major scale. The first and last note have the same name but are one octave apart. Examples:

See *Scales, *Major, *Key, *Signatures, *Minor.

Major triad A chord of three notes having a fundamental note or root with an interval of a major third and perfect fifth above the root. Example:

Major triad on G

See *Chord, *Major, *Interval.

Mal (Ger.) (mäl) Time. Das erste Mal (däs ĕ rs '—tå mäl) the first time.

Malagueña (Sp.) (mä—lä—gā '—nyä) (1) A Spanish folk dance originating in Malága. A Spanish dance much like the fandango. (2) An older dance form in which the music moves to a succession of parallel chords above an ostinato type bass pattern. The melody was improvised. (3) A type of Spanish folk song. (4) Pieces written in the style of the Malagueña, e.g., "Malagueña" from *Suite Andalucia for Piano* by Ernesto Lecuna (b. 1900).

Male choir A choir made up of men or men and boys.

Malinconia (It.) (mä—li n̠—kō—nē '—ä) Melancholy.

Malinconioso (It.) (mä—li n—kō—nē—ō '—zō) In a sorrowful style.

Man. Abbreviation for manual. Used in organ music.

Mancando (It.) (män—kän '—dō) Dying away.

Manche (Fr.) (mä(n)sh) Sleeve. The neck of a cello, viola, violin, etc.

Mandola (It.) (män—dō '—lä) A large instrument of the lute family much like a large sized mandolin. It was often used during the 16th and 17th centuries. Also, mandore. See *Manodlin.

Mandolin (Mandolino (It.) (män—dō—lē '—nō)) A small stringed pear-shaped, fretted neck instrument of the lute family. It has four pairs of strings tuned like the violin (E, A, D, G) with a compass of some three octaves beginning on the low g string just below the treble clef. It is plucked with a plectrum and fingered with the left hand like the violin, and has a wooden body. Some mandolins have 10 strings tuned in fifths using double-courses. The mandolin is popular in Italy and Spain. See *Mandola, *Lute.

Mandriale (It.) (män—drē—ä '—lä) Pastorale poem. See *Madrigal.

Mani (It.) (mä '—nē) Hands.

Manica (It.) (mä '—nē—kä) Sleeve. Shift. Related to fingering and positions on a finger board.

Manichorde (Fr.) (mä—nē—kôrd) Clavichord.

Manico (It.) (mä '—nē—kō) Handle. Fingerboard on a stringed instrument.

Maniera (It.) (mä—nē—ä '—rä) Manner or fashion. Style of composing music in relationship to nature.

Manière (Fr.) (mȧ —nyĕr) Manner or style.

Manieren (Ger.) (mä—nē '—rȧ n) (1) In a style or manner. (2) Ornaments or grace notes.

Mannerism A style of music and art developed in Europe during the 16th century, a period of formal structure and form. The late Renaissance.

Mannheim School A group of musicians at Mannheim, Germany around the middle of the 18th century developed a style of orchestra music which influenced the classical style of composition of such men as Haydn and Mozart. Johann Stamitz (1717-1757), a conductor of the Mannheim orchestra, did much to develop the performance style of this music and was one of its most important composers. The work of the composers and performers of this school set the style for the later Viennese classics. Characteristics of the Mannheim School: homophonic style, tempo styles like those of the classical period, greater use of dyanmic changes, the development of new orchestra techniques and instrumentation, and new innovations in orchestration.

Mano (It.) (mä'—nō) Hand.

Mano destra (It.) (mä'—nō děs'—trä) Right hand.

Mano sinistra (It.) (mä'—nō sē—nēs'—trä) Left hand.

Manual Usually used with reference to the organ or harpsichord hand keyboard. Generally, a hand keyboard.

Manual controller In electronic music, voltage outputs that respond to hand movements.

Maraca A gourd filled with pebbles. A rattle type percussion instrument. A rhythm instrument used in orchestras or bands and in rhythmic dance music.

Marcato (It.) (mär—kä'—tō) Also, marcando (It.) (mär—kän'—dō) Marked. Ben marcato (It.) (bān mär—kä'—tō) Well marked.

March Music to which a group may march. Music, in duple time, having a constant and recurring beat.

Marche (Fr.) (märsh) March; walk.

Marcia (It.) (mär'—chē—ä) March; alla marcia (It.) In the style of a march.

Marimba A percussion instrument which originated in Africa, and became popular in Latin American and the U.S. It has a set of graduating wooden bars which sound a half-step apart, in the manner of the piano keyboard structure, which are struck by mallets. The tone resonates through tubular resonators which hang in a vertical position below the bars. It is used in ensembles and in solo work. A very popular instrument in jazz circles.

Marine trumpet A large bowed instrument called a monochord. Not to be confused with a trumpet. See *Tromba marina.

Markieren (Ger.) (mär—kē '—rȧ n) Mark; accent.

Marqué (Fr.) (mär—kā) Marked, determined.

Marsch (Ger.) (märsh) March.

Martellato (It.) (mär—tĕll—ä'—tō) Also, martelé (Fr.) (mär—tĕ—lā). Distinct or hammered. (1) A bow stroke; hammered stroke. The bow is drawn with force in short accented strokes. Markes as follows:

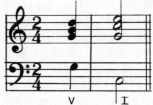

(2) A technique for piano which calls for a hammer-like action of the hands resulting in strongly accented notes.

Martellement (Fr.) (mär—tĕll—mä(n)) A mordent or trill.

Marziale (It.) (mär—tsē—ä'—lā) Martial style.

Marzo (It.) (mär'—tsō) March.

Masculine ending Music that ends on an accented syllable or on a strong beat. A feminine ending calls for the music to end on an unaccented syllable or weak beat. E.g., of masculine ending:

See *Feminine ending.

Mask (maske, Ger. (mäs'—kȧ); Masque, (Fr.) (mäsk)) A form of entertainment for the English nobility during the 16th and 17th centuries which included dancing, poetry, dialogue, song and pantomime. It also included scenery, costumes and instrumental music. A type of musical play.

Mass The main service of the Roman Catholic Church. The celebration of the Holy Eucharist. The high point of the Mass is the Consecration of the Host. The Low Mass is spoken. The High Mass is sung. The Mass has been sung in Latin for many centuries but today it is sung primarily in the vernacular. The Ordinary of the Mass is the part in which the text and the order of text of the Mass stay constant. In the Proper of the Mass the text changes with the religious calendar. Following are the first words of each section of the Ordinary of the (unchangeable parts of the Mass): (1) "Kyrie eleison." "Christe eleison" (Lord, have mercy. Christ, have mercy); (2) "Gloria in excelsis Deo" (Glory to God in the highest). (3) The Nicene Creed or Credo, "Credo in unum Deum, Patrem omnipotentem" (I believe in one God, the Father Almighty). (4) "Sanctus, Sanctus, Sanctus" (Holy, Holy, Holy) and "Benedictus qui venit in nomine Domini" (Blessed is He Who comes in the name of the Lord). (5) "Agnus Dei, qui tollis peccata mundi, miserere nobis" (Lamb of God, You Who take away the sins of the world, have mercy on us). The Proper of the Mass — the changing parts — are as follows: Introit, Prayer and Collect, Epistle, Gradual, Alleluia, Tract, Gospel, Offertory, Secret, Preface, Canon, Communion, Post-communion, Ite, Missa est (dismissal). Also, at solemn Mass the priest sings, "Ite Missa est" (go, you are dismissed) or "Benedicamus Domino" (Let us bless the Lord). In the Requiem Mass the priest says "Requiescant in pace" (May they rest in peace). The early Latin Mass was sung in Gregorian chant. Early polyphonic settings of the Mass came during the 13th and 14th centuries. Complete Masses were written during the 15th and 16th centuries. An example of a 16th century setting is *Missa Papae Marcelli* by Giovanni Peirluigi da Palestrina (1524-1594) which includes "Kyrie Eleison", "Gloria in excelsis Deo", "Credo", "Sanctus", "Benedictus", and "Agnus Dei". Examples of later Masses: J. S. Bach (1685-1750) wrote the famous *Mass in B Minor;* Mozart (1756-1791) *Mass in C Minor,* K 427; Franz Joseph Haydn (1732-1809) *Mass in D, No. 3* (The Imperial or Lord

Nelson); Vaughan Williams (1872-1958) *Mass in G Minor.* Current polyphonic masses are now being written in the U.S., in English, for use during High Mass. The "Credo" is spoken during the current (1970) Mass, and therefore is omitted from the musical portion of The Mass. The text has also been changed. The following sections are sung in the 1970 Mass by the choir, the celebrant, and often with the congregation: (1) "Lord Have Mercy" — full 1970 text, "Lord, have mercy. Lord, have mercy. Christ, have mercy. Christ, have mercy. Lord, have mercy. Lord, have mercy." (2) "Gloria" — full 1970 text, "Glory to God in the highest and peace to his people on earth. Lord God, heavenly King, almighty God and Father, we worship you, we give you thanks, we praise you for your glory. Lord Jesus Christ, only Son of the Father, Lord God, Lamb of God, you take away the sin of the world: have mercy on us· you are seated at the right hand of the Father, receive our prayer. For you alone are the Holy One, you alone are the Lord, you alone are the Most High, Jesus Christ, with the Holy Spirit, in the glory of God the Father. Amen." (3) "Holy, Holy, Holy" — full 1970 text, "Holy, holy, holy Lord, God of power and might, heaven and earth are full of your glory. Hosanna in the highest. Blessed is he who comes in the name of the Lord, Hosanna in the highest." (4) Lamb of God" — full 1970 text, "Lamb of God, you take away the sins of the world: have mercy on us. Lamb of God, you take away the sins of the world: have mercy on us. Lamb of God, you take away the sins of the world: grant us peace." See *each separate entry of the Ordinary of the Mass.

Mässig (Ger.) (měss'–ĭk) Moderate, as in tempo.

Massima (It.) (mäs'–ē–mä) Maxim. Largest single note or time value in mensural notation. The figure: ⊨

Mastersinger See *Meistersinger.

Masurek (Polish) Mazurka. See *Mazurka.

Matins (1) The first of the Office hours of the Roman Catholic Church which begin at midnight or during the night, although they often begin at early morning. (2) Morning songs or Prayer in the Anglican Church.

Matricale (It.) (mä—trē—kä'—lä) A rustic song performed in the vernacular. See *Madrigal.

Mattinata (It.) (mä—tēn—ä'—tä) Morning song.

Matinée (Fr.) (mä—tē—nä) (1) Morning performance. (2) Performance during the day, usually in the afternoon.

Maul-trommel (Ger.) (mowl trō'—mäl) Mouth-drum. Jew's harp.

Maxima (Lat.) Maxim. See *Massima.

Mazurka A Polish (mazur) country dance in triple time and in various tempos. It is strongly accented on the 2nd or 3rd beat of the measure and has a dotted rhythm which moves in a skipping style. The rhythm:

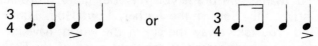

or a variation of the rhythm such as

etc. Frédéric Chopin (1810-1849) adopted the style for many of his piano pieces entitled Mazurka.

Me (mā) (1) In the sol-fa system when the note identified with the syllable mi is lowered one-half step by an accidental it is called me. E.g.

(2) The anglicized syllable for the Italian mi.

Meane Mean or mene. The middle voice, part, string, or instrument.

Meantone tuning A system of tuning keyboard instruments before the system of equal temperament. It worked for the key of C as well as for keys having no more than two sharps or flats. When more sharps or flats were required other devices had to be applied to the instrument in order to produce the proper altered pitch. See *Equal temperament.

Measure (1) A metrical unit. The music which is included between two vertical bars on a staff. Also called a bar. Jazz musicians prefer calling measures, bars. (2) A melody or air. (3) A slow dance.

Medesimo tempo (It.) (mā—dā'—zē—mō těm'—pō) When a piece of music changes from one meter to another, the above terminology indicates that the tempo should continue at the same speed. In the same tempo. See *L'istesso tempo.

Medial Median or middle.

Mediant (Lat.) Middle. The third note of the diatonic scale is called the mediant as it is mid-way between the first (tonic) note of the scale and the fifth (dominant) note of the scale. For example: A in F major; C in A minor. See *Diatonic.

Medieval music Music of the period also called the Middle Ages which extended from about the year 500 A.D. to the year 1500 A.D. Sometimes referred to as the period of music from 1100 A.D. to the Renaissance.

Medley A piece of music consisting of several musical pieces or sections which are taken from many sources. A mixture.

Medium per (Lat.) In half. Alla breve.

Mehr (Ger.) (mār) More.

Mehrstimmig (Ger.) (mār'—shtim—īk) Several voices.

Mehrstimmigkeit (Ger.) (mār'—shtim—ik—kit) Polyphony.

Meistersänger (Ger.) (mis'—tě r—zě ng—å r) See *Meistersinger.

Meistersinger (Ger.) (mīs'—tě r—zǐng—å r) Master singer. A working man or craftsman who was a member of a guild which flourished in many German major cities during the 15th and 16th centuries. They continued in the traditions of the minnesingers. Their primary purpose was to cultivate and foster good poetry and music. The music is generally monophonic and in bar form. *Die Meistersinger von Nürnberg,* by Richard Wagner (1813-1883) is an opera in three acts which depicts the life and times of the 16th century guilds of the meistersinger.

Melisma (Greek) Song or tune. (1) The technique of singing several notes on one syllable in plainsong. (2) A florid style. For example, the final "Amen Chrous" from the *Messiah* by George Frideric Handel (1685-1759), is in this melismatic style:
Final Amen Chorus:

Allegro moderato

f A — — — — — men, A — — — — — men, A — — — — — men

Melismatic The florid and ornamental style of singing a melisma. See *Melisma.

Mellophone A brass instrument that looks, plays, and sounds similar to the French horn. It has three piston-type valves rather than the rotary-type valves of the French horn. It is easier to play than the French horn and is often used in school bands and on occassion in dance bands. See *French Horn.

Melodeon A type of small reed organ which was developed in the U.S. during the first half of the 19th century. It had bellows and a three octave keyboard.

Melodia (It.) (mā—lō—dē '—ä) Melody.

Melodic interval The distance between two notes as they are sounded one after another.

Melodic inversion The inversion of a melody by playing successive intervals of the melody from note to note in the opposite direction by size of intervals. For example: an interval ascending a major second would descend a major second, etc. A melodic inversion may be tonal or real. See *Inversion.

Melodic minor A form of minor scale. The pure form of minor becomes melodic when the sixth and seventh degrees of the scale are raised by a semitone when

228

ascending and the descending scale is the pure form of minor. E.g.,

d minor
(Melodic form)

See *Minor.

Mélodie (Fr.) (mā–lō–dē) (1) Melody. (2) A song with accompaniment.

Melodioso (It.) (mā–lō–dē–ō'–zō) Melodious or in a tuneful manner.

Melodrama (melo-song, drame - drama (Greek)) (1) Often used in the sense of being over sentimental or emotional. (2) In the 17th and 18th centuries a romantic work which included spoken dialogue with instrumental accompaniment. It can be a work or part of a work. An example of the style can be found in scenes of Weber's (1786-1826) opera *Der Freischütz.*

Melodramma (It.) (mā–lō–dräm'–mä) ,An Italian term which means opera.

Melody A meaningful horizontal arrangement of notes. A succession of notes having rhythmic movement, pitch, and conceived in a horizontal pattern. It is the horizontal element of musical texture. Melody is related to three basic textures: monophonic (one horizontal line, alone); homophonic (one horizontal line with chordal accompaniment); polyphonic (two or more independent melodies whose relationship is not vertical but horizontal). See *Harmony, *Rhythm, *Texture, *Counterpoint.

Melos (Greek) Song. Melody. Wagner used the term to identify musical lines of later operas which did not have the symmetry of earlier opera melodies.

Membranophones Instruments that use stretched membrane to produce sound.

Même (Fr.) (mĕm) Same.

Mêmement (Fr.) (mĕm–mä(n)) The same.

Meno (It.) (mā'–nō) Less.

Meno mosso (It.) (mā'–nō mŏs'–sō) Less motion.

Mensural (mensur, Lat.) Measure, meter.

229

Mensural music A medieval term used to describe music in which each note had a relative time value as opposed to music done in the style of plainsong.

Mensural notation Musical notation (13th—16th centuries.) This system included note signs, a relationship of values among notes, altered or combinations of notes, dotted notes, coloration of notes (e.g., three black notes = 2 white notes), and the equivalent of meters or bar lines which are called divisions. Examples of notational signs: (Large) Maxima (note) ⊨⊨ ; (Long) Longa (note) ⊨ ; (Breve) Brevis (note) ⊨ = (|o|) oo; (Semibreve) Semibrevis (note) ◊ = O (whole note); (Minim) Minima (note) ◊ = ♩ (half note); (Semiminim) Semiminima (note) ↓ or ◊ = ♩ (quarter note); (Fusa) Fusa (note) ♦ or ♪ = ♪ (eighth note); (Semifusa) Semifusa (note) ♦ = ♪ (sixteenth note). A dot indicated: (1) to add to a note half the value of the note; (2) a division or group. Rest signs of equivalent values were also used. See *Prolation, *Punctus, *separate entry for each notational term.

Menuet (Fr.) (mĕ—nü—ā) See *Minuet.

Mescolanza (It.) (mĕ—skŏ—län'—tsä) Mixture. A medley.

Messa (It.) (mĕs'—ä) Mass.

Messa di voce (It.) (mĕs'—ä dē vō'—chä) A technique for voice which is an increase and decrease in intensity on a long tone. E.g., ⟨⟩

Messanza (It.) (mĕs—sän'—tsä) A medley or potpourri. Singing several different tunes at the same time or in succession.

Messa per i Defunti (It.) (mĕs'—ä pĕr ē dä—foŏn'—tē) Mass for the Dead. Requiem Mass.

Messe (Fr.) (mĕss) and Ger.) (mĕs—så) A Mass.

Mesto (It.) (mĕs'—tō) Sad.

Mesure (Fr.) (mĕ—zhür) Measure, bar, metre, time.

Meta (It.) (mā'—tä) Half.

Metamorphosis Changing a musical theme or musical line by altering the meter, notes, rhythm, etc., but maintaining the basic idea and shape of the line.

230

Meter (Metre) (1) The relationship of rhythm and accents of the meter. The number of beats in a measure related to the kind of note that receives a beat is indicated by the time signature. Bar lines indicate the normal strong accents. (2) Poetic meter. See *Time, *Time signatures, *Rhythm, *Compound meter, *Simple time.

Metric Symmetrical groupings of accented and unaccented notes. See *Meter.

Metrical psalms A psalm put into metrical meter or metrical verse.

Metric modulation In modulation, the time unit which links one tempo to the next tempo. See *Meter.

Metronome An instrument generally identified with Johann Maelzel (1770-1838) who developed a model around 1815 which keeps a steady beat at an indicated time interval. This mechanical device (a box with a wind-up spring) can be set to maintain a beat ranging from a slow M.M. of 40 to a rapid M.M. of 208. The pendulum swings back and forth making a clicking sound for each beat. Using a quarter note as a unit of beat, at M.M. ♩ = 60, the pendulum would swing at a pace of 60 times per minute or once each second. M.M. ♩ = 120 would be a march tempo or two beats per second, and so on. Current electronic metronomes are now available that produce a ping and show a light flashing for each pulse. See *M.M.

Metronomic marks The marking by which a composer indicates the tempo. E.g., using the quarter note as a unit of beat a M.M. ♩ = 60 would indicate one quarter note played per second. See *Metronome, *M.M.

Mezza voce (It.) (mĕt'–tsä vō'–chā) Half voice; softly; half power.

Mezzo (It.) (mĕt'–tsō) Half, middle, medium.

Mezzo forte (It.) (mĕt'–tsō fôr'–tā) Half loud. A term indicating that the music is to be played at an intensity between mezzo piano (mp) and forte (f), i.e., medium loud. The abbreviation for the term is mf. See *Dynamics.

Mezzo piano (It.) (mĕt'–tsō pē–ä'–nō) Half soft. A

term indicating that the music is to be played at an intensity which is louder than piano (p) and softer than mezzo forte (mf). The abbreviation for the term is mp. See *Dynamics.

Mezzo Soprano A female voice, lower than soprano, but higher than alto. The range is generally:

Mezzo Soprano clef Middle C is on the second line of the staff.

Mi (It.) (mē) and (Fr.) (mē) (1) The Pitch E in the fixed do system. (2) The third syllable and step of the major scale in the movable do system.

Microtones Intervals smaller than the semitone (half-step). E.g., a quarter tone, a sixth-tone, etc. For example, a system of quarter tones is used in the *String Quartet,* Op. 87, No. 11 by Alois Hába (b. 1893).

Middle C The note of the first ledger line below the treble clef   or the first ledger line above

the bass   staff. Often identified as

c', an octave above being c'', and an octave below being c.

Mi dièse (Fr.) (mē dē—ĕz) E sharp (E#).

Mikrokosmos A set of 153 short piano works by composer Béla Bartók (1881-1945) which is essentially a course of study in piano technique.

Milieu (Fr.) (mē—lyû) Medium, mean.

Military band A large ensemble maintained by an armed service that includes woodwinds, brass, and percussion instruments. It is used as a marching band and as a concert band for special events and entertainment. The size and structure differ from country to country. See

232

*Band, *Brass band.

Minaccevole (It.) (mē—nät—chā '—vō—lā) Threatening.

Minacciando (It.) (mē—nät—chē—än '—dō) Threatening.

Mindern (Ger.) (mi n '—då rn) Diminish, lessen.

Mineur (Fr.) (mē—nû r) Minor.

Minim Half note (♩) or half rest (━). Half or a semi-breve which is equal to a whole note (o) or a whole rest (━). See *Mensural notation.

Minne (Ger.) (mi '—nå) Love (poetic).

Minnesinger (Ger.) Love-singer. A guild of musicians and lyric poets who were from the class of aristocrats during the 12th through the 14th centuries. They were German troubadours who corresponded to the troubadours of France. The principal form used was the bar form and the name implies that the text dealt with the subject of love. The Meistersingers followed later and were of the working class. See *Meistersinger.

Minor Less; smaller. A minor scale, interval, chord, triad, mode, etc. See *Minor chord, *Minor intervals, *Minor key, *Minor scale, *Minor triad, *Major.

Minor chord A chord which in root position has an interval of a minor third and a perfect fifth above the root or fundamental of the chord. E.g., F—A♭—C—F

See *Intervals, *Perfect.

Minore (It.) (mē—nō '—rā) Minor.

Minor intervals The intervals of a 2nd, 3rd, 6th and 7th may be major, minor, augmented or diminished intervals. Intervals of the 4th and 5th may be perfect, augmented or diminished. A minor interval is a half step smaller than the major interval. Examples:

Minor 2nd   Minor 3rd   Minor 6th   Minor 7th

See *Intervals, *Minor.

Minor key (Minor mode) The key and harmony are based on the minor scale. For example, in the key of A minor the fundamental or tonic of the A minor scale is the note A, the tonic is the anchor tone and the key center. All notes in the key are related to that tonic note A. Each minor key shares a key signature with a major key. Using the sol-fa syllable system, the major scale begins on do, while the minor scale begins on la. Following are the key signatures, minor keys, and tonic note of each minor key:

Minor mode See *Minor key, *Minor scale.

Minor scale A succession of tones moving in whole and half steps within an octave. There are seven different notes in the minor scale, the eighth being the octave. The half steps appear between the 2nd and 3rd degrees of the scale and between the 5th and 6th degrees with the remaining intervals being whole steps. There are three forms of the minor scale: (1) pure form (described above) e.g.,

a minor scale-pure form:

(2) Harmonic form of minor scale — an altered form of the pure minor scale with the seventh degree of the scale raised a semitone in the ascending the scale and remaining raised when the scale descends. E.g.:

A Minor Scale — Harmonic Form

(3) Melodic form of minor scale — an altered form of the pure minor scale with the sixth and seventh degrees of the scale raised a semitone in the ascending scale and returned to the pure minor when the scale descends

A Minor Scale — Melodic Form

See *Scales, *Major, *Key, *Signature, *Minor.

Minor triad A chord of three notes having a fundamental note or root with an interval of a minor third and a perfect fifth above the root. Example:

Minor Triad on G

See *Chord, *Interval, *Minor.

Minstrels (1) Musicians or court entertainers of the Middle Ages who sang or recited poetry to the accompaniment of instruments. (2) Today, players in a minstrel show. Those who render songs, jokes, etc. See *Minstrel show.

Minstrel show Entertainment or stage show given by black face actors during the 19th century. It precedes and is related to vaudeville. The show had song and dance numbers, comic dialogue, an interlocutor, end men, a chorus, tambourines, etc.

Minuet A slow dignified dance in triple meter introduced in the French court during the mid-17th century. It was originally a rustic dance of the French peasants but later became quite reserved when performed at the courts. The term menu (Fr.) means small and the steps of the minuet (menuet) became small. The minuet style was often used in the instrumental music of the Baroque and Classical periods in forms such as the suite, sonata, classical sonata form, three part form of minuet-trio-minuet, piano pieces, string quartets, third movement of the classical symphony, etc. The minuet of the classical symphony is most often followed by a "trio" which ends with a da capo. An example of the minuet (plus trio with minuet repeated, da capo) is clearly seen in the third movement (Minuet in G major, allegro molto) of *Symphony in G,* No. 94 "Surprise" by Franz Joseph Haydn (1732-1809). See *Symphony, *Trio, *Da capo.

Minuetto (It.) (mē—noo—ĕt '—tō) Minuet.

Minugia (It.) (mē—noo'—jē—ä) Catgut. See *Catgut.

Mirliton (Fr.) (mēr—lē—tō(n)) Reed-pipe. A kazoo. See *Flûte eunuque.

Mirror canon A canon which is repeated backwards (retrograde). It can also mean that the melody is played in an inverted form. See *Canon.

Mirror fugue In a fugue the subject is repeated in contrary movement, that is, inverted from or in retrograde form. See *Fugue.

Miscuglio (It.) (mis—kool'—yō) Medley or hodge-podge.

Miserere (Lat.) (mē—zä—rä '—rä) "Miserere mei Deus, secundum magnam misericordiam tuam." (Lord, have mercy on me, according to thy loving kindness.) Pslam 50 from the Douay Bible which was prepared by the Roman Catholic Church from the Vulgate. Especially sung at Tenebrae during Holy Week. See *Psalm, *Tenebrae.

Miskin A type of bagpipe.

Missa (Lat.) Mass.

Missa Brevis (Lat.) (1) A short Mass. (2) A setting of the "Kyrie" and the "Gloria". For example, the *Missa Brevis* by Dietrich Buxtehude (1637-1707).

Missa Cantata (Lat.) A sung Mass.

Missa de angelis (Lat.) A Mass sung in unison in the style of the plainsong.

Missal A book of prayers and service used in celebrating the Mass.

Missa lecta (Lat.) Mass that is read. The Low Mass which may include hymn singing.

Missa parodia (Lat.) Parody Mass.

Missa pro defunctis (Lat.) Mass for the Dead. Requiem Mass.

Missa solemnis (Lat.) Solemn High Mass. Name of Ludwig Van Beethoven's (1770-1827) *Mass in D,* Opus 123 (published in 1827) "Kyrie", "Gloria in excelsis Deo", "Credo", "Sanctus", "Benedictus" and "Agnus Dei".

Missklang (Ger.) (mi s'—kläng) Discord or dissonance.

Misterioso (It.) (mis—tā—rē—ō'—zō) Mysterious.

Mistico (It.) (mis'—tē—kō) Mystic.

Misura (It.) (mē—zoo'—rä) Measure.

Misurato (It.) (mē—zoo —rä'—tō) Measured; measured time.

Mit (Ger.) (mĭt) With.

Mitemente (It.) (mē—tā—měn'—tā) Gently.

Mittel (Ger.) (mit'—ål) Middle or mean.

Mixed cadence A cadence that includes both subdominant and dominant harmonies in the last three or four chords of a final progression. E.g., II, IV, V, and I chords. E.g., I, IV, V$_7$, I; II—V—I; etc.

Mixed choir or chorus A choir or chorus comprised of both male and female voices.

Mixed voices (1) A group of voices of various ranges. (2) Male and female voices.

Mixolydian mode One of the authentic church modes. The range is from g—g', the final is g and the dominant is d'. It can be sounded by playing the white keys on the piano form g—g' in a diatonic ascending scale. See *Church modes.

Mixture An organ stop having two or more ranks of organ pipes, which produces tones of the harmonic series above the foundation tone. There are a variety of mixtures and they are referred to as compound stops. See *Harmonic series.

M.M. Abbreviation for Maelzel's Metronome. See *Metronome.

M.M. marking A marking which means Maelzel's Metronome. A tempo marking. See *Metronome, *Metronome mark, *Tempo.

Mobile (It.) (mō'—bē—lā) Moveable. E.g., changes in tempo, etc.

Mock trumpet A chalumeau. An instrument of the clarinet variety.

Mod. Abbreviation for moderate or moderato (It.).

Modal The term pertains to the mode of the music, usually church modes or rhythmic modes. See *Mode, *Church modes.

Modality Being modal. The relationship of the tones within the octave. The oldest basic system of a diatonic progression of seven notes within the octave. A melodic or harmonic structure based on church modes. See *Mode, *Church modes.

Modal rhythm See *Rhythmic modes.

Mode Scales, keys; rhythmic modes. The key center or the arrangement of notes within a scale structure. The term mode also relates to Greek modes, oriental modes, medieval modes, church modes, scales of the major and minor, etc. See *Church modes, *Key, *Modal, *Modality.

Mode final The finalis. The note on which a melody ends in a given mode is called its final. E.g., the Dorian mode (authentic) has a range from D—D; The final is D. The Hypodorian mode (plagal) has a range from A—A. The final is D. See *Church modes, *Finalis, *Mode.

Moderato (It.) (mō—dā—rä'—tō) Moderate tempo.

Modern jazz The development of jazz from the 1940's. A complex, melodic, rhythmic, and harmonic style. Identified by many names: Be-bop, Cool jazz, Funky jazz, hard bop, progressive jazz, third stream music, etc. See *Jazz.

Modifier An electronic instrument which is used to alter the tone quality of sounds in electronic music.

238

Modo (It.) (mō'–dō) Manner, way, style, mode.

Modulation A change of key. The movement from one key to another within a piece of music through the formal shifting of the tonal center. The key shift can take place in many ways, through transitions, abrupt modulations, those based on the use of enharmonic notes or chords, chromatic notes or chords or diatonic chord relationships. The authentic cadence is often used to establish a new key. E.g., the old key of C: I chord G modulates to the new key of G, Key I Key V_7
of of
C C G D_7
I IV V_7 I New key established is key of G.
G C D_7 G.

Modus (Lat.) Mode.

Modus lascivus The medieval mode that is called the Ionian mode. It has a range from c' to c'' and a tonality of the C major scale. See *Church modes, *Major scale.

Mögen (Ger.) (mĕ(r)'–gȧn) Like; may.

Moitié (Fr.) (mwä–tyā') Half.

Moll (Ger.) (mawl) Minor; minor key.

Molle (It.) (mŏl'–lä) Soft.

Mollemente (It.) (mŏl'–lä–mĕn'–tä) Gently.

Molto (It.) (mŏl'–tō) Much, very.

Monochord An ancient instrument used to demonstrate the mathematical relationships of musical intervals. It consisted of one string which was strung across a wooden oblong box. The length of the string was changed by adjusting a moveable bridge. Instruments using this principle were the marine trumpet and the clavichord.

Monocordo (It.) (mō–nō–kôr'–dō) (monocorde, Fr. (mŏ–nŏ–kôrd)) The principle of playing a passage or an entire composition on a single string.

Monodic One voice. Relates to monody. See *Monody.

Monody Music written for one voice. The term is usually applied when describing a style of accompanied solo songs used during the 16th and 17th centuries. E.g., 16th century songs with lute accompaniment; solo acc-

239

ompaniment in the 17th century Italian arias and recitatives.

Monophonic (monophony) A single musical line. No accompaniment. E.g., Gregorian chant. See *Homophonic,
*Polyphonic.

Monothematic A musical composition which is based on a
single theme.

Monotone One tone. Singing on one note. A recitation on
one pitch. A declamation on one tone. To chant on
one tone.

Mood Mode. The relationship between the maxima and
the longa or between large and brevis in mensural notation. See *Longa, *Maxima, *Mensural notation.

Mood music Music which is designed to establish or in-
duce a particular state of mind in the listener. It can
be either programmatic or absolute music. E.g., music
for dining, for relaxing, etc.

Moog Electronic Music Synthesizer An Electronic instrument invented in the 1960's by an engineer, Robert
A. Moog of Trumansburg, New York. The moog has
tape recorders and synthesizer keyboards which are
on circuit modules that can be interconnected to produce tones of varied qualities. The tones are monitored
through a loudspeaker. Tone shapes are pre-programmed
on the moog. The time element and sequence are controlled by playing a keyboard. This human element
allows new timing and variable phrasing. The manual
controls allow smooth and continuous movement. A
great many musical variables and elements can be controlled e.g., pitch, timbre, vibrato, attack, duration,
dynamics, glissando, etc. An example of music played
on the instrument: Bach performed on a Moog Electronic Synthesizer by composer and synthesist Walter
Carlos assisted by musicologist Benjamin Folkman. See
*Electronic music, *Electronic musical instruments.

Morality play A type of drama during the 14th through
16th centuries which dealt with virtue and vice. Also
called mystery play.

Morbido (It.) (môr'—bē—dō) (morbidezza) Soft; softness.

Morceau (Fr.) (môr—sō) A piece or fragment. A concerted piece of music.

Mordent An ornament or embellishment on a note. It is a melodic embellishment played from the given note to the note immediately below it. The mordent takes time value from the written note. It is played in a rapid succession and begins on the written note. It can be played once or twice depending on the length and tempo of the note. The usual sign is (𝄉) E.g.

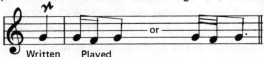

Written   Played

or sometimes played double.

Morendo (It.) (mō—rĕn'—dō) Dying away. Usually used to indicate a decrescendo in a final cadence, but may be used with an intermediate cadence.

Mosso (It.) (mŏs'—sō) Moved or motion. Meno mosso; less motion. Piu mosso; more motion.

Motet From the French "mot" which means "word". Generally, a polyphonic choral composition in anthem style. It was sacred music and based on biblical or sacred Latin prose. The early medieval motet was a composition of measured organum. The upper voice or voices had added text (mots). The texted duplum was referred to as motetus. Therefore, the general style of writing was called motet. The motet during the medieval period of music usually had three parts which were called: tenor (lower part, called cantus firmus, with a Latin text, taken from Gregorian chant, and had a separate rhythm from the upper parts); the middle voice called motetus had a text in the vernacular; third voice called the triplum also had a text in the vernacular. The later motet of the Renaissance period was in polyphonic style and had several voices

(4 to 8) singing the same text at various times in all parts. There were also solo motets with accompaniment and various types with two or more voices with accompaniment. Examples of motets are given in *Historical Anthology of Music,* ed. Davison and Apel. Many examples of the 16th century motet were written by Giovanni Palestrina (1524-1594). Nineteenth century composers also used the motet style. For instance, the *O Heiland, reiss die Himmel auf,* Op. 74, No. 2 by Johannes Brahms (1833-1897).

Motetus (1) Latin for motet. (2) In a medieval motet, the motetus was the middle voice above the tenor. Motetus had the principal text. The duplum with the added text was called motetus. (3) Name given to the whole composition (motet).

Motif (Fr.) (mŏ—tēf) See *Motive.

Motion Direction or pitch changes. The movement or progression of a musical line. Melodies move in parallel motion, contrary motion, or oblique motion. Intervals move by small steps or large steps. See *Similar motion, *Oblique motion, *Contrary motion.

Motiv (Ger.) (mō—tēf') See *Motive.

Motive A fragment or idea, usually from a theme, which is used to develop and build larger musical units.

Moto (It.) (mō'—tō) Motion or movement. Con moto (It.) with motion.

Mouth-organ See *Harmonica.

Mouthpiece The section of a blowing musical instrument with which the lips come in contact. E.g., brass instrument cup mouthpiece; single reed mouthpiece on woodwind instruments; the double reed which is the actual mouthpiece; the open hole type of horizontal flute; the beak or fipple type mouthpiece, or the open end hole mouthpiece.

Mouthpipe In brass instruments, the section of the tube into which the mouthpiece is inserted.

Mouvement (Fr.) (mōov—mä(n)) Movement, tempo, motion, march.

Mouvementé (Fr.) (mōov—mä(n)—tā) Animated or vivacious.

Movable do system The system of solmization (do, re, mi, fa, sol, la, ti, do) where do represents the tonic note of any major key. In the system called fixed do the note C is always do regardless of the key.

Movement A section or a principal division of a larger work such as a sonata, concerto, symphony, etc. The movements are separate and complete but are relative to other movements in tempo, form, etc.

Movente (It.) (mō—věn'—tā) Moving.

Movimento (It.) (mō—vē—měnt'—tō) (1) A movement of a work. (2) Motion.

Mozarteum A concert hall and institution devoted to and named for Wolfgang Amadeus Mozart (1756-1791). It is located in Salzburg, Austria the town of Mozart's birth.

Mp Abbreviation for mezzo-piano meaning half-soft.

M.S. The abbreviation for mano sinistra, which is Italian for left hand. It is used in keyboard music.

Multiple stop An interval or chord sounded on a stringed instrument such as the violin, viola, etc. See *Double stop.

Musette (Fr.) (mü—zě t) (musetta, (It.) (mōo—zě t'—tä)) (1) A French bagpipe of the 17th and 18th centuries. The wind is supplied by bellows and it has many chambers. A small type shawm. (2) A musical piece that has a drone bass below the melodic line. A section of a suite. The musette often followed the Gavotte in the Baroque suite. An example of a musette within a Baroque Suite: J.S. Bach (1685-1750). *English Suite No. 3, in G Minor for Piano* (Prelude, Allemande, Sarabande, Gavotte, Musette and Gigue.) (3) A reed organ stop.

Music Music is the art of communicating an idea. It is emotion; a mood; an artistic expression of ideas; technical; psychological; organized; a sound; a skill; and a concept. It has meaning and is expressed through several media. Music includes many parts or elements such as: melody, harmony, rhythm, meter, time, form or structure, dynamics, tempo, phrasing, style, timber, and pitch.

Musica (Lat.) Music.

243

Musica antiqua (Lat.) (1) Antique or old music. (2) A collection of music (hymns, motets, madrigals, etc.) from the 12th to the 18th century. Compiled by John Smith and published in 1812.

Musica da camera (It.) (moo'-ze-kä dä kä'-mä-rä) Chamber music.

Musica Divina (1853-1863) A collection of vocal church music of the 16th century. The early collection was done by Father Proske. After his death in 1861 the later series was edited by Schremo and Haberi.

Musicae Magister (Lat.) Music master. The degree of Master of Music.

Musica Enchiriadis An early writing (c. 9th century) on the subject of polyphony, types of organum such as parallel organum, and containing music written in Daseian notation.

Musica falsa (Lat.) See *Musica ficta.

Musica ficta (Lat.) False music or false tones. The use of chromatic tones outside the diatonic scale or hexachord. The term is used to identify the practice of using altered tones in the performance of contrapuntal music during the Middle Ages. Non-diatonic (chromatic) tones became necessary as church modes were modified. Musica falsa was the term used by theorists in the 13th century. The term Musica ficta was adopted later.

Musica figurata (Lat.) An embellishment. In medieval music, the added musical line above the cantus firmus.

Musical (1) Musical entertainment. (2) Producing music. (3) A musical play.

Musical box A mechanical box that produces music by means of a revolving cylinder having protruding pins which hit against a comb plate which sounds different pitches.

Musical comedy A light musical play with singing, dancing, chorus, orchestra, costumes, and staging.

Musicale A musical evening or program of music in an informal or social situation.

Musical glasses (1) The glass harmonica. (2) Graduated glass strips, tubes or bowls. See *Glass harmonica.

Musical style The techniques and forms used in a particular school, period of music, area, movement, etc. E.g., classical style, virtuoso style, Wagnerian style, etc.

Musica mensurata (Lat.) Measured or mensural music.

Musica plana (Lat.) Plainsong music.

Music Appreciation An academic and musical course of study in which the student is exposed to many musical experiences that are designed to provide a better understanding of the musical score and to develop various skills. It is hoped that through this understanding and experience, appreciation for music will follow.

Musica reservata (Lat.) A term used to describe the expressive style of music of Josquin Des Prés (c. 1450-1521). Later, the term was applied to the distinct expression and meaning of the text of musical compositions.

Musica Sacra (Lat.) Sacred music or church music. A collection of sacred music of the 16th and 17th centuries.

Musica Transalpina (Lat.) The first printed collection of Italian madrigals with English words. Compiled by Nicholas Yonge and published in 1588.

Musica vulgaris (Lat.) Secular music.

Music criticism A review of a musical performance which is published in a newspaper, periodical, or magazine.

Music drama The term used to identify Wagner's operas beginning with Lohengrin. These operas were dramatic; had continuous lines of music moving to and from the vocal and instrumental parts; had melodies that were flexible and free rather than organized in a sequence of aria, recitative, etc.; used thematic development in the orchestral parts; used an enlarged orchestra; were unified by means of the leit-motif. The music drama is conceived as a whole rather than a collection of many parts. Examples: *Der Ring des Nibelungen,* Wagner (1813-1883); *Tristan and Isolde,* Wagner; *Parsifal,* Wagner.

Music education The instruction of music in the public and private schools and colleges at all levels. The purpose: to make the student musically literate; to per-

245

form and create music; to become skilled, etc. Music education is also taking place in the concert hall, on radio and T.V., etc. Informal experiences are very valuable to becoming musically educated.

Musicology The scholarly study of music. This includes historical research, theory of music, science of sound, the investigation and systematization of music and knowledge of music, the performance and publication of musical scores relative to its historical significance, etc. An academic approach to music and to the history of music.

Musique concrète (Fr.) (mü—zēk kō(n)—krĕt) Concrete music. A form of electronic music which was originated by P. Schaeffer in Paris beginning in 1948. The music is constructed by using tapes of musical and natural sounds rather than purely electronically produced sounds. These sounds can be electronically distorted or kept unchanged. The sounds are then arranged and organized into a meaningful work. Example of musique concrète: *Visage V* by Luc Ferrari (b. 1929) See *Electronic music.

Musique de chambre (Fr.) (mü—zēk dû shä(m)—br) Chamber music.

Muta (It.) (mōo'—tä) Change. Change to another instrument, another crook, another key, another tuning, etc. E.g., change from one timapni to another or change from F horn to Eb horn, etc.

Mutation Changing. (1) A change of voice. (2) A shift in hand position. (3) A change in syllables from one hexachord to another. See *Hexachord, *Syllables.

Mutation stops Organ stops that sound a pitch other than the fundamental note which is played. The tone is from the harmonic series of the basic tone.

Mute A mechanical device that muffles the sound of a musical instrument. Examples: a device (mute) placed in the bell of brass instruments; a three pronged device (mute) placed on the bridge of a violin, cello, etc.

Mutevole (It.) (mōo—tä '—vō—lä) Changeable.

Mutig (Ger.) (mōo'—ti k) Courageous, bold.

Mutwillig (Ger.) (mo͞ot'–vĭl–ĭ k) Deliberate.

Mystery play A medieval sacred drama. See *Morality play.

Mystic chord The name given to a chord invented by Alexander Scriabin (1872-1915) that consisted of intervals of fourths. E.g., C – F# – Bb – E – A – D.

Mystique (Fr.) (mēs–tēk) Mystic. Spiritually significant.

Nacaire (Fr.) (nä–kĕ r) The French name for small Arabian kettledrums used in pairs during the medieval period of music. Called nakers in England.

Nacchera (It.) (nä'–kā–rä) Timpano or kettledrum.

Nacchere (It.) (nä'–kā–rä) Castanets.

Nach (Ger.) (näkh) Towards, to; after, at.

Nachahmung (Ger.) (näkh'–ä–moŏng) Imitation.

Nach belieben (Ger.) (näkh bā–lē '–bà n) At your pleasure or discretion. See *Ad libitum.

Nachdruck (Ger.) (näkh'–droŏk) Emphasis, accent.

Nachfolge (Ger.) (näkh'–fŏl–gà) Succession; imitation.

Nachlassen (Ger.) (näkh'–läs–à n) Abate, slacken in tempo.

Nachschlag (Ger.) (näkh'–shläk) After beat; after stroke. An agrément (Fr.). (1) An ornamental note which is played between two notes which are often a third apart. The nachschlag note is performed after the main note and takes its value from the note it leaves. Example of this 17th and 18th century nachschlag:

(2) The term is also used to describe the two notes which close a trill. (3) An anticipation. E.g.,

See *Agrément, *Springer.

Nachspiel (Ger.) (näkh'–shpēl) Postlude.

Nacht (Ger.) (näkht) Night.

Nachtanz (Ger.) (näkh'–tänts) After dance or follow dance. A lively dance in three which follows a slow dance in two. For example, Pavan (slow, duple meter) followed by a galliard (fast, triple meter) or the allemande (moderate $\frac{4}{4}$ meter) followed by the courante (fast triple meter). This pairing of dances was common during the 16th and 17th centuries.

Nachtmusik (Ger.) (näkht'–moo–zēk') Night music. A serenade. For example: *Eine Kleine Nachtmusik: Serenade in G,* K525 for Strings by Wolfgang Amadeus Mozart (1756-1791).

Nachtstück (Ger.) (näkht'–shtük) Nocturne.

Nagarah (Naggarah) Small Arabian kettle drums. See *Nacaire.

Nagelclavier (Ger.) (nä'–gål–klä–vēr) Nail piano. The tone is produced by a friction wheel.

Nagelgeige (Ger.) (nä'–gål–gī–gå) Nail violin. An 18th century instrument having a wooden cylinder in which U-shaped nails or pins protrude. A bow was used to produce the sound.

Nail violin See *Nagelgeige.

Naked fifth An interval of an open fifth. E.g., a triad without a third. See *Interval, *Triad.

Nakers Small kettledrums. See *Nacaire, *Nagarah.

Nallari A reed instrument of Korea.

Nämlich (Ger.) (něm'–likh) The same.

Narrare (It.) (nä–rä'–rä) Narrate.

Narrativo (It.) (nä–rä–tē'–vō) Narration.

Narrator One who recites a text to music or some other action. One who gives a descriptive narrative.

National music Music that reflects characteristics of a country. It relates to the people, heroes, events, folk literature, folk songs, etc. Examples: Bedřich Smetana (1824-1884), *My Country;* Jean Sibelius (1865-1957), *Finlandia,* Op. 26; Modest Murssorgsky (1839-1881), *Boris Godunov* (opera).

Natural A note that is neither flat nor sharp. A natural sign (♮) cancels out a flat or a sharp. See *Accidentals.

Naturale (It.) (nä–too–rä'–lä) Natural. An indication to play or sing in a natural way or normal range.

Natural harmonic Written ♪ . A natural harmonic is produced by lightly touching an open string at a given point. For example, when an open string is touched at mid-point, a sound an octave higher than the open string will result.

Natural horn A horn without keys or valves. It plays the tones within the harmonic series of the fundamental pitch of the instrument. Some tones can be altered by stopping the horn. The key of the instrument is determined by the length of the tubing. Also called hunting horn.

Natural key A key having no flats or sharps, e.g., the key of C major.

Natural minor The pure form of minor. E.g., the relative minor scale of the major scale without alterations, such as the pure minor of C major, which is A minor. See *Minor scale.

Natural scale A scale without sharps or flats. E.g., the C scale and the pure A minor scale which can be played by using only the white keys of the piano.

Natural sign The sign (♮) which is used to indicate that a sharped or flatted note is to revert to the natural note of the same letter name. E.g.,

Natural tones The harmonic tones sounded above the fundamental tone. See *Harmonics.

Natural trumpet A trumpet without keys or valves. The key is determined by the length of the tubing. Only the tones of the harmonic series above the fundamental can be sounded.

Neapolitan Sixth A chord that is a first inversion of a supertonic triad in a given key, with the root of the chord and the fifth of the chord lowered one half-step. E.g., in the key of G major the N_6 chord would be

spelled C — E♭ — A♭

Nebel, Nabla (Heb.) An ancient Hebrew instrument having ten strings that are sounded by plucking the strings with the fingers.

Neck The part of the violin, guitar, etc. which extends from the body of the instrument to the peg box. A finger board runs above it and the strings stretch over the finger board. See *Fingerboard, *Violin, *Guitar.

Negligente (It.) (nāl—yē—jĕn'—tā) (Nelgigentemente, (It.) (nāl—yē—jĕn—tā—mĕn'—tā) Remiss; indifferently.

Negro spiritual A religious folk song sung by the American Negro.

Neighboring tone A tone found in either melodic or harmonic writing which is a non-chord tone. E.g.,

Neighboring tone

See   *Appoggiatura.

Nénies (Fr.) (nā—nē) Funeral dirges.

Neo-classicism An early twentieth century movement which used contemporary sounds and techniques with the characteristics of the Baroque and Classical periods of music. It was a reaction against the very emotional music of the Romantic period; a return to formal structure and form; a revival of the principles of the classic sonata; use of the Baroque contrapuntal treatments; a revival of early forms, such as the concerto grosso and other small instrumental forms; a return to the use of smaller instrumental combinations; and an emphasis on absolute music rather than the Romantic program music. Example of some composers: Hindemith, Piston, Stravinsky.

Neo-modal A twentieth century revival and return to using scales which have a relationship to the modal system rather than to the major-minor system. The use in 20th century music of folk songs, etc. based on a modal system. See *Modes, *Church modes, *Scales.

Neo-romanticism A term generally used to identify the twentieth century composers who use some of the attitudes and elements of Romantic composers. For example, the composer might use expressive and emotional melodic lines, rich textures and rich harmonies, such as those found in 19th century Romantic music.

Nero (It.) |(nā '—rō) Black. A black note, such as the crotchet. (♩).

Net (Fr.) (nĕt) Clear, distinct.

Netto (It.) (nĕt '—tō) Clear-cut, distinct.

Neu (Ger.) (noi) New.

Neue Musik (Ger.) (noi'—å mōo—zēk ') New music. A term used in connection with the new innovations and new movements within the twentieth century. It is a reaction to nineteenth century Romanticism.

Neuf (Fr.) (nûf) Nine or ninth. Also, new.

Neuma (1) A melodic line used by medieval theorists to demonstrate the characteristic of a mode. (2) A term used to describe the style of singing a group of notes on a syllable. See *Mellismatic, *Neumes.

Neumatic style A style of singing groups of notes on one syllable in plainsong. In this style fewer notes (two, three, four, etc.) are sung than in melismatic style. See *Melismatic, *Neumes, *Melisma.

Neumes Symbols of early musical notation. Neumes date back to an Oriental and Greek system of symbols that were used in speech recitation called ekphonetic notation. A group of symbols called neumes developed throughout the 6th and 7th centuries. These neumes did not identify the pitch or rhythm, but gave a general shape of the melodic line. By the eighth century, letters were added in order to develop a more accurate system. During the 9th century a color line was added, then later, a second color line to identify the tones more accurately. Guido d'Arrezzo (c. 990—c. 1050) used three and then four lines on which neumes represented fixed pitches. The four line staff is the one used for Gregorian chant notation. During the 12th and 13th centuries neumes evolved into square and diamond shaped notes. The square shaped neumes are used in the liturgical books of the Roman Catholic Church. Examples of neumes using the four line staff: Gregorian notation:

etc.

Modern notation:

etc.

Another form of neumes were those first symbols used above the words which gave the rise and fall of the musical line. A rise was indicated by an upward line (/), a downward line (\), and a rise and fall by the combination of the two signs (∧), etc. Examples of some symbols used for groups of notes:

Neun (Ger.) (noin) Nine.

Neuntel (Ger.) (noin '–tål) Ninth.

New music Generally, a term used to describe new periods or movements in music throughout the history of music. A reaction against the old. Innovation in music. See *Neue Musik.

Nicht (Ger.) (nĭkht) Not.

Nicht gedämpft (Ger.) (nĭkht gå–dĕmpft) Not muffled, not muted.

Nicht schleppen (Ger.) (nĭkht shlĕp '–ån) Not dragged. Keep the tempo moving.

Nieder (Ger.) (nē '–dår) Down.

Niederschlag (Ger.) (nē '–dår–shälk) Down-stroke. Downbeat.

253

Niederstrich (Ger.) (nē '–dår–shtrĭkh)Down-stroke. Down-bow.

Niedrig (Ger.) (nēd '–rĭk) Low.

Night piece A nocturne or evening song. For example, the many "Nocturnes" by Frédéric Chopin (1810-1849).

Nigun In Jewish music, a chassidic melodic line with or without a text.

Nineteenth An organ stop producing a note two octaves and a fifth above the fundamental.

Ninth A compound interval of a ninth. Examples of intervals of a ninth on the note of F, key of F major:

Maj 9th   min 9th   Dim 9th   Aug 9th

See *Intervals.

Ninth chord A chord that includes a root, 3rd, 5th, 7th, and 9th. Usually a dominant ninth chord in a given key. See *Chord.

Nobile (It.) (nō'–bē–lā) Noble or grand. Nobilmente, (It.) (nō–bēl–měn'–tā) Nobly.

Noch (Ger.) (nŏkh) Still, yet.

Noche (Sp.) (nō'–chā) Evening, night.

Nochmalig (Ger.) (nŏkh'–mäl–ĭk) Repeated.

Nocturn (nocturnus, Lat.) By night. The office "Matins" of the Roman Catholic Church. See *Office hours, *Matins.

Nocturne (Fr.) (nŏk–türn) Nocturnal. Night piece. A serenade or evening song. A sentimental piece of instrumental music. Frédéric Chopin (1810-1849) used Nocturne as a title for many of his piano compositions.

Node A point in a wave length at which there is little or no vibration. A point between two vibrating sections of an air column or a vibrating string.

Noël (Fr.) (nŏ–ĕl) Yule-tide. Christmas carol.

Noire (Fr.) (nwär) Crotchet. A quarter note. See *Nero.

Nomos (Greek) Custom; rule; law. (1) To compose by rules. (2) Early Greek traditional melodies used in recitation.

Non (Fr. (nō(n)) and It. (nōn)) No; not.

None, Nona (Lat.) Ninth. (Nona hora, (Lat.) ninth hour). The Roman Catholic Office hour which is celebrated around 3:00 P.M. See *Office hours.

Nonet (1) A piece for nine performers. (2) A piece for nine instruments. E.g., a work for string quartet (quintet) and winds. *Serenade-Nonet in F* for Strings and Winds, Op. 95 by Charles Villiers Stanford (1852-1924); Instruments; string quartet, string bass, flute, clarinet, bassoon, and horn.

Nonharmonic notes A note that is not part of the chord with which it is sounded. A non-chord tone. See *Appoggiatura, *Non-chord tone, *Passing tone, *Cambiata, *Auxiliary note, *Échappée, *Anticipation.

Nonnengeige (Ger.) (nōn'—ĕn—gi—gä) Nun's violin. See *Nun's fiddle, *Tromba marina.

Nono (It.) (nō'—nō) Ninth.

Non-strophic song A through-composed song. A song in which the music changes with each verse. Example: Franz Schubert (1797-1828), *Der Erlkönig*. See *Through-composed, *Strophic.

Non tanto allegro (It.) (nōn tän'—tō äl—lě'—grō) Not too fast.

Non troppo (It.) (nōn trŏ'—pō) Not too much.

Noodling Isolated passages or independent groups of notes played by a musician during a warm-up period or pause in a rehearsal.

Normalton (Ger.) (nôrm'—äl—tōn) Normal tone. The orchestra tuning note A.

Nota cambiata (It.) (nō'—ta käm—bē—ä'—tä) Shifting or changing note. A non-harmonic tone. See *Cambiata.

Notation Signs, characters, and symbols which represent musical tones. Neumes developed from an early system of symbols used by the Greeks and Orientals in speech recitation called ekphonetic notation. During the 6th and 7th centuries, neumes identified the general shape of a musical line. Around the 8th century letters were added to make the system more accurate. During the 9th century a color line was added, then two colored lines to identify the tones more accurately. During the 10th and 11th centuries three and four lines were added on which the neumes were placed and represented fixed pitches. During the 12th and 13th centuries neumes evolved into square and diamond shaped notes. During the 13th century a smaller note value called semibreve was used along with the longa and brevis. The system of mensural notation followed. In the 14th century mixed notation was developed followed by the white mensural notation of the 15th century. The system known as tablatures was developed during the 15th and 16th centuries for keyboard and lute music. Then, the modern system of notes and rests was generally agreed upon in the 17th century. Some examples of signs and symbols of notation: Greek accents / or \ above a syllable or word;

Early Neumes ⌣ ⌐ ⌒ ⌒ (direction of line);

Neumes ⌐ ▪ ◆ ⌐ ⌐ ⫽ (14th century ⌐ ⌐;

15th century white mensural notation — ⌐ Maxima, ⌐ longa, ⊨ brevis, ◇ semibrevis, ♩ minima, ♪ semiminima, ♪ fusa. 17th century to the present

form: (◇) (♩) (♩) (♪) ♪ ♪ ♪ etc.
　　　　○ ♩ ♩ ♪ ♪ ♪

and the corresponding rests. See *Notes, *Neumes, *Mensural notation, *Maxima, *Longa, *Brevis, *Semibrevis, *Minima, *Semiminima, *Fusa, *Tablatures, *"Selected Annotated Bibliography"

Note A sign or symbol on a staff that represents a given sound (tone) or pitch. The basic notes are: ○ Whole note (semibreve); ♩ half note (minim); ♩ quarter note (crotchet); ♪ eighth note (quaver); ♪ sixteenth note (semiquaver); ♪ thirty-second note (demisemiquaver); sixty-fourth note (hemidemisemiquaver). Each note also has an equal rest in time. The term can also be applied to earlier "notes" such as neumes. Also, in modern abstract music, composers find it necessary to use other types of "notes" to sound quarter tones and other sounds not identified by standard pitch. Composers of electronic music require a whole new system of notes, terms and notation, such as electronic switch, filtered, square-wave cluster, sine tones, non-pitch clusters, etc. For examples see the score from *Dramatic Pantomime* by Vladimir Ussachevsky. See *Notation.

Note-against-note See *Counterpoint.

Note row See *Tone-row, *Twelve-tone row.

Notes éagles (Fr.) (nŏt sā—gäl) A term used in French music of the 17th and 18th centuries to indicate that groups of notes of the same value were to be played as written rather than in the customary interpretation of long and short. See *Notes inégales.

Note sensible (Fr.) (nŏt să(n)—sēbl) Obvious note. Leading tone.

Notes inégales (Fr.) (nŏt sēn—ā—gäl) Unequal notes. A practice in the French school during the 17th and 18th centuries of playing a succession of certain shorter notes of the same value in an uneven (long-short) pattern. For example, a written succession of notes in C time, e.g.,

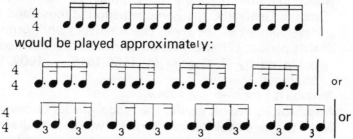

would be played approximately:

more unequal or less unequal depending on the passage and the performer. No directions were given as this was the accepted custom. The notes would be played in an equal manner if a term such as détaché was indicated or staccato marks were placed above the notes. Ex-

257

amples of other note patterns in some other meters (L = long, S = short):

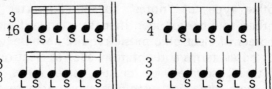

Notre Dame The School of Notre Dame is important to the development of polyphonic music (organum) during the late 12th and 13th century Ars Antiqua. Two leaders in the Notre Dame school were Leoninus and Perotinus.

Notturno (It.) (nŏt—tōor'—nō) Nocturne.

Novachord A one manual electronic keyboard insturment the shape of an up-right piano. It is able to produce a variety of tone colors.

Nove (It.) (nō'—vā) Nine.

Novellette (Ger.) (nō—vĕ l—ĕ t'—tå) Short story. A short romantic piece of free form. E.g., Robert Schumann (1810-1856), piano works, *Novelette,* Op. 21; *Novelette,* Op. 99.

Nuances (Fr.) (nü—ä(n)s) Subtleties in shades, meanings, and expression. Subtle variations in dynamics, tempo, intonation, etc.

Nuove musiche (It.) (nōo—ō'—vā mōo'—zē—kā) (1) New music. Generally, the Baroque period of music and the development of the style, characteristics, and forms of that period. (2) A collection of monophonic melodies published by G. Caccini (c. 1550-1618) in 1602. See *Baroque.

Nuovo (It.) (nōo—ō'—vō) New.

Nuschaot In Jewish music, the modal chants or prayers.

Nut (1) The movable screw at the lower end of the bow (violin, viola, etc.) which is used to tighten and loosen the bow hair. (2) The small ledge across the upper end of the finger board which prevents the strings from touching the finger board.

Nychelharpa A Scandanavian stringed instrument much like the hurdy-gurdy. The tone is produced with a bow rather than a wheel as is the case with the hurdy-gurdy. See *Hurdy-gurdy.

O

O (1) An abbreviation for octavo. (2) Indicates an open string on a stringed instrument, e.g., cello. (3) A sign used in keyboard fingering for the thumb.

O (It.) (ō) Or.

Ob. The abbreviation for oboe.

Obbligato (It.) (ŏb—lē—gä'—tō) (obbligatorio, (It.) (ŏb—lē—gä—tō'—rē—ō)) Obligatory or compulsory. (1) A second melodic line which is played with the basic melody. For example, it is obligatory to play this part in music of the Baroque period. It is usually an instrumental part. (2) In the 19th and 20th century music the term usually has the opposite meaning, that of ad libitum (at your pleasure) and the part may be omitted. Also, obligat.

Ober (Ger.) (ō'—bå r) Over, upper, higher.

Oberdominante (Ger.) (ō—bå r—dō—mē—nän'—tĕ) Dominant. The specific name of the fifth degree of a scale or a chord built on that degree.

Ober-manual (Ger.) (ō'—bå r—mä—noŏ—äl') Upper-manual.

Oberstimme (Ger.) (ō'—bå r—shtĭm—å) Upper voice.

Obertöne (Ger.) (ō'—bå r—tĕ (r)n—å) Overtone(s). The upper partial(s) of the note. Upper harmonic(s).

Oberwerk (Ger.) (ō'—bå r—vĕ rk) Over-work. Swell organ.

Obligat (Ger.) (ŏb—lē—gät') Necessary. Obbligato. See *Obbligato.

Oblique motion The relative movement of two melodies. One part remains stationary while the other part moves. E.g.:

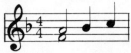

Oblique piano A small piano with the strings strung diagonally. The purpose of stringing the piano in this fashion was to have a greater length on the low strings.

Oboe (oboe, (Ger.) (ō—bō'—å); hautbois, (Fr.) (ō—bwä)) Hautboy, oboe. A double reed instrument having a narrow, tubular, and concial bore. It has a range of approximately two and one-half octaves ranging from b flat below middle c' to g'''. The oboe plays in concert pitch; the note sounds as written. The abbreviation is Ob.

Oboe da caccia (It.) (ō—bō'—ā dä kät'—chē—ä) Tenor hautboy; (taille, (Fr.) (tä—yä)) The "hunting oboe". A double reed instrument having a range of a fifth below the oboe. The predecessor of the English horn. See *Oboe.

Oboe d'amore (It.) (ō—bō'—ā dä—mō'—rä) An early 18th century oboe pitched a minor third lower than the oboe and with a mellow sound. It had a pear-shaped bell similar to that of the English Horn. See *Oboe.

Oboe lungo A long oboe similar to the oboe d'amore. See *Oboe, *Oboe d'amore.

Ocarina A sweet potato. An egg-shpaed instrument with finger holes and a mouthpiece.

Ochetto (It.) (ŏ—kĕt'—tō) See *Hocket.

Octachord (1) A musical instrument having eight strings (2) A series of eight tones. For example, a major scale of one octave. See *Scale.

Octave (1) A note an eighth degree above or below a given note. The octave can be perfect (e.g., g to g), diminished (g to g♭), or augmented (e.g., g to g♯). A tone a perfect octave higher than a given tone vibrates twice the number of vibrations per second as the given tone. Notes in octaves share the same letter name. The abbreviation con 8va would mean, with the octave doubling; 8va alone would mean, transpose an octave above or below. (2) A principal organ stop of 4 foot on the manual, an 8 foot stop on the pedal.

Octave coupler A device on an organ that adds the octave to a note played. Super-octave coupler (add the octave above). Sub-octave coupler (add octave below). See *Octave.

Octave flute (flauto piccolo, (It.)) A small flute sounding an octave higher than the ordinary flute with a range

of approximately three octaves (actual sound) d" to
c'''''. See *Piccolo.

Octave key A lever used on a wind instrument, such as the
saxophone, to produce a tone one octave higher while
using the same fingering as the lower octave.

Octave scale An organized set of tones used to compose
a scale within an octave. For example, a diatonic scale
made up of seven different notes, five whole steps and
two half-steps, and the octave note. See *Scale.

Octave spinet (1) In the 18th century, a four foot triangular shaped harpsichord that had the strings strung
at a 45 degree angle to the keyboard. See *Spinet. (2)
A small 17th century German keyboard instrument
approximately the size of a sewing box with very narrow
keys and a high pitch. It was probably designed as a
child's instrument.

Octavin (Fr.) (ŏk–tä–vă(n)) Octave-flute. An organ stop.

Octet (1) A group of eight. Eight instruments, voices, or
a mixture. (2) A composition for eight instruments. For
example, Franz Schubert (1797-1828); *Octet in F,* Op.
166, for String Quintet (string quartet and double bass,
plus bassoon, clarinet, and horn).

Octobasse (Fr.) (ŏk–tō–bäs) A mid-nineteenth century
huge double-bass, which ranged in height from 13 to
15 feet, having three strings which were stopped with
mechanical devices.

Od (It.) (ōd) Or.

Ode From the Greek word aoide which means song. Poetry to be sung or put to music. Example: Henry Purcell (c. 1659-1695), *Ode to Queen Mary.*

Oder (Ger.) (ō'–dar) Or.

Ode symphony A symphony that includes a chorus. For
example: Ludwig Van Beethoven (1770-1827), *Symphony No. 9 in D Minor,* Opus 125, "Choral Symphony".

Odhecaton (Greek) The earliest published collection of
polyphonic music. It was published by Petrucci in
1501.

Oeuvre (Fr.) (û–vr) A work of a musician. An opus.

Offen (Ger.) (ŏ'–få n) Open.

Offertory (offertorium, Lat.) The music (plainchant, polyphonic setting, anthem, or verses) sung or recited at the offerings at a religious service. An anthem in the Anglican Church. In the Roman Catholic Mass it is sung or said after the "Creed". Originally, it was a psalm with an antiphon. Today, it is just the antiphon. See *Mass.

Office hours Divine hours. The services, prayers, psalms, and readings that are held throughout an entire day in the Roman Catholic Church. Matins (during the night); Lauds (at daybreak; Prime (about six o'clock in the morning); Terce (early morning); Sext (at noon); None (early afternoon); Vespers (in the evening around sunset); Compline (at darkness).

Ogni (It.) (ōn '–yē) Every; all.

Ohne (Ger.) (ō '–nå) Without.

Ohne dämpfer (Ger.) (ō '–nä dĕ mp '–få r) Play an instrument open, that is, without a mute.

Oktave (Ger.) (ŏk–tä '–vå) Octave.

Oktavgeige (Ger.) (ŏk–täv '–gi '–gå) Octave fiddle.

Oliphant horn The word oliphant is Old English for elephant. An Oliphant horn is an old medieval hunting horn carved from an elephant tusk.

Ondeggiare (It.) (ŏn–dĕ d–jē–ä '–rā) Undulate, tremolo or vibrate. See *Ondulé.

Ondulé (Fr.) (ō(n)–dü–lā) Undulating. An obsolete form of tremolo in string playing. A single note or several notes are played with an undulating movement of the bow. See *Tremolo.

One step dance A quick round dance in duple meter. A ballroom variety dance done by a couple to ragtime music.

Ongarese (It.) (ŏn–gä–rā '–zā) Hungarian.

Onion flute A kazoo or mirliton.

Onze (Fr.) (ō(n)z) Eleven.

Onzième (Fr.) (ō(n)–zē–ĕm) Eleventh.

Op. The abbreviation for opus. Work.

Open (1) An open string; one not stopped. (2) An open horn; one not muted.

263

Open chord A term used when the three upper voices of a chord are not close together, but are spread to the octave or beyond.

Open diapason An open organ pipe made of wood or metal.

Open fifth A triad or chord with the third of the chord omitted. See *Chord.

Open flam See *Flam.

Open harmony Chords that have a wide spacing between notes. A wide distance from voice line to voice line. The opposite of close harmony.

Open key On a wind instrument, an open hole not covered by a finger or mechanical key.

Open notes (1) Notes that are produced on wind instruments which are the harmonic tones of the fundamental note. (2) The note of the open string.

Open pedal See *Damper pedal.

Open roll Clear and rapid strokes on the drum head. Each stroke is heard more distinctly than in the press roll.

Open score A full score in which every instrument or voice is notated on a separate staff. See *Score.

Open strings The entire string is allowed to vibrate. The symbol (o) above the note indicates that the note should be played open rather than fingered.

Open tones (1) The tones produced on instruments without the aid of keys or valves. (2) On string instruments the fingers are not pressed on the strings. (3) A French horn tone which is not stopped.

Open triad A triad without the third of the chord. Open fifth. See *Triad.

Open valves The valves on an instrument which are not depressed.

Oper (Ger.) (ō'–pĕ r) Opera.

Opera (It.) (ō'–pā–rä) Work. An extended musical work in which all or most of the parts are sung to instrumental accompaniment. Elements of the opera; aria, recitative, chorus, dance, scenery, action, dialogue (in some 18th and 19th century operas), drama or comedy, vocal and instrumental music, duets, and other ensembles. The idea of opera dates back to the Greek dramas in which stories were acted out and choruses recited the text. It is also related to the medieval church plays, such as the Liturgical Dramas and the Mysteries of the 11th through 16th centuries. During the 17th through the 20th centuries the opera developed through several styles. For example: the Italian (17th century) Florentine opera, Roman opera, Venetian opera, French opera, English opera, German opera, Neapolitan opera (18th century), Russian opera, 19th century Music-Drama, and Contemporary opera. See the following entries plus others listed for specific details on types of operas and musical plays: *Opera ballad, *Opéra bouffe, *Opera buffa, Opéra comique, *Opera di camera, *Opera seria, *Operetta, *Spingspiel, *Ballad opera, *Music-Drama, *Bel canto, *Neapolitan opera, *Liturgical Dramas, and *Mysteries.

Opera ballad See *Ballad opera.

Opéra bouffe (Fr.) (ŏ—pā—rä boōf) A French variety of comic or light opera more like a musical or operetta than an opera. A farce or satire. It should not be confused with opera buffa or opéra comique. Example: Jacques Offenbach (1819-1880), *Orpheus in the Underworld.*

Opera buffa (It.) (ŏ'—pā—rä boō'—fa) Italian comic opera which included dialogue called recitativo secco. The speaking parts came between the various vocal solos, vocal ensembles, patter songs, or airs. The story was comical, about everyday people, or of a very light nature. The opera buffa was related to the Italian intermezzo of the 16th and 17th centuries and was usually in two acts. The form was developed to a high point during the 18th century. Examples: Giovanni Pergolesi (1710-1736), *La Serva Padrona;* Wolfgang Amadeus Mozart (1756-1791), *Marriage of Figaro;* Gioacchino Rossini (1792-1868), *Barber of Seville.* See *Recitative, *Secco.

Opéra comique (Fr.) (ŏ—pā—rä kŏ—mēk) An early 18th century form of comic opera in France. It began as a light musical play with spoken dialogue. During the 19th century the meaning of opéra comique changed to include, frequently, operas of a tragic or serious nature which had passages of spoken dialogue. Examples: Jacques Offenbach (1838-1880), *The Tales of Hoffman;* Georges Bizet (1838-1875), *Carmen.*

Opera di camera (It.) (ō'–pā–rä dē kä'–mā–rä) Chamber opera.

Opéra, L' (Fr.) (lŏ–pā–rä) Academie de Musique. The first opera house built in France in 1671.

Opera seria (It.) (ō'–pā–rä sä'–rē–ä) A serious or tragic opera in three acts which was important during the 17th and 18th centuries. It included the use of the aria da capo and the recitative. The arias were elaborate and greatly ornamented. The story often centered on legendary characters and the scenes were elaborate. A term applied to Italian opera and Italian style operas such as: Wolfgang Amadeus Mozart (1756-1791). *La Clemenza di Tito.*

Operetta Small opera or light opera. A play which includes songs, dances, orchestral accompaniment, spoken parts, and romantic melodies. Examples: Franz von Suppé (1819–1895), *Boccaccio;* Gilbert and Sullivan (1842-1900), *H.M.S. Pinafore;* Victor Herbert (1859-1924), *Babes in Toyland.*

Ophicleide (1) On the organ, a 16 foot pedal reed. (2) A 19th century keyed instrument of the brass family. It was a bass instrument having a conical metal tube which was bent double, a cup mouthpiece like a brass instrument, keys similar to the present day saxophone, a range of three octaves, and was an imporevement over the Serpent and bass horn in design and addition of keys. It was replaced by the brass tuba during the mid-nineteenth century.

Opus (Lat.) A work. A composition numbered according to the order of the publication of the work or to indicate the order in which the works have been composed.

Or (Fr.) (ŏr) But.

Orageuse (Fr.) (ŏ–rä–gûz) Agitated.

Oratorio The term comes from the Latin oratori(um) which means oratory. Oratory was a religious service with music held in the Church of the Oratory of St.

Philip Neri in Rome during the 16th century. An oratorio is a work with a sacred or contemplative text in a musical setting which includes solo voices, chorus and orchestra. It has some characteristics of an operatic work, but without action, dance, scenery, or costumes and was, and still is, performed in a concert hall or a church. Examples: George Frideric Handel (1685-1759), *Messiah;* Franz Josef Haydn (1732-1809), *The Creation;* Arthur Honegger (1892-1955), *King David;* Felix Mendelssohn (1809-1847), *Elijah;* Carl Orff (b. 1895), *Carmina Burana.*

Oratoria volgare (It.) (ō—rä—tō'—rē—ō vŏl—ga'—rä) The text of the oratorio is in the vernacular. See *Oratorio.

Orchestra A group of instrumentalists who perform as a separate unit or are associated with a larger work, such as opera. The term orchestra as an organized ensemble dates back to the 17th century opera houses. The term today has several meanings: a symphony orchestra, a chamber orchestra, show orchestra, dance orchestra, string orchestra, jazz orchestra, etc. The common large concert orchestra of the Romantic period and Contemporary period is comprised of the following four basic sections as listed on a full orchestra score: woodwind section, brass section, percussion section, and string section. Instruments in each section from a high range to a low are as follows: Woodwinds; piccolo (1), flutes (3), oboes, (3), English horn (1) clarinets (3), bass clarinet (1), bassoons (3), contra-bassoon (1), added for special works are alto clarinet (1), saxophones (1—3) (soprano, alto, tenor, baritone); Brasses; French horns (6—8), trumpets, (4), trombones (4), tuba (1); Percussion; timpani (4), bass drum (1), snare drum (1), side drum (1), tenor drum (1), set of bells (1), cymbals (1 set), piano (1), etc.; Strings; violins (18 first, 18 second), violas (12—14), celli (10—12), string bass (8—10), harp (1—2). The major orchestra of today has a complement of about 100 musicians.

Orchestral An organ stop that sounds like an orchestral instrument.

Orchestral score A full score in which each instrument has its part written on a separate staff. The sections from top to bottom are arranged as follows: woodwinds, brass, percussion, and strings. See *Score.

Orchestra pit The area in which the theatre orchestra or opera orchestra is seated. It is a lowered area just in front of the stage.

Orchestration The instrumentation of a musical score. To orchestrate or bandstrate music in order that it can be played by instrumentalists. The arranging or scoring of a musical work keeping in mind the range of instruments, the tone color of instruments, and combination of instruments, the transposition of music for certain instruments, the technical facility of the instruments, the style, etc.

Orchestrion A large 19th century mechanical organ that produces a sound similar to that of the orchestra.

Ordinaire (Fr.) (ŏr—dē—nĕr) Ordinary. Ordinario (It.) (ŏr—dē—nä'—rē—ō) Ordinary.

Ordinary of the Mass The text of the Mass that remains the same ("Kyrie", "Gloria", "Credo", "Sanctus" and "Benedictus", "Agnus Dei") as opposed to the Proper of the Mass which changes with the day or feast. See *Mass.

Ordre (Fr.) (ŏr—dr) Order. A suite.

Oremus (Lat.) "Let us pray". Sung or recited just before prayers of the Mass.

Organ A keyboard instrument having a wind chest, a blower to supply a continuous flow of air, manuals (from one to seven), and a pedal keyboard. The manuals and pedal keyboard are connected with the pipes by means of rods (trackers), pneumatic devices, or electric action. The pipes are flue type (whistle types) or reed type (beating reed and resonator). The stops admit wind to each pipe or to each register. There are many different stops which allow a variety of mixtures and tone colors. Couplers are used to join manuals and make divisions available to various keyboards. The divisions of the organ are called: Pedal, Choir, Great,

Swell, Positive, Solo, and Echo. An organ is quite complete with three manuals (Choir, Great, and Swell). It is not uncommon to find organs with two manuals (Great and Swell). The Great organ includes the most powerful stops while the Swell organ includes the softest stops. The Solo manual has stops of more individual timbre. The larger organs have a complete Pedal organ and the Echo organ. A five manual keyboard would include Choir (the lowest), Great, Swell, Solo, and Echo. There are a variety of instruments which use the name organ. See *Barrel organ, *Electric organ, *Mouth organ, *Hammond organ. Also see *Great organ, *Pipe organ, *Reed organ, *Extension organ (unit organ), *Double diapason, *Divisions, *Diapason, *Flue pipes, *Manual, *Mixture, *Stops, *Mutation stops, *Pedal keyboard, *Swell, *Electronic musical instruments, *Choir organ.

Organ chorale A polyphonic organ work based on the melodic line of a church chorale or hymn. See *Chorale, *Hymn, *Chorale prelude.

Organe (Fr.) (ŏr—gän) Organ.

Organetto (It.) (ŏr—gä—nĕt'—tō) A small medieval organ which was portable.

Organista (It.) (ŏr—gä—nĭs'—tä) Organist.

Organistrum (Lat.) Hurdy-gurdy.

Organ Mass The Mass sung in plainchant alternating with the organ playing in polyphonic style.

Organo (It.) (ŏr'—gä—nō) Organ. Organo d'eco (It.) (ŏr'—gä—nō dä'—kō) See *Echo organ. Organo di coro, (It.) (ŏr'—gä—nō dē kō'—rō) See *Choir organ. Organo pieno, (It.) (ŏr'—gä—nō pē—ā'—nō) Full organ.

Organo pleno (Lat.) Full organ.

Organ point Pedal point. A tone sustained below a moving voice (s).

Organum (Lat.) (1) Organ. (2) A system of writing music in polyphonic style from the 9th century into the 13th century. It consisted of adding one or more voices to a plainchant or cantus firmus. There are several types of organum. Early parallel organum, in which the added voices started and ended in unison and moved throughout the work with the cantus firmus at intervals of the 4th, 5th, and octave. The harmony moved with each note of the cantus firmus. Early examples of this strict organum can be found in the 9th century document called *Musica Enchiriadis.* Simple organum included two voices, composite organum, three or four voices. Free organum followed with the added part keeping the same rhythm but moving in different directions (e.g., oblique and contrary motion) in 4ths, 5ths, octaves and sometimes 3rds. In this free organum the lower voice is called the vox principalis (called tenor). Later, (12th century on) the melismatic style of organum introduced elaborate melodic movement on one syllable while the cantus firmus maintained the basic musical line, i.e., several notes in the added part against one note in the tenor. The later development of measured organum introduces the element of measured rhythmic modes to the upper parts and often to the cantus firmus. During the 13th century polyphonic music was developed further through the motet. The addition of 4ths, 5ths, and octaves is also known as diaphony. Music in thirds was known as gymel. A study of early organum if found in *Musica Enchiriadis.* Other sources: *Masterpieces of Music Before 1750* by Parrish and Ohl; *Source Readings in Music History from Classical Antiquity Through the Romantic Era* by W. O. Strunk; (See *"A Selected Annotated Bibliography").

Orgel (Ger.) (ŏr'–gȧl) Organ.

Orgelbüchlein (Ger.) *Little Organ Book.* Forty-six chorale preludes for organ by J. S. Bach (1685-1750).

Orgelmesse (Ger.) (ôr'–gȧl–mĕs–sȧ) See *Organ Mass.

Orgelpunkt (Ger.) (ôr'–gȧl–po͝ongkt) Pedal point.

Orgue (Fr.) (ôrg) Organ.

Orgue expressif (Fr.) (ôrg ĕk–sprĕs–ēf) Expressive organ. A reed organ.

Orgue plein (Fr.) (ôrg plă(n)) Full organ.

Orgue positif (Fr.) (ôrg pō–zē–tēf) Positive organ. Choir organ.

Ornaments Embellishments or notes added to a musical line. See *Appoggiatura, *Agréments, *Mordent, *Nachschlag, *Trill, *Turn.

Orotund A clear, full rich voice, tone, or style of singing.

Orphéon (Fr.) (ôr—fā—ō(n)) Choral singing. Choral society.

O Salutaris Hostia (Lat.) "O Saving Host". A hymn sung in the Roman Catholic Church at the service of Benediction or after the "Benedictus" during the Mass.

Oscillator A device used in creating electronic music. It produces pitch sounds.

Oscilloscope An instrument which shows a graphic representation of amplitude, frequency, etc., of signals produced by musical instruments, voices, etc.

Ossia (It.) (ōs—sē'—ä) Or else. A term which indicates an alternative version to a given musical section.

Ostinato (It.) (ŏs—tē—nä'—tō) Obstinate. A figure which is repeated over and over, in succession throughout a composition, usually at the same pitch level. When the figure is in the bass it is called basso ostinato (which means obstinate bass) or ground bass. The principle of ostinato is a characteristic of the chaconne and passacaglia. An example of the ostinato treatment is found in the J. S. Bach (1685-1750), *Passacaglia in C Minor for Organ.* The following ostinato theme is repeated many times in exact form or in some variation. It stays primarily in the bass line. Theme: J. S. Bach, *Passacaglia in C Minor:*

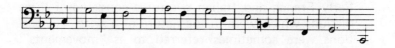

See *Ground bass, *Chaconne, *Passacaglia.

Ôter (Fr.) (ō—tā) To remove; to take off.

Ottava (It.) (ŏt—tä'—vä) Eighth or octave. Indicated by 8va. Ottava alta, (It.) (ŏt—tä'—vä äl'—tä) An octave

271

above. Ottava bassa, (It.) (ŏ t–tä '–vä bäs '–sä) 8va bassa. An octave below. Ottava sopra, (It.) (ŏt–tä '–vä sŏp '–rä) An octave above. Ottava sotto, (It.) (ŏt–tä '–vä sŏt '–tō) 8va bassa. An octave below.

Ottavino (It.) (ŏt–tä–vē '–nō) Flauto Piccolo (It.). Small flute. Piccolo.

Otto (It.) (ŏt '–tō) The number eight.

Ottone (It.) (ŏt–tō '–nä) Brass.

Ottoni (It.) (ŏt–tō '–nē) Brass instruments.

Ou (Fr.) (ōo) Either, or.

Out-chorus In jazz, the last chorus of music played by the entire band. A climax of the music.

Outré (Fr.) (ōo–trä) Exaggerated or excessive.

Ouvert (Fr.) (ōo –vĕr) Open.

Ouvrage (Fr.)) (ōo–vräzh) Work of art.

Overblow To blow excessively into a wind instrument in order to produce overtones or harmonics.

Overstring A method of stringing the piano so that the bass strings cross diagonally with the treble strings. It adds length.

Overtones The partials that vibrate above the fundamental tone. The notes above the first in the harmonic series. See *Harmonics.

Overture (Ouverture, (Fr.) (ōo–vĕ r–tür)) (1) An instrumental composition performed as a prelude to an opera, etc. (2) An independent piece for orchestra in one movement and in sonata-allegro form. (3) A programmatic piece which is played as a concert overture. (4) A potpourri overture which is a group of melodies and excerpts played before a musical comedy, etc. (5) Early French and Italian overtures consisted of three sections which were in the nature of a suite. The sections were sometimes referred to as "movements". (6) Preludes in free form. The three section overture or orchestral overture grew out of the Italian and French opera. The Baroque Italian overture used the order fast, slow, fast, e.g., the *Overture to Dal Malo II Bene* by Alessandro Scarlatti (1660–1725). The French overture used the order slow, fast (fugal section), slow, e.g., *Overture to Alcidiane* by Jean Baptiste Lully (1632—1687). The Classical overture followed the Baroque French and Italian overture and was in sonata-allegro form, e.g., *Overture to the Marriage of Figaro* by Wolfgang Amadeus Mozart (1756-1791). The 19th century Romantic concert overture also used sonata-allegro form and free "Vorspeil". (Johannes Brahms (1833—1897), *Academic Festival Overture,* Opus 80; Peter Ilyich Tchaikovsky (1840-1893), *Romeo and Juliet).* The 20th century single movement overture is much like the symphonic poem (Aaron Copland (b. 1900), *Outdoor Overture).*

273

P (1) The abbreviation for piano which means soft; (2) for pedal in piano music; (3) for positif in organ music.

Pace The speed or tempo of the music. Movement.

Pacifico (It.) (pä—chē '—fē—kō) Peaceful. The passage is to be played in a quiet or peaceful manner.

Pad (1) The soft material used on the metal keys of the clarinet, saxophone, etc. to allow the keys to close tightly. (2) The cushion or felt on the piano hammers.

Paean A song of praise or joy. A hymn of thanksgiving.

Pai-hsiao A Chinese flute-type instrument. Ten to sixteen pipes are tied together forming pan pipes. Each pipe produces a specific pitch.

Pair (Fr.) (pĕ r) Equal, even.

Paix (Fr.) (pā) Quiet, rest.

Paléographie musicale (Fr.) (pā—lā—ō—grä—fē mü—zē—käl) A collection of facsimiles of manuscripts of plain-song along with discussions of the works published by the Benedictines of Solesmes beginning in 1889.

Palestrinastile (It.) (pä—lĕs —trē—näs'—tē—lā) In the style of Palestrina. The 16th century Italian style of polyphonic music as is found in the works of Palestrina. The unaccompanied, a cappella style of Palestrina.

Pamba A small drum of India.

Pandean pipes An ancient Greek instrument. See *Pan pipes.

Pandiatonicism The use of the tones of the diatonic scale without adhering to the standard practice of writing tonal progressions, resolutions, voice leadings, etc. A freer use of tones in contemporary music. It was a reaction against Romantic chromaticism and resulted in diatonic dissonance rather than the chromatic dissonance of tone-row music. The term was coined by Nicolas Slonimsky. Igor Stravinsky (b. 1882) for example, illustrates this technique in many of his works. For instance, in his *Sonata for Two Pianos.*

Pandora See *Pandore.

Pandore A family of citterns invented in the 16th century which had a flat front and back sides having three lobes, pegs and wire strings and was played by plucking the strings. They were especially popular in England. They were called by many names such as pandora, bandora, bandoer, bandore.

Pandura An ancient lute-type instrument of Greece. It was the long-neck variety of lute.

Pandurina (It.) (pän–doo–re ʹ–nä) A small lute.

Panpipes An ancient Greek instrument. It consists of vertical pipes of varying lengths tied together as one instrument. The tone is produced by blowing across the upper ends of the pipes. Tones are changed by moving the instrument across the lips. Each pipe has its own pitch. See *Pandean.

Pantaleon (1) A large and elaborate dulcimer used during the 18th century. One instrument is said to have had 185 strings and another 276 strings. These strings were played by two small hammers. See *Dulcimer. (2) A late 18th century name used in Germany for horizontal pianos having a hammer that used a downward stroke.

Pantonality Pan is taken from the Greek meaning all. Pantonality means combining all tones or all keys. When several keys are used the tonal center would be lost, therefore, it would move away from tonal music to the atonal concept in composition. See *Atonal, *Bitonality, *Polytonality, *Twelve-tone row.

Parallel chords Chords moving in succession on a scale pattern. If chords progressed step by step on a diatonic scale in root position the result would be parallel 5ths and octaves. Generally, in classical harmony this is to be avoided when writing triads, etc. See *Parallel 5ths, *Parallel octaves.

Parallel fifths The harmonization of two voices moving at the interval of a fifth. This is to be generally avoided in classical harmonic writing. However, composers do use "hidden" fifth, or "fifths" for certain effects. See *Horn fifths.

Parallel intervals Intervals of the same size moving consecutively.

Parallel keys The same note serving as the tonic for both a major and a minor key. For example, F major and F minor.

Parallel motion Two or more parts moving at the same interval.

Parallel octaves The harmonization of two voices moving at the interval of an octave. This is to be generally avoided in classical harmony. However, composers do write the "hidden" octave or "octaves" for certain effects.

Parallel organum (1) The added voice moves with the cantus firmus in parallel motion at an interval of an octave, fourth, or fifth. See *organum. E.g.,

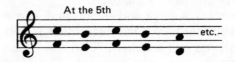

(2) Later, parallel thirds (gymel). See *Gymel.

Paraphrase An arrangement, transcription, or elaboration or a musical work or line. A rewriting of a text.

Parlando (It.) (pär—län '—dō) In vocal music, to perform in a spoken style. An imitation of speech pattern especially in rapid passages.

Parlante (It.) (pär—län '—tā) To speak. A spoken style in either vocal or instrumental music. See *Parlando.

Parody A humorous imitation of a work, person, etc.

Parody Mass The use of borrowed music in writing a musical setting of the Mass during the Renaissance period. The music was borrowed from existing motets, chansons, etc. Many of the Masses of Giovanni Palestrina (1524-1594) are Parody Masses.

Part (1) A single line of a composition. A vocal part; an instrumental part; a section of a score for an instrument(s) or voice(s). (2) A division of a work; a movement. (3) A part-book, separate parts under one cover for each voice. E.g., the tenor part for several works would be contained in a separate book, bass part in another, etc.

Parte (It.) (pär'—tā) Part. See *Colla parte.

Partials A frequency component. Notes of the harmonic series. The fundamental (lowest partial) and the upper tone or upper partials. See *Harmonic series..

Partial score A part score.

Partial signature A method of notation before the 16th century in which some parts, usually the upper parts, in a polyphonic piece did not use a full signature. For example, the lower part might have one or two flats while the upper part had none.

Partial tone The fundamental or harmonic of a tone. A pure tone. See *Partials.

Partie (Fr.) (pär—tē) Part, section or movement.

Partie (Ger.) (pär—tē ') Part, partita.

Partimento (It.) (pär—tē—mĕn'—tō) Division. A practice used in the 17th & 18th centuries which was an improvization or exercise on a figured bass. See *Figured bass, *Division.

Partita (It.) (pär—tē '—tä) Divided. A term used in the 17th & 18th centuries for an instrumental suite or a set of variations. For example, it is treated as a suite by J. S. Bach (1685-1750) in his "Six Partitas for Clavier" (Clavierübung, Part I). The original meaning is variation, as used by Girolamo Frescobaldi (1583-1643) in his *Toccate e Partite d'Intavolatura di Cembalo.* See *Suite.

Partition (Fr.) (pär—tē—sē—ō(n)) Score.

Partitur (Ger.) (pär—tē—toor ') Full score; Partitura (It.) (pär—tē—too'—rä) Full score.

Partsong A term used chiefly to describe the homophonic style of writing of a choral composition. The upper melody is most important while the other voices are secondary. Used in the 19th century writing.

Part-writing The interest in the composition is horizontal. That is, in each separate melody. Each musical line is equally important and has good voicing. See *Counterpoint, *Voice leading.

Pas (Fr.) (pä) (1) No; not. (2) Step; pace; gait; dance, e.g., pas de deux, a duet in ballet.

Passacaglia (It.) (pä—sä—käl'—yä); passecaille (Fr.) (päs—cä—yå). (Possibly from Pasacalle (Sp.) (pä—sä—cäl'—lyā) defined as street music or an ancient dance). Originally, a moderately slow dance in triple time. During the 17th and 18th centuries, the passacaglia became an important form of instrumental music. Early suites incorporated the passacaglia. The passacaglia is generally defined as a continuous variation based on an ostinato. The ostinato is usually in the bass, but could be in another part. It is in triple meter and in polyphonic style. Many contemporary composers use this Baroque form in their compositions. The passacaglia is usually in variation form over a ground bass as is found in an example from J. S. Bach (1685-1750), *Passacaglia in C minor for Organ.* The ground bass is as follows:

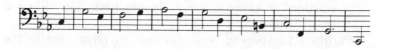

An example of the passacaglia as used by a contemporary composer is found in Part I of the *Symphony No. 3* by William Schuman (b. 1910). The 1st theme (ostinato bass) of the passacaglia. See *Chaconne, *Ground bass, *Ostinato, *Variation.

Passage A phrase, part, section, etc. of a composition.

Passaggio (It.) (pä—säd'—jē—ō) Passage or crossing. A transition.

Passecaille (Fr.) (päs—kä—yå) Passacaglia.

Passepied (Fr.) (pas—pyā) Called paspy in England during the 17th century. A moderately fast dance of the 17th and 18th centuries in $\frac{3}{8}$ or $\frac{6}{8}$. It probably originally came from Brittany and was later incorporated into the Baroque suite. Example: J. S. Bach (1685-1750), *Suite No. 1 in C for Orchestra* (Overture and first theme, 2nd theme ($\frac{4}{4}$), Courante ($\frac{3}{2}$),

Gavotte (¢), Forlane ($\frac{6}{4}$), Minuet ($\frac{3}{4}$), Bourée
(¢) and Passepied ($\frac{3}{4}$).) Another example of the
dance is found in the W. A. Mozart (1756-1791) opera,
Idomeneo, K. 366. See *Suite.

Passing modulation A temporary or transient modulation.

Passing note or tone A non-harmonic note that moves
stepwise between two notes which are consonant with
the harmony. E.g.,

The melody notes A and F are consonant with the F
chord. G is the passing note.

Passione (It.) (päs—sē—ō'—nā) Passion.

Passion music A musical setting of the Passion taken from
the gospel of Mathew, Mark, Luke or John. Settings of
these texts are used in the Roman Catholic Church
during Holy Week. There are several varieties of Passion
music. The Passion of the Middle Ages was sung as a
Plainsong Passion. It was sung in Latin in the fashion
of a play which included the roles of Christ, the
Narrator and the Crowd (Turba). Later the part of the
Crowd was done in part singing. From about the middle
of the 15th century the text was set in polyphonic
style. When the polyphonic Turba section was contras-
ted with the plainsong section it was called Scenic or
Responsorial Passion. When the entire text was done
in polyphonic (motet) style it was called Motet Passion.
The Luthern Reformation led to a homophonic style
and the use of the vernacular. In the 17th century the
Oratorio Passion developed which included the many
innovations of the Baroque period such as aria, chorus,
orchestra, recitative, etc. and a freer treatment of the
text. With all the paraphrases, the application of the
Baroque technique, the free use of texts, the Passion
Oratorio became more an opera than an oratorio. J. S.
Bach assimilated all these developments and returned
the oratorio to the Passion style in his *St. John Passion*
and the *St. Mathew Passion*.

Pasticcio (It.) (päs–tē'–chē–ō) Mess, patch work. A work that consists of borrowed material from many sources. A medley of operatic airs. Popular during the 18th century. The term also applies to a collaboration on a work.

Pastiche (Fr.) (päs–tēsh) Medley. See *Pasticcio.

Pastorale Music that reflects the mood of a pastoral scene. An opera, cantata, or other vocal work based on a pastoral or mythological subject. An instrumental piece reflecting a pastoral scene. Example: Ludwig Van Beethoven (1770–1827), "Pastoral" *Symphony No. 6 in F,* Op. 68.

Pastourelle (Fr.) (päs–tōo r–ĕ l) (1) A French dance. (2) A medieval type of verse. (3) A song of pastoral nature.

Patetico (It.) (pä–tā'–tē–kō) Pathetic. Sadness or sorrow.

Pathétique (Fr.) (pä–tā–tēk) Pathetic or moving. Name used to describe a work. Example: Peter IlyichTschaikovsky (1840–1893), *Symphony No. 6 in B Minor,* Opus 74 is called "Pathétique".

Patter-song The rapid flow of words or syllables done to a simple melody and usually comic in nature. Used in opera and operetta. Example: Gioacchino Rossini (1792–1868), "Largo al factotum" from the *Barber of Seville.*

Pauken (Ger.) (powk'–å n) Kettledrums, timpani.

Pauroso (It.) (pä–ōo–rō'–zō) Fearful.

Pausa (It.) (pä'–ōo–zä) Pause, rest.

Pause (English) (Fr.) (pōz) (Ger.) (pow'–zå) A rest.

Pause sign (fermata, (It.))Hold. The sign ⌒ over a note or rest indicates that the note or rest should be held longer than the value indicated. See *Fermata, *General pause.

Pavane (Fr.) (pä–vän) A slow stately dance in $\frac{2}{4}$ or $\frac{4}{4}$ of the 16th and 17th centuries. Originally a Spanish folk dance, it found its way into the instrumental suite and was usually followed by the quicker galliarde. A modern example is Maurice Ravel's (1875–1937), *Pavane for a Dead Infanta* for Piano, and orchestrated for small orchestra.

Pavillon (Fr.) (pä—vē—yō(n)) Bell of a horn, trumpet, etc.

Peal Loud ringing of bells. A set of bells tuned to each other.

Pedal board The set of keys (keyboard) on the organ operated by the feet. The board consists of thirty (or thirty-two) notes with a range of two and one-half octaves from C below the bass staff up to f' (or g') in the treble clef.

Pedal clarinet Contra-bass clarinet.

Pedale (It.) (pā—dä'—lā) Pedal.

Pedal harp A harp having pedals that allow for chromatic notes.

Pédalier (Fr.) (pā—däl—yā) Pedal-board.

Pedalklavier (Ger.) (pā—däl'—klä—vēr') Pedal piano.

Pedalkoppel (Ger.) (pā—däl'—kŏp—ål) Pedal coupler. Used in organ playing.

Pedal note The basic or fundamental note of a harmonic series.

Pedal organ A division of the organ. See *Division.

Pedalpauken (Ger.) (pā—däl'—powk'—ån) Pedal-timpani. Timpani that use pedals for tuning and changing pitch. Some timpani have only turn screws around the rim to tune the timpani heads.

Pedal piano A piano used during the 19th century that had a pedal board added which was used to play the bass line.

Pedal point A tone in the bass part which is held for a considerable time while the harmony above changes. When the tone is held in a part other than the bass line, it is called inverted pedal. An example: The pedal note G in the last six measures of the bass line in the vocal fugue, "Kyrie eleison", from the *Missa Brevis No. 4* in .G by J. S. Bach (1685-1750). (Text omitted).

EXAMPLE – NEXT PAGE ►

Pedals The levers depressed by the feet on the organ, piano, harpsichord, etc.

Pedal tone The low or fundamental tone that can be "lipped" on some instruments such as the trombone or French horn. See *Harmonic series, *Pedal note.

Pentacorde (Fr.) (pă (n)—tä—kôrd) Pentachord. (1) A scale of five diatonic tones. (2) An instrument of five strings.

Pentatonic scale A scale that has a succession of five different tones within the octave, e.g., c, d, f, g, a, (c). Another example would be the black keys of the piano, e.g., c#, d#, f#, g#, a#, to the octave c#.

Per (Ger.) (pĕr) By; with.

Per (It.) (pĕr) For; through; by.

Percosse (It.) (pĕr—kŏs'—sā) Beating. Percussion instruments.

Percussion instruments Those instruments that are either shaken or struck to produce a sound. Some percussion instruments have drum heads made of skin, plastic, etc., while other percussion instruments are made of metal, wood, bone, etc. Some of these instruments such as timpani, bells, vibraphone, xylophone, celesta, etc. have definite pitch. The kettle drums can be tuned

282

by hand or by a pedal. Other percussion instruments are not of definite pitch, such as bass drum, cymbal, snare drum, maraca, triangle, tambourine, gong, etc. See *Kettle drum, *Glockenspiel, *Membranophone, *Idiophone, *See the individual entries.

Perdendosi (It.) (pĕr—dĕn—dō'—zē) Dying away. Softer and slower.

Perfect Time A time division (second division) in mensural notation. A note in perfect time equalled three of the lower note values. For example, in perfect time the breve equalled three semibreves. See *Prolation, *Imperfect time.

Perfect cadence Full close or final cadence. The cadence ends on a one chord in root position with the root of the chord in the bass and soprano. (1) In the perfect authentic cadence the leading chord is the dominant (V) in root position. (2) In the perfect plagal cadence the leading chord is the subdominant (IV) in root position. E.g.

Key of Bb Major:

PERFECT AUTHENTIC CADENCE　　PERFECT PLAGAL CADENCE

See *Cadence.

Perfect intervals Normally, intervals of the fourth, fifth and octave are perfect. Examples: perfect 4th = two whole steps and one half step; perfect 5th = three whole and one half step; perfect octave = five whole steps and two half steps.

Examples: NEXT PAGE ➤

P.4th P.5th P.octave(8th)

When a perfect interval is made smaller by a semitone it becomes diminished. When it is made larger by a semitone it becomes augmented. See *Intervals.

Perfect pitch Absolute pitch. Perfect pitch is the ability to identify by name a tone (pitch) that is heard, or to sing a note at the correct pitch without the aid of any instrument.

Period A musical sentence or natural division of a composition. It usually falls into eight or sixteen measures, or two or more phrases which end in a cadence.

Perpetual canon A circle canon. Each voice repeats its part over and over again, e.g., a round. See *Canon, *Circle canon.

Perpetual motion A fast piece of music with rapid and repeated note patterns.

Pesado (Sp.) (pā—sä'—dō) Heavy, dull.

Pesant (Fr.) (på—zä(n)) Pesante (It.) (pā—zän'—tā) Heavy, slow, ponderous.

Petit (Fr.) (på—tē) Also, petite (på—tēt) Small, short, low, miniature.

Petite flûte (Fr.) (på—tēt flüt) Piccolo.

Peu (Fr.) (pû) Not much, little, few. Peu à peu - by degrees, little by little.

Pezzo (It.) (pĕt'—tsō) A piece.

Phantasie (Ger.) (fän—tä—zē') Imagination, fancy, fantasy, fantasia, whim. See *Fantasia.

Phantasy or Fantasy (1) An instrumental piece of free structure. (2) An imaginative character piece. (3) A contrapuntal piece of the 16th and 17th centuries. Also called Fancy. Examples: Robert Schumann (1810—1856), *Phantasy in C,* Opus 17 for Piano; Wolfgang Amadeus Mozart (1756—1791), *Fantasia in D Minor,* K. 397 for Piano. (4) Compositions written for the W. W. Cobbett Competitions held in the early 20th century See *Fantasia, *Fantasia section.

Philharmonic (philharmonique, Fr.; Filarmonico, It.) Friend of music. The name used for societies of music or musical organizations.

Philharmonic pitches Old Philharmonic pitch and New Philharmonic pitch were two standards of pitch. Both are obsolete. See *Pitch, *Concert pitch.

Phrase A musical idea or musical thought. A unit, or group of notes, that have meaning. A natural grouping of notes or measures. It includes one or more motives and usually ends in a cadence. A phrase is often a unit of four measures, although it may have fewer or more measures. An example of a four measure phrase, the first theme, 4th movement, of *Symphone No. 9*, in D minor, Op. 125, "Choral" by Ludwig Van Beethoven (1770–1827).

Phrase Mark

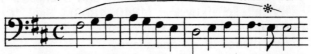

See *Phrase mark, *Phrasing.

Phrase mark The curved line that indicates the notes that form a phrase. An articulation mark that helps in performing a phrase. See *Phrase.

Phrasing The division of a musical sentence into phrases. The articulation of a musical line.

Phrygian mode An authentic church mode ranging from e—e' with a final of e and the dominant of c'. It can be sounded on the piano keyboard by playing the white keys in an ascending scale form E to E. See *Church modes, *Modes.

Piacere (It.) (pē—ä—chä '—rā) Pleasure; ad libitum.

Piacevolmente (It.) (pē—ä—chä—vōl—měn '—tā) Pleasingly or genially.

Pianamente (It.) (pē—än—ä—měn '—tā) Softly.

Pianino (Ger.) (pē—ä—nē '—nō) A cottage piano, upright piano, or cabinet piano. A pianette would be a small upright piano.

Pianissimo (It.) (pē—än—is '—sē—mō) Very soft. The term indicates that the music is to be played at an intensity softer than piano, i.e. very soft. The abbreviation for the term is pp. See *Dynamics.

Pianist One who performs professionally on the piano. Pianism refers to the technique or performance of a pianist.

Piano (1) A term meaning soft. The music is to be played at a soft dynamic level. The abbreviation for piano is the letter p. (2) An abbreviation for the instrument, pianoforte.

Piano-accordian An accordian that has a vertical piano-type keyboard which is played with the right hand. See *Accordian.

Piano concerto A concerto that features piano and orchestra. A popular example is: *Concerto No. 1 in B Flat Minor,* Op. 23, for Piano and Orchestra by Peter Ilyich Tchaikovsky (1840–1893). See *Concerto.

Piano duet Music for two pianists. It may be played on two pianos or on one piano.

Pianoforte (It.) (pē–ä'–nō–fŏr'–tā) Piano. Literally soft-loud, a term which distinguished it from the earlier harpsichord which could not sound gradations of loudness. The pianoforte followed the clavichord and harpsichord. A form of the piano was invented in Italy by B. Cristofori in 1709 and by the end of the 18th century the piano had just about displaced the harpsichord. The name for the Cristofori invention was *gravicembalo col piano e forte* which indicates that it was a type of cembalo (harpsichord) that produced dynamic levels of soft (piano) and loud (forte). It had hammer action and a "grand" shape. This instrument led to the present day piano after many developments such as the perfection of the piano action (escapement and hammer check), perfection of the pedals, changes in the shape, etc. The modern piano comes in many sizes, either as an upright or a grand. It has a series of strings which graduate in length, thickness, and tension. The lowest strings are thick and there is a single string for each note. Other notes are assigned two or three strings. The strings are sounded by a hammer which is activated by keys on the finger board. The standard finger board has 88 keys that progress in semitones ranging from A" to c'''''. Many pianos have three pedals which are operated by the feet. The left pedal (soft pedal) shifts the action and hammers a little to the left so that the hammers hit fewer strings than usual. The center pedal (sostenuto) raises the dampers from only the notes played so that only they are sustained as the pedal is held. The right pedal (sustaining or damper pedal) raises all the dampers which permits the strings to continue vibrating after the keys are released. The piano has a sound board and is a combination of a stringed instrument and a percussion instrument. Varieties of pianos: Grand type pianos in many sizes; upright pianos in many sizes, spinet, and square. See *Una corda, *Tre corde.

Pianola A type of player piano which is pumped with the feet.

Piano organ Street organ.

Piano quartet A composition for one piano and usually a string trio (1 violin, 1 viola, and 1 cello). Example: W. A. Mozart (1756-1791), *Quartet in G Minor, K. 4, Piano and Strings.*

Piano quintet Usually music written for a piano plus a string quartet (2 violins, 1 viola and 1 cello) Example: Robert Schumann (1810—1856), *Quintet in E^b,* Op. 44, Piano and Strings.

Piano roll The keys of a player piano are activated by the perforations on the piano roll.

Piano trio Music usually written for one piano, one violin and one cello. Example: Ludwig Van Beethoven (1770 —1827), *Trio in B^b,* Op. 97, Violin, Cello, Piano.

Piatto (It.) (pē—ät'—tō) Cymbal.

Pibgorn (Welsh) A Celtic reed-type instrument made from an animal shin-bone with a bell made of horn.

Pibroch The most important form of bagpipe music. It consists of ornamental variations on a theme (urlar) with each variation increasing in speed and difficulty.

Picardy third or "Tierce de Picardie" When a piece in a

minor mode (17th — 18th centuries) or modal piece (16th century) ends with a major chord (major 3rd), that major 3rd is called a Picardy 3rd. A final chord, during the 16th century, was usually a major chord regardless of the mode. An example of a "Picardy third" is illustrated in the Baroque fugue in G minor by J. S. Bach (1685–1750), "Little Fugue" in G minor, for Organ. Example: (last two measures)

g minor_____→ G Major

Picchettato (It.) (pē̄—kĕ t—tä̈'—tō) A type of spiccato bowing. A short bowing stroke. See *Bowing.

Piccolo (It.) (pē̄'—kō̄—lō̄) Small. (1) A small flute pitched one octave above the flute. It sounds from d" to c"'''' but the part is written an octave lower. (2) An organ stop. The abbreviation is picc. See *Flute.

Pickelflöte (Ger.) (pē̄'—kå̊ l—flĕ (r)—tå̊) Octave-flute or piccolo.

Pieno (It.) (pē̄—ā̈'—nō̄) Full.

Pietà (It.) (pē̄—ā̈—tä̈') Mercy, pity.

Pietoso (It.) (pē̄—ā̈—tō̄'—zō̄) Merciful; tenderly.

Piffero (It.) (pē̄'—fā̈—rō̄) An 18th century Italian term for a fife or shepherd's pipe.

Pincer (Fr.) (pă̈ (n)—sā̈) (1) To pinch, to pluck, to play, as to pluck a stringed instrument. (2) A mordent.

P'ip'a A Chinese short lute.

Pipe (1) A tube of a musical instrument. (2) A single tube instrument such as flute, piccolo, etc. (3) An organ pipe. (4) An end-blown flute called pipe which is played with one hand, while a small drum is played with the other hand. See *Farandole, *Tabor. (5) Bagpipe, panpipes, etc.

Piqué (Fr.) (pē—kā) A type of short bow stroke in string playing indicated by a dot over or under the note. Spiccato bowing. See *Spiccato, *Bowing.

Piston (1) A piston valve. Piston or valve on a brass instrument such as the trumpet. (2) Cornet à pistons, (Fr.) (kôr—nā tä pēs—tō(n)) The modern cornet. See *Valve.

Pitch The relative position of a note in a series. The highness or lowness of a tone. The number of vibrations per second of a tone determine the pitch. The vps double at the octave. Many different tunings were used throughout the history of music. There were different tuning pitches for choir, organ, wind instruments, etc., depending on the area and time in history. Today the standard pitch for a' is 440 double vibrations per second (adopted in 1939). The old instrumental pitch or concert pitch adopted in 1859 was a' = 435 vps at 59º F or 439 vps at 68º F. See *Concert pitch.

Pitch letter names Several systems are used to identify the several octaves or the location of a pitch on the grand staff. The one used to identify pitches and octaves throughout this book is as follows:

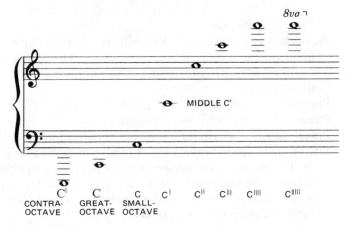

CONTRA- GREAT- SMALL-
OCTAVE OCTAVE OCTAVE

Other systems identify middle c' as c with the other octaves having relative markings. See *Keyboard, *Letter names, *Scales, *Syllables.

Pitch pipe A small reed or flue pipe used to produce tones for tuning instruments or to establish a pitch for singing. The early ones were pipes with a stopper which was used to vary the pitch. Today, there are circular reed pitch pipes (based on the harmonica principle) which sound the semitones within the octave.

Piu (It.) (pē–ōo') More. E.g., piu allegro — faster.

Piu mosso (It.) (pē–ōo' mŏs'–sō) More motion.

Piuttosto (It.) (pē–ōo–tŏs'–tō) Rather.

Pivotchord A chord common to the old and new key when progressing through modulation. Example:

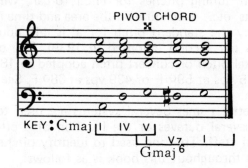

See *Modulation.

Pizzicato (It.) (pit–tsē–kä'–tō) A direction used for an instrument that is usually bowed. The string is to be plucked with the finger. The abbreviation pizz, is usually used.

Placare (It.) (plä–kä'–rā) Placate. To calm.

Placido (It.) (plä–chē'–dō) Placid.

Plagal cadence A perfect cadence moving from IV to I. The harmonic cadence IV–I. The subdominant is the leading chord and moves to the tonic with the chord in root position and the tonic note in the top voice. Also known as the Amen Cadence. See *Cadence, *Perfect Cadence. Example: NEXT PAGE ➤

Key of B♭ Major

IV   I

Plagal modes In the system of church modes, each of the finalis belongs to two church modes, one authentic and the other plagal. The authentic modes begin with the finalis and end one octave higher. The plagal modes begin a fourth below the finalis and end an octave higher or a fifth above the finalis. See *Church modes, *Modes.

Plainchant See *Plainsong.

Plainsong A single line of vocal music (monophonic), unaccompanied, and having a free rhythm. The style is used in many liturgies, a well-known example being the Gregorian chant. The rhythm is dependent on the text and in early times special notation (neumes) was used. It is modal music with a liturgical text. See *Gregorian chant, *Neumes.

Plainte (Fr.) (plă(n)t) Accent. An ornament of the Baroque period. See *Nachschlag.

Plat (Fr.) (plä) Flat; dish. Cymbal.

Player-piano A piano that is played by means of a pneumatic device which responds to a piano roll.

Plectrum (1) A small piece of plastic, wood, ivory, etc. that is used to pluck strings of instruments such as the banjo, guitar, etc. (2) A quill of a harpsichord.

Plein jeu (Fr.) (plĕ(n) zhû) Full play. Full organ.

Plénitude (Fr.) (plā—nē—tüd) Fullness.

Pleno (Sp.) (plā '—nō) Full.

Plica (plicare, Lat., a fold) An ornament of the Medieval period which was indicated by a vertical mark added to neumes. The mark indicated than an ornamented note was to be added higher (plica went up (⊔) from the note) or lower (plica went down (┌) from the note) than the main note. The interval was usually that of a second. See *Neumes.

Plunger In jazz, a regular toilet plunger used as a mute by trumpet and trombone players.

Plus (Fr.) (plü) More.

Pochette (Fr.) (pŏ—shĕ t) A small fiddle. Pocket violin.

Pochetto (It.) (pŏ—kĕt'—tō) Very little.

Poco (It.) (pō'—kō) Little.

Poco a poco (It.) (pō'—kō ä pō'—kō) Little by little.

Podium The platform on which a conductor stands.

Poi (It.) (pō'—ē) Then.

Point Dot; point; full stop; mark. (1) The point of a bow. (2) An imitative passage on a subject or theme in the 16th century motet.

Point d'orgue (Fr.) (pwă(n) dôrg) (1) Pause (⌒) (2) Pedal point. (3) The cadenza of a concerto indicated by the sign ⌒ placed over the chord which precedes the beginning of the cadenza.

Pointe (Fr.) (pwă(n)t) Tip (of the bow). Play at the tip end of the bow.

Polacca (It.) (pō—läk'—kä) See *Polonaise.

Polka A lively dance for couples, in $\frac{2}{4}$ time, which originated in Bohemia in the early 19th century.

Polo (Sp.) (pō'—lō) A Spanish dance in moderate triple time accompanied by singing. It has frequent syncopations and fast ornamental phrases sung on a syllable such as Ay.

Polonaise A graceful Polish dance in $\frac{3}{4}$ time having a basic rhythmic figure such as: $\frac{3}{4}$ ♪♪♪ ♪♪♪♪etc. It is in moderate tempo and the accent in the rhythmic motive falls on the second beat. Example: the Polonaises of Frédérick Chopin (1810—1849). It characteristically closes with a feminine ending with a strong accent on the second beat and the close of the third beat.

Polymetric The use of several meter or various accents at the same time. A device which is often used by contemporary composers such as: Elliott Carter (b. 1908), Paul Hindemith (1895—1963), Igor Stravinsky (1882—1971), and many others.

Polyphonic Many sounds. A composition having two or

more voices which are important as individual lines. These melodies move simultaneously. The interest is horizontal rather than vertical as in homophonic music. Examples of polyphonic styles are: the later examples of organum; round; motet; canzona; ricercar; fugue; etc. See *Counterpoint, *Homophonic.

Polyrhythm The use of many different contrasting rhythms at the same time.

Polythematic A composition is polythematic when it is based on or developed from two or more themes of equal importance.

Polytonality The use of two or more keys (tonalities) at the same time. The use of two keys at the same time is called bitonality. E.g., Béla Bartók (1881—1945), two Sonatas for Violin and Piano (1921—1922), *Sonata for Two Pianos and Percussion* (1937); Igor Stravinsky (1882—1971) *Petrouchka* and other composers such as Hindemith, Milhaud, etc.

Pommer (Ger.) (pŏm'—å r) A large double reed instrument of the shawm family. A forerunner of the bassoon and oboe. See *Shawm.

Pomposo (It.) (pŏm—pō'—zō) Pompous.

Ponticello (It.) (pŏn—tē—chě'—lō) Ponte (It.) (pŏn'—tā) (1) The bridge of a string instrument. (2) A term instructing the string player to play near the bridge. Also, sul ponticello.

Pop Rock A combination of folk music, pop music, and rock and roll. The rhythm and blues style of the 1900's developed into rock and roll during the 1950's. This rock style of performance combined with the pop music or temporal music is called pop rock. See *Jazz.

Pop tunes Tunes or songs popular at a given time.

Portamento (It.) (pôr—tä—měn'—tō) To carry across. An indication (slur) in vocal music and music played on bowed stringed instruments to glide from one note to the next in a smooth manner without a break in tone.

Portando (It.) (pôr—tän'—dō) Carrying. See *Portamento.

Portative organ A portable organ used during the Middle Ages.

Portato (It.) (pôr—tä'—tō) Half-staccato.

Portée (Fr.) (pŏr—tä) Stave.

Porte-musique (Fr.) (pôrt—mü—zēk) Music stand.

Posaune (Ger.) (pō—zow'—nå) (1) Trombone. (2) A 16 foot or 8 foot organ reed stop.

Posément (Fr.) (pō—zā—mä(n)) Sedately.

Poser (Fr.) (pō—zā) To give a musical pitch.

Positif (Fr.) (pō—zē—tēf) Choir-organ. An organ manual.

Position (1) The left hand positions on the finger board of stringed instruments. (2) The slide position on the trombone which changes the length of the tubing which changes pitches. (3) The placement of chords in root position, 1st, 2nd, or 3rd inversions. See *Inversions. (4) The position of the hands in keyboard music.

Positive organ A small (medieval) chamber pipe organ. A fixed type of small organ, rather than the portable variety.

Post-impressionsim The transition from Impressionism to Expressionism. Impressionism was a French movement away from the 19th century Romantic style. Expressionism was a German reaction to the Impressionistic movement.

Postlude A piece that concludes. An organ piece played at the end or after a service.

Post-Romanticism During the last decades of the 19th century, the grand style characteristics of the Romantic period declined. It became a period of transition to the new music of the 20th century. The music of Hugo Wolf, Richard Strauss, and Gustav Mahler represented this Post-Romantic style and transition.

Potpourri (Fr.) (pō—poo—rē) Hotchpotch. A medley of tunes.

Poussé (Fr.) (poo—sā) Up-bow.

Pousser (Fr.) (poo—sā) To push, e.g., to move the tempo.

Pracht (Ger.) (präkht) Splendor.

Pralltriller (Ger.) (präl'—tri l—å r) An inverted mordent. See *Mordent.

Precentor The director of music at a cathedral, church, etc.

Precipitoso (It.) (prā—chē—pē—tō '—zō) Rushing.

Preciso (It.) (prā—chē '—zō) Precise.

Prelude A work that introduces something else. A prelude to an act of an opera; an introduction to a fugue; a prelude or voluntary before a service; or a section of a suite. Also, a short independent piece for piano, organ, virginal, etc. Examples: J. S. Bach (1685—1750), *Prelude and Fugue in A Minor for Organ;* J. S. Bach — *English Suite, No. 2, in A Minor for Piano* (the suite begins with a prelude); J. S. Bach — Preludes in the *Well-tempered Clavichord* Books 1 and 2. An operatic prelude: "Prelude" to *Tristan und Isolde* by Richard Wagner (1813—1883).

Preparation To prepare a discord in harmony. The introduction of a dissonant note as a consonant note in the preceeding chord.

Près (Fr.) (prĕ) By, near; about; on the point of.

Presse (Fr.) (près) Hurry.

Presto (It.) (près '—tō) Quick. Quickly; fast tempo.

Prick song (Old English) prick; to mark or dot. A song that was written down as distinguished from the plainsong or folk song.

Prima (It.) (prē '—mä) First; before; premiere.

Prima donna (It.) (prē '—mä dŏn '—nä) First lady. The principal female singer in opera.

Primary chord The prime chord or I chord within tonal music. Tonic chord.

Primary triads Chords. The I, IV, V triads used in the diatonic tonal system.

Prima volta (It.) (prē '—mä vŏl '—tä) First time. Repeating music e.g., 1st ending (prima volta), then second ending (seconda volta). Written. ⌐1‾‾‾ AND ⌐2‾‾‾

Prime (1) In the Office hours-of the Roman Catholic Church, the canonical hour that follows Lauds. (2) The "interval" of a unison.

Primo (It.) (prē '—mō) Prime; first; foremost. E.g., tempo primo, play as in the original tempo. Also, it identifies the first part or upper part e.g., primo violino.

Primo uomo (It.) (prē '—mō ōo—ō '—mō) In opera, first

man or leading man. In the 18th century the singer of the tenor and castrato role.

Principal (1) An open diapason organ stop. (2) The "first" chair player in the orchestra.

Probe (Ger.) (prō'–bå) Rehearsal. **Proben** (Ger.) (prō'–bå n) To rehearse.

Processional A book that contains chants which are used in religious processions.

Programme music Music associated with or illustrative of an event, scene, picture, story, etc. It suggests an image or mood, conveys an impression, is imitative, etc. The opposite of absolute music. Examples: Peter Ilyich Tchaikovsky (1840–1893), *1812 Overture, Festival Overture,* Op. 49, and his *Romeo and Juliet Fantasy Overture.*

Progression In succession or sequence. The movement of a tone to the next tone or chord to chord in an organized manner. An example of a simple chord progression: Key of C,

$$\text{I} \qquad \text{IV}\,^6_4 \qquad \text{I} \qquad \text{V}_6 \qquad \text{I}$$

Progressive Jazz A modern style of jazz (1945–1955) which encompasses many styles of jazz with non-jazz elements. Progressive jazz was played by larger groups with the addition of varied instruments. It was influenced by contemporary composers in its use of dissonance, varied meters, polymeters, and tone-row techniques. It was an attempt to move forward in the development of jazz music. Representative composers of this style are Stan Kenton and Pete Rugolo.

Prolation The third division of mensural notation during the medieval period, (the oldest was the "moods," the second was time) prolation was the relationship between a semibreve (♦) and a minum. (♩). One relationship was called prolation major, where one semibreve is equal to three minums (♦ = ♩♩♩), another relationship was called prolation minor where one semibreve is equal to two minums (♦ = ♩♩). Several symbols were devised to indicate the prolation major or prolation minor. Symbols were also used to show the time relationship between the breve and the semibreve, which were called tempus perfectus (one breve equals three semibreves) and tempus imperfectus (one breve equal to two semibreves). E.g., O = tempus perfectus; C = tempus imperfectus. A dot placed within the circle or half circle indicated a prolation major; without the dot a prolation minor. See *Mensural notation, *Perfect time.

Prologue An introductory presentation before the first act of an opera, etc. Examples: Ruggiero Leoncavallo (1858–1919), the "Prologue" to the opera *Pagliacci.*

Pronto (It.) (prŏn '—tō) Prompt; quick.

Proper of the Mass The changing parts of the Roman Catholic Mass. The text and music change with the church calendar. "Introit", "Gradual", "Alleluia" or "Tract", "Offertory" and "Communion". See *Mass, *Ordinary of the Mass.

Proportion The ratio or relationship between: (1) a note and its augmentation or diminution; (2) strings, tones, scales and their relative vibrations; (3) rhythm and time elements; (4) balance in writing and orchestrating.

Prunkvoll (Ger.) (prŏongk '—fŏl) Pompous.

Psalm (1) A sacred hymn or a song with a sacred text. (2) "Psalms", a book of the Bible having 150 Psalms.

Psalmody Setting Psalms to music. The method of singing Psalms or hymns. Psalms are sung in (1) unison and direct style (recitation), (2) antiphonal style (alternation of two choirs), (3) responsorial style (alternation between soloist and choir).

Psalter The book of Psalms in the vernacular, sometimes with music.

Psaltery A medieval instrument similar to a dulcimer with a sound-box, but plucked with the fingers or a plectrum. This type of instrument dates back to ancient times. They were made in various shapes and forms.

Punctus (Lat.) Point, dot. (1) A note. (2) A dot after a note in mensural notation which adds half the value of the note. (3) The repeated section of an estampie is called punctus. The estampie (13th and 14th centuries) has four to seven sections called "puncti", each repeated with a first and second ending. See *Estampie.

Punta (It.) (po͝on'–tä) Tip. Punta d'arco indicates that a string player should bow at the tip of the bow. See *Arco.

Pure tone A complex tone consists of a fundamental and upper partials. One single part of the compound tone is called a pure tone.

Pyrotechnics A brilliant display of musicianship and technique.

Pythagorean scale A diatonic scale developed acoustically from the perfect fifth by Phythagoras.

Q

Qanon An Arabic psaltery. Kanûn.

Quadrat (Ger.) (kväd—rät') Natural (♮).

Quadrille Dance; square. An early 19th century square dance for two to four couples. It consisted of five parts or sections that alternated between $\frac{6}{8}$ time and $\frac{2}{4}$ time. The melodic lines were taken from current tunes or from operatic literature.

Quadripartie (Fr.) (kä—drē—pär—tē) Consisting of four parts. (1) A musical piece having four parts. (2) A quartet. (3) A composition for four voices or instruments.

Quadrivium (Lat.) The medieval universities based their studies on the seven liberal arts. The quadrivium included the mathematical studies: arithmetic, astronomy, geometry, and music. The other three arts, called trivium were grammar, dialetics, and rhetoric.

Quadruple Four. Music having four beats to a measure.

Quadruple counterpoint Four part counterpoint in which the parts may be inverted. See *Counterpoint, *Invertible counterpoint.

Quadruple-croche (Fr.) (kä—drü—pl—crŏsh) Sixty-fourth note (♬) or hemidemisemiquaver.

Quadruple fugue A fugue having four subjects. The subjects or countersubjects may be developed separately and then together or at the same time. See *Fugue.

Quadruple meter Four beats to a measure. Examples: $\frac{4}{4}$, $\frac{4}{2}$, $\frac{4}{1}$, $\frac{4}{8}$, $\frac{4}{16}$.

Quadruple stop A stop refers to placing the finger on a string in order to shorten the string, thereby changing the pitch. When the string player stops four strings at the same time forming a chord of four notes, that is a quadruple stop. See *Double stop, *Stopping.

Quadruplet A grouping of four notes of equal value being played in the time value of three of the notes. E.g.,

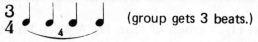 (group gets 3 beats.)

Quadruple time Four pulses or beats to a measure. The strongest accent falls on the first beat, the second strongest accent on the third beat. E.g.,

$$\frac{4}{4}\ \downarrow\ \downarrow\ \downarrow\ \downarrow\ \bigg|\bigg|\ \frac{4}{2}\ \downarrow\ \downarrow\ \downarrow\ \downarrow\ \bigg|\bigg|\ \text{etc.}$$

Quadruplum (Lat.) The fourth part above the tenor. See *Duplum.

Quality The texture or timbre of a tone. See *Timbre.

Qualvoll (Ger.) (kvāl'–fŏl) Agonizing.

Quand même (Fr.) (kä(n) mĕm) All the same. Even.

Quantity The length or time values assigned to a given note or rest. The measured aspect of music.

Quanto (It.) (koo–än'–tō) How . much, so much.

Quart (Fr.) (kär) (quarte, (Ger.) (kvärt'–å)) A fourth.

Quartal (Harmony) Chords built on superimposed fourths rather than thirds. For example:

Examples are found in the music of Charles Ives (1874–1954), Anton von Webern (1883–1945), Paul Hindemith (1895–1963), et. al.

Quarter-note A crotchet (English) ($\downarrow$); viertel (Ger.); noire (Fr.).

Quarter-rest A pause equal to the value of the quarter-note. A quarter-rest symbol (ξ). E.g.:

Quarter-tone Half of a semitone. For example, a note placed halfway between two keys representing a half-step on the piano keyboard. The quarter tone is used in modern music, Eastern music, and was referred to in the discussions of the enharmonic tetrachord in Greek music.

Quartet (1) A group of four. (2) A piece for four voices or instruments. Examples: string quartet; two violins, one viola, one cello; mixed vocal quartet; soprano, alto, tenor, bass. An example of string quartet music: W. A. Mozart (1756–1791), *Quartet in G,* K 387.

Quartetto (It.) (ko͞o–är–tĕt'–tō) Quartet.

Quartfagott (Ger.) (kvärt'–fä–gŏt') (Quartfagotto, (It.) (ko͞o–ärt'–fä–gŏt'–tō)) A bassoon that is a perfect fourth lower than the regular bassoon. See *Bassoon.

Quartflöte (Ger.) (kvärt'–flĕ(r)–tå) A flute that is a perfect fourth higher than the regular flute. See *Flute.

Quartgeige (Ger.) (kvärt'–gi–gå) A violin that is tuned a perfect fourth higher than the standard violin. Pochette (Fr.); Violino Piccolo (It.). See *Violin.

Quarto (It.) (ko͞o–är'–tō) Fourth; quarter.

Quartolet (Fr.) (kär–tō–lā) Quadruplet.

Quartposaune (Ger.) (kvärt'–pō–zow'–nå) The trombone pitched a perfect fourth below the standard Bb trombone. See *Trombone.

Quasi (It.) (ko͞o–ä'–zē) Nearly; as if.

Quasi arpa (It.) (ko͞o–ä'–zē är'–pä) Play the notes "as if" playing on a harp. For example, playing broken chords.

Quatre (Fr.) (kä–tr) Four; fourth.

Quatrième (Fr.) (kä–trē–ĕm) Fourth.

Quattro voci (It.) (ko͞o–ät'–trō vō'–chē) Four voices.

Quatuor (Fr.) (kä–tü–ôr) Quartet.

Quatuor à cordes (Fr.) (kä–tü–ôr ä kôrd) String quartet.

Quaver (Achtel, (Ger.); Croche, (Fr.)) Eighth note (♪); eighth rest (𝄿).

Quedo (Sp.) (kä'–dō) Quiet; soft.

Querflöte (Ger.) (kvĕr'–flĕ(r)–tå) Cross-flute. Transverse flute. The modern flute.

Querstand (Ger.) (kvĕr'–shtänt) A cross relation or false relation in the harmonization of voice leadings. See *Cross relation, *False relation.

Queue (Fr.) (kü) Tail; end; stem. E.g., note stem; tailpiece.

301

Quick march, quick-step march A fast march in two. Either in $\frac{2}{4}$ or $\frac{6}{8}$ time.

Quieto (It.) (kōo–ē–ā'–tō) Quiet.

Quilisma (Lat.) The sign ($\sim$) or neume usually placed between two notes a third apart, indicating a trill, roll, or tremolo.

Quindicesimo (It.) (kōo –ĭ n'–dē–chā'–zē–mō) Fifteenth. E.g., an interval of two octaves.

Quint (Ger.) (kvĭnt) (1) A fifth. (2) An organ stop which sounds a fifth above the foundation stop.

Quinta falsa (Lat.) False fifth. The interval of a diminished fifth.

Quintatön (Ger.) (kvĭn'–tä–tĕ(r)n) An organ stop that produces the fundamental tone and the tone a twelfth above.

Quinte (Fr.) (kă(n)t) Fifth. A tenor violin (viola). A five-stringed tenor viol. The strings were tuned a fifth lower than the standard violin.

Quinte (Ger.) (kvĭnt'–å) Fifth. The e string of the violin. The first string.

Quinte de viole (Fr.) (kă(n)t dû vyŏļ) Viola.

Quintenkriesen (Ger.) (kvĭnt'–ån–kri'–zån) Circle of fifths.

Quintet (Quintette, (Fr.) (kă(n)–tĕt)) A work for five voices or instruments. A string quintet either has an additional viola or cello added to a regular string quartet. The piano is usually added to a standard string quartet (piano quintet). The standard woodwind quintet consists of flute, oboe, clarinet, bassoon, and horn. A brass quintet varies and might consist of 2 trumpets, French horn, trombone, and tuba, or, trumpet, French horn, baritone horn, trombone, and tuba. Other brass quintets might consist of several combinations of brass instruments of varying range and timbre. A vocal quintet might consist of two sopranos, alto, tenor, and bass. Examples: W. A. Mozart (1756–1791) *Quintet in C,* K 515 for Strings; Mozart, *Quintet in A,* K 581, for Clarinet and Strings; Ernest Block (1880–1959), *Quintet for Piano and Strings.*

Quintfagott (Ger.) (kvĭnt'–fä–gŏt') A bassoon pitched a

fifth above the standard bassoon. Also called Tenoroon.

Quinto (It.) (koo̅—i̯ n '—to̅) Fifth.

Quinton (Fr.) (kă(n)—to̅(n)) A violin having five strings (tuned g, d', a', d", g") used during the 18th century in France.

Quintposaune (Ger.) (kvi̯nt'—po̅—zow'—nå̊) The trombone a fifth below the regular trombone in B♭.

Quintsaite (Ger.) (kvi̯nt'—zī—tå̊) The violin E string.

Quintuor (Fr.) (kă (n)—tû̂—ô̂r) Quintet.

Quintuple counterpoint Five voices employed in invertible counterpoint. See *Counterpoint, *Invertible counterpoint.

Quintuplet A group of five notes of equal value being played in the time value of four of the notes. E.g.,

   (group gets 4 beats).

Quintuple time Five beats to a measure. A measure of combined time with 2 and 3. For example: $\frac{2}{4}$ meter plus $\frac{3}{4}$ meter or $\frac{3}{4}$ meter plus $\frac{2}{4}$ meter. The accent falls on one and three or on one and four. Example: Peter Ilyich Tchaikovsky (1840—1893), *Symphony No. 6 In B Minor,* Op. 74, "Pathetique", Second Movement.

Quintus (Lat.) The fifth part in a composition having five or more parts. In 15th and 16th century compositions this fifth part had the same compass as one of the other four.

Quinze (Fr.) (kă(n)z) Fifteen; fifteenth.

Qui tollis peccata mundi (Lat.) (kwe̅ to̅l'—le̅s pĕ—kä'—tä moŏn'—de̅) A part of the "Gloria" and the "Agnus Dei" in the Roman Catholic Mass which translated into English reads: "You who take away the sins of the world". See *Mass.

Quodlibet (Lat.) Two or more unrelated melodies played or sung in succession or at the same time in polyphonic style. The melodies may be fragmented. Some-

times, the texts are borrowed and the melodies are ex-
temporized. The effect can be humorous. The technique of combining folk tunes was popular during the
15th and 16th centuries. The 16th century composer
Ludwig Senfl (c. 1492—1555) wrote many "quodlibet".
The technique was used by J. S. Bach (1685—1750)
in his *Goldberg Variations,* and by Arthur Honegger
(1892—1955) in his *Christmas Cantata.*

R (1) The letter used for the super-tonic (re) in the syllable sol-fa system. (2) Letter for Récit in French organ music.

Ra (rä) Used to identify the syllable re lowered one-half step in the syllable system. See *Solmization.

Rabbia (It.) (rä'–bē–ä) Anger, rage.

Racket, Rackett An obsolete and odd double reed instrument used during the 16th and 17th centuries. It was a small instrument with complex inside coiling concealed by the body of the instrument. The holes were closed by the tips and joints of the fingers or the soft parts of the hand. It was related to the early instruments of the oboe family. Also called sausage-bassoon or ranket.

Raddolcente (It.) (rä–dŏl–chĕn'–tä) Calmer.

Raddoppiamento (It.) (rä–dŏp–pē–ä–mĕn'–tō) Doubling, usually the octave below.

Raddoppiate (It.) (rä–dŏp–pē–ä'–tä)   To double or repeat (e.g., a note).

Radical The fundamental or root. E.g., fundamental bass or root of a chord. See *Fundamental bass.

Radoucir (Fr.) (rä–dōo–sēr) Quiet, soften.

Raffrenare (It.) (rä–frĕn–ä'–rä) Restrain. From frenare, to brake or check.

Raga A melodic structure in Hindu music.

Ragtime A style of Jazz from the end of the 19th century to about 1915. It was primarily a piano style with or without a group of instruments. It was written in $\frac{2}{4}$ or $\frac{4}{4}$ and used various types of syncopation. Some of the rhythms used were:

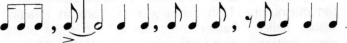

The popularity of Ragtime began to decline around 1910 and it was followed by the Blues. See *Jazz.

Ralentissement (Fr.) (räl–ă(n)–tēz–mä(n)) Slackening.

Rallentando (It.) (räl–lĕn–tän'–dō) Slowing down. The abbreviation is rall.

Range The total compass of a voice or musical instrument.

Rank A set of organ pipes of the same kind belonging to one stop.

Rankett A sausage-bassoon. See *Racket.

Ranz (Fr.) (rä(n)) An air or tune.

Ranz des vaches (Fr.) (rä(n) dā väsh) A melody played on an alphorn or sung by Swiss herdsmen. The ranz des vaches have been used by many composers, as for example: Gioacchino Rossini (1792–1868), "Overture" to the opera *William Tell;* William Walton (1902–   ), *Facade, Suite No. 1* for Orchestra in the "Parody on William Tell".

Rapidement (Fr.) (rä–pēd–mä(n)) Rapidly, fast; suddenly.

Rapsode (Fr.) (räp–sŏd) Rhapsody.

Rasch (Ger.) (räsh) Lively, quick.

Ratsche (Ger.) (rät'–shå) Rattle.

Rattles Instruments of the percussion section that are rattled, turned, or shaken, e.g., gourds, cogwheel and maracas. See *Idiophone.

Rausch (Ger.) (rowsh) Rush.

Rauscher (Ger.) (rowsh'–å r) (1) A German 18th century term for arpeggio. (2) A rapidly executed figure which includes repeated notes.

Rauschwerk (Ger.) (rowsh'–vĕrk) Loud alto on the organ.

Ravvivare (It.) (rä–vĕ–vä'–rā) Enliven; quicken.

Ray The supertonic syllable of the scale in the tonic sol-fa system. See *Tonic sol-fa.

Re (It.) (rā) (Ré, (Fr.) (rā)) (1) The note D in the system of fixed do. (2) The supertonic syllable of the scale in the movable do system.

Reading Rota A round. The name given to a canon written during the 13th century by a monk at Reading Abbey called "Sumer is icumen in". It is the oldest piece written in this style using six parts. See *Canon.

Real answer See *Answer.

Realization The act of realizing a figured bass. That is, providing a harmonization or accompaniment for a 17th or 18th century work based on the indication of a figured bass. See *Figured bass.

Rebaba (rebab) A bowed instrument with one, two, or three strings used in Moslem countries, Java, Egypt, and the northern parts of Africa.

Rebec A medieval bowed string instrument with three or four strings and shaped somewhat like a pear. It was used in Europe and preceded the viol and violin.

Re-bop The bop or be-bop jazz music popular during the 1940's and early 1950's. Some characteristics of bop are: the use of vibraphones, which were important to the style; many unisons or octaves were used rather than the contrapuntal style; improvisations. See *Be-bop.

Recapitulation The modified restatement of the material used in the exposition. It follows the development section and is found in sonata form or a similar structure. See *Sonata form.

Rechts (Ger.) (rĕkts) On the right hand.

Récit (Fr.) (rā—sē) Recital. (1) A recitative. (2) An organ stop.

Recital A public performance by a soloist or a soloist with accompaniment.

Récitant (Fr.) (rā—sē—tä(n)) Solo.

Recitare (It.) (rā—chē—tä '—rē) Play; recite.

Recitative (Recitativo, (It.) (rā—chē—tä—tē '—vō); (récit (Fr.) (rā—sē)) To recite or perform in a declamatory style. It is partly spoken and partly sung. Used in opera and oratorios. See *Recitativo accompagnato, *Recitative secco, *Recitativo stromentato.

Recitativo accompagnato (It.) (rā—chē—tä—tē '—vō äk— kŏ m—pän—yä '—tō) An accompanied recitative. The continuous accompaniment was written out and was done by a full ensemble or orchestra.

Recitativo secco (It.) (rā—chē—tä—tē '—vō sĕk '—kō) Secco means dry. The freer or simple declamatory style used in the 18th century Italian opera. A style of recitative in which the recitative was more flexible and had a limited thoroughbass accompaniment played on a keyboard instrument with periodic chords being played on accents, or a simple accompaniment by a keyboard instrument with some added instruments. See *Recitative, *Recitativo accompagnato, *Recitativo stromentato.

Recitativo stromentato (It.) (rā—chē—tä—tē '—vō strō—mĕ n—tä'—tō) A recitative with orchestral accompaniment. See *Recitativo accompagnato, *Recitative.

Réciter (Fr.) (rā—sē—tä) To sing or play in recitative.

Reciting note The important note of a psalm tone in Gregorian chant on which most of each verse of a psalm is sung. The note is the dominant of the mode of the psalm tone.

Recorder An end-blown flute with a fipple mouthpiece and a mellow sound. It was used during the Middle Ages and is very popular today. The instrument is made in various sizes which range from treble to bass. Today it is usually made in four sizes, Soprano, Alto, Tenor, and Bass.

Recorder (Fr.) (rû—kôr—dā) To rehearse.

Recording bass A modern upright tuba used in concert bands and orchestras. The bell faces forward. See *Tuba.

Récrire (Fr.) (rā—krēr) To rewrite.

Recte et retro, per (Lat.) Retrograde motion.

Redire (Fr.) (rû—dēr) To repeat.

Redoublé (Fr.) (rû—doō —blā) Accelerated; repeated. Pas redoublé — double pace or double time.

Redowa A dance popular in Bohemia which is done in several styles. One is similar to the waltz, another is similar to a mazurka, and one is similar to a polka.

Reduktion (Ger.) (rā—doŏk—si —ōn ') A reduction of a full orchestral score, vocal score, etc. For example, reducing a full score so it can be played on a keyboard instrument for rehearsals.

Reed A piece of cane, plastic, or metal used on musical instruments. It is the sound producing part and is set to vibrating by an air column. It is used on reed organs, clarinets, harmonicas, etc. The single reed is used on such instruments as the clarinets and saxophones. A double reed is used on the oboe, English horn, and bassoon.

Reed organ An organ on which the sound is produced by air moving through small metal reeds. The American organ and the harmonium are good examples.

Reed stop The stop that controls a set of reed pipes.

Reel A lively dance in duple meter. The music is in four or eight measure phrases.

Refrain A chorus that recurs after each stanza. A melody. The section that keeps returning in a composition.

Regal A very small portable keyboard reed organ. It was used during the 16th and 17th centuries. One model folded like a book. See *Bible regal.

Register A part of the compass of a voice or instrument. (1) The various qualities within the divisions of the voice or instruments. For example: voice qualities of the so-called head register, throat register and chest register; on the clarinet, the clarion (higher) register and the chalumeau (lower) register. (2) A set of organ pipes controlled by a stop.

Registrate To combine pipe organ stops for a particular composition.

Reigen (Ger.) (rī'—gȧn) (1) A roundelay; song. (2) A round dance.

Rein (Ger.) (rīn) Clear, pure.

Reine Stimme (Ger.) (rī'—nȧ shtĭm'—mȧ) Clear voice.

Réjoui (Fr.) (rā—zhoo—ē) Joyous.

Relâche (Fr.) (rṹ—läsh) Intermission.

Relative keys The relationship of the major mode and minor mode to a given key signature. The relative major and minor use the same key signature. See *Relative major, *Relative minor.

Relative major The major scale that begins a minor third above the relative minor scale. The two keys and scales share the same key signature. E.g.,

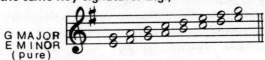

G MAJOR
E MINOR
(pure)

See *Keys, *Major, *Minor.

Relative minor The minor scale that begins a minor third below the relative major scale. The two keys and scales share the same key signature. E.g.,

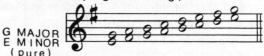

G MAJOR
E MINOR
(pure)

See *Keys, *Minor, *Major.

Relative pitch (1) The relationship of one tone to another or to a given scale. (2) The ability to produce a pitch or identify a pitch from another given pitch. See *Absolute pitch.

Release A name given to the bridge section of a jazz or pop piece of music.

Religioso (It.) (rā—lē—jē—ō '—zō) To be played in a solemn manner.

Remettez (Fr.) (rŭ—mĕ t—tā) To take off an organ stop.

Remote keys Keys that are not closely related. The greater the difference in the numbers of sharps or flats in the key signature the more remote the relationship. For example, the key of F would be less remote from the key of Bb than from the key of Cb. See *Key relationship.

Renaissance music An indefinite era in music, usually referring to the period between c. 1430 and c. 1600. It was a period during which music developed as an art. Sacred music continued with the Mass and motet, which were developed to a high point by Palestrina, Lasso, Victoria, Byrd, Dunstable, Ockeghem, etc. For example: Giovanni Pierluigi da Palestrina (c. 1525—1594), Motet: *Stabat Mater;* Mass: *Missa Papal Marcelli* (Pope Marcellus Mass). In secular music, both vocal and instrumental, new forms were developed including, in vocal music, the frottola, madrigal, chanson, and quodlibet, and in instrumental music, the ricercar, canzona, prelude, variation, and dance forms. For example: Adrian Willaert (c. 1490—1562), *Ricercar No. 7;* Orlando Gibbons (1583—1625), *Three part Fantasia No. 3.* The cantus firmus was used in the tenor voice. Canonic devices were used for the sake of variety. Melodies were modal, rhythm was complex and free from metrical accent, and the texture was polyphonic, although later works were of a homophonic nature. Music was primarily vocal, with instrumental music developing later in the period.

Renverser (Fr.) (rằ(n)—vĕr—sā) To invert.

Renvoi (Fr.) (rằ(n)—vwä) Repeat; return.

Repeat marks Signs which indicate that music is to be replayed. (1) The music falls between the following signs ( ) and these measures between the parallel lines and dots are to be repeated. The music is to be repeated from the beginning if no dots or double bars are indicated before the eye reaches the beginning. (2) Repeats are also made by measure or measures. The sign is (repeat the previous measure). (3) a first and second ending indicates a repeat of a section with the second ending to be used the second time through rather than the first ending. The signs are . See *Da capo, *Dal segno.

Repercussion (Lat.) The reciting note of psalm tones. See *Reciting note.

Repertoire (Fr.) (rû—pĕr—twär) Repertory. Works prepared for performance.

Répéter (Fr.) (rā—pā—tā)To rehearse. To repeat.

Répétition générale (Fr.) (rā—pā—tē—sē—ō(n) zhā—nā—räl) A dress rehearsal with invited guests.

Repetitore (It.) (rā—pā—tē—tō'—rā) A coach or choral director of an opera company.

Replicare (It.) (rā—plē—kä'—rā) Repeat. Replicato, (It.) (rā—plē—kä'—tō) repeated. Replicazione, (It.) (rā—plē—kä—tsē—ō'—nā) repetition.

Réplique (Fr.) (rā—plēk) Repeat.

Répondre (Fr.) (rā—pō(n)—dr) To answer; to make responses.

Répons (Fr.) (rā—pō(n)) A response in church.

Repos (Fr.) (rû—pō) Rest; pause.

Reprendre (Fr.) (rû—prä(n)—dr) To resume; to return to.

Repris (Fr.) (rû—prē) (reprise, (Fr.) (rû—prēz)) Repetition. A refrain. (1) The repetition of the exposition before the development. (2) A return of the exposition after the development (recapitulation). (3) A repeated chorus of a song. (4) The B section of binary (AB) form.

Requiem (Lat.) Also, Requies (rest). A Requiem Mass is a Mass for the dead. It is a musical work in honor of the dead. It is sung in plainsong or in polyphonic settings. Included in the Mass are: (1) "Introit" "Requiem aeternam dona eis, Domine" (Eternal rest give to them, O Lord); (2) "Kyrie" (Lord, have mercy); (3) "Gradual" and "Tract" ("Requiem aeternam" and "Absolve, Domine"); (4) "Sequence", "Dies Irae" (Day of wrath); (5) "Offertory", "Domine Jesu Christe": (6) "Sanctus" (Holy); (7) "Benedictus" (Blessed is He Who comes in the name of the Lord); (8) "Agnus Dei" (Lamb of God); (9) "Communion", "Lux Aeterna"; Final prayers, "Requiescant in pace" (May they rest in peace). The Responsorium, "Libera Me", is sometimes added at the end. The "Gloria" and "Credo" are omitted. Later settings of the Requiem use various texts from the Bible and include orchestra (Verdi, Brahms, Berlioz, etc.) Examples: Johannes Brahms (1833—1897), *Ein Deutches Requiem,* Op. 45, No. 1 (A German Requiem); Giuseppe Verdi (1813—1901), *Requiem* (Requiem and "Kyrie", "Dies Irae", "Domine Jesu", "Sanctus", "Agnus Dei", "Lux aeternam", "Libera me"). See *Mass.

Resin Rosin. A substance used on bows (violin, viola, etc.)

Résolument (Fr.) (rā—zō—lü—mä(n)) Boldly.

Resolution A progression to resolve a discord. A dissonance followed by a consonance.

Resonance The transmission of vibrations from one body to another. Overtones vibrate from the fundamental; sound boards reinforce vibrations; strings respond in vibration to other strings. Also, the reflection of sound.

312

A resonator would be the sound box or other materials that make up the instrument.

Response (1) The answer of the choir or congregation in a service. (2) A response in the fugue is the repetition of the theme in another voice.

Responsorial psalmody The alternation between soloist and a response by the choir or congregation. The "Alleluias" and "Graduals" are important examples of this style. Many examples are available in the "Liber Usualis". See "A Selected Annotated Bibliography".

Rest Time values which are equal to note values but silence is maintained. Examples:

etc.

See *Notes.

Resultant bass Organ pipes whose tone is based on combination tones. See *Combination tones, *Resultant tone.

Resultant tone Combination tone. A tone that sounds when two different tones are played together. A tone sounds as a result of the difference between frequencies (difference tone) or as a result of the total of the frequencies (summation tone). See *Acoustics, *Combination tone, *Difference tone, *Summation tone.

Retardation A suspension which resolves upwards. See *Suspension.

Retenir (Fr.) (rû—těn—ēr) Hold back.

Retentissant (Fr.) (rû—tă(n)—tē—să(n)) Ringing, sonorous.

Retrograde canon A canon in which, when the imitative parts enters, the original melody is read backwards. Also called crab canon. A canon performed in reverse. See *Crab motion, *Cancrizans, *Retrograde motion.

Retrograde motion The writing or performance of a musical line from the end to the beginning (backwards). One of the common canonic devices. Retrograde inversion would be backwards and upside-down. Examples: a canon in retrograde is found in the *Musical Offering* by J. S. Bach (1685—1750). Retrograde motion is used in the fourth movement of *Sonata No. 29 in B♭,* Op. 106, for Piano, "Hammerklavier", by Ludwig Van Beethoven (1770—1827). See *Crab motion, *Cancrizans, *Retrograde canon.

Rhapsody Essentially an instrumental form in the nature of a fantasy. The rhapsody is in a free style and based on folk songs or melodies of a folk song style. It is an uninterrupted succession of short, contrasting passages. The character of the rhapsody may be heroic, in a ballad style, of free spirit, etc. The title is used by many 19th and 20th century composers. Examples: Franz Liszt (1811—1886), *Hungarian Rhapsodies;* Claude Debussy (1862—1918) *Rhapsody for Saxophone and Orchestra, Rhapsody for Clarinet and Orchestra;* Béla Bartók (1881—1945), *Rhapsody No. 1, Violin and Orchestra.*

Rhythm The movement or motion in music. The relationship among note values. The organization of the measurement of music. The stress, accents, and pulse of music. The relationship of notes to time, meters, and measures. Much of modern music rejects the pattern of recurring beats and rigid rhythm. It becomes a matter of pulse. Very early music relied on syllables and words to reflect the rhythm. Yet, other music between the very early and modern music, relies on patterns of notes regulated by meters. For example, a waltz has three beats in a measure with an accent on the first beat of each measure. A march is in duple time with an accent on one. Music in four would have an accent on one and three. Accents vary as compound and combined meters are used. The accents remain at the same position, but the rhythm or note values vary. See *Meter, *Mensural notation, *Plainsong.

Rhythm band An ensemble of rhythm instruments. It is used as a basic music education program in the primary grades.

Rhythmic modes A system of rhythmic notation used during the 13th century. An arrangement of longs and breves in patterns. The six modes are: Mode I (Trochee) (– ⌣) long - breve; Mode II (Iambus (⌣–) breve - long; Mode III (Dactyl) (– ⌣⌣) long - breve - breve; Mode IV (Anapaest) (⌣⌣ –) breve - breve - long; Mode V (Molossus) (– – –) long - long - long; Mode VI (Tribrach) (⌣⌣⌣) breve - breve - breve.

Rhythmicon An electronic instrument that sounds various complex rhythmic patterns. Invented by L. Theremin and H. Cowell.

Rhythm section The percussion instruments of an orchestra, band, or jazz ensemble.

Ribs The side sections of the violin, viola, cello, etc.

Ricercar (It.) (rē '–chĕr–kär) (recercare, (It.) (rē–chĕr–kär '–ā) "To search out", "study". A 16th and 17th century term. A most important form is the polyphonic instrumental work in the style of the 16th century vocal motet. There were several themes and sections that were developed in imitative style. The organ ricercar had fewer themes which were highly developed. There were ricercar written for instruments which were not in imitative style, but were freer and more in the nature of study pieces. Later ricercars were monomatic. Some ricercar were sung or played. A Renaissance and Baroque form. E.g., several monothematic and polythematic ricercars were written by Andrea Gabrieli (c. 1520–1586); Girolamo Frescobaldi (1583–1643), *Ricercar Cromatico Post II Credo,* organ. J. S. Bach (1685–1750) used the term in his six-part fugue in his work ("The Musical Offering") *Musikalisches Opfer.* Sixteenth century instrumental ricercars were written by Adrian Willaert (c. 1490–1562) et. al, and by 17th century composers, such as Domenico Gabrielli (c. 1655–1690) et. al.

Ricochet (Fr.) (rē–kō–shā) Rebound. The upper third of the bow is used. It is dropped on the strings and allowed to bounce. Several notes are played on one stroke. Also, jeté.

Riddle canon A canon in which directions are not complete. The performer must determine entrances and the pitch on which to enter. See *Canon.

Ridurre (It.) (rē—dŏor'—rā) Arrange. To arrange a piece of music.

Riff In jazz, the riff is a modified instrumental and vocal call-and-response pattern much like that used in various churches. A repeated phrase.

Rigaudon (Fr.) (rē—gō—dō(n)) A 17th century French dance in duple time in a lively tempo. It was later used in the suite. An example of a "Rigaudon" is found in the *Suite in E Minor for Harpsichord* by Jean Philippe Rameau (1683—1764). It was also adopted into the operatic ballets of the 17th century French opera. It is also found in the works of contemporary composers.

Rigo (It.) (rē'—gō) Line; staff.

Rigoroso (It.) (rē—gō—rō'—zō) Rigorous. E.g., strict time.

Rimettere (It.) (rē—mĕt'—tā—rā) Reinstate. E.g., go back to the old tempo.

Rinforzo (rin—fôr'—tsō) (rinforzando, (It.) (rin—fôr—tsän'—dō)) Reinforcement; reinforcing. (1) Give weight to a chord or note. The same as sforzando. (2) A short and sudden crescendo. Abbreviated rzf, rf, or rinf.

Ring shout In Negro folk music, a song that was sung outdoors. The participants formed a ring and the singing was accompanied by stomping, clapping, and movement in a circle.

Ripieno (It.) (rē—pē—ā'—nō) Stuffed; full. A Baroque orchestral term used especially with the concerto grosso. In the concerto grosso there are two contrasting groups. The ripieno section is the larger section (tutti) the concertino group is the smaller (a solo group of two, three or four performers) section. Examples: J. S. Bach (1685—1750) "Six Brandenburg Concertos" *No. 1 in F; No. 2 in F; No. 3 in G; No. 4 in G; No. 5 in D;* and *No. 6 in B♭ Major.* Numbers two, four and five are concerti grossi which use a ripieno section and a concertino section. For example, *No. 5 in D* consists of flute, violin, harpsichord, strings, and continuo. The concertino section includes harpsichord, flute and violins; the ripieno section includes strings and continuo. See *Concerto grosso, *Concertino, *Tutti, *Brandenburg concerti.

Riposante (It.) (rē—pō—zän '—tā) Restful.

Ripresa (It.) (rē—prā '—zä) (1) Repeat. (2) The refrain in the 14th century ballata. (3) A 16th century variation of a dance movement. (4) Recapitulation.

Risoluto (It.) (rē—zō—lōo'—tō) Determined.

Risposta (It.) (rē—spôs '—tä) Response. The answer in a fugue.

Risvegliato (It.) (rēs—vāl—yē—ä '—tō) Stirring; lively; rousing.

Ritardando (It.) (rē—tär—dän '—dō) Retarding; slowing down. The same as rallentando (Rall). The abbreviations are rit. and ritard.

Ritenuto (It.) (rē—tĕ n—ōo'—tō) Held back. Hold down the tempo. The abbreviation is rit.

Ritmico (It.) (rēt '—mē—kō) Rhythmical.

Ritournelle (Fr.) (rē—tōor—nĕl) (ritornellō, (It.) (rē—tôr—nĕ l '—lō)) Flourish. (1) The instrumental interlude between scenes, acts, and arias in the 17th century operas. (2) An instrumental section played after each verse in 17th century German songs. (3) An instrumental section within early forms of opera. (4) A recurring section of a work. (5) A 17th century dance in triple time. (6) The two-line stanza which followed the verses of the 14th century madrigal (in a different meter) was called the ritornello stanza.

Rivista (It.) (rē—vi s '—tä) Musical comedy.

Rivoltato (It.) (rē—vŏ l—tä '—tō) Also, rivolto. Inverted; inversion.

Rock Music of the young. It has been described as music of revolt, of the 1960's. A hybrid of blues and country-western music. It incorporates the blues, styles from Indian classical raga, as well as techniques of Bach, Stockhausen, Cage, and others. It is a new culture, a sense of involvement, a type of "tribal" music. A person attends a Rock concert, not to listen, but to partic-

317

ipate in an event.

Rococo (Fr.) (rō—kō—kō) A decorative style of music between c. 1710 to 1780 and at its peak from 1725 to 1775. It overlaps the Baroque period (1600—1750) and the Classical period (1725—1800) of music. It is called the gallant style, and is marked by elegance and ornamentation. See *Gallant style, *Emfindsamer Stil.

Rohr (Ger.) (rōr) Reed.

Rohrflöte (Ger.) (rōr'—flĕ(r)—tå) Reed-pipe. Flue stop of the organ.

Rohrwerk (Ger.) (rōr'—vĕrk) Reed work. Organ reed stops.

Rôle (Fr.) (rōl) Roll; catalogue.

Roll The continuous sound produced by rapid drum beats.

Rolle (Ger.) (rŏl'—lå) Roll; scroll.

Rolltrommel (Ger.) (rŏl'—trŏm—ål) Roll drum. A side drum or tenor drum.

Romance (English and Fr.) Song or ballad. A name given to a simple vocal or instrumental piece in a tender or sentimental vein. Examples: Camille Saint Saëns (1835—1921), *Romance,* Op. 36, French Horn and Orchestra; Claude Debussy (1862—1918), *Deux Romances* (text by Bourget).

Romanticism An era in music from about 1800 to 1910. The Romantic composer was interested in the individual and was concerned with the emotional element in music. The melodies were long and melodic; the rhythm complex; the tempo varied; the harmony was still tonal but used much chromaticism, modes were used in the nationalistic movement; the texture was thick, the media was a continuation of the classical forms in a less rigid style and the addition of piano and vocal literature; orchestral and operatic literature was developed further. Program music became important (forms; symphonic poem, concert overture, program symphony, and incidental music). Nationalistic music was another important movement, e.g., Russian Five (Balakirev, Cui, Borodin, Rimsky-Korsakov, and Mussorgsky). Example of national music: Alexander Borodin (1833—1887), the opera *Prince Igor.* The emphasis on the individaul can be seen in the music written for solo voice by Franz Schubert (1797—1828) and Robert Schumann (1810—1856). The music for solo piano also exemplifies this spirit of the individual, e.g., Frédéric Chopin (1810—1849). The large forms, opera, oratorio, and symphony, show the grand side of the Romantic period in the melodic lines, harmonies, elaborate texture, and orchestration. The use of large forms can be seen in the operas of Giuseppe Verdi (1813—1901) and Richard Wagner (1813—1883); the symphonies of Johannes Brahms (1883—1897) and Peter Ilyich Tchaikovsky (1840—1893), and the large vocal works of Brahms and Felix Mendelssohn (1809—1847). During the last part of the Romantic era a new French movement called Impressionism was introduced and led to the modern music of today.

Romanza (It.) (rō—män '—zä) (romanze, (Ger.)) See *Romance.

Ronde (Fr.) (rō(n)d) Round. (1) A semibreve. (2) A roundelay.

Rondeau (Fr.) (rō(n)—dō) Rondo; rondel. (1) A French vocal form practiced during the medieval period having two phrases repeated many times. It was based on a six or eight line poem. The refrain (lines 1 and 2) at the beginning returns in its entirety at the end. The trouvère settings were monophonic. Later settings are polyphonic. (2) A 17th century instrumental form with a recurring refrain. It led to the 18th century sonata-rondo form. See *Rondo form.

Rondelay A roundelay. The often repeated refrain identifies this type of song.

Rondo form A form developed from the 17th century rondeau. An instrumental form in which the main theme keeps returning after each new section. A rondo may be done in several schemes, e.g., ABACABA would be symmetrical or third rondo form or alternating sections such as ABACADA, plus other arrangements. Section A would be the principal theme, the other letters are contrasting sections. The rondo is used in the last movement of the concerto and in movements of the sonata and symphony. Example: Felix Mendelssohn (1809–1847), the third movement of the *Concerto in E Minor for Violin and Orchestra*, Op. 64; Ludwig Van Beethoven (1770–1827) the third movement of the *Concerto in D,* Op. 61 for Violin and Orchestra.

Ronzio (It.) (rŏn–tsē '–ō) Drone.

Root The fundamental note of any chord. Root position; the fundamental note is the lowest note of the chord. When any other note of the chord is.the lowest note it is called an inversion.

Rosin See *Resin.

Rota (Lat.) Round. (1) A strict canon, e.g., the famous "Reading rota", *Sumer is icumen in,* by John Fornsete (13th century) of Reading Abbey. See *Reading rota, *Canon. (2) Hurdy-gurdy.

Rote (1) Learning by memory. (2) A crwth or crowd. See *Crwth.

Roulade (Fr.) (roo – läd) Trill, shake. A vocal embellishment or florid passage.

Round An imitative vocal piece or continuous variety of canon. The same melodic line is sung as each voice enters at the different times, e.g., "Frère Jacques".

Round dance (1) A couple moves in a circle or revolving manner. A folk-dance done in a circle. (2) Music for these dances.

Rovesciare (It.) (rō–vĕ–shē–ä '–rā) (rovescio, (It.) (rō–vĕ'–shē–ō) Reverse. Play backwards or by inversion.

Rubato (It.) (roo–bä '–tō) Robbed. The freedom to give and take when playing the rhythm and tempo. Flexibility.

Ruhen (Ger.) (roo'–å n) Repose.

Ruhezeichen (Ger.) (roo'–å –tsi kh–å n) A pause or rest in music.

Ruhig (Ger.) (roo'–ĭ k) Calm.

Rühren (Ger.) (rü'–rå n) Beat; as in beating a drum.

Rührtrommel (Ger.) (rür '–trŏm–å l) Tenor drum.

Rumba (Rhumba) A rhythmic ballroom dance of Cuban

origin. It is in $\frac{4}{4}$ time and requires many rhythm instruments, such as the gourd, claves, etc. It has a basic pulse of 3+3+2 beats. The rhumba style is sometimes adapted by contemporary composers. For example, the "Rhumba" from *Symphony No. 2* by H. McDonald (1899–1955).

Run A rapid flow of successive notes.

Russian bassoon An obsolete brass bass horn. An upright serpent. See *Serpent.

Russian Five An organized group of Russian composers dedicated to writing Nationalistic music for the glory of Russia. They were: Mily Balakireff (1837–1910), César Cui (1835–1918), Modest Mussorgsky (1839–1881), Alexander Borodin (1833–1887), Nicolas Rimsky-Korsakoff (1844–1908).

Rustico (It.) (roŏ s'–tē–kō) (rustique, (Fr.) (rūs–tēk)) Rustic; simple.

Rhythmique (Fr.) (rēt–mēk) Rhythmic.

S. The abbreviation for: (1) soh (sol) in the syllable system; (2) segno; (3) subtio; (4) senza; (5) soprano; (6) soft; (7) sinistra.

Sabaoth (Lat.) Part of the text in the "Sanctus" which is sung in the Roman Catholic Mass. "Dominus Deus Sabaoth" (Lord God of Hosts). See *Mass.

Sabi An ancient Egyptian flute.

Saccadé (Fr.) (sä–kä–dā) Abrupt; irregular.

Sacht (Ger.) (zäkht) Soft.

Sackbut (saquebute, sagbut, sachbut, sambute) An English name for the medieval trombone.

Sackgeige (Ger.) (zäk '–gī –gå) Kit-violin.

Sackpfeife (Ger.) (zäk–pfī –få) Bagpipe.

Sacred music Religious music.

Saite (Ger.) (zā '–tå) String.

Saiteninstrument (Ger.)　　　(zā–tå n–ĭn–strōō–měnt ') Stringed instrument.

Salicional An 8 or 16 foot organ stop having a soft string or reedy quality.

Salmo (It.) (säl '–mō) Psalm.

Salon music Music of an emotional and simple nature performed by a small group. Mood music played in a salon.

Salpinx (Greek) An obsolete trumpet-shaped instrument of Greece. A straight trumpet.

Saltando (It.) (säl–tän '–dō) (Saltato, It. (säl–tä '–tō); sautillé, Fr. (sō–tē–yā)) A bowing technique in which the bow is bounced lightly on the string.

Saltarello (It.) (säl–tä–rěl '–lō) (saltare, to jump) A lively Italian dance in triple time which has a leaping motion. The style was often used in instrumental compositions during the Renaissance and Baroque periods. For example, the passamezzo (slow, in duple meter) would be followed by the saltarello (fast, in triple meter) when dances were used in pairs. This technique was used in the suite or in variation form. Both dances were composed from the same musical line, harmony, etc. The galliard is essentially the same musical style as the saltarello. An example of the passamezzo and saltarello is available in the "Fitzwilliam Virginal Book", *"Galiarda Passamezzo"* by Peter Philips (c. 1561—c. 1628).

Salterio (It.) (säl—tā'—rē—ō) Psaltery.

Salterio tedesco (It.) (säl—tā'—rē—ō tā—dĕs'—kō) Dulcimer.

Salto (It.) (sal—to) Jump, spring, hop.

Salve Regina (Lat.) "Hail queen". Antiphons sung to the Virgin Mother, Mary. The text has been set to music by many composers.

Samba A dance, originally from Africa, but introduced into America from Brazil. It is a rhythmic and syncopated ballroom dance in duple time.

Sambuca (1) An ancient Greek psaltery. (2) A name given to the hurdy-gurdy during the medieval period in music.

Samisen A plucked string instrument of Japan. It has three strings, a small body and long neck. A plectrum is used to start the tone.

Sämtlich (Ger.) (zĕmt'—li k) Entire.

Sanctus and Benedictus (Lat.) (sänk'—tōos) "Holy, Holy; Blessed is he who comes." In the Roman Catholic Mass, the fourth part or section of the Ordinary of the Mass. It follows the "Credo" (in the Ordinary). The Latin text is: "Sanctus, Sanctus, Sanctus, Dominus Deus Sabaoth. Pleni sunt Coeli et terra gloria tuo. Hosanna in excelsis. Benedictus qui venit in nomine Domini. Hosanna in excelsis." For centuries, the Latin text was used. Today, it is sung in the vernacular. The English translation is as follows: "Holy, Holy, Holy, Lord God of Hosts. Heaven and earth are filled with your glory. Hosanna in the highest. Blessed is He Who comes in the name of the Lord. Hosanna in the Highest." The "Sanctus" is used in musical settings by many composers. A good example is found in the *Mass in B minor* by J. S. Bach (1685—1750), section XIX, "Sanctus", and section XXI, "Benedictus". See *Mass, *Ordinary of the Mass.

Sanftmütig (Ger.) (zänft '–mü–tǐ k) Soft; gentle.

Sänger (Ger.) (zĕng '–å r) Singer.

Sangsaite (Ger.) (zäng '–zā–tå) See *Cantino.

Sans (Fr.) (sä(n)) Without.

Sapphic form A type of hymn meter used in stanzas having four lines.

Sarabande (Fr.) (sä–rä–bä(n)d) A slow Spanish dance in triple meter. Later introduced in Europe and used in the Baroque suite or partita. Example: J. S. Bach (1685–1750), *French Suite, No. 3 in B Minor for Piano* (Allemande, Sarabande, Minuetto, Anglaise). See *Suite.

Sardana (Sp.) (sär–dä '–nä) A regional dance of northern Spain. A circle dance accompanied by a small drum and tiny flute. See *Tabor, *Farandole.

Sardina A stringed instrument of India.

Sarrusophone A 19th century double-reed instrument made in various sizes. The larger varieties are used in bands and the contra-bass size is sometimes used in the orchestra instead of the contra-bassoon. Invented by Sarrus in 1856.

Sassofono (It.) (säs–ō '–fō–nō) Saxophone.

S.A.T.B. music Vocal music written for four mixed voices. Soprano, Alto, Tenor and Bass.

Satire To ridicule. A parody or burlesque.

Satz (Ger.) (zäts) Phrase; a movement of a composition.

Saudade (Portuguese) Yearning or a sense of longing.

Sausage bassoon Wurstfagott (Ger.) An odd shaped bassoon. See *Racket.

Saut (Fr.) (sō) Jump, hop.

Sautillé (Fr.) (sō–tē–yā) Short bowing. Spiccato bowing. See *Saltando, *Bowing.

Sautillement (Fr.) (sō–tē–yå –mä(n)) Skipping; jerky style.

Sax The abbreviation for saxophone.

Saxhorn A family of brass instruments invented by Adolphe Sax (1814–1894) ranging from the high soprano ⸲ to the bass. Examples of types: Flügelhorn, tenor horn, baritone horn, saxtuba, etc.

Saxophone A family of single reed instruments of the woodwind family, although they are made of brass or other metals. They have a conical bore and have keys like the clarinet. They range in size and pitch from E♭ soprano to the B♭ bass saxophone (E♭ soprano, B♭ soprano, E♭ alto, C melody, B♭ tenor, E♭ baritone, B♭ bass and E♭ contrabass). They are used in bands, dance band ensembles, and in special cases in orchestras. They can produce a light reedy tone and blend with woodwinds or a heavy tone in order to blend with the brasses. Invented by Adolphe Sax in the mid-19th century. The abbreviation is sax.

Saxtromba A variation on the saxhorn. It is more like the instruments of the trumpet and tuba family.

Saxtuba Bass saxhorn.

Sbarra (It.) (zbär'–rä) Bar.

Scala (It.) (skä'–lä) Scale.

Scalar A passage moving in a scale-wise pattern as opposed to wide skips.

Scale A meaningful arrangement of tones ascending or descending. See *Chromatic scale, *Diatonic scale, *Major scale, *Minor scale, *Modal scale, *Pentatonic scale, *Quarter-tone, *Twelve-tone, *Whole tone scale, also, *Harmonic minor, *Melodic minor, *Pure minor.

Scale names Specific names that are used to identify each step of the major and minor scales. The 1st degree is tonic, 2nd degree, supertonic, 3rd degree, mediant, 4th degree, subdominant, 5th degree, dominant, 6th degree, submediant, 7th degree, leading tone (in pure minor the subtonic) and 8th degree, the tonic.

Scampare (It.) (skäm–pä'–rä) Also, scampanio. Chime.

Scan To analyze the metrical structure of a verse. To determine the accents and non-accents of a text in order to write a melody to a text.

Scat singing A jazz singer substitutes nonsense syllables for the words of a song. The singer tries to imitate the sound of an instrument.

Scemando (It.) (shā–män'–dō) See *Diminuendo.

Scena (It.) (shā'–nä) Scene. (1) A scene of an opera. (2)

An independent composition for voice which has the characteristics of an opera aria or recitative.

Scenario An outline of a work such as a play, opera, etc., giving the plot, characters, situations, etc.

Scene A subdivision of an act of a play, opera, etc. A unit of action.

Schale (Ger.) (shä'—lå) Saucer; cymbal.

Schalkhaft (Ger.) (shälk'—häft) Also, schelmisch. Crafty; playful.

Schall (Ger.) (shäl) Sound; ring. Schallbecken, (Ger.) (shäl'—bĕk—å n) Cymbals. Schallboden, (Ger.) (shäl'—bōd—å n) Sounding-board. Schallplatte, (Ger.) (shäl'—plät—å) Phonograph record. Shcallrohr, (Ger.) (shäl'—rọr) Wind instrument. Schalltrichter, (Ger.) (shäl'—trikht—å r) Horn.

Schalmei (Ger.) (shäl'—mī) Shawm.

Scharf (Ger.) (shärf) Sharp; strict.

Schauspiel (Ger.) (show'—shpēl) Drama.

Schelle (Ger.) (shĕl'—å) Bell.

Schellen (Ger.) (shĕl'—å n) Ring.

Schellentrommel (Ger.) (shĕl'—å n—trŏm—å l) Tambourine.

Scherz (Ger.) (shĕrts) Jest.

Scherzando (It.) (skĕr—tsän'—dō) In a playful manner.

Scherzetto (It.) (shĕr—tsĕt'—ō) Little scherzo; short scherzo.

Scherzevole (It.) (skĕ r—tsä'—vō—lä) In a playful style.

Scherzo (It.) (skĕ r'—tsō) Joke or jest. (1) A title for a lively piece of music. Example of a scherzo as a separate instrumental piece: Frédéric Chopin (1810—1849), *Scherzo in B Minor,* Op. 20. (2) A third movement of a symphony, quartet, or sonata. Beethoven replaced the usual classical movement called the minuet with the scherzo movement in his symphonies and sonatas (all of the symphonies except the 8th). The scherzo is usually in a lively $\frac{3}{4}$ meter. It is not always of a humorous nature, but it is not sentimental. It was frequently used by Nationalistic composers. (3) A Baroque term used for light vocal and instrumental pieces.

Schietto (It.) (skē—ĕ̆ t'—o) Simple.

Schlachtgesang (Ger.) (shläkht'—gä—zäng) Battle song.

Schlag (Ger.) (shläk) Beat; pulsation; rhythm; measure.

Schlägel (Ger.) (shlĕg—å l) Also, schlegel. Drum-stick.

Schlager-melodie (Ger.) (shläg'—å r—mä—lō—dē ') Song-hit.

Schlaginstrumente (Ger.) (shläg'—ĭ̆ n—stroō—mĕn'—tå) Also, Schlagzeug. Percussion instruments.

Schlagring (Ger.) (shläg'—ring) Plectrum

Schlagzither (Ger.) (shläg'—tsit—å r) Zither.

Schlangenrohr (Ger.) (shlǎng'—å n—rōr) Schlange means snake. Name of an instrument called serpent. See *Serpent.

Schleichen (Ger.) (shlīkh'—å n) Flow; gentle movement.

Schleifbügel (Ger.) (shlī f'—büg—å l) Sliding-bow.

Schleifen (Ger.) (shlī f'—å n) Slide; slur.

Schleifer (Ger.) (shlī f'—å r) A schleifer is an ornament used in 17th and 18th century music. It is called a "slide" or slur and is an appoggiatura (ascending or descending) consisting of two grace notes. For example:

Or a direct (⌇) may be used in place of the grace notes for example:

The appoggiatura is played on the beat. See *Appoggiatura, *Direct.

Schleppen (Ger.) (shlĕp'—å n) Move slowly, drag.

Schleunig (Ger.) (shloin'—ik) Swift, quick.

Schlummerlied (Ger.) (shloōm'—å r—lēt) Lullaby.

Schluss (Ger.) (shloŏs) Conclusion; cadence; finale.

Schlüssel (Ger.) (shlüs'—å l) Clef.

Schluss-kadenz (Ger.) (shloŏs'—kä—dĕnts) Final-cadence.

Schluss-satz (Ger.) (shloŏs'—zäts) Last movement.

Schmachtend (Ger.) (shmäkht'—å nt) Languishing

Schmeizen (Ger.) (shmī '—tså n) Blend.

Schmelzend (Ger.) (shmĕl'–tsȧnt) Melodious.
Schmerzlich (Ger.) (shmĕrts'–lĭkh) Grievous.
Schmetter (Ger.) (shĕmt'–å r) Resound; blare.
Schnabel (Ger.) (shnäb'–å l) Beak. Mouthpiece of an instrument.
Schnabelflöte (Ger.) (shnäb'–ål–flĕ(r)–tå) Beaked-flute, e.g., recorder.
Schnarrbass (Ger.) (shnär'–bäs) Drone bass.
Schnarre (Ger.) (shnär'–å) Rattle.
Schnarrtrommel (Ger.) (shnär'–trŏm–må l) Snare drum.
ᵥSchnell (Ger.) (shnĕl) Fast; presto.
Schneller (Ger.) (shnĕl'–å r) (1) Faster. (2) An 18th century ornament in the fashion of a quick trill. (3) Inverted mordent.
Schola cantorum (Lat.) Choir school; ecclesiastical choir; papal choir.
Schottische (Ger.) (shŏt'–ĭsh–å) Scottish. A 19th century round dance like a slow polka. German polka.

Schwächung (Ger.) (shvĕ kh'–o͝ong) Weakening; diminution.
Schwank (Ger.) (shvänk) Flexible.
Schwebung (Ger.) (shvā'–bo͝o ng) Fluctuation. Beats in acoustics.
Schweinskopf (Ger.) (shvīns'–kŏ pf) An instrument of Europe. A psaltery.
Schweller (Ger.) (shvĕl'–å r) Swell.
Schwellton (Ger.) (shvĕl'–tōn) Louder tone; crescendo.
Schwellwerk (Ger.) (shvĕl'–vĕ rk) Swell organ.
Schwindend (Ger.) (shvin'–då nt) Dying away.
Schwingung (Ger.) (shving'–o͝ong) Oscillation.
Scialumo (It.) (shē–ä'–lo͞o–mō) (chalumeau, Fr. (shä–lü–mō)) 1. Lower register of the clarinet. 2. Shawm.
Scinder (Fr.) (să (n̠)–dā) To divide.
Scintillare (It.) (shi n–tē–lä'–rā) (scintillant, Fr. (să(n)–tē–lä(n)) Glitter; sparkle.
Scioltezza (It.) (shē–ōl–tĕt'–tsä) Freedom.
Sciolto (It.) (shē–ŏl'–tō) Easy; loose, free.
Scissione (It.) (shē–zē–ō'–nā) Division.
Scivolando (It.) (shē–vō–lăn'–dō) Glissando.

328

Scordatura (It.) (skôr–dä–tōo'–rä) Mis-tuning. The tuning of a string instrument in a way other than the normal tuning to simplify the playing of a difficult passage or to achieve a special effect.

Score The printed copy of music showing the parts in a given order. The orchestration, bandstration, the voicing, the ranges, the keys, etc. are included in a score. Several types of scores are used in the conducting and study of music. The full score, which has all the instrumental and vocal parts; the instrumental score, which has only the instrumental parts; the piano score, which is a reduction of a larger score or a piano work; the short score, which is a reduction; the vocal score, which shows the voice parts and the text along with a reduction of the orchestra parts; the miniature score (study score or pocket score) which is a full score but in a smaller size in order to cut down on expense; and a full open score, which has each part on a separate line. See the individual entries.

Scoring Organizing all the parts into a unit. Orchestrating; making a score.

Scorrendo (It.) (skôr–ĕn'–dō) Gliding or flowing.

Scotch snap A typical rhythm used in the folk music of Scotland. It is short-long (♪♩.). It is also a typical rhythm of jazz, 16th century French songs, early Baroque music, and is frequent in 17th century English and Italian music.

Scrittura (It.) (skrē'–tōo–rä) Writing. A contract to write an opera.

Scroll The curved head of the violin, viola, etc.

Sdrucciolando (It.) (sdrōo–chē–ō–län'–dō) Also sdrucciolare (sdrōo–chē–ō–lä'–rä) Sliding; glissando.

Se (It.) (sā) If.

Sea trumpet See *Tromba marina.

Seba A flute of ancient Egypt.

Sec (Fr.) (sĕk) Dry; sharp; plain.

Secco (It.) (sĕ'–kō) Dry, e.g., secco recitativo. See *Recitativo.

Sechsachtel-takt (Ger.) (zĕks–äkht'–ål–täkt) Six-eight

time.

Sechzehntel-note (Ger.) (zĕk–tsān'–tal–nō'–tå) Semi-quaver note (♪).

Sechzehntel-pause (Ger.) (zĕk–tsān'–tål–pow'–zå) Semiquaver rest. (𝄿).

Second (1) An interval consisting of two tones with one note on the next degree to a given note. A major second consists of two semitones (e.g., C – D); a minor second of one semitone (e.g., C – Db); and an augmented second consists of three semitones (e.g., C – D#). See *Intervals. (2) A second part is the lower part of two parts that are assigned to the same instrument or voice. E.g., 1st trumpet and 2nd trumpet; 1st soprano and 2nd soprano; etc.

Seconda volta (It.) (sā–kŏn'–dä vôl'–tä) Second time. The second ending. See *Prima volta.

Second inversion A triad or chord is in second inversion when the fifth of the chord is the lowest note. E.g.,

Root position   2ⁿᵈ inversion

See *Inversion.

Secondo (It.) (sā–cŏn–dō) Second. The second part or player.

Section A subdivision of a complete musical period.

Secular music Music that does not pertain to religion. Not sacred music.

Seele (Ger.) (zā'–lå) The sounding-post of a stringed instrument (violin, etc).

Segno (It.) (sĕn'–yō) A repeat sign which is indicated in the music with a sign (𝄋). The term dal segno indicates that the music is to be repeated from the sign. See *Dal segno, *Al segno.

Segue (It.) (sā'–gōo–ā) Follows. (1) A direction to go on to the next section without a puase. (2) Continue the style. E.g., if a part has been doubled the doubling is to be continued.

Seguidilla (Sp.) (sā–gē–dēl'–lyä) A lively Spanish dance in triple time. The instruments used for accompaniment are castanets and guitars. Example: Issac Albéniz (1860–1909), *Sequidillas.*

Sehr (Ger.) (zār) Greatly; very.

Sei (It.) (sä'–ē) Six.

Sekundieren (Ger.) (zā–ko͝on–dē'–rå n) Second; accompany.

Semi (Lat.) Half.

Semibiscroma (It.) (sĕ–mē–bēs–krō'–mä) Sixty-fourth note (♬).

Semibreve Whole-note (𝅝). It is equal to half a breve or two minims.

Semicroma (It.) (sĕ–mē–krō'–mä) Semiquaver. Sixteenth-note (♪).

Semicrotchet An eighth note (♩). A quaver.

Semidemisemiquaver A sixty-fourth note (♬). Hemidemisemiquaver.

Semiditas (Lat.) Diminution. A version of "cut time" used in mensural notation and indicated by a line through a time signature.

Semiminima (It.) (sā–mē–mē'–nē–mä) A crotchet. A quarter-note (♩).

Semiquaver A sixteenth note (♪). Semicroma in Italian.

Semiseria (It.) (sā–mē–sā'–rē–ä); **Semiserio** (It.) (sā–mē–sā'–rē–ō) Half-serious. An opera having some serious parts with other parts less serious or comic.

Semitone A half-tone. A half-step. For example, the distance from a white key to the next black key on the piano keyboard such as from F to F sharp. Or, from B to C or E to F.

Semplice (It.) (sĕm'–plē–chä); **Semplicemente** (It.) (sĕm–plē–chä–mĕn'–tā) Simple; simply.

Sempre (It.) (sĕm'–prä) Always; yet; still.

Sensibile (It.) (sĕn–sē'–bē–lä) Sensitive.

Sensible (Fr.) (sä (n)–sē–bl) Obvious. Leading note.

Sentence A complete musical idea. A period.

Sentire (It.) (sĕn–tē'–rä) Feel.

Senza (It.) (sĕn'–tsä) Without; Senza replicare, (It.) (sĕn'–tsä rā–plē–kä'–rä) Without a repeat. Senza

331

sordino, (It.) (sĕn'–tsä sôr–dē'–nō) Without mute.

Septet A work for seven parts, seven voices, or seven instruments. An example, Camille Saint – Saëns (1835–1921) *Septet,* Opus 65, for String Quintet, Trumpet, and Piano.

Septième (Fr.) (sĕp–tē–ĕ m) Seventh.

Septolet, septuplet, septimole A group of seven notes and /or rests of equal value that is played in the time value equal to four or six notes of the same time value. An example,

Septuor (Fr.) (sĕp–tü–ōr) Septet.

Sequence The repetition of a part of a musical phrase on a different pitch. (1) Melodic sequence: the repetition is only in the melody. (2) Harmonic sequence: the repetition is in all parts. (3) Tonal or diatonic sequence: the repetition does not use accidentals. (4) Real or modulating sequence: the repetition preserves the exact intervals through the use of accidentals. (5) A hymn sung after the gradual. Example of a melodic and rhythmic sequence: from *Symphony No. 5, in C Minor,* Op. 67 by Ludwig von Beethoven (1770–1827), "4th movement, 3rd theme."

Seraphine An early 19th century reed organ which preceded the harmonium.

Serenade An evening song or piece of music for evening entertainment. (1) A love song. (2) An instrumental piece of music during the 18th century written for small ensemble in several movements. The style is similar to the divertimento and the cassation, and used for entertainment. Examples: W. A. Mozart (1756–1791), *Serenade in Bᵇ,* K 361, for Woodwinds and

Brass; W. A. Mozart; *Serenade in G,* K 525, for String Orchestra called "Eine Kleine Nachtmusik." See *Divertimento, *Cassation.

Serenata (It.) (sā—rā—nä'—tä) (1) A short opera written to honor a patron. A secular cantata. (2) Serenade. Example: A. Casella (1883—1947) *Serenata for Clarinet, Bassoon, Trumpet, Violin, and Cello.*

Sereno (It.) (sā—rā'—nō) (1) Serene, clear. (2) Evening song.

Serial technique The use, in composition, of an organized order of tones as a basis for a composition. The rules are applied rigorously to the order of the tones and to the rhythm. The twelve-tone system which is used by Schoenberg is one example. Many varied series are possible. The technique is used by such composers as Stockhausen, Boulez, among others. See *Twelve-tone system.

Serio (It.) (sā'—rē—ō) Serious.

Serpent A large 19th century bass wood instrument in the shape of an S or in the shape of a serpentine. It was used in bands and played by blowing into a cup-shaped mouthpiece like that of the trumpet. See *Russian bassoon.

Serré (Fr.) (sĕr—rā) Concise, terse.

Service Divine service. Musical settings of the liturgy used in church services.

Sesqui (Lat.) Means one and one-half. A prefix used with many words. Used in proportions.

Sestetto (It.) (sĕs—tĕ'—tō) Sextet.

Sesto (It.) (sĕs'—tō) Sixth.

Setting Music written to a set of words; for a medium; or an arrangement.

Seule (Fr.) (sûl) By oneself. A solo.

Seventeenth The 17th in a series. The interval of two octaves plus a third.

Seventh A series from one to seven. From the tonic upwards to the seventh degree in a diatonic scale. The interval of a seventh. An interval of a major seventh has eleven half-steps; a minor seventh, ten half-steps; and a diminished seventh, nine half-steps. See *Intervals, *Chords.

Seventh chord A chord comprised of a root, third, fifth, and seventh. A chord consisting of three intervals of a third each

Sextet A work for six parts, six voices (accompanied or unaccompanied), or six instruments. An example: J. Brahms (1833—1897) *Sextet in B flat,* Opus 18, for Strings.

Sextole (Lat.); Sextuplet (Lat.) A group of six equal notes and/or rests played in the same time value as four of the notes/rests. Example ⟶

Sextolet (Fr.) (sĕks—tō—lā) Sextuplet.

Sextuplet See *Sextole.

Sextus (Lat.) Sixth part.

Sfogato (It.) (sfō—gä'—tō) In a light manner.

Sforzando (It.) (sfôrt—tsän'—dō); Sforzato (It.) (sfôrt—tsä'—tō); Sforzo (It.) (sfôrt'—tsō) Stress. The term indicates that the note or chord should be played with accent or strength. The abbreviation for the term is sfz or sf.

Shake To trill a tone. Also, to literally "shake" the horn or lip, in jazz playing, in order to achieve a wide vibrato. To agitate a tone.

Shako A military-type hat, cylindrical in shape with a visor and plume, sometimes worn by the players in school marching bands.

Shanty Sailors work-songs. Also called chantey or chanty, See *Chantey.

Sharp The sign (#). A sharp raises a tone one-half step from the given note. See *Keys, *Double-sharp.

Shawm An early double-reed instrument that preceded the oboe.

Sheng (Chinese) A Chinese gourd played by the mouth. A mouth organ.

Shift (1) Changing of the hand position in playing guitar, violin, piano, etc. (2) Changing the slide position on trombone.

Shofar An ancient wind instrument made from a ram's horn. It is used in the Synagogue service to celebrate Rosh Hashanah and Yom Kippur.

Short octave At a time when the complete cycle of keys was not generally used, there was little need for most chromatic notes of the lowest octave of the keyboard. Therefore, the strings and pipes for such chromatic keys were omitted from the lower section of the keyboard and were replaced with those bass notes most used. This arrangement of the lowest octave of the keyboard had a compass of a sixth. For example, rather than an octave extending from what is normally the C key to the octave C above, the short octave would begin with the C placed on the key which is normally E and extend up to C (a sixth). This short octave made easily playable chords that otherwise extended beyond the reach of one hand. The short octave was in general use in the 17th century and was also used in earlier times. The following chart (keyboard) will demonstrate a possible arrangement of a short ocatve (C—C) in relation to a regular octave (C—C). An example of one possible arrangement:

   *The keys F, G, A, A# (Bb), B usually remain in regular position.

xxC replaces E, D replaces F#, E replaces G#.

  Regular keyboard:

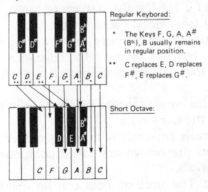

Regular Keyborad:

* The Keys F, G, A, A# (Bb), B usually remains in regular position.

** C replaces E, D replaces F#, E replaces G#.

Short Octave:

335

Short score A reduced score. See *Score.

Si (Fr.) (sē) (1) If, in French. (2) The note B in the syllable system of fixed do. (3) The French and Italian syllable for ti. (4) The syllable used when sol is raised a semitone.

Si bémol (Fr.) (sē bā—mŏl) B flat (B♭).

Siciliana (It.) (sē—chē—lē—ä'—nä); Siciliano (It.) (sē—chē—lē—ä'—nō); Sicilienne (Fr.) (sē—sē—lyěn) A slow Sicilian dance of the Baroque period written in six or twelve. It is similar in style and rhythm (♩.♩♩) to the pastorale.

Si dièse (Fr.) (sē dē—ěz) B sharp (B♯).

Side drum A snare drum used in orchestras, bands, dance bands, and marching bands.

Sideman A player in a dance band other than the lead man or first player.

Sight-singing or sight-reading To read the score without prior practice or study.

Signature See *Key signature, *Time signature.

Signs The symbols and signs that give directions. Following are some examples: a slur (♩♪); a tie (♩♩), a sustained tone (♩ or); a crescendo mark (＜); a decrescendo mark (＞); an accent (♩); an up bow (∨); downbow (⊓); a measure repeat (✕.); a double sharp (✗); a repeat (‖: :‖) a turn (∿); a trill ( ); a coda mark (⊕); a pedal (⌒); a grace note ( ); a first and second ending (⌐1   ⌐2   ); alla breve (¢); a flat (b); a sharp (♯); etc.

Silence (Fr.) (sē—lä(n)s) Pause or rest.

Similar motion Two or more lines moving in the same direction, but not at the same distance, at the same time. If the distance does not change the motion is parallel.

Simile (It.) (sē'—mē—lä) Similar. To continue the performance in the same style.

Simple intervals Intervals within the octave. Those that go beyond the octave are called compound intervals. See *Intervals.

Simple time The unit of beat can be divided by two.

Examples: $\frac{2}{4}$ ˘, $\frac{3}{4}$, $\frac{4}{4}$ time. See *Compound time.

Sinfonia (It.) (si n–fō'–nē–ä) (1) Symphony. (2) An instrumental piece that was played before the start of Italian operas during the 17th and 18th centuries. An overture.

Sinfonie (Ger.) (zi n–fō'–nē) Symphony.

Sinfonietta (It.) (si n–fō–nē–ĕ t'–tä) (1) A short symphony. (2) A small orchestra.

Sinfonische Dichtung (Ger.) (zi n–fōn'–ĭ sh–å dĭkh'– tŏong) Symphonic poem.

Singbar (Ger.) (zi ng'–bär) Vocal.

Singchor (Ger.) (zi ng'–kôr) Choir of singers.

Singing (1) Melodious vocal sounds. (2) The vocal performance of a song.

Singlehrer (Ger.) (zi ng'–lā–rå r) Singing master.

Singoper (Ger.) (zi ng'–ō–på r) Grand opera.

Singschlüssel (Ger.) (zi ng'–shlüs–å l) Clef.

Singschule (Ger.) (zi ng'–shōo–lå) Singing school.

Singstimme (Ger.) (zi ng'–shtim–å) Vocal part.

Singspiel (Ger.) (zing'–shpēl) Operetta. A light sung-play done in the vernacular with spoken dialogue included. They are modeled after the English ballad opera. Example: Wolfgang Amadeus Mozart (1756–1791), *The Abduction from the Seraglio,* K. 384.

Singstück (Ger.) (zing'–shtük) Song, ballad.

Sinistra (It.) (sē–nēs'–trä) Left.

Si replica (It.) (sē (rĕ–plē'–kä) Yes; repeat.

Sistema (It.) (sis–tā'–mä) System; staff.

Sistrum An Egyptian idiophone. The sound was produced by rattling the instrument. A variety of a rattle-type instrument.

Six-four chord The second inversion of a chord. The fifth of a chord is the lowest note. Above that note is the interval of a fourth and a sixth. A six-four chord of G, B, D follows: e.g., key of G

SEE * INVERSIONS   ROOT G $\frac{6}{4}$ or V $\frac{6}{4}$

Six, Les (Fr.) (lā sēs) Six French composers that were associated as a group about 1920. Eric Satie and Jean Cocteau had a great influence on the members. The six: Georges Auric (1899–   ), Louis Edmond Durey (1888–   ), Arthur Honegger (1892–1955), Darius Milhaud (1892–1974), Francis Poulenc (1899–1963), Germaine Tailleferre (1892–   ).

Sixteenth-note A semiquaver (♪).

Sixteenth-rest The pause equal to a semiquaver or sixteenth-note (♪).

Sixth A series from one to six. From the tonic upwards to the sixth degree in a diatonic scale. The interval of a sixth. An interval of a major sixth has nine half-steps; a minor sixth, eight half-steps; a diminished sixth has seven half-steps; and an augmented sixth has ten half-steps. See *Intervals, *Chords.

Sixth chord See *French sixth chord, *German sixth chord, *Neapolitan sixth chord, *Italian sixth chord.

Six-three chord A first inversion of a chord. The third of the chord is the lowest note. Above that note are the intervals of a third and a sixth. A six-three chord, G, B, D follows: e.g., key of C.

SEE * INVERSIONS

ROOT   G 6/3 or V 6/3

Sixty-fourth note Hemidemisemiquaver (♬).

Skala (Ger.) (skä'–lä) Scale.

Slentando (It.) (zlĕn–tän'–dō) Gradually slower.

Slide (1) A slide on the trombone used to change pitches. (2) Slides on brass instruments used to tune various parts of the horn. (3) Movement from one note to another using the same finger when playing a stringed instrument. (4) Ornaments or a short portamento. An embellishment of two or three notes moving up or down to a main note.

Slide horns Another name for slide trombone, slide trumpet, or a French horn with slides rather than valves.

Slide trombone Another name for the standard trombone.

There is a valved trombone used in jazz bands and for marching bands. See *Trombone.

Slur A group of notes of different pitch that are grouped by a curved line. E.g.,

They are to be played or sung on one breath or played with one bow stroke in a legato style. When notes of the same pitch are connected by this curve it is called . a tie.

Small octave The notes between c and c' on the bass staff. That is, beginning with c on the second space of the bass clef and going up one octave. See *Pitch letter names.

Smaniato (It.) (zmän–ē̱–ä'–tō) Vehement.

Smettere (It.) (zmĕt'–tä–rä) Stop.

Smorzando (It.) (zmôrt–tsän'–dō) Also, smorzato (zmôrt–tsä'–tō) Diminishing. Dying away.

Snare drum A circular drum having two heads with snares (strings or wires) stretched across the bottom head which add a rattling sound when the top head is struck with sticks. A percussion instrument used in orchestra, bands, etc. See *Side drum.

Snares Wires or strings of catgut stretched across the bottom head of a drum to produce a rattling effect.

Soave (It.) (sō–ä'–vä) Soft; tender.

Soft pedal The piano pedal to the left which is depressed in order to place the hammers in a position to strike fewer strings. The action produces less volume. Also called una corda pedal. See *Pianoforte, *Una corda.

Soggetto (It.) (sōd–jĕt'–tō) Subject. E.g., of a fugue.

Soh (Sol) (1) The fifth syllable in the system of movable do. (2) The note G when using the syllable system of fixed do.

Sol (sōl) The Italian syllable for the fifth note in the system of movable do. The syllable sol is identified with the note B in Italian and French in the fixed do system.

Sol dièse (Fr.) (sŏl dē–ĕz) G sharp (G#).

Solenne (It.) (sōl–ĕn '–nā) Solemn.

Solennellement (Fr.) (sŏl–ä–nĕl–mä(n)) Solemnly.

Solesmes A group of Benedictine monks, in Solesmes, France are known for their researching, editing, performing, and the establishment of rules relative to the Gregorian chant. See *A Selected Annotated Bibliography. (The Liber Usualis, Paléographic Musicale).

Sol-fa system An English tonic sol-fa system. It is the movable do system. Syllables are: 1 2 3 4 5 6 7 8 doh ray me fah sol lah te doh. See Movable do, *Solmization.

Solfège (Fr.) (sŏl–fĕ zh) See *Solfeggio.

Solfeggio (It.) (sŏl–fĕ d '–jē–ō) Vocal exercises to develop the musical ear using the system of syllables. Ear training by singing various tones by syllable names. See *Solmization.

Soli (It.) (sō '–lē) In orchestra or band music, one performer to a part.

Solmization The notes of the scale are designated by syllables rather than letter names. The system was developed by Guido D'Arezzo in the 11th century, who used ut, re, mi, fa, sol, la. Later the seventh syllable (si) was added. The syllables do and ti replaced ut and si, so that the syllables read (ascending) 1 2 3 4 5 6 7 8 do re mi fa sol la ti do. The English tonic sol-fa system reads (movable 1 2 3 4 5 6 7 8 doh): doh ray me fah sol lah te doh. The syllables do, re, mi, fa, sol, la, ti, do may be used in two ways: the system of fixed do means that do is always C, re is always D, mi is E, Fa is F, etc.; the moveable do system allows the syllable do to be the tonic of any key, for example, do is C in the key of C, do is F in the key of F, do is Bb in the key of Bb, etc. All other tones and syllables are relative. See *Sol-fa system.

Solo To play alone or with accompaniment. One main performer.

Solo anthem An anthem with solo parts and chorus. See *Anthem.

Solo organ A manual of the organ that has stops used for solo playing. Stops which give the sounds of orchestral instruments.

Solo pitch A tuning a little higher than the regular pitch.

Solovox An electronic keyboard that is attached below the right end of the piano keyboard. It produces many timbres sounding like an organ. The left hand can accompany on the regular piano keyboard.

Soltanto (It.) (sŏl—tän'—tō) Only.

Son (Fr.) (sō(n)) Sound. Son du tambour (Fr.), drumbeat.

Sonance Voice or sound Sonant — sounding.

Sonare (It.) (sō—nä'—rā) To sound.

Sonata (suonare, (It.)(sōō—ō—nä'—rā)) Meaning, to sound. Generally, a musical composition having several contrasting movements written for one or more instruments. Toward the end of the 16th century and during the first of the 17th century the Italians used the name canzone da sonar to identify many pieces of instrumental music. These 'pre-sonata' pieces had several contrasting long and short sections. A. Gabrielli (c. 1510—1586) and G. Gabrielli (1557—1612) wrote pieces having sections in contrasting styles. Later, a piece of this type was called sonata (an instrumental composition in polyphonic style). At the beginning of the 17th century, in Italy, the sonata was a fusion of canzone and the suite. It was also used as an introduction to a larger work. During the first half of the 17th century the sections of the sonata became larger, more like movements rather than sections of suites. Between 1650 and 1750 the sonata had 3, 4, 5, or more movements. About 1670, the Italians made a clear distinction between sonata da chiesa (fugue-like style) and the sonata da camera (suite of dances). Both were generally four movement works (in a general pattern of slow-fast-slow-fast), and usually written for violin and basso continuo or as a trio-sonata (two violins and basso continuo, usually performed by four players, some by fewer than three players). Example: A. Corelli (1653—

1713) *Sonata da Camera,* B flat, Op. 2, No. 5 for 2 Violins, Viola Da Gamba, Harpsichord. Around the mid-18th century, the classical sonata developed its own identity and lost its relationship with the suite. Through such composers as K.P.E. Bach (1714—1788), K. Stamitz (1745—1801), et al., the ternary and bi-thematic structure of the sonata was established. K.P.E. Bach (1714—1788) used the classical scheme (allegro-adagio-allegro) in his piano sonatas. However, D. Scarlatti (1685—1757) wrote more than 550 one movement sonatas (called 'Exercises') which exploited the binary form. The Baroque sonata was written for one, two, three, four, or more instruments (parts). See the various J. S. Bach sonatas; for violin alone; cello alone, plus those for several instruments. The "developmental" aspects of the sonata flourished through such composers as Haydn (1732—1809), Mozart (1756—1791), and Beethoven (1770—1827). By the end of the 18th century, the sonata was established and became a basic structure used in chamber music and symphonic music, e.g., solo sonata, chamber sonata and orchestral sonata. **The pre-classical sonata.** The 17th century trio-sonata was in polyphonic style with an instrumentation of two violins and basso continuo or cello doubled by the harpsichord, organ, or lute. The sonata at the beginning of the 18th century was more monodic and was written for one violin and basso continuo. At the end of the 17th century, it was difficult to distinquish between a sonata and a suite. Corelli (1653—1713) generally used the binary form of the suite although in some works he followed a pattern of ternary form. He generally wrote in four movements e.g., (slow, fast, slow, fast). Some of the church sonatas were in five or more movements. **The Classical sonata.** The classical (three movement) scheme was allegro—adagio—allegro (e.g., the sonatas of K.P.E. Bach, (1714—1788). The four movement scheme was allegro—adagio—minuet—allegro. Beethoven (1770—1827) however, used the scherzo instead of the minuet. An important development in the classical sonata was the re-entry of the theme in the opening key. The emphasis placed on the devleopment section of the structure during the mid-18th century was most important. In general, the following scheme is an example of a possible structure of the classical sonata (a sample guide only). It is bithematic. (I) **exposition:** theme A in the main key — transition toward the dominant — theme B in the dominant — cadence in dominant; (II) **development:** of theme A & B — modulations; (III) **Re-capitulation or re-exposition:** theme A, main key — bridge to main key — theme B in main key — cadence in the main key. The mid-18th century sonata is usually in three movements, some are in four, some in two movements. Some types of sonatas: Beethoven (1770—1827) wrote sonatas for such instruments as piano, violin, and cello. They are usually in three movements, some in two or four movements, with a scherzo rather than the minuet. Elaborate development sections are found in Beethoven's sonatas. Franck (1822—1890) wrote the sonata in cyclical form, e.g., *Sonata for Violin and Piano.* Liszt (1811—1886) used free construction and wrote his B Minor Piano Sonata in one movement. It is an elaborate work having six themes within the one movement. Brahms (1833—1897) also used the cyclical device in his sonatas. Schoenberg (1874—1951) uses a structure called sonata-suite. Musical examples: for one instrument, Beethoven (1770—1827), *Sonata No. 1 in F Minor,* Opus 2, No. 1 for piano; for two instruments, Beethoven, *Sonata No. 2 in G Minor,* Opus 5, No. 2 for Cello and Piano; for three instruments, Mozart (1756—1791) *Trio in B^b,* K. 502 for Piano, Violin and Cello; for four instruments, Mozart, *Quartet in G,* K. 387 Strings; for five instruments, Mozart, *Quintet in E^b,* K. 452 for Piano and Woodwinds. See *Sonata-form, *Sonata da chiesa, *Sonata da camera.

Sonata da camera Chamber sonata. A Baroque instrumental work having several varied movements. See *Sonata.

Sonata da chiesa Church sonata. A Baroque instrumental

form having several varied movements. See *Sonata.

Sonata form A design used within the form of the sonata for single movements. It is often used in the first or last movement (as well as other movements) of a sonata symphony, quartet, etc. Also called sonata—allegro-form. The basic structure of the form is in three parts: Exposition — Development — Recapitulation. An introduction, bridge material, and a coda may be used with the three basic parts. The Exposition: usually two (or three) themes are exposed in this part, the first theme in the home key, the second theme is usually in the dominant key of the major or in a related key. A closing section ends the Exposition and leads to the second section called Development. The themes of the Exposition are developed. Many techniques are used such as, fragmentation, modulations, canonic devices, fugal treatment, instrumentation, dynamic changes, etc. The development section leads back to the Recapitulation where the first theme is presented in the home key. The second theme is presented in the home key in this section which makes the movement end in the tonic key. Some new material or varied accompaniment may be introduced in the Recapitulation. Sometimes, a coda is used to round off the movement. The 18th century overture was also in sonata-allegro form. Examples: Wolfgang Amadeus Mozart (1756—1791), *Overture to the Marriage of Figaro,* K 492; Franz Joseph Haydn (1732—1809), *Symphony No. 101,* D Major (The Clock) Movement I. See *Sonata, *Sonata-rondo.

Sonata-rondo A piece of music having a combination of the sonata form and rondo form. The sonata-rondo form is also called the third rondo form. Sonata form may be outlined as follows: An example:

Intro — Exposition (repeated) — Development — Recapitulation — Coda (optional)

Theme I — Home Key	Several	Theme I — Home Key
Theme II — Dominant or	Keys:	Theme II — Home Key
related key.	transition	

The Sonata-rondo form may be outlined as follows: An example:

Theme I — Tonic Key	Theme III	Theme I — Tonic Key —	Coda
Theme II — (a second key)	(a third key) Theme II' — Tonic Key		
Theme I — (Tonic Key)		Theme I — Tonic Key	

An example of Sonata-rondo form: *Sonata No. 3 in C, Op. 2, No. 3*, Piano, "Fourth movement" by Ludwig von Beethoven.

Sonatina A small or short sonata. It is used in two instances: (1) A three movement work (sonatina or sonatine); (2) A single movement work (sonatina form or sonatine form).

Song A musical piece intended for singing with or without accompaniment. Words set to a melody which is written to heighten the effect of the words. There are many contexts in which song may be discussed. See *Folk-song, *Plainsong, *Ballad, *Frottola, *Duets, *Motet, *Madrigal, *Lied, *Minnesinger, *Meistersinger, *Strophic song, *Through-composed song, *Art song, *Song cycle, etc.

Song cycle A group of songs based on a unifying idea. The texts are by one poet and the music by one composer. E.g., Franz Schubert (1797—1828), *Die Winterreise, Opus 89*, and *Die Schöne Müllerin, Op. 25*.

Song form (1) Often used when referring to ternary form or da capo aria. (2) Binary song form.

Sonner (Fr.) (sŏ—nā) To ring; to sound.

Sonore (Fr.) (sŏ—nŏr) Sonorous.

Sonority Deep or resonant.

Sonorous Full sound. Rich and deep sound.

Sons bouchés (Fr.) (sō(n) bōo—shā) Placing of the right hand into the bell of the French horn to muffle the sound or change the pitch. Stopped horn.

Sons étoufflés (Fr.) (sō(n) ā—tōo—flā) Damped.

Sopra (It.) (sŏp '—rä) Above.

Sopran (Ger.) (zō—prän ') Soprano.

Sopranino (It.) (sŏ—prä—nē '—nō) Little soprano. Above the soprano, e.g., sopranino saxophone, which is the

345

size above the soprano saxophone.

Soprano (It.) (sŏ–prän'–ō) (1) The highest female voice having a range from around middle c' upwards to about two octaves. It is also identified as lyric soprano, coloratura soprano and dramatic soprano. (2) A male voice of a similar range, either the unchanged voice or a castrato. (3) The term soprano can be used to identify an instrument, usually the highest in a family. E.g., soprano saxophone. The abbreviation for soprano is sop.

Soprano clef C clef. Middle c is on the lower (first) line of the staff. E.g.,

Soprano string (chanterelle (Fr.)) The highest or first string on a stringed instrument.

Sordamente (It.) (sôr–dä–měn'–tā) Muffled.

Sordino (It.) (sôr–dē'–nō) Mute or damper.

Sospiro (It.) (sŏs–pē'–rō) Sighing; Sospirando (It.) (sŏs–pē–rän'–dō) Sigh. A crotchet rest.

Sostare (It.) (sŏs–tä'–rā) Stop.

Sostenuto (It.) (sŏs–těn–ōō'–tō) Sustained.

Sotto (It.) (sŏt'–tō) Under or below; Sotto voce (It.) (sŏt'–tō vō'–chā) Subdued voice.

Sound board The wooden plate of a musical instrument placed close to the strings which acts as a resonator.

Sound box The chamber of an instrument which helps the tone to be more resonant.

Soundholes (1) The f holes cut in the upper part of a violin, cello, etc. (2) The circle cut in lutes and guitars.

Sound post The vertical post between the back and the table of the violin, cello, etc. It gives support to the table which is under pressure from the bridge and strings and carries vibrations.

Soupir (Fr.) (sōō–pir) A quarter rest (𝄾). A crochet rest.

Sourde (Fr.) (sōōrd) Muffled.

Sourdine (Fr.) (sōō r–děn) (1) An obsolete double reed instrument that had a muffled sound. (2) Mute.

Sousaphone The bass tuba named for John Philip Sousa, (1854–1933), a bandsman. It is made in a circular shape which is large enough to circle the body so it can be carried easily on the march. The bell faces forward. A form of helicon.

Sparta (It.) (spär'–tä) To score.

Spassen (Ger.) (shpäs'–å n) Jest.

Speaker keys Keys that are used to aid a player to produce higher notes (harmonics) by overblowing. E.g., clarinet, etc.

Species Types of counterpoint.

Spezzato (It.) (spĕt–tsä'–tō) Separated or divided.

Spianar la voce (It.) (spē–ä–när'lä vō'–chä) Smooth or even voice.

Spianato (It.) (spē̱–ä–nä'–tō) Even.

Spiccato (It.) (spi–kä'–tō) Bowing. Detached bowing. Short and rapid bouncing bow strokes in the middle of the bow. See *Sautillé.

Spiel (Ger.) (shpē l) Style of playing.

Spinet (1) A small single keyboard square piano. (2) Now used to identify a small upright piano with indirect action.

Spirito (It.) (spē'–rē–tō) Spirit. Con spirito, with spirit.

Spiritoso (It.) (spē–rē–tō'–zō) Spirited.

Spiritual In Negro folk music, a religious song that is usually improvised. The style is usually that of call and response.

Spitze (Ger.) (shpit'–tså) (1) For violin, at the point of the bow. (2) For organ, the toe.

Sprechgesang (Ger.) (shprĕkh'–gå–zäng) (1) Recitative. (2) Half sung and half spoken. See *Sprechstimme.

Sprechstimme (Ger.) (shprĕkh'–sti m–å) A term indicating a part which is not sustained enough to be considered singing but the composer has written a notational line indicating the approximate pitch at which the part is to be spoken.

Springer A type of agrément which was used in 17th century English music. It is the same as one form of Nachschlag in which the time value for the 'extra' note is taken from the main note and played before the next main note. For example,

WRITTEN   PLAYED
(WITH THE SIGN / TO THE RIGHT OF MAIN NOTE)
The springer was often used in 17th century viol and-lute music. The *extra note was played by simply touching the string, for that note, at the very end of the main note before playing the next main note. See Nachschlag.

Stabat Mater (Lat.) A medieval poem concerned with Mary's Vigil at the Cross which was adopted into liturgical use. Many composers have written settings for the text, e.g., des Prés, Pergolesi, Haydn, Verdi, Dvořák, etc.

Stabile (It.) (stä'—bē—lā) Stable.

Staccato (It.) (stä—kä'—tō) Separate; detached. It is written: $\frac{2}{4}$ ♩♩♩♩ . A dot or the sign ▼ is placed over or under the note and the note is shortened by more than half its length.

Staff (stave) The five horizontal lines and spaces on which notes are placed. When a clef is added the notes identify pitches. Early staves had one, two, or three lines and some composers experimented with a six line staff. Now, standard music is written on five lines. See *Treble clef, *Alto clef, *Tenor clef, *Bass clef, and *Grand staff.

Stamm (Ger.) (shtäm) Stem.

Standard tunes Well established popular vocal or instrumental tunes in the field of jazz.

Ständchen (Ger.) (shtĕnd'—khå n) Serenade.

Stark (Ger.) (shtärk) Forte. Loud.

Statement A theme, subject, motif, exposition presented in a composition.

Stave See *Staff.

Steam Calliope A callipoe that has a keyboard which operates steam valves which force steam through various sized whistles. Used at carnivals.

Steg (Ger.) (shtāk) Bridge used on violins, cello, etc.

Stegreif-musiker (Ger.) (shtāg '–ri f–moo–zē–kå r) One who improvises music.

Stem The vertical line that is drawn from a note head.

Stentado (It.) (stĕn–tä '–dō) Forced.

Stentando (It.) ((stĕn–tän '–dō) Dragging.

Step An adjacent degree in music.

Sterben (Ger.) (shtĕr '–bå n) Die away.

Stesso (It.) (stĕs '–sō) (steso, stessa) Same.

Stil (Ger.) (shtēl); stile (It.) (stē '–lä) Style. E.g., stile galante means gallant style. Stile reappresentativo – declamatory style.

Stimmbuch (Ger.) (shtim '–bookh) Part-book.

Stimme (Ger.) (shtim '–å) (1) Voice. (2) Part. (3) Organ stop. (4) Sound-post.

Stimmer (Ger.) (shtim '–å r) Tuner.

Stimmung (Ger.) (shtim '–oong) Tuning; pitch.

Stochastic music A term used by Yannis Xenakis, a 20th century Roumanian-born Greek composer, to describe his music. Example: *Metastaseis and Pithoprakta* by Xenakis.

Stock arrangement In jazz music, a commercial or standard published arrangement.

Stomp In Jazz, a type of blues song with a strong or marked beat.

Stop (1) A lever that controls a set of pipes. (2) A set of organ pipes forming registers (3) To stop a string is to change pitch. See *Stopping.

Stopped diapason See *Diapason.

Stopping Stopped notes. (1) On stringed instruments, pitch changes as the finger stops the string at a given point. (2) To stop a horn.

Strain A tune, melody, phrase, or period of music.

Streich (Ger.) (shtrīkh) Stroke. Streich instrumente, (Ger.) (shtrīkh i n–stroo –mĕn '–tå) Stringed instrument. Streich-quartett, (Ger.) (shtrīkh–kvär–tĕ t ') String quartet. Streich zither (Ger.) (shtrīkh–tsit '–å r) Zither played using a bow.

Strepitoso (It.) (strā—pē—tō '—zō) Noisy.

Stretto (It.) (strĕt'—tō) Narrow or close. (1) The closing section of a piece at a faster tempo. (2) An overlapping subject and answer in a fugue.

Strich (Ger.) (shtrĭkh) Bar line. Stroke.

Stringed instruments Chordaphones. Those musical instruments using strings to produce sound. The strings struck by hammers (piano, etc.); those bowed (cello, etc.); and those plucked (harps, etc.).

Stringendo (It.) (strin—jĕn '—dō) Pressing to speed up the music.

String quartet An ensemble almost always consisting of two violins (1st and 2nd), one viola and one cello.

String quintet An ensemble usually consisting of two violins, two violas, and one cello. Some composers have used the combination of two violins, one viola, and two celli.

Strings (1) Usually identified as the string section of the orchestra. (2) Any instrument having a string or strings.

String trio An ensemble usually consisting of one violin, one viola, and one cello.

Strisciare (Ir.) (strē—shē—ä '—rā) Creep. Slurred.

Stromento (It.) (strō—mĕn '—tō) Instrument.

Strophic song Each stanza of text is sung to the same music. Strophic bass means using the same bass for all verses. See *Through-composed.

Strum The act of running the thumb or fingers across the strings. To strum a guitar.

Strumentale (It.) (strōo —mĕ n—tä'—lā) Instrumental.

Stück (Ger.) (shtük) Piece.

Studien (Ger.) (shtōo'—di — å n) Studies.

Studio piano An upright piano as opposed to a grand piano.

Study piece Étude. A piece practiced to master specific problems.

Stufe (Ger.) (shtōof '—å) Step. Scale degree.

Stumm (Ger.) (shtŏom) Silent.

Style brisé (Fr.) (stēl—brē—zā) Broken style. A style in lute music where rapid successions of notes in different ranges gives the impression of contrapuntal texture.

Style galant (Fr.) (stēl gä—lä(n)) The elegant style of the Rococo period. See *Gallant style.

Suavita (It.) (sōō—ä—vē—tä´) Sweetness.

Subdominant The fourth degree of the diatonic sacle. In the key of G major it would be C.

Subito (It.) (sōō'—bē—tō) Suddenly. Subito forte, suddenly loud.

Subject The theme of a fugue. The motive or main theme of a piece. See *Fugue.

Submediant The sixth degree of a diatonic scale. In the key of G it would be E.

Subtonic The tone below the tonic. The seventh tone of the pure minor scale would be called subtonic as it is one full step below the tonic. The seventh tone in the major scale, harmonic minor, or melodic minor (ascending) would be a leading-tone as it leads one-half step to the tonic.

Sudden modulation A modulation that is not prepared. See *Modulation.

Suite An instrumental composition having several movements. (1) A series of dances (usually from four to eight movements) played one after another, all in the same key (Baroque suite). Dances used in the Baroque suite are: Allemande, Courante, Sarabande, Gigue, Bourée, Galliard, Hornpipe, Loure, Minuet, Musette, Gavotte, Pavan, Passepied, Rigaudon, Polonaise, Saltarello, and Siciliana. E.g., Baroque Suite: J. S. Bach (1685—1750), *French Suite, No. 2 in C Minor for Piano* (Courante, Sarabande, Air, Minuet, Gigue). The Baroque suite emerged from a practice (16th and 17th century) of playing dances in pairs, e.g., a passamezzo (slow, in duple time) followed by a saltarello (fast, in triple time). The second dance was a variation of the first. This technique was applied to all the dances of the 17th century variation suite. A good example may be seen in the *Banchetto Musicale, Suite No. 1,* for string quintet by Johann H. Schein (1586—1630). All five movements (padouna ($\mathbf{C}$). galliarde ($\frac{3}{2}$), courente ($\frac{6}{4}$), allemande (₵), tripla ($\frac{3}{2}$), are variations of the same theme. (2) The modern suite consists of a series of melodies or ideas taken from a larger work.

Sul (It.) (sool) On the. E.g., Sul G string — play the section or piece on the G string.

Sul ponticello (It.) (sool pŏn—tē—chĕl'—lō) Near the bridge.

Sul tasto (It.) (sool täs'—tō) On the finger board.

Sumer is icumen in A 13th century canon which is the oldest known six-part work. See *Reading rota.

Summation tone A tone which is heard when two tones are sounded together. It is a result of the total of the frequencies of the two notes. See *Combination tone.

Superius (Lat.) The top voice (vocal or instrumental) in a 16th century polyphonic composition.

Superoctave A coupler on an organ which produces an octave above.

Supertonic The second degree of a diatonic scale, the next above the tonic. In the key of G it would be A.

Sur (Fr.) (sür) On; above.

Suspension A nonharmonic tone. In harmony, a note of a chord which is extended to the next different chord. It forms a discord which is resolved when that note becomes a note within the next chord.

Süss (Ger.) (züs) Sweet.

Sustaining pedal The right foot pedal on the piano that removes the dampers from all strings permitting them to continue to vibrate. The tone continues to sound.

Swell (1) Increased volume. (2) A manual of the organ. (3) An enclosed division on the organ. See *Swell box.

Swell box An enclosed division of the organ. The shutters on the box are opened by a pedal causing a crescendo or dimuendo effect by the organ pipes that are enclosed.

Swell organ The manual which is just above the Great organ manual.

Swing music A style of arranged jazz music during the 1930's and 1940's. The music was played by large dance bands and had an easy beat for dancing.

Syllabic style A style used in singing Gregorian chant where one syllable is used for each tone. Occasionally one syllable is used for two or three tones but it remains an inflected monotone rather than a melody.

Syllables See *Solmization.

Sympathetic strings Strings that are not played but vibrate in sympathy with other strings which are either bowed or plucked. See *Viola d'amore, *Viola bastarda.

Symphonette A small symphonic orchestra.

Symphonia (Lat.) (1) Unison. (2) Medieval musical instruments such as the early organistrum and hurdy-gurdy. (3) Later, a name used for virginals. (4) Orchestral music; symphony.

Symphonic Related to the style of the symphony or the symphonic orchestra.

Symphonic jazz Jazz incorporated with symphonic music. For example, music by Gershwin, Grofé, etc.

Symphonic poem A one movement poem for orchestra. It is a program piece which is based on extra-musical ideas such as: a literary or pictorial idea, narrative or dramatic in style, poetic or realistic. The symphonic poem was developed by Liszt (1811–1886). It was preceded by the concert overture and the program symphony. However, Liszt did not use the sonata form or multiple movements in the symphonic poem but rather several motives (in the form of theme and variation) in one movement. Examples: Franz Liszt (1811–1886), *Symphonic Poem No. 3, Les Préludes,* Liszt, *Funeral Triumph of Tasso, Symphonic Poem No. 2A;* Bedřich Smetana (1824–1884), *Mà Vlast* (My Country). Later composers adopted and further developed the symphonic poem. For example: R. Strauss (1864–1949), *Domestic Symphony;* C. Debussy (1862–1918), *La Mer;* P. Dukas (1865–1935), *The Sorcerer's Apprentice;* O. Respighi (1879–1936), *The Fountains of Rome.*

Symphonie (Fr.) (sǎ (m)–fŏ–nē) Symphony.

Symphonic concertante (Fr.) (sǎ (m)–fŏ–nē kō(n)–sår–tä(n)t) A sonata for orchestra using several solo instru-

353

ments. Its style was characteristic of the 18th century German Mannheim School.

Symphony A term used in early music for instrumental music or for instruments and voices, such as an instrumental piece in an opera or in a sacred choral work. The classical symphony had its roots in such forms as the concerto grosso, trio sonata, and the overture. During the 18th century the symphony was identified as a sonata for orchestra. The symphony is generally defined as a large scale work having several movements which was written for a full orchestra or in some cases for part of an orchestra (e.g., a symphony for strings). The symphony first appeared in mid-18th century and had three or four movements and followed the pattern of the sonata. Such composers as G. B. Sammartini (1698–1775), J. W. Stamitz (1717–1757), K. P. E. Bach (1714–1788), and C. D. von Dittersdorf (1739–1799) contributed much to the development of this form. Two masters of the classical symphony were F. J. Haydn (1732–1809) with 104 symphonies and W. A. Mozart (1756–1791) with 41. The classical symphony usually had four movements. Movement I was usually allegro, often with a slow introduction, in sonata form; Movement II, slow (andante or adagio), in lyrical form; Movement III, minuet in the form of minuet and trio; Movement IV, finale, fast, in sonata form, sometimes rondo form. Some symphonies had three movements. Generally, the classical orchestra (e.g., Mozart orchestra) consisted of a string section (violins 1, violins 2, celli, violas, string basses) 2 flutes, 2 oboes, 2 bassoons, 2 French horns, and later added trumpets, clarinets, and timpani. Beethoven (1770–1827) increased the size of the orchestra and expanded the symphony. He added piccolo, trombones, contra-bassoon, and enlarged the number of players in the string section, enlarged the percussion section, and added more horns. He extended the coda, replaced the minuet with a scherzo, used variation form, fugue, and more complex rhythms, accents, and a wide range of dynamic levels. He bridged the gap between 18th century Classicism and 19th century Romanticism. The 19th century Romantic composer was less inclined to follow strict form and more interested in conveying the emotional feeling of the time. For instance Berlioz (1803—1869) wrote a program piece, with a title for each of the five movements, called *Symphony Fantastique,* Brahms (1833—1897) was interested in structure and was a master manipulator of thematic material. His melodies were emotional and lyrical. Tchaikovsky (1840—1893) was a vivid orchestrator and a creator of the rich extended melody. Bruckner (1824—1896), Mahler (1860—1911), and Wagner (1813—1883) wrote for the very large orchestra. The symphony was used as a vehicle by many composers to express the national spirit of a country, for example, the Sibelius (1865—1957) symphonies. The 20th century composer is making a great contribution to the symphonic repertoire. He writes for both large and small orchestra combining the basic principles of the symphony with style of the 20th century. For example, some few representatives are: Schoenberg — (1874—1951) *Chamber Symphonies, Opus 9 and Opus 38,* Shostakovich (b. 1906) — *Symphonies 1—13;* W. Schuman (b. 1910), *Symphonies 1—8;* plus many more, e.g., Vaughan Williams, Piston, Stravinsky, Hindemith, Ives, Copland, Hanson, Mennin, et al.

Syncopation (1) The elimination of an accent or the displacement of a strong beat. (2) The accent on a weak beat or on the weak part of a beat. For example: (1)

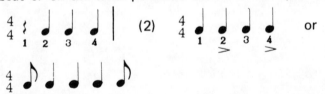

Synthesizer An electronic instrument used to create certain types of abstract music. The synthesizer creates and produces sounds in an organized and meaningful way using generators, controllers, and modifiers. Examples are the RCA electronic music synthesizer and the Moog electronic music synthesizer. See *Moog Electronic Music Synthesizer.

System A group of staves; a score. Liniensystem (Ger.) line system. Staff.

T An abbreviation for: (1) ti in the syllable system; (2) tasto; (3) tenor; (4) tonic; (5) trill (7th century); (6) tutti.

Tablature Systems of writing music during the 15th, 16th and 17th centuries for lute, keyboard instruments, etc. The pitch and duration were indicated by signs, symbols, letters, and numbers rather than by notation. This type of system can be found today in the music written for fretted instruments such as the guitar. An example of an F chord placed on a guitar tablature:

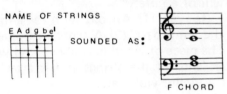

NAME OF STRINGS
E A d g be¹

SOUNDED AS:

F CHORD

See *Guitar.

Table d'harmonie (Fr.) (tä—bl där—mō—nē) The sound board of a musical instrument.

Tabor A small drum that was played by one hand while the other hand played a pipe (galoubet). A tambourin. It was used to accompany dances and is sometimes used in the orchestra. See *Farandole, *Sardana.

Tabourement (Fr.) (tä—boor—mä(n)) Drumming; strumming on an instrument.

Tacere (It.) (tä—chä '—rä); Tacet (Lat.) Keep quiet; is silent. The term is used to indicate to a player or group of players that they should not play or sing in a section or movement of a piece.

Tacit Silent.

Tactus (Lat.) Beat. A pulse in music. A term used in medieval and Renaissance music. The 15th and 16th century tactus had a stable tempo of about M.M. (semibreve) 𝅝 = c.60. The basic unit was the semi-breve (whole-note, 𝅝) and the tempo varied only slightly from this tempo. Later, when the bar line was introduced, the semibreve became a basic unit for a measure and the tactus became the metrical beat of a given measure. A great variety of tempi became available.

Tafelklavier (Ger.) (tä'–få l–klä–vēr') Table keyboard. A square piano.

Tafelmusik (Ger.) (tä'–få l–mōō –zēk') Dinner music. Title for a composition for chamber orchestra; *Tafelmusik* by George Philip Telemann (1681–1767).

Tag-ending In jazz, a term which identifies that extra music added to the end of a composition.

Tagliare (It.) (täl–yē–ä'–rā); Tagliato (It.) (täl–yē–ä'–tō) Cut; cut time (₵). An obsolete term.

Tail The stem of a note.

Taille (Fr.) (tä–yå) (1) An old term for a middle part, usually the tenor part. (2) A tenor instrument.

Tail-piece The piece of wood (usually ebony) which holds the lower ends of the strings and is attached to the body of a violin, viola, etc.

Takt (Ger.) (täkt) (1) Beat. (2) Measure. (3) Time. Taktart (Ger.) (täkt'–ärt) measure or time. Taktieren (Ger.) (täk–tē'–rå n) beat time. Taktierstab (Ger.) (täk'–tēr–shtäp) the baton. Taktmesser (Ger.) (täkt'–mĕs–å r) the metronome. Takstrich (Ger.) (täkt'–shtrīkh) a cadence or bar. Taktteil (Ger.) (täkt'–tīl) accent. Taktzeichen (Ger.) (täkt'–tsī kh–å n) or Taktbezeichnung (Ger.) (täkt–bå–tsīkh'–nŏŏng) time signature.

Taknote (Ger.) (täkt'–nōt–å) Semibreve.

Talon (Fr.) (tä–lō(n)) Heel. The lower end of the bow (violin, viola, etc).

Tambour (Fr.) (tä(m)–bōōr) Drum.

Tambour de basque (Fr.) (tä(m)–bōō r dû bäsk); Tambourino (It.) (täm–bōō–rē'–nō) Tambourine.

Tambourin (Fr.) (tä(m)–bōōr–ă(n)) (1) Provencal tabor. (2) In modern usage a tambourine.

Tambourin à cordes (Fr.) (tä(m)–bōōr–ă(n) ä kôrd) A tabor with strings.

Tambourine Also, tamburino (It.) A small circular drum

with one head and a series of small double plates or tiny cymbals placed around the rim that jingle as the head of the instrument is shaken or struck by the hand.

Tambour voilé (Fr.) (tä(m)—boor vwä—lā) Muffled drum.

Tambura (Also tamboura, tambur, tanbur, etc.) A lute instrument of Asia. It has a long neck and a small round body. A plucked-stringed instrument with four strings.

Tamburo (It.) (täm—boo'—rō) Drum. Tamburo maggior (It.) (täm—boo'—rō mäd—jē—ō'—rā) Drum major. Tamburo militare (It.) (täm—boo'—rō mē—lē—tä'—rā) Side drum or an orchestral snare drum.

Tampon (Fr.) (tä(m)—pō(n)) A drum-stick having a beater-head on each end. A roll may be played on a bass drum by holding the stick in the center and moving the wrist back and fourth.

Tamtam (Fr.) (täm—täm) Gong.

Tanbur Tambura.

Tangent A blade which is attached to the end of a clavichord. key. It strikes the string when the key is pressed. It divides the string into two parts. One part is damped by a cloth while the other part is free to vibrate. On some clavichords a single string may serve two notes by having two separate tangents each of which strike the string at a different point.

Tango A dance popular in South America and later in the United States. It is in duple time and has a moderatley

slow syncopated rhythm (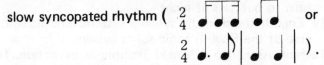 or).

The style is used in various compositions. Example Issac Albéniz (1860—1909), *Tango in D.*

Tanto (It.) (tän'—tō) So much.

Tanz (Ger.) (tänts) Dance.

Tanzmusik (Ger.) (tänts'—moo —zēk') Dance music.

Tape music A form of electronic music. Music that is assembled and composed through the use of magnetic tape, not by live performance.

Tarantella (It.) (tä—rän—tĕl'—lä) A lively Italian dance in

$\frac{6}{8}$ time in which sections alternate between major and minor. Examples: Felix Mendelssohn (1809–1847), *Italian Symphony No. 4, in A,* Opus 90; "Tarantella" for Piano No. 45 in C, from *Songs Without Words for Piano.*

Tardamente (It.) (tär–dä–měn '–tā) Slowly.

Tardo (It.) (tär '–dō) Late; slow.

Tartini tone The differential tones discovered by G. Tartini. See *Combination tone, *Difference tone, *Summation tone.

Taschengeige (Ger.) (täsh '–å n–gī–gå) Pocket violin.

Tastar (It.) (täs '–tär) Touching. A 16th century Italian name for pieces in a free prelude style written for the lute.

Tastatur (Ger.) (täs–tä–toor ') Keyboard. Keys.

Taste (Ger.) (täst '–å) Key.

Tasten-instrumente (Ger.) (täst '–å n ǐ n–stroo –měn '–tå) Keyed instruments.

Tasten-lager (Ger.) (täst '–å n–läg–å r) Key-board.

Tastiera (It.) (täs–tē–ā '–rä) Finger board; keyboard.

Tasto (It.) (täs '–tō) Key. Finger board; sul tasto, near the finger board.

Tasto solo (It.) (täs '–tō sō '–lō) (1) One key. (2) Play the continuo part alone without the chords.

Tattoo (1) Strong beat or pulse. (2) An outdoor military display. (3) A military bugle call which signals the return to quarters at night.

Te English for si in the syllable system. The seventh degree of the English tonic sol-fa system.

Technik)Ger.) (tě kh '–ni k) Technique; execution. Technique — The skill and virtuosity in performance.

Tedesca (It.) (tā–dě s '–kä) Also, tedesco. (1) German (German dance style). (2) A name used at various times for the allemande, Ländler or dances in triple meter.

Te deum laudamus (Lat.) (tā dā '–oom low–dä '–moos) "We praise Thee, O God". A hymn of praise to God. It is sung at Matins of joyful feast days in the Roman Catholic Church and at Morning Prayer in the Anglican

Church. It is often used outside religious services in settings by many composers for special festivals, celebrations and national thanksgiving.

Temperament The tuning of instruments in order that all keys (signatures) may be used without re-tuning. Prior to equal temperament there were systems of unequal temperament such as the mean-tone system. See *Equal temperament, *Tempered tuning.

Tempered tuning A system of tuning the octave on the keyboard into 12 equal half steps.

Tempestoso (It.) (tĕ m—pē s—tō '—zō) Gusty, tempestous.

Temple blocks A hollow piece of wood used in the rhythm section of a dance band. A hollow sound is produced when it is struck with a drum stick. The various sizes have an approximate pitch but are not tuned to a note.

Tempo (It.) (tĕ m '—pō) Time. The speed of the music. Some of the terms used to indicate tempo (from slow to fast) are: largo, lento, adagio, adagietto, andante, andantino, moderato, allegretto, allegro, presto, vivace, and prestissimo. See *M.M.

Tempo commodo (It.) (tĕm '—pō kō—mō '—dō) Moderate tempo. Tempo giusto (It.) (tĕ m '—pō jē—ōŏs '—tō) Exact time. Tempo Ordinario (It.) (tĕm '—pō ôr—dē—nä '—rē—ō) Moderate speed. Tempo perdito (It,) (tĕ m '—pō pĕr—dē '—tō) Uneven tempo. Tempo primo (It.) (tĕm '—pō prē '—mō) Go back to the first tempo. Tempo reggiato (It.) (tĕ m '—pō rĕ d—jē—ä '—tō) Adjust the tempo for the soliost. Tempo rubato (It.) (tĕm '—pō rōo—bä '—tō) Robbed time, An unsteady tempo. See *Rubato.

Temps (Fr.) (tä(n)) Time; measure; duration. Temps faible (Fr.) (tä(n) fĕbl) Weak beat. Temps fort (Fr.) (tä(n) .for) Strong beat. Temps frappé (Fr.) (tä(n) frä—pā) Fall; down beat. Temps levé (Fr.) (tä(n) lĕ —vā) Rise; up beat.

Tempus (Lat.) Time.

Tenebrae (Lat.) Darkness. The Office hours of Matins and Lauds sung in the Roman Catholic Church on the last three days of Holy Week. See *Office hours.

Tenere (It.) (tā—nā '—rā) Hold.

Tenerezza (It.) (tā—nā—rĕt '—tsä) Tenderness.

Teneur (Fr.) (tĕn—ûr) Tenor.

Tenor (1) The highest natural male voice. The tenor voice is approximately from B to g'. (2) An instrument within approximately the same voice range such as tenor saxophone, tenor horn, etc. (3) The cantus firmus in early polyphony. (4) An obsolete English term for the viola was tenor violin. (5) The recitation note in psalmody.

Tenor clef The C clef indicating that middle C is on the fourth line of the staff. The tenor clef:

MIDDLE C →

It is sometimes used for the upper range of cello, bassoon and tenor trombone.

Tenor drum The drum sized between the snare drum and the bass drum. It is usually used in marching bands.

Tenore (It.) (tĕ—nō '—rā) Tenor.

Tenorhorn (Ger.) (tān—ōr '—hôrn) A brass instrument, with valves, from the saxhorn family. See *Saxhorn.

Tenor Mass A medieval polyphonic Mass based on the cantus firmus.

Tenoroon A double-reed instrument pitched a fifth above the bassoon. Bassoon quinte (Fr.); Fagottino (It.) (small bassoon).

Tenor saxophone The B flat saxophone sized between the alto saxophone and the baritone saxophone. See *Saxophone.

Tenorschlüssel (Ger.) (tān—ōr '—shlüs—å l) Tenor clef.

Tenor staff See *Tenor cleff; *Clef; *Staff.

Tenor trombone The B flat slide trombone. See *Trombone.

Tenor tuba A euphonium; small tuba.

Tenor violin Viola

Tenth An interval (compound) of an octave and a third. See *Intervals.

Tenute (It.) (tĕn—ōo'—tā); tenuto (It.) (tĕn—ōo'—tō) Held; sustained. The abbreviation is ten.

362

Ter (Fr.) (tĕr) Three times.

Terce (Lat.) The morning Office hour between Prime and Sext in the Roman Catholic Church. See *Office hours.

Tercet (Fr.) (tĕr—sĕ) Triplet.

Ternary form A three-part form (e.g., ABA or AABA). The third (A) section may be an exact repetition of the first section. Each section is complete by itself beginning and ending in the same key. Often a different key is used for the middle section (e.g., the dominant key, parallel key, or relative key) and different thematic material is also used. See *Da capo aria.

Ternary time Rhythmic structure having units of three.

Terraced dynamics The change back and forth between levels of loud and soft in Baroque music. The subtle changes in dynamic levels were not practiced during this period as in later periods. For example, dynamic changes would come with the addition or deletion of instruments. A good example of this technique is found in the concerto grosso which alternates the use of smaller and larger groups of instruments. Generally a sharp change in dynamic level.

Tertiary harmony Chords built on intervals of thirds, i.e., triads.

Terz (Ger.) (tĕrts); **Terzo** (It.) (tĕrt'—tsō) Third.

Terzen-folge (Ger.) (tĕr'—tsån—fŏl—gå) A series of thirds.

Terzett (Ger.) (tĕrts—ĕt'); **Terzetto** (It.) (tĕrt—tsĕt'—ō) A vocal trio; three part song.

Terzflöte (Ger.) (tĕrts'—flĕ(r)—tå) A flute pitched a third higher than the (C) flute.

Terzina (It.) (tĕrt—tsē'—nä) Triplet.

Tessitura (It.) (tĕs—sē—too'—rä) The average lie of a piece of music. It is concerned with the majority of notes rather than a few high or low tones. The length of phrases and pauses is also a consideration.

Testo (It.) (tĕs'—tō) Text. Narrator.

Tetrachord (1) The ancient Greek tetrachord having four descending notes (whole-step, whole-step, half-step) within a perfect fourth. This forms the basis of the diatonic scale. (2) A four stringed instrument. (3) Four tones within a perfect fourth.

Texture The weave. The vertical and horizontal relationship of notes. The arrangement of voices, instruments, chords, etc. For example: homophonic texture; polyphonic texture.

Thema (Ger.) (tā '–mä); Thème (Fr.) (tĕm) Theme. (1) A short melody. (2) The subject of a work. The motive. The idea to be developed.

Thematic development The building of a composition on a basic idea through varied devices and techniques. The principal subject used in variation.

Theme and variations The presentation of a musical idea followed by a number of treatments but the original idea can still be recognized. The theme is usually sixteen to thirty-two measures long. It may be original or borrowed. Some methods of varying a theme are — by using several voices, different ranges, many keys, varied instruments, etc. in polyphonic treatment, or the melody can be changed while the harmonic structure remains the same, plus the treatment of any element of the theme or any part of the theme. Examples of theme and variations: J. S. Bach (1685–1750) *Goldberg Variations;* Franz Joseph Haydn (1732–1809) *Symphony in G,* No. 94, "Suprise Symphony" — Movement No. 2.

Theme song (1) The dominant melody in a large vocal work. (2) The melody always used to identify an ensemble or program.

Theorbo A large bass lute of the 17th and early 18th centuries. The plucked instrument had two peg boxes and two sets of strings. Generally used as a concert or accompanying instrument.

Theory of music The principles by which music is written. The science of music.

Theremin A melodic electronic instrument invented in the 1920's by Leo Theremin (b. 1896).

Thesis (Greek) (1) Strong beat. (2) A down beat in conducting. See *Arsis.

Third An interval of a third. Three degrees of a diatonic scale. Some examples of some types of thirds:

364

(F–A)
Major 3rd
(Four Semitones)

(F–Ab) (F#–A♮)
Minor 3rd
(Three Semitones)

(F–Abb) (F#–Ab)
Diminished 3rd
(Two Semitones)

(F–A#)
Augmented 3rd
(Five Semitones)

See *Intervals, *Scale.

Third inversion A chord is in the third inversion when the seventh of the chord is the lowest note. The third inversion is possible only when a seventh is added to a triad (chord). An example of a chord in the third inversion: key of G major, the V7 or D7 chord in third inversion:

It is identified as a D2 or V2 chord. See *Inversions.

Third-stream music A style of modern jazz which uses both jazz and classical elements. This is done in two ways: (1) the composition can be developed by incorporating both elements into one piece and played by a symphony orchestra; (2) the other method would have a jazz group and a symphony orchestra each maintain its identity while each group contributes to a new sound. The new sound is the third-stream. Examples: John Graas (b. 1924) *Jazz Symphony No. 1;* Dave Brubeck (b. 1920) *Dialogues for Jazz Combo and Symphony Orchestra.*

Thirty-second note A demisemiquaver ( ).

Thorough-bass See *Basso continuo, *Figured bass.

Three-quarter time Three-four time ($\frac{3}{4}$). A meter having three beats to a measure with the quarter note ( ) receiving one beat.

Threnody A funeral song. A dirge.

Throat voice A term sometimes used to identify the voice register above the chest register. It is also referred to as the middle register.

Through-composed A song that has different music throughout the work. The music changes with each stanza. Example: *Erlkönig* By Franz Schubert (1797–1828). See *Strophic song, *Durch komponiert.

Thrum A crude way of plucking or strumming strings.

Ti (tē) (1) The seventh syllable in the major scale in the movable do system. (2) The note B in the fixed do syllable system.

Tie A curved line that ties together two or more notes of the same pitch. The tied notes are held as one note for the total duration of the notes.

Tiento (Sp.) (tē–ě n'–tō) A Spanish term for the 16th century organ ricercar.

Tierce (Fr.) (tyěrs) Third. See *Picardy third.

Tierce de Picardie (Fr.) (tyěrs dû pē–cär–dē) See *Picardy third.

Timbal A kettledrum.

Timbale (Fr.) (tă(m)–bäl) Kettledrum; timpani.

Timbre Bell; sound, tone. The tone color. Those characteristics in a tone that identify the instrument or voice. See *Tone color.

Timbrel Any instrument in the tambourine group.

Time (1) Meter, tempo, duration, rhythm, the metrical aspects of the music, and mensural notation. Meters or time signatures (simple, combined, and compound) establish the number of beats in a measure and the kind of note that receives a beat. All other notes and rests are relative to the time signature. Meters ($\frac{2}{4}$, $\frac{3}{4}$, $\frac{4}{4}$, $\frac{5}{4}$, $\frac{6}{8}$, $\frac{9}{8}$, etc.). (2) Time is used in reference to style: waltz time, march time, etc. See *Meter, *Mensural notation.

Time signature Meter. The two numbers, one above the other, at the beginning of a piece of music or a section of music which indicate the number of beats in a measure (upper number) and the kind of note that receives a beat (lower number). The letter C, often used, is for common time ($\frac{4}{4}$), Some examples of meters: $\frac{2}{4}$ time (simple duple time) two beats to a measure and a quarter note equals one beat; $\frac{3}{4}$ time (simple triple meter) three beats to a measure and a quarter note equals one beat, plus many other combinations. Combined meters (e.g., $\frac{3}{4}$, $\frac{5}{8}$, $\frac{7}{4}$, $\frac{7}{16}$, etc.) are those having two different simple meters combined. Compound meters are multiples of the simple meters (e.g., $\frac{6}{4}$, $\frac{6}{8}$, $\frac{9}{8}$, $\frac{12}{4}$, etc.). See *Compound time or meter, *Meter.

Timpani (It.) (tim'—pä—nē) The large kettledrums used in the percussion section of the orchestra and concert band. They have definite pitch and are tuned by turnkeys around the top rim or by turning the rim of the instrument. The head of skin or plastic is tuned by varying the degree of tension. The timpani (two, three, or more) are tuned for each separate composition. Pitches are changed during the performance by a foot-pedal or by hand. The tone can vary in intensity and a tone may be short, or continuous by means of a roll with the sticks.

Tirasse (Fr.) (tē—rä'—tō) Pull; draw. An ornamental scale passage of several notes moving between two main notes.

Tirasse (Fr.) (tē—räs) An organ pedal coupler.

Tirata (It.) (tē—rä'—tō) Pull; draw. An ornamental scale passage of several notes moving between two main notes.

Tiré (Fr.) (tē—rä) Pull. E.g., pull the bow downward.

Toccare (It.) (tŏ—kä'—rä) Touch.

Toccata (It.) (tŏ —kä'—tä) (1) A Renaissance piece for keyboard. It was an imitative piece in a florid style. During the Baroque period the toccata continued as a one movement keyboard piece in contrapuntal style. Example: J. S. Bach (1685—1750) *Toccata and Fugue in C,* for Organ. It included fugal style, as well as an improvisatory style. (2) Brass music somewhat like a fanfare.

Todesgesang (Ger.) (tōd'—å s—gå —zäng) Todeslied (Ger.) (tōd'—å s—lēt) Dirge.

Tolling To sound a large bell in a slow and repeated manner.

Tom-tom An oriental drum with skin stretched across both circular ends. It has no definite pitch and is played by the fingers and hand. It comes in several sizes. It is used in dance bands of today and jazz combos. It is also the type of drum used by the American Indian.

Ton (Fr.) (tō(n)) Tone. Pitch.

Ton (Ger.) (tōn) Note; timbre; tone.

Tonabstand (Ger.) (tōn '–äb–stänt) Interval.

Tonada (Sp.) (tō–nä '–dä) Tune or song.

Tonal Tonality.

Tonal answer See *Answer.

Tonal center The key or key tone around which a piece of music is centered.

Tonality Music having a key center. Polytonality — having several keys. Bitonality — having two keys.

Tonart (Ger.) (tōn '–ärt) Key.

Tonbild (Ger.) (tōn–bilt) Tone poem.

Tondichtung (Ger.) (tōn '–dikht–ŏong) Musical composition. Tone poem.

Tone (1) A musical sound or timbre having a definite pitch. (2) The fundamental and its partials. (3) The Gregorian formula for plainchant. (4) A whole-tone, which is the sum of two half-steps. (5) The term is also used in modern systems to identify tone row or twelve-tone row. (6) Pure tone, which is a tone without its overtones. (7) Also used in the sense of referring to a flat tone, an open tone, a pleasing tone, etc.

Tone cluster A group of tones consisting of several adjacent tones being played at the same time. Henry Cowell (1897–1966) introduced this technique of playing in 1913. This device was used mainly in his piano works. Later, it was applied in his orchestral works. For example, in his piano concerto (1929), the technique of tone-clusters is used in both the solo part and orchestral part.

Tone color The timbre. Those characteristics in accoustics which make it possible to identify one instrument from another or one voice from another. The purity or richness of a tone. The orchestration or relationship of instruments and voices.

Tone holes The finger-holes of some flutes, clarinets, etc.

368

Tone painting A mood or descriptive piece of music.

Tone poem A one movement programmatic piece of music based on a poetic idea. The form is similar to that of theme and variations. It may have several themes. The orchestral piece in this style is called symphonic poem. Examples: Arnold Schönberg (1874–1951), *Verklärte Nacht,* Opus 4 for String Sextet; Franz Liszt (1811–1886), *Funeral Triumph of Tasso,* Symphonic Poem; Franz Liszt, *Les Préludes, Symphonic Poem No. 3.* See *Symphonic poem.

Tone row The twelve notes of the chromatic scale are reassembled into a pattern without reference to a key. The basic row is used throughout a composition in variation. It may be imitated, reversed, augmented, diminished, inverted, or the row played as a cluster of tones. The tones may be arranged in 48 forms. A key must not be established at any point. It is possible to transpose the row to any degree of the twelve chromatic notes used. The system was developed by Arnold Schoenberg. An example: Arnold Schoenberg (1874–1951), *Violin Concerto,* Opus 36. See *Twelve-tone system.

Tonette An end-blown flute having a whistle-type mouthpiece and open finger holes. It is similar to the soprano recorder.

Tonfall (Ger.) (tōn'–fäl) (1) Intonation. (2) Cadence.

Tonfolge (Ger.) (tōn'–fŏl–gä) Scale.

Tonführung (Ger.) (tōn'–für–ŏong) Modulation.

Tonfülle (Ger.) (tōn'–fül–å) Sonority.

Tongue A vibrating reed on the clarinet, organ, etc.

Tonguing Articulation in playing a wind instrument. There are several techniques, for example: soft-tonguing using the syllable (dew); short and sharp tonguing using the syllable (tat) for single tonuging; double-tonguing using the syllables (ta-ka, ta-ka, etc.) in very rapid succession; triple-tonguing using the syllables (ta-ta-ka, ta-ta-ka, etc.) in very rapid succession; and a buzz or flutter-type tonguing as is used in flute playing.

Tonhöhe (Ger.) (tōn'–hě(r)–å) Pitch.

Tonic (1) One, or the first degree of the scale. (2) The name of the key.

Tonic sol-fa See *Sol-fa system.

Tonisch (Ger.) (tōn '–i sh); **Tonika** (Ger.) (ton '–i k–ä) Tonic or key-note.

Tonkunst (Ger.) (tōn '–kŏonst) Musical art.

Tonleiter (Ger.) (tōn '–li t–å r) Scale.

Tono (It.) (tō '–nō) (Sp.) Tone, pitch, key.

Tonometer Tuning fork. An instrument that measures frequencies of a tone.

Tonreihe (Ger.) (tōn '–ri –å) Tone-row.

Tonsatz (Ger.) (tōn '–zäts) Phrase.

Tonschlüssel (Ger.) (tōn '–shlüs–å l) Key note, key-tone.

Tonschrift (Ger.) (tōn '–shrift) Note-writing; notation.

Tonstufe (Ger.) (tōn '–shtōof–å) Pitch.

Tonübergang (Ger.) (tōn–üb '–å r–gäng) Modulation.

Tonus (Lat.) (1) Gregorian tones. Psalm tones. (2) A whole-tone. (3) Mode.

Tonus lascivus (Lat.) Name for the Ionian mode (c' to c''). It can be played on the piano keyboard by playing all white keys from c' up one octave (the c major scale).

Tonus peregrinus (Lat.) An irregular psalm tone which has a different reciting note for its first and second half. It is used in the Roman Catholic Church to Psalm 114.

Tonzeichen (Ger.) (tōn '–tsi kh–å n) Accent.

Tosto (It.) (tŏs '–tō) Quick.

Totenlied (Ger.) (tōt '–å n–lē t); **Totengesang** (Ger.) (tōt '–å n–gå –zäng) Dirge.

Totenmesse (Ger.) (tōt '–å n–mĕ s–å) Mass for the dead. See *Requiem Mass.

Touch The weight applied, by the fingers, to the keyboard by a pianist. The touch is related to the tone produced when the hammers hit the strings. The touch is important in the interpretation of the many styles of music.

Touche (Fr.) (tōosh) Touch. (1) Fingerboard. (2) A key of the piano. (3) A 17th century term for toccata.

Toy A light piece of music written during the 16th and 17th centuries for the virginal.

Tract Sung after the Gradual in the Roman Catholic Mass. It is part of the Proper of the Mass and is sung during Lent and on somber occassions. It replaces the Alleluia which is sung on other occassions. See *Mass.

Tradolce (It.) (trä—dŏl '—chā) Very sweet.

Traduzione (It.) (trä—doo—tsē—ō '—nā) (1) Transposition; (2) arrangement.

Träge (Ger.) (trĕg '—å) Slow; sluggish.

Trällern (Ger.) (trĕl '—å rn) Trill.

Tranquille (Fr.) (trä(n)—kēl); **Tranquillo** (It.) (trän—koo— ēl '—lō) Quiet, calm.

Transcripteur (Fr.) (trä(n)—skrip—tûr) Transcription.

Transcription (1) To adapt a piece of music for another medium. For example, to transcribe a piano piece for orchestra, or an orchestral piece for band, etc. (2) An arrangement of a piece of music.

Transient modulation A temporary or passing modulation. A transitory modulation.

Transient overtones Harmonics that are present for a short time, usually as the tone is sounded.

Transient trill A half-trill. A short trill. See *Trill.

Transition (1) A bridge between two themes, sections, movements, etc. (2) An abrupt modulation. (3) A passing modulation. See *Modulation.

Transposed, transposition To change the key. For example, in order that a trumpet play music from a piano part, the music must be transposed for the B flat instrument. The trumpet player must read the piano part one step higher. To sing or play a work higher or lower, i.e. in another key.

Transposing instruments Some instruments are in concert pitch while others are transposing instruments. A transposing instrument plays a note that is different from the actual pitch. For example, using the note C on piano, the note C would be played as a C by violin, flute, oboe, among others; but the same C on the piano would be played as a d on the trumpet and other B flat instruments. Some transposing instruments: A clarinet; B♭ trumpet and cornet; F and B♭ French horns; F English horn; E flat alto saxophone; B flat alto clarinet; A trumpet, among others. The instruments are built in various keys in order to facilitate adequate finger patterns, to attain the best tone quality, and to make it possible to play within the key structure and proper range.

Transverse flute The modern flute. Flutes that have a mouth hole on the side and are held in a transverse position. See *Flute.

Transverse trumpet A primitive side-blown trumpet of Africa or South America which was made from animal horns.

Trapezoid A box fiddle.

Traps A general term used to describe the standard percussion instruments plus the special noise and sound devices used by a drummer in dance orchestras and bands.

Trattenere (It.) (trä—tā—nä '—rā) Restrain, hold back.

Trauer (Ger.) (trow '—å r) Mourning.

Travesti (Fr.) (trä—věs—tē) To parody.

Tre (It.) (trā) Three.

Treble (1) The highest voice. (2) A high pitched member of an instrumental family.

Treble clef The sign on a staff. →

The G clef. The note G in on the second line. The higher instruments and voices read in this clef.

Treble staff The staff that uses the G clef (treble clef) sign.

Tre corde (It.) (trā kôr '—dā) Three strings. An indication to release the left-pedal on the piano in order that all the strings are struck by the hammers. See *Una corda.

Tremando (It.) (trā—män '—dō) Trembling; tremolo.

Tremblement (Fr.) (trä(m)—blå—mä(n)) Shake; trill.

Tremolo (It.) (trā '—mō—lō) (1) On a stringed instrument the rapid repetition of a note on down and up bows. (2) Playing two notes back and forth (very fast) on any instrument. (3) The fluctuation of the voice on a tone.

Tremulant (Ger.) (trā—moo—länt ') A tremolo stop on the organ.

Trepak A lively Russian Cossack dance in duple meter.

Très (Fr.) (tre̬) Very much; most.

Triad A chord having three notes, the root, third, and fifth. There are four basic triads: (1) major triad (root, major third, plus a perfect fifth); (2) minor triad (root, minor third, plus a perfect fifth); (3) diminished triad (root, minor third, plus a diminished fifth); (4) augmented triad (root, major third, plus an augmented fifth). Examples:

See *Intervals, *Chords.

Triangle (Triangel (Ger.) (tre̅ '–ängl); Triangle (Fr.) (tre̅—ä(n)gl);Triangolo (It.) (tre̅—än '–go̅—lo̅) A non-pitched instrument used in the percussion section. It is a metal rod bent in the shape of a triangle which rings when struck with a metal stick. See *Idiophone.

Tricinium (Lat.) A three part vocal work (16th and early 17th centuries).

Trill Also called shake; Triller in German; Trillo in Italian; Tremblement, Trille, Cadence in French. (1) Generally, the trill is the repetition of a written note and the next note above alternating in rapid succession for the length of time of the main written note. The variety of trill used in 16th century choral music was used in the cadence. The resolution of the suspension was done using an ornamental trill. During the 17th and 18th centuries the trill was not written out but was marked above the note(s) by the abbreviation tr or by such symbols as (𝄢~), (~~), or (𝓵,~𝆪). Up through the time of Beethoven the shake usually began on the upper or subsidiary note. For example:

There are times during this period when the shake began on the principal note. For instance, after a rest, after a downward leap, or at the beginning of a phrase. A trill might begin, for example with an appoggiatura (upper or lower), for example: (lower appoggiatura)

or, with a turn, for example:

The trill ends on the main written note. A turn usually precedes the last main note. Some composers write in the notation for the extra notes in the turn, for example:

A turn usually includes a triplet or a quintuplet. An example:

The modern trill or 19th century trill usually begins on the main note, for example:

If the trill is to start on the upper note, the grace note is used, for example:

As a general rule, in any period, a shake begins on the upper note when the main note is preceded by the

374

same note. e.g.

WRITTEN   PLAYED

The trill differs according to periods, styles, composers, and performers. The above brief outline simply gives some examples. Many additional varieties and treatments exist.

Trillo (It.) (tril'–ō); Triller (Ger.) (tril'–år) Trill, shake.

Trio (1) Three performers. (2) Music written for three performers. Examples: string trio, piano trio, woodwind trio, vocal trio, etc. (3) The contrasting middle section of a minuet or scherzo movement, called trio because it was originally written in three parts. Example: Ludwig von Beethoven (1770–1827), *Symphony No. 5, in C Minor,* Opus 67, Movement Three is an example of Scherzo-Trio-Scherzo.

Triole (Ger.) (trē'–ol–å) See *Triolet.

Triolet (Fr.) (trē–ō–lā) A triplet. See *Triplet.

Trio sonata A Baroque instrumental chamber sonata having two melodic parts written above a continuo. During the Baroque period, the trio-sonata was often played by four instruments: two solo or treble instruments, a bass instrument to play the continuo part, and a keyboard instrument to complete the figured bass part. They were also written for one keyboard instrument or three instruments. Example: Arcangelo Corelli (1653–1713), *Sonata Da Camera in Bb* Opus 2, No. 5 for Two Violins, Viola Da Gamba and Harpsichord.

Tripeltakt (Ger.) (trē'–på l–täkt) Triple time.

Triple concerto A concerto having three solo instruments.

Triple counterpoint Counterpoint in three parts that may be inverted. That is, the parts may be placed in any voice. See *Counterpoint.

Triple-croche (Fr.) (trēpl krôsh) Demisemiquaver; a thrity-second note (𝅘𝅥𝅯).

Triple fugue A fugue on three independent subjects and a

375

combination of the subjects. Examples are available in *The Art of Fugue* (Die Kunst der Fuge) by J. S. Bach (1685–1750). See *Fugue.

Triple measure A measure having a total of three beats.

Triple stop The string player plays three separate notes, each on a separate string, at the same time. Playing a triad on a bowed, stringed instrument. See *Double stop.

Triplet A group of three notes or rests played in the time equal to two of the same notes or rests. Examples:

$\frac{2}{4}$ ♩♩♩ $\underset{3}{\smile}$ = 2 beats or $\frac{2}{4}$ ♪♪♪ $\underset{3}{\smile}$ = 1 beat.

Triple time Each measure is divided into three basic beats and can be in simple or compound time. Examples: $\frac{3}{1}$, $\frac{3}{2}$, $\frac{3}{4}$, $\frac{3}{8}$, etc; $\frac{6}{1}$, $\frac{6}{2}$, $\frac{6}{4}$, $\frac{6}{8}$, etc.; $\frac{9}{1}$, $\frac{9}{2}$, $\frac{9}{4}$, $\frac{9}{8}$, etc.

Triple tonguing The rapid succession of tones that are to be played faster than can be done by single tonguing. It is articulated on the syllables: TA-TA-KA, TA-TA-KA, etc. or TA-KA-TA, TA-KA-TA, etc.

Triplicare (It.) (trĭ–plē–kä'–rä) Triple.

Triplum (Lat.) The name for the third part in organum and the 13th century motet. The part above the tenor and duplum.

Tritone The interval consisting of three whole steps. An augmented fourth or a diminished fifth. Half an octave. E.g.,

Trochaic meter (Trochae, Lat.) See *Trochee.

Trochee In meter, a foot of two syllables, a long followed with a short (♩ ♪ | ♩ ♪). An accent followed by an unaccented beat.

Trois (Fr.) (trwä) Three; third.

Tromba (It.) (trŏm'–bä) Trumpet.

Tromba cromatica (It.) (trŏm'–bä krō–mä'–tē–kä) A trumpet having valves which enable it to play chromatic notes as well as the overtones.

Tromba da tirarsi (It.) /ˌtrŏm—bä dä tē—rär'—sē) The trumpet with a slide rather than valves.

Tromba marina (It.) (trŏm—bä mä—rē'—nä) A bowed stringed instrument, not a trumpet. See *A Marine trumpet.

Trombetta (It.) (trŏm—bĕt'—tä) Little trumpet.

Trombettiere (It.) (trŏm—bĕt—tē—ā'—rä) Trumpeter.

Trombone A slide brass instrument. It has a cylindrical bore, a bell, and a cupped mouthpiece. The slide extends the length of the tubing and is divided into seven positions. The trombone is made in several sizes ranging from alto, tenor, tenor-bass, bass, to contra-bass. The ones most often used in orchestra, bands and dance groups are the Bb tenor trombone and the G or F bass trombone, although the tenor-bass trombone with a larger bore and an extra key which adds a fourth below the tenor is replacing the bass trombone. The range of the tenor trombone is approximately from E to bb' with the addition of some pedal tones, e.g., the positions (1, 2, and 3) which go down to the notes Bb', A', Ab' below the bass clef. The bass trombone is pitched a fourth below the tenor trombone. Valve trombones are sometimes used in dance bands, marching bands and, on occasion, in other ensembles.

Trommel (Ger.) (trŏm'—ål) Drum.

Trompete (Ger.) (trŏm—pā'—tå); Trompette (Fr.) (trō(m)—pĕt) Trumpet.

Trop (Fr.) (trō) Too much.

Trope (1) A liturgical text (with or without music) that varied in length and was used to embellish the standard text.

Troppo (It.) (trŏp'—pō) Too much. Non troppo means not too much.

Troubadours (Fr.) (troo—bä—door) The poet-musicians from the nobility of southern France during the Medieval Period (12th and 13th centuries). Many of their songs and poems have been preserved. Two popular forms were: (1) Canzo in binary form and (2) the vers, a melody sung to several stanzas. The melodies are

377

monophonic.

Trouvères (Fr.) (troo—vĕ r) Medieval (12th and 13th centuries) poet-musicians of northern France, usually of the aristocracy. About 1,400 trouvère melodies and texts are preserved and represent many forms. For example, the chanson (strophic), ballade (binary form), rotrouenge (several stanzas), rondeau (rounded), etc. The melodies are monophonic.

Trumpet (tromba, It.; trompete, Ger.; trompette, Fr.) The 19th and 20th century trumpet is a brass treble instrument with a cylindrical bore, a cupped mouthpiece, three valves and a bell. It is a transposing instrument pitched in Bb, A, D, F, etc. as well as the non-transposing instrument of C. The C trumpet has a range from f# to c''' including all chromatics. Trumpets pitched in other keys have a relative range. The smaller trumpets are used in works of Bach while larger trumpets are used in Wagner's music. There are many other sizes and varities of trumpets. For example, long fanfare trumpets, trumpets without valves, slide trumpets, and keyed trumpets. The abbreviation for trumpet is trpt.

Tuba (1) The large bass instrument having a conical bore, a cupped mouthpiece, a flaring bell and three to five piston-valves. There are several sizes: tenor tuba in Bb; the bass tuba in Eb or F; the double-bass tuba in BBb. There are several other members of the tuba family: the large saxhorns, baritone horn, euphonium, helicon, and sousaphone. (2) An organ stop. (3) An old Roman trumpet. (4) In the plainsong (Gregorian chant) the reciting note of the psalm tones (recitation melodies).

Tuba mirum (too'—bä mē '—roo m) The opening words: "Tuba mirum spargens sonum (the trumpet, spreading a wonderful sound), in the "Dies Irae". Example: Giuseppe Verdi (1813—1901), *Requiem, II* "Dies Irae". See *Requiem Mass.

Tucket A fanfare by trumpets.

Tune Melody, air, song. (1) The melodic line or horizontal succession of tones. (2) To tune in agreement, one

378

pitch with another. In tune, piano tuning, etc. See *Melody.

Tuning Tuning instruments in proper accord. For example, the strings of the cello in proper intervals of open fifths from low C up to G, D, A or the flute a' to concert pitch a' with all other tones relatively in tune, etc.

Tuning fork A steel, two-pronged instrument used to tune musical instruments. They are built in different sizes and definite pitches and produce a pure tone (without the upper partials). The pitch is very accurate.

Tuning hammer The steel tuning bar used by piano tuners. It is struck and the vibrations are amplified when it is placed on a board.

Tuning slide (1) The slides on brass instruments which allow each valve to be tuned as well as the whole instrument. Each tube can be lengthened by pulling the slide which lowers the pitch. (2) The clip used to tune an organ flue-pipe.

Tuono (It.) (too—ō '—nō) Tone.

Turmmusik (Ger.) (toorm '—moo —zēk) Steeple music. Music played from a tower.

Turn (turno, It.) (too r '—nō)) An ornamental group of notes played, for example, starting on the note above the printed note, then the printed note, the tone below the printed note, back to the printed note. E.g.,

WRITTEN   PLAYED

Or, it may start with the printed note. It may be done on one note or between two notes. It may also be inverted. The notes may be written out or a sign (∞ or ?) may indicate a turn.

Tusch (Ger.) (toosh) Flourish (of trumpets).

Tuten (Ger.) (too t '—å n) Blow (a trumpet, horn, etc.).

Tutti (It.) (too'—tē) Also, tutte, tutto. All. The whole group performs Solo would be one player.

Twelfth (1) An interval of an octave and a fifth. (2) An organ stop sounding a twelfth.

Twelve-tone music Dodecaphony. Music using a twelve-tone set. See *Twelve-tone system, *Tone row, *Dodecaphonic, *Dodecaphony.

Twelve-note system See *Tone row, *Twelve-tone system.

Twelve-tone row See *Tone row, *Twelve-tone system.

Twelve-tone system A method of compoistion developed by Schoenberg in the early 1920's. The pattern of notes or musical line that governs a particular musical work is a special arrangement, by the composer, of twelve notes of the semitonal scale. This pattern which is arranged before each composition is written is called the "row", the "series", or the "set". Certain rules apply to each set. For example, the set includes the twelve tones of the semitonal (a scale divided into twelve equal parts) scale established as a musical line. Each note of the semitonal scale appears just once in the set. The set may be used in imitation, inversion, retrograde, or retrograde-inversion. The set can be stated on any degree of the semitonal scale using each of four devices (imitation, inversion, retrograde, or retrograde-inversion). Forty-eight different forms of a set may be developed when a particular set is started on each of the twelve pitch levels using each of the four devices. A few additional comments about the "rules" applied to the twelve-tone system are in order. For instance, the theme need not include all twelve notes. Although the rule states that each note appears once in a set, the repetition of a single note without an intervening note may be used. Also, the interval relationships between adjacent notes are not affected when the set is inverted or when the set is transposed to each of the four devices. Schoenberg's twelve-tone compositions evolve around many varied restatements of the set. Examples: A. Schoenberg (1874—1951) *Fourth Quartet;* Schoenberg, *Klavierstück* Opus 33a; Schoenberg, *Klavierstück,* Opus 33b.

Twelve-tone technique See *Tone row, *Twelve-tone system.

Two part design See *Binary form.

Two-step A ballroom dance in duple meter and slower than the one-step. The dancers glide.

Tymbal Also, timbal. Kettledrum.

Tympan (Fr.) (tă(m)—pä(n)) Drum.

Tympani Kettledrums. See *Timpani.

Tympanon (Fr.) (tă(m)—pä(n)—ō(n)) Dulcimer. See *Dulcimer.

Tympanum (Greek) Drum.

Tyrolean (tryolien or tyrolienne, Fr.) (1) A dance of the peasants of Tyrol which is an area of western Austria and northern Italy. (2) A song which includes yodeling. See *Yodel.

U

U The abbreviation for upper. Also, u.c. for una corda.

Übelklang (Ger.) (ü'—bȧl—kläng) Dissonance, discord.

Übenung (Ger.) (ü'—bȧn—ŏong) Practice, exercise.

Über (Ger.) (ü'—bȧr) Over, higher, above. Überein-stimmen, (Ger.) (ü—bȧr—in'—shtim—ȧn) Accord, harmony. Übergang, (Ger.) (ü'—bȧr—gäng) Transition; modulation. Übergreifen, (Ger.) (ü'—bȧr—grif—ȧn) Shift or glide. (1) Shift the hand position on a violin. (2) Cross the hands on piano. Übermässig, (Ger.) (ü'—bȧr—mĕs—ik) Excessive. Augmented. Über-treiben, (Ger.) (ü'—bȧr—tri—bȧn) Exaggerate.

Übung (Ger.) (ü'—bŏong) An exercise.

Uguale (It.) (ōo—gōo—ä'—lā) Equal.

Uke A short form of the word ukulele.

Ukulele (Ukelele) A small, four stringed Hawaiian instrument of the guitar family. It is strummed and the music written in tablature form. It has a long fretted finger board.

Ultimo (It.) (ŭl'—tē—mō) End; last; most.

Umfang (Ger.) (ŏom'—fäng) (1) Volume. (2) Compass (of an instrument, etc.).

Umkehrung (Ger.) (ŏom'—kĕr—ŏong) Overtuning; inversion.

Umoristico (It.) (ōo—mō—ris'—tē—kō) Humorous.

Umschriften (Ger.) (ŏom'—shrift—ȧn) Transcription.

Umsetzen (Ger.) (ōom'—zēts—ȧn) Transpose.

Umstimmen (Ger.) (ŏom'—shtim—ȧn) Make a change. To re-tune. To tune to another pitch.

Un (It.) (ōon) (una, (ōo'—nä); uno (ōo'—nō)) One; a.

Unaccented Unstressed. A weak stress in music.

Una corda (It.) (ōo'—nä kôr'—dä) (1) Play on one string. (2) On the piano, the soft or left pedal. See *Soft pedal.

Und (Ger.) (ŏont) And.

Undicesimo (It.) (ŏon—dē—chä'—zē—mō) Eleventh.

Undulation Wavy motion, Vibrato.

Un, Une (å (n), ün) One; a; an; first.

Uneben (Ger.) (ŏon '–āb–å n) Uneven.

Unequal temperament A system of tuning in which pure intervals are used for some keys and adjustments are made for remote keys. See *Temperament, *Equal temperament.

Ungebunden (ŏon '–gå –bŏond–å n) Free.

Ungeniert (Ger.) (ŏon '–gå –nē rt) Easy; free.

Ungerade (Ger.) (ŏon '–gå –rä–då) Uneven.

Ungeradertakt (Ger.) (ŏon '–gå –rä–då r–täkt) Uneven rhythm.

Ungestüm (Ger.) (ŏon '–gå –shtüm) Impetuous.

Ungezügelt (Ger.) (ŏon '–gå –tsü–gå lt) Not restrained.

Ungleich (Ger.) (ŏon '–glikh) Uneven.

Uni, Unie (Fr.) (ü–nē) Even; smooth.

Unico (It.) (ōo'–nē–kō) Only; single.

Unison (1) Two or more performers playing or singing the same tune either on the same notes or in octaves. (2) The interval formed by sounding a pitch and it's duplication simultaneously. E.g.,

Unit organ See *Extension organ.

Unmeasured Music which is not bound by strict measure bars or meter.

Un peu (Fr.) (å (n) pû) A little.

Un poco (It.) (ōon pō '–kō) A little.

Unregelmässig (Ger.) (ŏon '–rā–gå l–mĕ s–ĭ k) Irregular.

Unruhig (Ger.) (ŏon'–rōo–i k) Uneasy.

Unten (Ger.) (ŏont '–å n) Down; below.

Unter (Ger.) (ŏon–å r) Under; below.

Unterbass (Ger.) (ŏont '–å r–bäs) Contra-bass.

Unterstimme (Ger.) (ŏont '–å r–shtim–å) Lower part.

Unterwerk (Ger.) (ŏont '–å r–vĕ rk) Choir organ.

Up-beat (1) The beat preceding the bar line. (2) The up-stroke given by the conductor, usually on the beat before the bar line.

Upbow The movement of the bow from the tip-end to the frog-end. The sign $\vee$ is used above the note(s).

Upper partials The harmonics or overtones. See *Partials.

Upright piano A piano in which the strings are stretched vertically and the body stands up-right as opposed to the horizontal position of the grand piano.

Upright tuba The tuba that is played in a vertical position.

Ut Originally the note C. The French and Italian name for C.

Ut bémol (Fr.) (üt bā—mŏl) C flat (Cb).

Ut dièse (Fr.) (üt dē—ĕz) C sharp (C#).

Ut supra (Lat.) As above.

V The abbreviation for: (1) valve; (2) violin; (3) voice.

Va. The abbreviation used for viola. Vla. is also used as an abbreviation for viola.

Va (Fr.) (It.) (vä) Go.

Vacillant (Fr.) (vä–sē–lä(n)) Wavering. Vacillare, (It.) (vä–chē–lä'–rā) Waver.

Vago (It.) (vä'–gō) Dreamy; vague.

Vals (Sp.) (väls) (Valse, (Fr.) (väls)) Waltz.

Value The duration of a note.

Valve The mechanical device used on brass instruments to allow the air to move through additional tubing, thus lowering the tone. The valves used alone or in combination allow the instrument to play all the chromatic notes within the range of the instrument. The instruments of the trumpet variety use piston valves while the French horn uses rotary valves. Valves are used on such instruments as: trumpet, cornet, flügelhorn, saxhorns, baritone horn, euphonium, tuba, sousaphones, some trombones, French horn, plus others. There are usually three valves, although four valves are used on the tuba and euphonium. The fourth valve lowers the range of these instruments a perfect fourth. The valves are pressed down by the fingers. For example, a note is lowered one-half step by depressing the second valve; a whole-step by pressing down the first valve; an interval of a minor third by depressing the third valve; and so on in various combinations throughout the scale. Alternate fingerings can be used for a given note and many combinations are used to play chromatics.

Valve instruments Instruments having piston or rotary valves. See *Valve.

Vamp An improvisation that is used as in introduction or an accompaniment. It is used to "fill in" while a soloist is preparing to begin or continue a performance.

Vamp-horn A variety of megaphone used to amplify the

voice when speaking or leading the congregation in singing. It was used during the 18th and 19th centuries during church services.

Variations A principle used in developing a musical subject or idea. Variation may be considered a form or a technical device. It embraces many other forms, such as the canzone, the fugue, the passacaglia, the chaconne, the chorale, etc. It may be used in several ways: an elaboration in melody, harmony, rhythm, etc., an ornamentation on a musical line, a varied series based on a theme, a variation on an accompaniment, the development section of a form, à variation on a mode, a variation on texture, etc. The idea of variation is old and basic to musical development. It can be found in the ornamentation of early plainchant, in 15th and 16th century motets, lute-songs, the polyphonic Mass based on the cantus firmus, etc. An often used variation during the 17th century was based on an ostinato or ground bass (e.g., used in many passacaglias). The Classical composer often used the style of variation called theme and variations (e.g., Mozart). The variation form and the techniques of variation were used widely by 19th century composers and continue to be important to the 20th century composer. Some composers borrow themes from other composers, e.g., Giuseppi Tartini (1692–1770), *Variations on a Theme of Corelli for Violin and Piano.* Others supply their own theme, e.g., Edward Elgar (1857–1934) *Engima Variations,* Opus 36, for Orchestra. Several methods of variation have been mentioned. The following are examples of some: (1) The variation in which a theme is repeated with ornamentation (i.e., rhythmic or melodic modification) E.g., Franz Josef Haydn (1732–1809) *Symphony in G,* No. 94 (Surprise), Movement Two (variations on a theme). (2) The variation in which a theme usually remains the same and the variations are developed in a polyphonic style. E.g., J. S. Bach (1685–1750), *Passacaglia in C Minor for Organ.* (3) The variation which centers on the retention of the harmonic functions of the thematic material. This is demonstrated in the chaconne, e.g., J. S. Bach (1685–1750), "Violin Chaconne" (D Minor) for solo violin (from his *Partita, No. 1, in B Minor,* Violin alone). The four measure theme is varied sixty-five times. The theme:

The Theme:

(4) The contrapuntal variation, e.g., imitation, canon, fugue, etc. Examples of contrapuntal type are found in J. S. Bach (1685–1750), *"Goldberg" Variations;* the theme as counterpoint in Felix Mendelssohn (1809–1847) *Variations Sérieuses,* Opus 54, for piano. (5) Other types of variation techniques, such as: the theme which is dissolved into fragments (e.g., in development sections); themes which are shaped from fragments of the theme; and free construction or free variation which shows little relation to the theme. See *Canzone, *Fugue, *Passacaglia, *Chaconne, *Chorale, *Ostinato, *Contrapuntal, *Theme and variations, *Canonic devices.

Variazione (It.) (vä–rē–ät–tsē–ō '–nä) Variation.

Varieté (Ger.) (vä–rē–tä ') Vaudeville; variety entertainment.

Vaudeville (English) (Fr.) (vōd–vēl)) (1) A ballad. (2) A satirical song. (3) A 19th century form of comedy that includes songs. (4) A 20th century variety show. (5) A song with verses which are sung by different characters in succession. A practice used in opera (e.g., by Mozart (1756–1791). (6) A type of song in early "opéra comique".

Vcl. An abbreviation for cello (violoncello).

Veloce (It.) (vä–lō '–chä) (véloce, (Fr.) (vä–lŏs)) Swift.

Velocita (It.) (vä–lō–chē–tä ') Speed.

Veloz (Sp.) (vä–lōth ') Fast.

Vent (Fr.) (vă(n)) Wind.

Ventage The fingerholes in a woodwind instrument.

Ventil (Ger.) (vĕn–tēl ') Valve.

Ventile (It.) (vĕn—tē'—lā) Valve.

Ventiltrompete (Ger.) (vĕn—tēl'—trŏm—pĕt'—å) Valve trumpet.

Verdoppelung (Ger.) (fĕr—dŏp'—ål—ŏong) Doubling.

Verfassen (fĕr—fäs'—ån) Compose.

Verghetta (It.) (vĕr—gĕt'—ä) Stem.

Vergrössern (Ger.) (vĕr—grĕ(r)s'—årn) Enlarge; augment.

Verhallen (Ger.) (fĕr—häl'—ån) Fade away.

Verismo (It.) (vĕr—iz'—mō) Realism; truth; naturalism. The use of realism in the plots of the 19th century Italian opera. For example, Leoncavallo (1858—1919), *Pagliacci.*

Verklärt (Ger.) (fĕr—klĕrt') Transfigured.

Verlängern (Ger.) (fĕr—lĕng'—årn) Prolong.

Verlöschen (Ger.) (fĕr—lĕ(r)sh'—ån) Go out; fade out.

Vermehren (Ger.) (fĕr—mā'—rån) Augment.

Vermindern (Ger.) (fĕr—min'—dårn) Diminish.

Vernacular Native language of a given country.

Verringern (Ger.) (fĕr—ring'—årn) Decrease.

Vers (Fr.) (vĕr) (Vers, (Ger.) (fĕrs)) Verse, stanza, strophe. Several stanzas sung to the same melody. A form popular with the troubadours.

Verschiebung (Ger.) (fĕr—shē'—bŏong) Shift.

Verschwiegen (Ger.) (fĕr—shvē'—gån) Silent. Reserved.

Verschwinden (Ger.) (fĕr—shvin'—dån) Disappear; die away.

Verse (1) A metrical line of a poem. (2) The musical ï line sung by a soloist. (3) The section that precedes the chorus.

Verse anthem An anthem in which sections are sung by solo voices. See *Anthem.

Verset A short organ piece which was used to replace a verse of a psalm in the Mass.

Versetzung (Ger.) (fĕr—zĕt'—tsŏong) Transposition.

Versicle Short phrases sung, spoken, or chanted by the officiant in a service. They are responded to by the choir or the congregation.

Verso (It.) (vĕr'—zō) Verse; song; toward.

Verstimmt (Ger.) (fĕr—shtimt') Not in tune.

Vertement (Fr.) (vĕr—tå—mä(n)) Briskly.

Vertical texture The term used to identify the relationship of simultaneous tones. Roughly, chords.

Vertönen (Ger.) (fĕr—tĕ(r)n '—å n) Die away.

Vertonung (Ger.) (fĕr—tōn '—ŏo ng) Composition.

Verve (Fr.) (vĕrv) Animation.

Verwegen (Ger.) (fĕr—vā '—gå n) Bold.

Verweilen (Ger.) (fĕr—vī '—lå n) Retard; linger.

Verzierung (Ger.) (fĕr—tsēr '—ŏong)　Embellishment, ornament.

Vesper hymn A hymn sung at Vesper service. See *Vespers.

Vespers The evening Office hour of the Roman Catholic Church between None and Compline. Included in the service are psalms, antiphons, hymn, and the "Magnificat".

Vezzosamente (It.) (vĕt—tsō—zä—mĕn '—tā)　Tenderly.

Via (It.) (vē '—ä) Away; off.

Vibraharp See Vibraphone.

Vibraphone A percussion instrument having a series of metal bars in chromatic progression as on the piano keyboard. The bars are struck with mallets. The sound is sustained by means of resonators that are opened and closed electrically.

Vibrare (It.) (vē—brä '—rā) (vibrieren, (Ger.) (vē—brē '—rå n) Vibrate.

Vibration Oscillation. Sound produced by: (1) movement of an air column; (2) the movement of the strings when plucked or bowed; (3) striking a surface.

Vibrato (It.) (vi—brä '—tō) The rapid and slight variation of a tone. (1) The wind player manipulates the tone by a slight jaw movement (lip vibrato) or by shaking the instrument (hand vibrato). (2) The string player uses an oscillation of the left hand without a noticeable change of pitch. (3) The clavichord player repeats the pressure of the finger on the key without raising the key. This changes the degree of pressure on the strings. (4) The vocal vibrato is the natural fluctuation of the voice without a noticeable change of pitch. A wide

389

vibrato becomes a tremolo.

Vide (Fr.) (vēd) Void; empty; open. An optional cut in the music.

Viel (Ger.) (fēl) Much.

Vielle (Fr.) (vyĕl) (1) Hurdy-gurdy. (2) The medieval bowed fiddle.

Vielstimmigkeit (Ger.) (fēl–shtĭm'–ĭg–kīt) Polyphony.

Vieltönig (Ger.) (fēl'–tĕ(r)n–ĭk) Many sounds.

Vier (Ger.) (fēr) Four. Vjertel, (Ger.) (fir'–tål) Quarter. Viertelnote, (Ger.) (fir'–tål–nōt–å) Quarter-note, Crotchet (♩). Viertelpause, (Ger.) (fir'–tål–pow'–zå) Quarter-rest, Crotchet-rest (♩); Viertelton, (ger.) (fir'–tål–tōn) Half a semi-tone, a quarter-tone.

Vif (Fr.) (vēf) Quick; animated.

Vihuela (Sp.) (vē–ōo–ā'–lä) A Spanish string instrument built in the shape of a guitar and played like the lute.

Villancico (vēl–lyän–thē'–kō) (1) A rustic song that starts with a refrain which is sung after each verse. (2) A cantata for soli and chorus with instrumental accompaniment that often uses a theme of Christmas. (3) Spanish name for Christmas carol.

Villanella (It.) (vil–lyä–nĕl'–lä) A sophisticated type of 17th century Italian song. A partsong which made great use of consecutive triads resulting in parallel fifths.

Villanelle (Fr.) (vē–lä–nĕl) A short pastoral poem or song.

Villotta (It.) (vĭ–lŏt'–tä) A 16th century rustic Italian folk-song, sung in parts. Identified with the northern part of Italy.

Viol A group of bowed string instruments used during the 16th and 17th centuries and made in various sizes of treble, tenor, and bass. They had a flat back, deep ribs, sloping shoulders, several strings (average, six), a finger board with gut frets, were played with an arched bow, and were either rested on or held between the knees. The normal set, known as the chest of viols, had two each of treble, tenor, and bass. Several names were given to the various sized viols. For example: Descant viol (treble); Viola da braccio (tenor viol); Viola d'

390

amore (treble or tenor viol with several sympathetic strings); Viol da gamba (bass viol); Violone (double-bass viol); and the Viola bastarda (sized between the tenor and bass viol); Division viol (small bass viol that was used to play variations on a bass line).

Viola (English and It.) (Alto (Fr.); Bratsche (Ger.)) A bowed stringed instrument of the violin family. It is tuned a fifth lower than the violin and is slightly larger than the violin and smaller than the cello. The strings are tuned a', d', g, c, from high to low. It is the alto of the violin family (violin, viola, cello, bass). The abbreviation for viola is va. or vla.

Viola alta A large viola with an added string tuned to e".

Viola bastarda (It.) (vē−ō'−lä bäs−tär'−dä) A bass viol with sympathetic strings, sized between the tenor and bass viol. Also called lyra viol.

Viola da braccio (It.) (vē−ō'−lä dä brät'−chē−ō) Arm viol. Tenor viol. The German name is Bratsche. See *Viol.

Viola da gamba (It.) (vē−ō'−lä dä gäm'− bä) A viol held between the legs. Bass viol. Used in solo playing and for accompaniment.

Viola d'amore (It.) (vē−ō'−lä dä−mō'−rä) Love viol. The name is from the shape of its scroll. A treble or tenor viol. Some varieties had sympathetic strings under the bowed strings. It was played under the chin like the viola. The finger board had no frets.

Viola da spalla (It.) (vē−ō'−lä dä spä'−lä) Shoulder viola. A large viola that was held by a strap across the shoulder. A type of cello of the 17th and 18th centuries.

Viola di bordone (It.) (vē−ō'−lä dē bôr−dō'−nä) A baryton. See *Baryton.

Viola pomposa (It.) (vē−ō'−lä pŏm−pō'−zä) An 18th century viola with a fifth string tuned to e". A member of the violin family.

Viole (Fr.) (vyŏl) Viol.

Violet A variety of viola d'amore.

Violetta (It.) (vē−ō−lĕt'−tä) (1) A small violin-type instrument of the 16th century having three strings. (2)

A name used for the viola during the 17th and 18th centuries.

Violin (Violine, (Ger.); Violino (It.); Violon (Fr.)). The first instrument of the string section of the orchestra and in string ensembles. A treble bowed stringed instrument having a table (sound board) and back, finger board, sound-post, sound holes, side walls (ribs), peg-box, tail-piece, neck, bridge, four strings, tuning pegs, and a scroll. The strings of the violin are tuned in fifths from the high note of e'', to a', d' and g. The instrument is held under the chin. The present day violin dates back to the 16th century. Several famous violin makers contributed to the development of the fine violins of today. For example: Andrea Amati (1520 to about 1580); his sons Antonio Amati and Girolamo Amati; A. Stradivari; D. Montagnana; A. Gagliano; A. Guarneri; J. Rayman; B. Banks; plus many others. The abbreviation for violin is V.; for violins Vv.

Violinbogen (Ger.) (vē—ō—lin'—bō—gån) Violin bow.

Violin concerto A concerto with the violin as the solo instrument. Examples: Johannes Brahms (1833—1897), *Concerto in D,* Opus 77, for Violin and Orchestra; Peter Ilyich Tchaikovsky (1840—1893), *Concerto in D,* Opus 35, for Violin and Orchestra; Felix Mendelssohn (1809—1847), *Concerto in E Minor,* Opus 64, for Violin and Orchestra. See *Concerto.

Violine (Ger.) (vē—ō—lin'—å) Violin.

Violin family The four bowed stringed instruments of the modern orchestra. The violin, viola, violoncello (cello), and the double-bass (string bass). They are discussed under separate entries. Other variations on the basic violin are also entered in various sections. For example: *Viola alta, *Violino piccolo, *Violoncello piccolo, *Violotta, *Viola, *Cello, *Double-bass, *Viola da spalla.

Violino (It.) (vē—ō—lē'—nō) Violin.

Violino piccolo (It.) (vē—ō—lē'—nō pē'—kō—lō) A small violin used during the 17th century and the first half of the 18th century. It was tuned an octave above the viola.

Violin-schlüssel(Ger.) (ve̅—o̅—lĭ n '—shlüs—å l) Treble clef.

Violon (Fr.) (ve̅—o̅—lo̅(n)) Violin. Violon (Sp.)   (ve̅—o̅—lo̅n ') Bass viol.

Violoncello (English) ((It.) (ve̅—o̅—lo̅n—chĕ'—lo̅)) (violon-cell (Ger.) (ve̅—o̅—lå n—chĕl ') (violoncelle (Fr.) (ve̅—o̅—lo̅(n)—sĕl). The abbreviated term (cello) is often used. See *Cello.

Violoncello piccolo (It.) (ve̅—o̅—lo̅n—chĕ l '—lo̅) A small cello used during the 17th and 18th centuries.

Violone (It.) (ve̅—o̅—lo̅ '—na̅) (1) A double-bass viol. (2) An organ stop.

Violotta A tenor violin tuned e', a, d, G, from high to low. It was sized and pitched to fall between the viola and cello.

Virelai (Fr.) (ve̅r—la̅) Virelay. A French poem running on two rhymes. A Medieval French song with the refrain sung before and after each stanza forming a modified ternary pattern.

Virginal A type of harpsichord in a rectangular, oblong, or wing shape, popular during the 16th and 17th centuries. Early harpsichords were placed on the table or held in the lap. Later varieties were built on legs. The Virginal has one keyboard which is placed to one side and strings run parallel to the keyboard. The strings are plucked. One of the large collections of 17th century music for the Virginals is contained in the *Fitzwilliam Virginal Book.* Some important English composers of Virginal music are O. Gibbons, J. Bull, W. Byrd, T. Morley, among others.

Virtuoso A performer who has a superior technique.

Vista (It.)(vĭ s '—tä) Sight.

Vistoso (It.) (vĭs—to̅ '—zo̅) Flashy.

Vitement (Fr.) (ve̅t—mä(n)) Quickly, rapidly.

Vivace (It.) (ve̅—vä'—cha̅) Brisk, lively.

Vivido (It.) (ve̅ '—ve̅—do̅) Vivid.

Vivo (It.) (ve̅ '—vo̅) Live; brisk.

Vl. The abbreviation for violin.

Vla. The abbreviation for viola.

Vlc. The abbreviation for violoncello (cello).

Vocal Music written for the voice or a group of voices, with or without instrumental accompaniment.

Vocalise (Fr.) (vö–käl–ēz) A vocal line sung on syllables (vowel sounds). An exercise.

Vocalize To exercise by singing scales, intervals, and varied phrases on a syllable or vowel. A warm-up procedure.

Vocal score A score that includes all voice parts and texts with a piano score. See *Score.

Voce (It.) (vō'–chā) Voice. E.g., sotto voce, subdued voice; mezza voce, half-voice.

Voce di gola (It.) (vō'–chā dē gō'–lä) Throat voice.

Voce de petto (It.) (vō'–chā dē pět'–tō) Chest voice.

Voce di testa (It.) (vō'–chā dē těs'–tä) (voce di capo (It.) (vō'–chā dē kä'–pō)) Head voice.

Voice (1) The tone produced by the vibration of the vocal cords. (2) To voice or regulate the tone of an organ pipe. (3) The parts or lines in harmonic or polyphonic writing. The voices of a fugue; voices or parts in vocal, choral, keyboard, or instrumental music.

Voice leading The progression of each part. The principles by which each voice moves in various parts. The German word is Stimmführung.

Voice ranges There are three basic classifications of voices for men and three for women. The general ranges are: Women: Soprano (range from middle c' to a''), Mezzo-soprano (range from a to f''), Contralto (alto) (range from f to d''); Men: Tenor (range from B to g'), Baritone (range from G to e'), Bass (range from E to c'). These ranges are approximate as some voices may be able to extend their range above or below the normal. The tone quality of the voice also identifies the type of voice. For example: Lyric Soprano, Dramatic Soprano, Lyric Tenor, Castrato, Falsetto, Wagnerian Tenor, Tenore Rubusto, Basso Profondo, Bass-Baritone, Coloratura Soprano, etc.

Voicing (1) The placement of notes in a given position within a chord. (2) Regulating organ pipes for a proper tone.

Voix (Fr.) (vwä) Voice; tone.

Voix céleste (Fr.) (vwä sā–lēst) Two ranks of pipes on the organ that produce a wavy tone when sounded together. This wavy tone results because one set of pipes is tuned sharper than the other.

Voix humain (Fr.) (vwä ü–må (n)) Human voice (sound). A reed organ stop that sounds somewhat like the human voice.

Vokal (Ger.) (vō–käl ') Vocal. Vowel.

Volkslied (Ger.) (fŏlks '–lēt) National song; folk song.

Volkstanz (Ger.) (fŏlks '–tänts) Folk dance.

Voll (Ger.) (fŏl) Full; entire; whole.

Vollenden (Ger.) (fŏl–ĕnd '–å n) Complete close; finish.

Volles Werk (Ger.) (fŏl '–å s vĕrk) Full work. Full organ.

Vollkommen (Ger.) (fŏl–kŏm '–å n) Perfect; full.

Voll-lautend (Ger.) (fŏl '–low–tĕnt) Full sound; sonorous.

Vollstimmig (Ger.) (fŏl '–shti m–ĭk) Full voiced. For example, full chorus or full orchestra.

Volltönig (Ger.) (fŏl '–tĕ(r)–ni k) Full sounding.

Volo (It.) (vō '–lō) Flight. For example, a run of notes.

Volta, Volto (It.) (vŏl '–tä, vŏl '–tō) (1) A lively 17th century dance in $\frac{6}{8}$ time. (2) Prima volta (1st ending) and seconda volta (2nd ending).

Volteggiando (It.) (vŏl–tĕ d–jē–än '–dō) The technique of crossing one hand over the other hand when playing on the keyboard.

Volti subito (It.) (vŏl '–tē soo '–bē–tō) Turn suddenly.

Volume Fullness; a quantity of tone; loudness.

Voluntary A piece of music of free structure or improvised. An organ piece played before or after a church service. At one time, a voluntary was also played during the middle of a service.

Vordersatz (Ger.) (fŏr '–då r–zäts) First movement; first theme; first subject.

Vorhalt (Ger.) (fŏr '–hält) Retard.

Vorhergehend (Ger.) (fŏr–hĕr '–gā–hĕnt) Previous.

Vorsänger (Ger.) (fŏr '–zĕng–å r) Choir leader; precentor.

Vorschlag (Ger.) (fŏr'—shläk) Appoggiatura.

Vorsetzungs-zeichen (Ger.) (fŏr—zĕt'—tsŏongs—tsĭkh'—ån) Sharp or flat, signature.

Vorspiel (Ger.) (fŏr'—shpēl) Prologue; prelude; overture.

Vortrag (Ger.) (fŏr'—träk) Recital; execution.

Vorwärts (Ger.) (fŏr'—vĕrts) Onward; move on.

Vorzeichen (Ger.) (fŏr'—tsĭ kh—ån) (Vorzeichnung, (Ger.) (fŏr'—tsĭ kh—nŏong) Signature; key signature.

Votive Mass A Mass for a special intention. It may be said or sung, at special times, in place of the Mass of the feria or feast of the day.

Vox (Lat.) Voice.

Vox Angelica (Lat.) A single or double rank of organ stops of a delicate tone. See *Voice céleste.

Voz (Sp.) (vōth) Voice.

Vuota (It.) (vōo—ō'—tä) (vuoto (It.) (vōo—ō'—tō))(vacant, blank, open. For example, a pause; open string (corda vuota); rest.

Wachsend (Ger.) (väkh '–sĕnt) Crescendo.

Wagner tubas The instruments designed for Wager's Ring operas. There were two tenor, two bass and a standard double-bass tuba. The tenor tubas were modified horns having a range from Bᵇ to f'' while the bass were also modified horns with a range approximately one octave lower. Each type of these modified horns uses a funnel shaped mouthpiece. The Wagner tubas bridge the gap between the trombone and French horn. The range is higher than the trombone and lower than the French horn. The Wagner tubas are generally played by the French horn players who alternate between the two instruments. These instruments are used in many works, e.g.: Richard Strauss (1864–1949) *Alpine Symphony, Elektra;* Igor Stravinsky (1882–1971) *Le Sacre du Printemps, The Firebird;* Anton Bruckner (1824–1896) Symphonies No. 7, No. 8, and No. 9.

Währen (Ger.) (vĕ'–rå n) Continue.

Wait (1) A medieval shawm. (2) A group of town musicians. (3) A street singer. (4) A caroler at Christmas time. (5) A night watchman who called out the time, etc. in the streets during the night. (6) A song sung by Waits.

Waldflöte (Ger.) (väld '–flĕ(r)–tå) Forest flute. An organ stop, an open stop of eight foot and four foot pitch.

Waldhorn (Ger.) (väld '–hô rn) Forest horn. The natural French horn or hunting horn.

Walking bass In jazz music, a technique in which a pizzacato bass line or left-hand piano accompaniment moves in a steady quarter note pattern (4 beats to a measure) using either a scalor or a chordal line.

Waltz A round dance in $\frac{3}{4}$ time. A ballroom dance in a moderately fast tempo that became very popular during the 19th century. The accent is on the first beat of each measure with a feeling of two measures to a unit. That is, a slightly stronger accent on each alternate measure beginning on the first measure (especially in the dance). Examples: Johann Strauss Jr. (1825–1899), "Du und Du", *Waltzes from Die Fledermaus, Opus 367 for Orchestra; Joseph Strauss (1827–1870), Wiener Kinder Waltzes, Opus 61 for Orchestra.*

Walzer (Ger.) (väl '–tsår) Waltz.

Wankend (Ger.) (vängk '–å nt) Unsteady; wavering.

Wärm (Ger.) (vĕrm) Ardour; warmth.

Wassail A festive song. A drinking song or salutation.

Wasserorgel (Ger.) (väs '–å r–ôr–gå l) An organ that is operated by hydraulic pressure.

Wayte An obsolete hautboy. See *Hautboy, *Wait.

Wechsel (Ger.) (vĕkh '–så l) Variation; turn. Wechseldominante, (Ger.) (vĕkh '–så l–dō–mē–nän '–tå) Dominant of the dominant. Wechselgesang, (Ger.) (vĕ kh '–så l–gå –zäng) Alternate song; antiphonal song. Wechselnoten, (Ger.) (vĕkh '–så l–nōt–å n) Appoggiatura; change-note. See *Cambiata.

Wegräumen (Ger.) (vĕg '–roim–å n) Remove.

Wehmütig (Ger.) (vā–mü '–tĭk) Melancholy.

Weiberstimme (Ger.) (vi '–bå r–shti m–å) Female voice.

Weich (Ger.) (vi kh) Smooth; delicate; soft.

Weihnachtslied (Ger.) (vi '–näkhts–lēt) Christmas carol.

Weise (Ger.) (vi '–zå) Motif; melody.

Weiten (Ger.) (vi t '–å n) Broaden.

Well-tempered Equal-tempered.

Well-Tempered Clavier The name applied to the two sets of preludes and fugues by J. S. Bach (1685–1750). Each set has twenty-four preludes and fugues written in all major and minor keys. It demonstrates the use of the system of equal temperament for keyboard instruments. The two groups have a total of forty-eight preludes and fugues. The first set dates to 1722 and the second 1744.

Wetlich (Ger.) (vĕlt '–lĭkh) Wordly. Secular.

Wenden (Ger.) (vĕnd '–å n) Turn.

Wenig (Ger.) (vā '–ni k) A small amount. Little.

Weniger (Ger.) (vā '–ni g–å r) Less.

Werk (Ger.) (vĕrk) Work; performance; opus.

Whiffle A flute or fife.

Whip A percussive instrument that produces the sound effect of the whip. Actually, two pieces of wood that are snapped together.

Whistle A fipple flute. A tin-whistle. An end-blown pipe.

Whole-note A semibreve. A round open note without a stem (o), equal to two half-notes.

Whole rest A pause equal to the semibreve (whole note). Also used for a whole measure rest. Example: (▬).

Whole step An interval of a major second. Two semitones. See *Whole tone.

Whole tone The interval having two semitones (two half-steps). For example, the interval of F to G.

Whole tone scale A scale of whole tones only, within the octave. The octave is divided into six equal parts. An example: C–D–E–F#–G#–A#–B# (C). The whole tone scale has six whole tones (steps). Used by Claude Debussy (1862–1918) and others.

Wieder (Ger.) (vēd '–å r) Again; back again. Wiederholen, (Ger.) (vēd '–å r–hōl–å n) Repeat. Wiederholungs-zeichen, (Ger.) (vēd '–å r–hōl–o͝ongs–tsi kh '–å n) Repetition sign.

Wiegend (Ger.) (vē '–gå nt) Move gently.

Wiegenlied (Ger.) (vē '–gå n–lēt) Lullaby.

Wind band A large ensemble of wind and percussion instruments. The Concert Band, Symphonic Wind Ensemble, Brass Band (no woodwinds) or Military Band.

Wind-chest The box that contains the air supply for the organ pipes. See *Organ.

Wind instruments Instruments which need wind or an air column to produce tone. Usually used to identify the woodwinds and brasses of the orchestra and band. See *Woodwinds, *Brass instruments, *Orchestra, *Band.

Wirbel (Ger.) (vi r '–bå l) Whirl. (1) A peg on a violin. (2) Roll of a drum.

Wire brushes Percussion sticks that have a metal or rubber handle and wire brushes extended from the handle. They are used to play on snare drums and on cymbals. Basic in dance bands.

Witzig (Ger.) (vi t '–tsi k) Humorous.

Wohlbedächtig (Ger.) (vŏl '–bå–dĕkh–tĭ k) Very deliberate.

Wohlgemerkt (Ger.) (vŏl '–gå–mĕrkt) Well marked. Nota bene.

Wohlklang (Ger.) (vŏl '–kläng) Melody.

Wohlklingend (Ger.)   (vŏl '–kli ng–å nt) Sonorous; harmonious.

Wolf (1) A discordant sound caused by poor tuning. (2) An undesirable tone on some notes on the violin and cello apparently due to the design of these instruments. (3) A discord heard as a result of unequal temperament.

Wood block A small hollow square or rectangular block of wood used in the percussion section. It is struck with a drum stick and has an indefinite pitch.

Woodwinds Wind instruments of the orchestra or band that are usually made of wood, although some (flute, piccolo, saxophones, etc.) are made of materials other than wood. The woodwinds are essentially tubes, with holes, that are end-blown, with a reed or double reed or are blown across an open hole (flute and piccolo). There are several woodwinds in the orchestra and band: piccolo, flute, alto flute, and bass flute, which require no reeds; oboe, English horn, bassoon, and contra-bassoon, which require a double-reed; and the various clarinets, alto clarinet, bass clarinet, contra-bass clarinet, soprano saxophone, alto saxophone, tenor saxophone, baritone saxophone, and bass saxophone which require a mouthpiece with a single reed. Many other instruments are also called woodwinds. For example, recorders. Individual instruments are discussed in separate entries.

Work song Songs in Negro folk music that are closely related to African work songs. The rhythm is regular and the music has a strong beat.

Wrest pins The tuning pins for strings on keyboard instruments.

Wucht (Ger.) (vōokht)   Weight; impetus; momentum.

Würdig (Ger.) (vür '–di k) With dignity.

Wut (Ger.) (vōot) Rage, fury.

X

Xylharmonicon An instrument that uses a series of graduated glass tubes for various pitches. A type of glass harmonica or musical glasses.

Xylophon (Ger.) (ksü—lō—fōn ') Xylophone.

Xylophone A percussion instrument that has a series of graduated wooden bars set in the order of the piano keyboard. Metal resonators are attached below the bars. The bars are struck with hammers. The instrument has a range from b♭' to c''''. The xylophone is used in the percussion section of the orchestra and the band. It is also very popular in small jazz combos.

Xylorimba A form of marimba.

Y

Yamato-koto (Jap.) A plucked stringed instrument of Japan having six strings. The melody is plucked with the little finger of the right hand and drone bass accompaniment is done with the tips of the other fingers.

Yigdal (Heb.) A hymn or prayer of faith sung by the cantor and the people at the end of a service on the Sabbath or at other religious services.

Yo (Chinese) Foot. A Chinese flute about a foot long.

Yodel A style of singing of the Swiss and Tyrolean mountain people. They sing on vowels and vary the voice back and forth rapidly from the chest voice to the falsetto voice. A kind of warbling. A song or a call.

Yüeh ch'in (Chinese) A guitar-like instrument of China having a round body, four strings, and a short neck. A flat lute.

Yu-hsiao (Chinese) A Chinese pipe or vertical flute instrument.

Z

Zagen (Ger.) (tsäg '–å n) Hesitate; timidity.

Zambra (Sp.) (thäm'–brä) A dance of the Spanish Moors.

Zampogna (It.) (dsäm–pŏn '–yä) Bagpipe, shawm, or an early chalumeau. An Italian bagpipe having two separate chanters.

Zapateado (Sp.) (thä–pä–tä–ä '–dō) A solo rhythmic Spanish dance in triple meter. The dancer marks the rhythm by the accented stamping of his heels.

Zarge (Ger.) (tsär '–gå) Case; side of a guitar, violin, etc.

Zart (Ger.) (tsärt) Tender, soft.

Zartflöte (Ger.) (tsärt '–flě (r)–tå) Soft flute. An organ stop.

Zartheit (Ger.) (tsärt '–hī t) Tenderness, softness.

Zärtlich (Ger.) (tsěrt '–li kh) Tender, soft.

Zarzuela (Sp.) (thär–thoo–ä '–lä) A type of Spanish opera, with dialogue, which dates back to the 17th century. It now refers to a serious opera in three acts or a satire or comic opera in one act.

Zehn (Ger.) (tsān) Ten.

Zehntel (Ger.) (tsān '–tå l) Tenth.

Zeichen (Ger.) (tsi kh '–å n) Sign or mark.

Zeit (Ger.) (tsit) Time in music.

Zeitlich (Ger.) (tsit '–likh) Secular; temporal.

Zeitmass (Ger.) (tsit '–mäs) Tempo.

Zeitmesser (Ger.) (tsit '–měs–å r) Metronome.

Zelo (It.) (zā '–lō) Zěle, (Fr.) (zě l); zeloso, (It.) (zā–lō '–zō)) Zeal, warmth; enthusiastic.

Zerteilen (Ger.) (tsěr '–ti l–å n) Divide.

Ziehharmonika(Ger.)(tsē '–här–mō–nē–kä) Accordian; concertina.

Ziemlich (Ger.) (tsēm '–li kh) Suitable; rather. (ziemlich spät – rather late).

Zier (Ger.) (tsēr) Embellishment, ornamentation or flourish.

Zierlich (Ger.) (tsēr '–li kh) Ornamental, delicate, graceful.

402

Zigeunermusik (Ger.) (tsĭ —goin '—å r—mōo—zēk) Gypsy music.

Zimbalon A large dulcimer used in Hungarian music. It is a popular instrument today in pop music and jazz.

Zimbel (Ger.) (tsim '—bå l) Cymbal.

Zingaro (It.) (zi n—gä '—rō) Gypsy. Alla zingaresca (It.) in a gypsy style.

Zinke (Ger.) (tsingk '—å) The old cornetto or cornet popular up to the 18th century. See *Cornet à bouquin.

Zirkelkanon (Ger.) (tsi rk '—å l—kän—ŏn) Circle canon.

Zither A plucked stringed instrument having a flat wooden sound box over which numerous strings are stretched and tuned. They may have forty or more strings. The five strings nearest the player have frets under them and, therefore, are the melody strings, while the away strings are played open. A plectrum is used to play on the melody strings while the fingers pluck the accompaniment on the open strings.

Zittern (Ger.) (tsit '—å rn) Shake; vibrate; waver.

Zitto (It.) (dsit '—ō) Silent.

Z'mirot In Jewish music, the hymns sung at meals during a festive occasion or on the Sabbath. The texts are devotional poems (piyutim).

Znamenny chant Early Russian chants that were written in neumatic symbols or signs.

Zögern (Ger.) (tsē(r) '—gå rn) Hesitate; retard.

Zokugakusempô (Jap.) A five-toned Japanese scale.

Zopfstil (Ger.) (tsŏpf '—shtēl) Zopf means pigtail. Zopfstil refers to the pedantic style of music common to the 18th century. Conventional; antiquated.

Zoppa (It.) (dsŏp '—pä) (zoppo, (It.) (dsŏp '—pō)) Limp; syncopated. See *Alla zoppa.

Zu (Ger.) (tsōo) Along with; at; by; for; in; to.

Zufällig (Ger.) (tsōo'—fēl—i k) Accidental.

Zuffolo (It.) (dsōo'—fō—lō) A pipe; whistle; shawm; flageolet.

Zug (Ger.) (tsōok) Pull; stress. Marching. (1) Organ register or stop. (2) Slide of an instrument.

Zugehen (Ger.) (tsōo'—gä—å n) Go faster; move toward.

Zugtrompete (Ger.) (tsōōg'—trŏm—pā—tå) Pull or slide trumpet.

Zukunftsmusik (Ger.) (tsōō'—kōōnfts—mōō—zēk') Music of Wagner. Music of the future.

Zumbido (Sp.) (thōōm—bē'—dō) Hum; buzz.

Zunehmen (Ger.) (tsōō'—nām—ån) Augment; swell; increase.

Zunge (Ger.) (tsōōng'—å) Reed; mouthpiece; tongue.

Zurla A Macedonian shawm.

Zurückgehen (Ger.) (tsōō—rük'—gā—ån) Go back.

Zurückhalten (Ger.) (tsōō—rük'—hält—ån) Detain; hold back; retardation.

Zusammen (Ger.) (tsōō—zäm'—ån) Jointly;   together.

Zwei (Ger.) (tsvi) Two. Zweigesang, (Ger.) (tsvi —gå—zäng) Duet in vocal music. Zweigestrichene Note, (Ger.) (tsvi'—gå—shtri kh—å—nå nō'—tå) Semiquaver. Zweimal, (Ger.) (tsvi'—mäl) Twice. Zweimalig, (Ger.) (tsvi'—mäl—ik) Repeated. Zweit, (Ger.) (tsvi t) Second.

Zwerchflöte (Ger.) (tsvĕrkh'—flĕ(r)—tå)   Cross-flute. Transverse flute.

Zwischen (Ger.) (tsvish'—ån) Between.

Zwischenbegebenheit (Ger.) (tsvich'—ån—bå—gā'—bån—hi t) Epsiode.

Zwischenspiel (Ger.) (tsvi sh'—ån—shpēl) Interlude, episode (in a fugue), intermezzo.

Zwölf (Ger.) (tsvĕ(r)lf) Twelve.

Zwölfachteltakt (Ger.) (tsvĕ(r)lf'—ăkh—tål—täkt) Twelve-eight time.

Zwölftonsystem (Ger.) (tsvĕ(r)lf'—tōn—süs—tĕm) Twleve-tone system.

Zyklus (Ger.) (tsē'—klōōs) Cycle. E.g., cycle or circle of fifths.

A SELECTED ANNOTATED BIBLIOGRAPHY

A SELECTED ANNOTATED BIBLIOGRAPHY

I.   Analysis, Interpretation, Appreciation.

Bernstein, Martin and Picker, Martin. *An Intro-duction to Music.* 3d. ed. Englewood Cliffs, N.J: Prentice-Hall, 1966.

A college textbook designed to be used in an introductory course in music literature. The book presents different styles of music by varied composers from selected periods of music. Includes some fundamentals of music such as rhythm,, melody, form, scales, etc.

Burk, C.; Meierhoffer, V.; Phillips, C. *America's Musical Heritage.* New York: Laidlaw Bros., 1942.

Not a history of music in America, but a textbook which points out the importance of music in the development of the culture of the people in America. Traces the development of some music in America from colonial days to 1942.

Fleming, William, and Veinus, Abraham. *Under-standing Music; Style, Structure, and History.* New York: Holt, 1958.

A textbook designed for a course in the intro-duction of music. Includes units on elements of music, the orchestra, the composer and his music, form and structure, and history of music.

Haggin, Bernard H. *The New Listener's Compan-ion and Record Guide.* 2nd ed. New York: Horizon Press, 1968.

Gives a description of musical procedures and forms, a survey of the literature of music, analysis of particular works, a chapter on critic-ism, a unit on jazz, and a comprehensive cover-age of "Recorded Performances of Works Listed

Under Names of Composers."

Machlis, Joseph. *Introduction to Contemporary Music.* New York: Norton, 1961.
    A textbook that surveys a broad panorama of the contemporary scene.
    Part one: materials of contemporary music.
    Part two: the European scene.
    Part three: the American scene.

McKinney, Howard Decker and Anderson, William Robert. *Discovering Music.* 4th ed. New York: American, 1962.
    A guidebook to more intelligent listening. A textbook for the uninitiated in music as well as for those having some background in music. Areas covered: how to listen, materials of music, forms, instruments, composers, musical works, etc.

Moore, Earl Vincent and Heger, Theodore E. *The Symphony and the Symphonic Poem.* 3d rev. ed. Ann Arbor, Mich., 1957.
    A detailed analysis of many symphonies and symphonic poems. For example, each of the Brahms four symphonies is analyzed by movement. Works of many other composers are analyzed such as Schubert, Beethoven, Haydn, etc.

Newman, William S. *Understanding Music.* 2d ed., rev. and enl. New York: Harper, 1961.
    A practical textbook and guide for the layman who wants an introductory survey. Also, one that can serve as a reference book for the initiated. Includes: historical viewpoints, elements and styles of music, and forms and the study of the music itself.

Scholes, Percy A. *The Listeners History of Music.* New York, London, Toronto: Vol. I, 7th ed., Vol. II, 4th ed., Vol. III, 5th ed.; Oxford University Press, 1954.

A course of study in music appreciation. The development of music from the 16th century to the 20th century. Vol. I. to Beethoven; Vol. II. the Romantic and Nationalist Schools of the 19th century; Vol. III. to the Composers of to-day.

Spaeth, Sigmund Gottfried. *Great Symphonies, How to Recognize and Remember Them.* Rev. ed. New York: Comet, 1952.

Designed for the laymen. Words are added to "symphonic tunes" to help remember them. Includes a "Glossary of Symphonic Terms."

_____. *A Guide to Great Orchestral Music.* New York: Modern Library, 1943.

For the layman or informed "music lover." The author gives the biographical background of the composer, history of the composition, elements and the themes of the composition— all in connection with an important orchestral work.

II. Articles

Babbitt, Milton. "An Introduction to the R.C.A. Synthesizer." *The Journal of Music Theory.* Vol. 8. (Winter 1964), p. 251.

Berger, Ivan. "The Switched-On Bach Story." *Saturday Review.* January 25, 1969, p. 45.

Davies, Hugh. "A Discography of Electronic Music and Musique Concrète." *Recorded Sound.* XIV. (April 1964), 205.

Hamilton, Donald. "A Synoptic View of the New Music." *High Fidelity.* XVIII (September 1968), 44.

Luening, Otto. "An Unfinished History of Electronic Music." *Music Educators Journal.* LV (November 1968), 42.

Schuller, Gunther. "The New German Music for Radio." *Saturday Review.* VL (January 1962), 62.

Ussachevsky, Vladimir A. "Sound Materials in the Experimental Media of Musique Concrète, Tape Music, and Electronic Music." (abstract). *Journal of the Acoustical Society of America.* XXIX (1957), 768.

_____. "The Making of Four Miniatunes: An Analysis." *Music Educators Journal,* LV (November 1968), 76.

III. Bibliography.

Basart,Ann Phillips. *Serial Music: A Classified Bibliography of Writings on Twelve-Tone and Electronic Music.* Berkeley and Los Angeles, California: University of California Press, 1963.
   A bibliography of significant writings on serial music (philosophical, historical, and analytical) arranged by subject: 1. Twelve-Tone music; 2. Electronic music; 3. The Viennese School; 4. Other composers who use serial techniques. The term "serial music" includes 12 tone music, electronic music, pre-dodecaphonic atonality, musique concrète, and "chance" music. There is an author index and a subject index. The entries number 823.

Cross, Lowell M. *A Bibliography of Electronic Music.* ed. Toronto, Canada: University of Toronto Press, 1967.

A bibliography of 1,562 books, articles, monographs, and abstracts on "music concrète," "elektronische Musik," "tape music," "computer music," and related experimental music.

Ewen, David. *American Popular Songs from the Revolutionary War to the Present.* New York: Random House, 1966.

An alphabetical guide to over 3,600 songs listed by title in alphabetical order. Also included are listings of composers, lyricists, musical comedies, and motion pictures. The title is followed by such information as: composer, lyricist, circumstances surrounding the writing of the song, facts on performance of the song, the production in which the song was heard, information about the recording of the song plus any other relevant historical facts related to the song. No musical examples.

Gillis, Frank and Merriam, Alan P. *Ethnomusicology and Folk Music: An International Bibliography of Dissertations and Theses.* Middletown, Conn.: Wesleyan University Press, 1966.

Linker, Robert White. *Music of the Minnesinger and Early Meistersinger,* a Bibliography. Chapel Hill, University of North Carolina, 1962.

The names of the composers are arranged alphabetically with songs listed in alphabetical order under each composer's name. Any general works about the composers are also added.

IV.   Church Music

The Liber Usualis. (with introduction and rubrics

in English) ed. Benedictines of Solesmes. Tournai (Belgium), New York, Desclee, 1962 (c 1961).

An important liturgical book of the Roman Catholic rites. It includes spoken texts as well as music for both the mass and the office. The text is in Latin except for the introduction and rubrics which are in English. Includes: 1. The Kyriale with Cantus ad libitum ; 2. The Mass of the Sundays and Feasts; 3. Prime, Terce, Sext, None, for Sundays and Feasts of the 1st and 2nd class; 4. Matins of Christmas, Easter, Pentecost, Corpus Christi, Lauds for Feasts of the 1st Class; 5. The Litanies: the Mass of Rogation Days, Ember Days, Easter and Whitsun weeks; the Vigils of Christmas, Epiphany and Whitsun; 6. The service of Ash Wednesday, the Triduum of Holy Week and Easter Day; 7. The principal Votive masses and the offices for the Dead. Also includes rules for interpretation of the plainsong used in the services, chants for special occasions, and a section on the common tones of the mass and office.

Macdougall, Hamilton Crawford. *Early New England Psalmody; an Historical Appreciation, 1620–1820.* Brattleboro: Stephen Daye Press, 1940.

Many illustrations of the music are included. Some areas covered are: Protestant Reformation; Ainsworth Psalters; Bay Psalm Book; Music of the Billings Period (1746–1800); the 'Fuguing' Tune; The Singing School.

Wellesz, Egon. *A History of Byzantine Music and Hymnography.* 2nd. ed. Oxford, Claredon Press, 1961.

Among the many excellent chapters on the subject are those dealing with the systems of

Byzantine musical notation, the transcription of Byzantine melodies, the structure of Byzantine melodies; and words and music. Many excellent musical examples of hymns from the Hirmologion, hymns from the Sticherarion, and melismatic chant are included.

V. Collections, Music, Addresses, Essays, Lectures, Anthologies, Composers, and Musicians.

Allen, Ware, and Garrison. *Slave Songs of the United States.* New York: Oak Publications, 1965.

Includes 136 sacred and secular slave songs (melodies and texts) from various parts of the U.S. Part I. Songs from South-Eastern Slave States. Part II. Northern Seaboard Slave States. Part III. Inland Slave States. Part IV. Gulf States.

Baldwin, Lillian. *A Listener's Anthology of Music.* New York: Silver Burdett Co., 1948.

Cage, John. *Silence; Lectures and Writings.* Middletown, Conn.: Wesleyan University, 1961.

John Cage, on composition, on the history of experimental music in the U.S. on Satie, on Varèse, statements on the dance, plus a "Lecture on Nothing," a "Lecture on Something," et. al.

Chávez, Carlos. *Musical Thought.* Cambridge: Harvard University, 1961.

The Charles Eliot Norton Lectures at Harvard (1958-1959) Contents:
I. A Latin American Composer
II. Art as Communication
III. Form in Music
IV. Repetition in Music
V. Composer and Public

VI. The Enjoyment of Music

Cowell, Henry. *Charles Ives and His Music.* New York: Oxford University Press, 1955.
    Part One: Life. Part Two: Music. The discussion of his music in part two centers on Ives use of the musical materials: polyphony, harmony, melody, rhythm, form, instrumentation and voice writing. The three works discussed in Chapter X are: 1. Paracelsus; 2. Sonata No. 2 for piano; 3. Universe Symphony.

Davidson, Archibald Thompson and Apel, Willi. *Historical Anthology of Music.* 2 vols. Rev. ed. Cambridge: Harvard University, 1966.
    Volume one contains important examples of Oriental, Medieval, and Renaissance Music. Volume two contains important examples of Baroque, Rococo, and Pre-Classical Music. The music appears in modern notation. Foreign texts are translated at the end of each volume and a commentary is given for each musical work. Each piece is a complete composition or a whole movement from a larger work.

Denkmäler der Tonkunst in Bayern. (DTB) 1900-1931. (published as *Denkmäler deutscher Tonkunst,* Zweite *Folge) (Monuments of Music in Bavaria).* 36 volumes.
    A series supplementary to *Denkmäler Deutscher Tonkunst* the Bavarian series is called *Zweite Folge* (second series). New revised edition now in progress.

Denkmäler der Tonkunst in Oesterreich (DTO); 115 volumes to date, first volume published in 1894. (Monuments of Music in Austria).
    A series of publications (reprints) of old Austrian music which includes works by foreign

composers written in Austria or works found in Austrian libraries.

Denkmäler deutscher Tonkunst (DdT);1892-1931. New revised edition 1957-1961. 65 volumes. (Monuments of German Music).

Publications of old music by German composers and works by foreign composers who lived in Germany. The series started in 1892. After the first two volumes were published, a long period elapsed during which time the Austrian musicians started their own series. The German series resumed in 1900 and was divided into two sections, one for Germany, the other for Bavaria *(Zweite Folge — second series).*

Einstein, Alfred. *Essays on Music.* New York: Norton, 1956.

Includes 22 articles, many of which are available in musical journals and periodicals. Covers many areas such as: opera, Elizabethan Madrigal and Musica Transalpina, manuscripts of Mozart, First Libretto of Don Giovanni, and articles about many composers such as Haydn, Mozart, Beethoven, Strauss, Wagner, et. al.

France. *Centre national de la recherche scientifique.* Debussy et l'evolution de la musique au xxe siecle. Paris, 24-31, Octobre 1962. Etudes réunies et présentées par Edith Weber. Paris, 1965.

Debussy and the evolution of 20th century music. A collection of writings by different scholars. The book is divided into three sections: I. The style of Debussy, II. The aesthetics of Debussy, III. The influence of Debussy. Text in French.

Geiringer, Karl. *The Bach Family: seven genera-*

tions of creative genius. New York: Oxford University Press, 1959.

A history of the Bach family from the 16th century to the middle of the 19th century. A "Geneological Table of the Bach Musicians" and an "Index of Compositions by Members of the Bach Family" are included. Many illustrations, plates, and musical examples are also included.

Gleason, Harold. *Examples of Music Before 1400.* New York: Crofts, 1946.

Morgenstern, Sam. *Composers on Music.* An anthology of composers' writings from Palestrina to Copland, ed. New York: Pantheon, 1956.

Composers' writings on their own and others' music. Sources for the material presented comes from: biographies, autobiographies, letters, prefaces, magazine articles, and lectures.

Paléographie Musicale. Edited by the Benedictines of Solesmes, Series I and II. 19 volumes. Tournai Belgium, 1889-.

A series of facsimiles, commentaries, and studies of plainsong. Nineteen volumes have been published since 1889, 17 volumes in the first series and 2 volumes in the second series. Subtitle: Les Principaux Manuscrits de chant. grégorien, ambrosien, mozarabe, gallican.

Schönberg, Arnold. *Style and Idea.* New York: Philosophical Library, 1950.

Essays of Schönberg on many ideas and people. For example, Gustav Mahler; Brahms the Progressive; Heart and Brain in Music; Criteria for the Evaluation of Music; and eleven more.

Weinstock, Herbert. *Donizetti and the World of Opera in Italy, Paris and Vienna in the First*

Half of the Nineteenth Century. New York: Pantheon, 1963.

A historical account of his life and his works. Includes a chronological list of Donizetti's operas, with commentary and performance date. Also, a list of Donizetti's non-operatic compositions.

Wellesz, Egon. *The Origins of Schönberg's Twelve-tone System.* A lecture delivered in the Whittall Pavilion of the Library of Congress, January 10, 1957. Washington: U. S. Government Printing Office, 1958.

VI. Dictionaries, Encyclopedias, Thematic Catalogs, Analytical Guides.

Apel, Willi. *Harvard Dictionary of Music.* 2d ed., rev. and enl. Cambridge, Mass.: Belknap Press of Harvard, University Press, 1969.

Baker, Theodore. *Biographical Dictionary of Musicians.* 5th ed. Completely rev. by Nicholas Slonimsky. New York: Schirmer, 1958.

_____. *A Dictionary of Musical Terms.* New York: Schirmer, 1923.

Barlow, Harold and Morgenstern, Sam. *A Dictionary of Musical Themes.* New York: Crown, 1948.

Part one contains ten thousand or more musical themes arranged by composers in alphabetical order. The second part is the notation-index or theme finder. When the letter names of the notes are identified within the melodic line (in the key of C major or C minor) the letter sequence is then found in the index. When the letter sequence is found in the index, you are referred to the musical theme and composer listed in part one. Does not contain vocal themes.

————. *A Dictionary of Vocal Themes.* London: Benn, 1956.

Themes from operas, cantatas, oratories, lieder, art songs, and other vocal pieces. Part one contains vocal themes with text, arranged by composers in alphabetical order. Part two is a notation index which is used to identify a sequence of notes by letter name. Each sequence refers back to the melody, title, and composers in part one. Part three has an "Index to Songs and First Lines."

Burrows, Raymond Murdock and Redmond, Bessie Carroll. *Concerto Themes.* comps. New York: Simon and Schuster, 1951.

————. *Symphony Themes.* comps. New York: Simon and Schuster, 1942.

Cooper, Martin. *The Concise Encyclopedia of Music and Musicians.* ed. New York: Hawthorn, 1958.

Ewen, David. *Encyclopedia of Concert Music.* New York: Hill and Want, 1959.

A guide and analysis of some 1500 instrumental compositions, over 300 biographies of foremost composers. Biographies of over 150 conductors and 250 instrumentalists. Histories of orchestras and ensembles. Included also, are over 500 musical terms, history and backgrounds of music, theories and theorists of music, and numerous special articles on varied subjects.

————. *Encyclopedia of the Opera.* New York: Wyn, 1955.

Grove, Sir George. *Dictionary of Music and Musicians.* 5th ed. Edited by Eric Blom. New York: St. Martin's Press, 1955. 9 vol. Vol. X—Supplementary Volume, 1961.
Volume I 1955 (A—Byzantine Music)
Volume II 1955 (C—Ezio)
Volume III 1955 (F—Gyulai)
Volume IV 1955 (H—Krie)
Volume V 1955 (L. H. —Myszhńska—Woyciechowska)
Volume VI 1955 (N.Z. Qvanten)
Volume VII 1955 (R. H. —Sowiński)
Volume VIII 1955 (Spadarius—Viotti)
Volume IX 1955 (Virchi—Zimmermann)
Volume X 1961 Supplementary Volume to the Fifth Edition (corrections, additions to existing articles, and new entries.)

Handel, Samuel. *A Dictionary of Electronics.* ed. Baltimore, Maryland: Penguin paperback, 1962.

Jacobs, Arthur. *A New Dictionary of Music.* Rev. Chicago: Aldine, 1962.

Lowenberg, Alfred. *Annals of Opera, 1597—1940.* 2d ed. rev. and corr. (Frank Walker) Compiled from original sources. Geneve, Societas Bibliographica, 1955.
Volume I—Text. Volume 2—Indexes.

Die Musik in Geschichte und Gegenwart; allgemeine Enzyklopädie der Musik. Hrsg. von Friedrich Blume. Kassel: *Bärenreiter-Verlag,* 1949—1968.
A general encyclopedia of music. 14 volumes from A—Z. Text in German.
Volumes:
Band I 1949—1951 (AACHEN—BLUMNER)
Band II 1952 (Boccherini—DAPONTE)

Band III 1954 (Daquin—Fechner)
Band IV 1955 (Fede—*Gesangspädagogik*)
Band V 1956 (Gesellschaften—Hayne)
Band VI 1957 (Head—Jenny)
Band VII 1958 (Jensen—Kyrie)
Band VIII 1960 (LAAFF—MEJTUS)
Band IX 1961 (DEL MEL—ONSLOW)
Band X 1962 (OPER—RAPPRESENTAZI-
ONE)
Band XI 1963 (RASCH—SCHNYDER VON
WARTENSEE)
Band XII 1965 (SCHOBERLECHNER—SYM-
PHONISCHE DICHTUNG)
Band XIII 1966 (SYRINX—VOLKSGESANG,
VOLKSMUSIK UND VOLKSTANZ)
Band XIV 1968 (VOLLERTHUN—ZYGA-
NOW)

O'Connell, Charles. *The Victor Book of Overtures, Tone Poems and Other Orchestral
Works.* New York: Simon and Schuster, 1950.
318 overtures, tone poems, and other orchestral works listed under the name of the
composer. Composers are arranged in alphabetical order. A biographical introduction
is given along with a discussion of the musical
work.

————. *The Victor Book of Symphonies.*
New York: Simon and Schuster, 1948.
138 symphonies are listed under the name
of the composer. Composers are arranged in
alphabetical order. A biographical introduction is given along with a discussion of the
musical work. Includes a discussion of the
modern orchestra and comments on the
specific instruments of the orchestra.

Sachs, Curt. *Real-Lexikon der Musikinstru-
mente, zugleich ein Polyglossar für das ge-*

samte Instrumententengebiet. Rev. and enl. ed. New York: Dover Publication, 1964. In German, a dictionary of musical instruments. An encyclopedia work having precise descriptions of instruments from all periods of history on a world-wide basis. Includes a great deal of ethnological and linquistic information. Emphasis is placed on the philological aspect of the names of instruments. Some names are written in such scripts as Sanscrit, Greek, Cyrillic, and Arabic.

Scholes, Percy Alfred. *The Concise Oxford Dictionary of Music.* 2nd ed. Edited by John Owen Ward, 1964. New York: Oxford University Press, 1952.

_____. *The Oxford Companion to Music.* 9th ed., completely rev. and reset. New York: Oxford Univ. Press, 1955. 10th ed. rev., 1970.
An encyclopedia of music and musicians. It is self-indexed, has a pronouncing glossary and over 1,100 portraits and pictures.

Thompson, Oscar. *The International Cyclopedia of Music and Musicians.* 8th ed. rev. Ed. by Nicolas Slonimsky. New York: Dodd, Mead, 1958. 9th ed., 1964.

Westrup, Jack Allan and Harrison, Frank Llewellyn. *The New College Encyclopedia of Music.* New York: Norton, 1960.

VII.   History and Criticism.

Apel, Willi. *Geschichte der orgel-und Klaviermusik bis 1700.* Kassel, Basel, Paris, London, New York: Bärenreiter-Verlag, 1967.
A history of organ and keyboard music until 1700. Text in German. Covers various

styles and forms of organ and keyboard music of several countries by many composers. Extensive use of musical examples.

————. *Masters of the Keyboard.* Cambridge, Harvard University, 1947.
This book contains material from a series of eight lectures given under the title "History of Music for the Pianoforte." It begins (Chapter I) with "The Keyboard Instruments," and follows with a discussion of pianoforte music from the late middle ages (1300—1500) and continues to New Music 1900—1940. Complete or nearly complete compositions played during the lectures are included.

Appleton, Jon H. *The Development and Practice of Electronic Music.* Englewood Cliffs, N. J.: Prentice-Hall, ,1975. Editors: Jon H. Appleton and Ronald C. Perera. Authors: Otto Luening [and others].

Austin, William. *Music in the 20th Century.* New York: W. W. Norton, 1966.
From Debussy through Stravinsky, much emphasis is placed on the music and achievements of Schoenberg, Bartók, and Stravinsky and the collective achievements of jazz. Also included are such composers as Debussy, Hindemith, and contemporaries from many countries. There is an extensive bibliography on composers and other musicians, an excellent bibliography on Jazz, and one on Experimental music.

Bauer, Marion and Peyser, Ethel Rose. *Music Through the Ages.* An introduction to music history. Edited and rev. by Elizabeth E. Rogers. 3d ed. completely rev. New York: G. P. Putnam's Sons, 1967.

Topics range from primitive and ancient music and lead in chronological sequences to new tendencies of the 20th century. A textbook for a survey course in music history and literature. Following each chapter, the authors give a selected bibliography, a discography, and a list of projects, and a list of terms related to the chapter.

_____. *Twentieth Century Music; How It Developed, How to Listen to It.* A new edition. completely rev. New York: Putnam, 1947.

The author relates to innovations of the past with those of the present. New terminology is explained such as polytonality, atonality, whole tone scales, etc. Many examples and illustrations of 20th Century music are freely used. Among the many 20th century composers included are Debussy, Ravel, Stravinsky, Kodály, Schoenberg, Hindemith, and Copland.

Brown, Howard Mayer. *Music in the French Secular Theater, 1400–1550.* Cambridge: Harvard University Press, 1963.

Not a history of popular music in the 15th and 16th centuries but a discussion of the normal musical practices of the theater. Contains an extensive catalogue (100 pages) of theatrical chansons and their sources.

Brussels. *Bibliothèque royale de Belgique.* The chanson albums of Marquerite of Austria. Mss. 228 and 11239 of the Bibliothèque royale de Belgique, Brussels. A critical edition and commentary by Martin Picker. Berkeley: U. of California Press, 1965.

The book contains a description and history of the manuscripts, a discussion on Marquerite and her court, music at the courts, biographical sketches of composers represented in the manuscripts, the music (transcriptions) contained in the manuscripts a critical commentary, and the texts of MS 11239 and 228. Manuscript 228 contains 58 compositions (40 French chansons, I Flemish song, 7 Latin motets, 7 works joining French and Latin texts, and 3 secular Latin pieces). Manuscript 11239 contains 24 compositions complete or in part (18 have French texts, 4 Latin texts, and 2 both French and Latin in different voices.)

Bukofzer, Manfred F. *Music in the Baroque Era*. From Monteverdi to Bach. New York: Norton, 1947.
A stylistic approach to the history of Baroque music. Some areas included: Italian music, French music, English music, on style, form, musical thought of the Baroque Era, and the sociology of Baroque music. Includes unique "checklist of Baroque Books On Music."

————. *Studies in Medieval and Renaissance Music*. New York: W. W. Norton & Co., 1950.
Interesting studies on the Old Hall manuscript (the edition, cantus-firmus, style) and Caput: a Liturgico-musical study (cyclic mass, caput melody, caput melisma, caput masses, and cantus firmi). Several other areas are covered such as: Holy Week music, carols, folk music, choral polyphony, polyphonic basse dance, etc.

Burney, Charles. *A General History of Music*. From the earliest ages to the present period (1789). New York: Dover, 1957.
A general history, not a period history, from music of the ancients through the 18th cen-

tury. A two volume work with critical and historical notes. Volume I, Book I—ancient music, Egyptian music, Hebrew music, Greek music; Volume I, Book 2—music of the church previous to the time of Guido to the middle of the 16th century; Volume II, Book 3—music in England during the 16th century to church music in England after the death of Purcell; Volume II, Book 4—the invention of recitative (opera in Italy) to music in England (18th century).

Cannon, Beekman Cox. *The Art of Music.* A short history of musical styles and ideas. et al. New York: Crowell, 1960.
    A textbook for an introduction to the history of music. A study of musical styles and ideas. Begins with a chapter on "The Legacy of Greece and Rome" and continues in historical order from the time of Gregorian chant through the 20th century. Some basic principles of music are presented in the Appendix.

Chase, Gilbert. *America's Music, From the Pilgrims to the Present.* Rev. 2nd ed. New York: McGraw-Hill Book Co., 1966.
    It is a text about America's music, the making of America's music. The text is based on historical principles. Starts with Puritan psalm singers of the 17th century and discusses revivals and camp meetings, Negro spirituals, jazz, 12 tone trends, and the scene in the sixties.

————. *The Music of* Spain. New York: W. W. Norton, 1941. (2nd rev. ed. Dover Publications, Inc. N. Y., 1959).
    Spanish music from the Middle Ages to the

present day. Includes a comprehensive account of Iberian music, secular songs of the Renaissance, masters of the guitar, rue of the zarzuela, chapters on Albéniz, Granados and de Falla, a unit on the dances of Spain, etc.

Cooper, Martin. *French Music*. From the death of Berlioz to the death of Fauré. New York: Oxford University Press, 1951.

A book on French composers and French music. Data on French composers (born, died, music, other arts) is given in a quick reference section entitled, "Table of Events 1870–1925".

Cowell, Henry. *American Composers on American Music*. A symposium. New York: Ungar, 1962.

Well-known composers review each other's compositions. The first section: "Composers in Review of other Composers." The example, Edgar Varèse by Henry Cowell; the second section: "Composers in Discussion of General Tendencies." An example, "Materials and Musical Creation," by Wallingford Riegger.

Einstein, Alfred. *The Italian Madrigal*. New Jersey: Princeton University Press, 1949.

Three Volumes. Volume one includes discussions on the Frottola, origins of the madrigal, the madrigal and poetry, the early madrigal of Verdelot, Arcadelt, Palestrina, Willarert, et. al., the lighter forms (e.g. Quodlibet) and the postclassic madrigal. Volume two continues with units on Orlando di Lasso, et. al., the new Canzonetta, Monteverdi, et. al. The third volume contains illustrations of complete compositions relative to the text in Volumes one and two.

_____. *Music in the Romantic Era*. New York: Norton, 1947.

A history of musical thought in the Romantic movement.

Part I. Antecedents, Concepts, and Ideals.

Part II. The History.

Part III. The Philosophy

_____. *A Short History of Music*. 4th American ed. rev. New York: Knopf, 1960, c 1938.

The development of music as a whole and the historical form of that development. The book is designed for those who have some understanding of the facts of musical history. Many representative examples of old music are given in the section at the end of the book — "Musical Examples and Notes."

Engel, Carl. *The Music of Most Ancient Nations, Particularly of the Assyrians, Egyptians, and Hebrews*. With special reference to recent discoveries in Western Asia and in Egypt. London: W. Reeves, 1929.

A great deal of attention is given to the description of early musical instruments, to examples of musical scales in use among nations at various times, to musical performances, and to the history of ancient music. Many illustrations throughout.

Ewen, David. *David Ewen Introduces Modern Music*. A history and appreciation from Wagner to Webern. Philadelphia: Chilton, 1962.

_____. *From Bach to Stravinsky*. ed; New York: W. W. Norton & Co., 1933.

A history of music from the 18th century to 1933. Emphasis is placed on lives of the composers, their works, and their personalities.

Fellowes, Edmund Horace. *The English Madrigal*. Reprinted 1935. London: Oxford University Press, 1925.

A discussion of its origin and etymology, form and technique, the part-books, the rhythm and underlaying, the harmony, the words, and the composers.

Ferguson, Donald Nivison. *A History of Musical Thought*. 3d ed. New York: Appleton-Century-Crofts, 1959.

A textbook on the history of music and a book on musical appreciation. Extends from principal modes of Greek Music to 20th century music including a unit on music in the U. S. Includes an extended and comprehensive bibliography.

Finney, Theodore Mitchell. *A History of Music*. Rev. ed. New York: Harcourt, Brace, 1947.

A textbook. The material in this text has been presented with the view to showing chronological growth and development from the ancient period to the 20th century.

Foote, H. W. *Three Centuries of American Hymnody*. Cambridge, Mass.: Harvard University Press, 1940.

The development of worship song in the U. S. from the first English settlements to 1940. It begins with English Psalmody, the Bay Psalm Book, et. al., to hymns of the 20th century. Excellent index of Psalm Books and Hymn Books.

Gleason, Harold. *Music Literature Outlines*. Series I—Music in the Middle Ages and Renaissance; Series II—Music in the Baroque; Series III—American Music from 1620–1920; Series V—Chamber Music from Haydn to

Ravel. Rochester, New York: Levis Music Stores (Series I) 1951, (Series II) 1951, (Series III) 1955, (Series V) 1955.

Recommended for use in classes in History of Music, Music Literature, and Introductory Musicology. Not only is each series an excellent outline, but a most valuable and extensive bibliogrpahy of books, periodicals, music, and a list of records is available at the end of each chapter. Well documented and illustrated.

Gosvami, O. *The Story of Indian Music.* Its Growth and Synthesis. Bombay, Calcutta, New Delhi, Madras, London, New York: Asia Publishing House, 1961.

A discussion of the basic principles of Indian music and its peculiar characteristics. Excellent sections on form, style, composition, and Indian musical instruments (Rabab, Sitar, Sarangi, and many others).

Gradenwitz, P. *The Music of Israel.* New York: W. W. Norton, 1949.

A survey of the music of Israel from the ancient Hebrews to the music of modern Palestine. Sections on the function of music in the ancient temple and in Jewish life, the influence of the ancient Hebrew culture and later Jewish achievements on music history and contributions of Jewish composers.

Grout, Donald Jay. *A History of Western Music.* New York: Norton, 1960. Rev. ed., 1973.

————. *A Short History of Opera.* New York: Columbia University, 1947.

A history of opera in 2 volumes. Vol. I, Music and Drama to the end of the 16th century; Renaissance and Baroque Opera; 18th

429

century, and Romantic Opera, Vol. II, from Romanticism to modernism. Special note should be made of the extensive bibliography (Bibliographies, Lexicons, Guides, Histories, and Other Works Dealing with the Opera in General) in Volume 2 (122 pages).

Harrison, Frank Llewellyn. *Music in Medieval Britian.* London, Routledge, and Paul, 1952.
A comprehensive treatment of the Liturgy and its Plainsong (examples: psalm, canticle, antiphon, tract, hymn, sequence, ordinary of the mass; tropes, Votive Mass, et. al.); the polyphony of the liturgy from 1100 to 1400 (examples: conductus; clausula, motet, descant of the 14th century, et. al); Mass and Motet (Fr. and Eng. style in 14th and 15th centuries, composers of the Old Hall Manuscript et. al.); Votive Antiphon and Magnificat; The Carol; et. al. Over 255 musical examples supplement the discussion.

Jones, A. M. *Studies in African Music.* London, New York: Oxford University Press, 1959.
Two separate volumes. Volume 1 is a series of essays on African music, technical analysis of the dances, and detailed commentaries on the music of Volume 2. Volume 2 contains full scores of songs and dances that are chiefly of the Ewe people in Ghana.

Kerman, Joseph. *The Elizabethan Madrigal;* a comparative study. New York: American Musicological Society; distributor: Galaxy Music Corp. 1962.
Emphasis is placed on the beginnings of the Elizabethan madrigal and its relation to the Italian development which preceded and

fathered it. Contents: English Madrigal Verse; Italian Music in Elizabethan England (discussion of Musica Transalpina 1588, the later anthologies); Madrigals of Alfonso Ferrabosco; Secular Song (Byrd and Gibbons); The Elizabethan Madrigal; T. Morley—Ballet, Canzonet, Light Madrigal; the Triumphes'of Oriana; Madrigal-Weelkes and Wilbye; the 'English Madrigal School.

Kolodin, Irving. *The Composer as Listener.* ed. A guide to music. New York: Collier, 1962.
Composers writing about composers (e.g. Beethoven by Tchaikowsky; Brahms by Maher); Composers on the compositions of other composers (e.g., Beethoven/nine symphonies by Berlioz; Chopin/opus 2 by Schumann); Composers comments on conducting and interpretation; plus comments on audiences and miscellaneous items.

Láng, Paul Henry. *Music in Western Civilization.* New York: Norton, 1941.
A history of music beginning with Ancient Greece. A chronicle of the participation of music in the development of Western civilization.

_____. *One Hundred Years of Music in America.* New York: G. Schirmer, 1961.
From 1861—1961 — a study of musical life during these 100 years: the publishing house, orchestra, bands, popular music, church music, opera, the American composer, music education, plus other general areas.

Láng, Paul Henry and Bettmann, Otto. *A Pictorial History of Music.* New York: Norton, 1960.

An adaption of Lãng's — *Music in Western Civilization.* The continuity and cultural viewpoint of Lãng's text is preserved. It extends from antiquity to the 20th century.

Leichtentritt, Hugo. *Music of the Western Nations.* Cambridge: Harvard Univeristy, 1956.
Slonimsky, in the forward of this volume, sums·up the purpose of the book as follows: "National developments are examined by Leichtentritt in their relation to international, cosmopolitan music, in the light of his central hypothesis that regional traits transcend their limited signifigance and attain international validity only when organized in an artistic creation at the hands of a truly great national composer." Contents: Greece, the Hebrews, Supranational Polyphony, the Netherlands, Italy, Germany, Austria, Switzerland, France, Belgium, Spain, Portugal, England, Scandinavia, Slavic Nations, Hungary, Rumania, Latin America, and United States.

McKinney, Howard Decker and Anderson, William Robert. *Music in History; the Evolution of an Art.* 2d ed. New York: American Book Co., 1957.
A general historical survey. The music is discussed against the general backgrounds of its time. Music is related to other arts: painting, literature, sculpture, and architecture.

Miller, Hugh Milton. *History of Music.* 3d ed. rev. and enl. New York: Barnes & Noble, 1960.

Moore, Douglas. *From Madrigal to Modern Music.* New York: W. W. Norton & Co., 1942.
A guide to musical styles. The periods cov-

ered are: Renaissance, Baroque, Classic, Romantic, and Modern. A general introduction to each period is given and at least one example of every important type of composition is examined. For example, in the Baroque period: fugue, suite, sonata, concerto grosso, solo concerto, chorale, mass, oratorio, passion, and opera. A "Dictionary of Musical Terms" is added.

Newman, William S. *The Sonata in the Baroque Era.* Rev. ed., 1966. Chapel Hill: University of North Carolina, 1959.
Part I. The Nature of the Baroque Sonata. Part II. The Composers and Their Sonatas. Eighty-five musical examples are used as illustration.

————. *The Sonata in the Classic Era.* Chapel Hill: University of North Carolina, 1963.
Part I. The Nature of the Classical Sonata. Part II. The Composers and their Sonatas. 133 musical examples are used as illustrations.

Parrish, Carl and Ohl, John F. *Masterpieces of Music Before 1750.* An anthology of musical examples from Gregorian chant to J. S. Bach. eds. New York: Norton, 1951.
A collection of musical examples with historical and analytical notes that illustrate the musical style from early Middle Ages to the mid-18th century. Some examples are given in short score; the complete text is given in each voice part, and Gregorian chants are transcribed into modern notation. Some examples of the music included in the text are: Antiphon, Psalm, Sequence, Trouvère Song, Virelai, Minnelied, Parallel Organum, Free Organum, Melismatic Organum, Motet,

433

Conductus, Estampie, Ballata, Chanson, Lute Dances, Madrigal, Cantata, Ricercar, Fugue, et. al.

Pincherle, Marc. *An Illustrated History of Music.* London: Macmillan and Co., 1960.

Contains a wealth of visual documentation (40 pages in color and 200 illustrations in black and white): samples of musical notation, front pieces from first editions of scores, portraits, photographs of famous musicians, photographs of paintings, sculpture, instruments, etc. The author presents a history of Western music from the time when the music of the Roman Catholic Church began to take a definite form through the contemporary scene.

Polin, Claire C. *Music of the Ancient Near East.* New York: Vantage Press, 1954.

The place of music in the life of the ancient Semitic cultures. A study of their instruments, their music, and the literary texts set to music. Chapters: I. Mesopotamia, II. Egypt, III. Palestine, IV. Arabia, V. Assyria, VI. Phoenicia, VII. Syria, and VIII. Abyssinia.

Reese, Gustave. *Music in the Middle Ages.* With an introduction on the music of ancient times. New York: Norton, 1940.

The main concern of the book is with style-analysis of the music from ancient times up through the year 1453. Part I. "Introduction: The Music of Ancient Times;" Part II. "Western European Monody to about 1300;" and Part III "Polyphony Based On the Perfect Consonances and its Displacement by Polyphony based on the Third." There are many musical examples and copious bibliographical references.

————. *Music in the Renaissance.* New York: W. W. Norton, 1954.

The first part deals with the central musical language of the 15th and 16th centuries in France, Italy, and the Low Countries. The second part deals with music of other lands. The author presents an extensive and comprehensive bibliography (over 60 pages).

Rothmüller, Aron Marko. *The Music of the Jews.* An Historical Appreciation. New York: A. S. Barnes and Company, Inc., 1960.

The book treats some four thousand years of cultural history of the Jews. Part I "From the Earliest Times to the Destruction of the Second Temple." Part II "The Synagogal Service and Jewish Music from the First to the Twentieth Century C. E." Part III "The New Jewish Music: Nineteenth and Twentieth Centuries."

Sachs, Curt. *Our Musical Heritage.* A short history of music. 2d ed. New York: Prentice-Hall, 1955.

A history of music textbook which gives the reader an idea of the essential trends of thought and style. Extends from the origins of primitive music through the year 1954 in a chronological sequence.

————. *The Rise of Music in the Ancient World, East and West.* New York: W. W. Norton & Co., 1943.

A study of the origins of music and of primitive styles. Oriental systems of music, of the theory and practice of the Greeks, and the evolution of major and minor.

Salazar, Adolfo. *Music in Our Time.* Trends in music since the romantic era. New York:

Norton, 1946.

Schering, Arnold. *Geschichte der Musik in Bei-spielen.* Leipzig, Breitkopf and Härtel, 1931.
A history of music in examples. 313 musical examples with commentary are presented in a general chronological order from very early music (Pindar (518-446) — "Melodie zur ersten pythischen ode"; and "Hymnus auf apollon" c. 150 v. chr.) to the musical examples of Mozart, Gluck, and Haydn. Text in German.

Scholes, Percy Alfred. *The Puritans and Music in England and New England.* A contribution to the cultural history of two nations. New York: Russell & Russell, 1962.
Includes extensive illustrations, a glossary of technical terms, and an excellent index of works cited.

Seamen, Gerald R. *History of Russian Music.* New York: F. A. Praeger, 1967.
Volume one is a history of Russian music from its origins to Alexander Sergeevich Dargomyzhsky (1813–1869). Emphasis is placed on the extent to which Russian music has been influenced by the folk element. Chapter one is devoted to an outline of Russian folk music.

Slonimsky, Nicolas. *Music of Latin America.* New York: Crowell, 1945.
A panorama of Latin American music. The music of each of the twenty republics of Latin America is discussed. Part III is a "Dictionary of Latin American Musicians, Songs and Dances, and Musical Instruments."

————. *Music Since 1900.* 3d ed. rev. and

enl. New York: Coleman-Ross, 1949.

Part I is a descriptive chronology: dates of musical events in chronological order.

Part II is a "Concise Biographical Dictionary of Twentieth Century Musicians." Includes corrections and additions to other dictionaries. Part III "Letters and Documents."

Southern, Eileen. *The Music of Black Americans: A History.* New York: W. W. Norton, 1971.

Strunk, William Oliver. *Source Readings in Music History from Classical Antiquity Through the Romantic Era.* comp. Reprinted in five volumes, 1965. New York: Norton, 1950.

Selected and annotated by Oliver Strunk. Vol. I — Antiquity and the Middle Ages; Vol. II — The Renaissance; Vol III — The Baroque Era; Vol. IV — The Classic Era; Vol. V — The Romantic Era.

Ulrich, Homer. *Chamber Music.* The growth and practice of an intimate art. New York: Columbia University, 1948.

An account of the evolution of chamber music to the beginning of contemporary works and a survey of many works during that evolution. Chapters 1—7 cover principal musical events, works, and tendencies over a period of 200 years prior to 1750. For example, there are discussions of chanson to canzone, on sonata da chiesa, on sonata da camera, et. al. Chapter 8—13 follow from the time of Haydn to the contemporary world.

Ulrich, Homer and Pisk, Paul Amadeus. *A History of Music and Musical Style.* New York: Harcourt, Brace & World, 1963.

Historical developments in musical style. Emphasis is placed on the music. Extends from music of Greece and Rome to 20th century music.

Vaughan Williams, Ralph. *National Music and Other Essays.* London: Oxford University, Press, 1963.

Contains lectures presented by R. V. Williams at Bryn Mawr College in 1932 and first published by Oxford U. Press under the titles 1. "National Music", and 2. "Some Thoughts on Beethoven's Choral Symphony with writings on other musical subjects." The third section "The Making of Music" was published by Cornell University Press in 1954. These essays are the substance of lectures given at Cornell University in 1954.

VIII. Instruction, Study, Manuals.

Bacon, Ernst. *Notes on the Piano.* Syracuse, N.Y.: Syracuse University, 1963.
Bacon states: "In short, the book is about the piano in music, or about music in the piano, I can't say which the more." The author comments on: The Performer: of Interpretation, of melody, of form and style, of the hands, of the fingers, of the pedals plus notes on the study, teaching, performance, and the observer.

Gleason, Harold. *Methods of Organ Playing.* 5th ed. New York: Appleton—Century—Crofts, 1962.

Jeans, James Hopwood. *Science and Music.* New York: Macmillan, 1953.
A discussion of those parts of science which are specially related to the questions and problems of music. The information is pre-

438

cise and presented in a simple non-technical way.

Newman, William S. *The Pianist's Problems.* A modern approach to efficient practice and musicianly performance. Rev. and enl. New York: Harper, 1956.
   Designed for the piano student. Chapters on musicianship, technique, practice, performance, steps to learning a new piece, and an approach through sight reading.

Picerno, Vincent. *Essentials of Music: A Course in Foundations of Music.* Minneapolis, Minnesota: T. S. Denison and Co., 1969.
   A basic course in music theory for the non-music student. Covers elements of music, rudiments of music, conducting patterns, score reading, melody writing, beginning harmony, and a brief introduction to a course in music history and literature.

IX.   Jazz Music, Folk Music, Popular Music, Musical Revue, Comedy.

Blesh, Rudi. *Shining Trumpets, A History of Jazz.* 2d ed. Rev. and enl. New York: Knopf, 1958.
   The author presents a broad coverage of the subject. For example, from Africa, from Negro folk music in America, from the fields, the blues, from New Orleans, and the beginning of jazz, classic jazz, Chicago jazz, etc. Musical examples referred to in the text are available in the appendices.

Blesh, Rudi and Janis, Harriet (Grossman). *They All Played Ragtime, the True Story of an American Music.* New York: Knopf, 1950.

The discography and reference lists are excellent. Note the following: the chronology of important Ragtime Dates, Lists of Ragtime Compositions, Record list (disks), Record list (cylinder phonograph records), and a list of Player-piano Rolls.

Charters, Samuel Barclay and Kundstadt, Leonard. *Jazz; A History of the New York Scene*. Garden City, N. Y.: Doubleday, 1962.
Take special note of the discography entitled: "Appendix of Available Recordings of New York Jazz."

Courlander, Harold. *Negro Folk Music, U. S. A.* New York: Columbia University Press, 1963.
Includes discussions on: anthems, spirituals, cries, calls, whooping, hollering, blues, ring games, Creole songs, ballads, minstrelsy, reels, and instruments. A section of over 60 pages is devoted to the actual music and texts.

Eisen, Jonathan. *The Age of Rock, Sounds of the American Cultural Revolution.* ed. New York: Vintage Books, A Division of Random House, 1969.
39 articles which explore some of the ramifications of the rock movement and its music. For example: Wolfe, *The New Music and the New Scene;* Kofsky, *The Scene;* Parsons, *Rolling Stones;* Kempton, *The Beatles;* etc.

Ewen, David. *Complete Book of the American Musical Theater.* New York: Henry, Holt, and Company, 1958.
A guide to more than 300 productions of the American Musical Theater from the Black Crook (1866) to the present; with plot, production history, stars, songs, composers, librettists, and lyricists. Illustrated with photo-

graphs.

Feather, Leonard. *The New Edition of the Encyclopedia of Jazz.* New York: Horizon Press, 1960.

Includes more than 2,000 biographies and chapters on the history and nature of jazz. A comprehensive and valuable reference work on the subject.

Fox Sidney. *The Origins and Development of Jazz.* Chicago: Follett Educational Corporation, 1968.

A study of jazz, contemporary folk music, pop music, and rock. An excellent chart on the "Origins and Development of Jazz" and one on the "Origins and Development of Folk Pop, and Rock." Includes discussions on such developments as Third Stream Jazz, Cool Jazz, Symphonic Jazz, Bop, Progressive Jazz, Folk Rock, Pop Rock, Soul Rock, and many others.

Keil, Charles. *Urban Blues.* Chicago, Illinois: University of Chicago Press, 1966.

The author is primarily concerned with the contemporary "bluesman" and the male role within urban lower-class Negro culture. Included are good chapters on Afro-American music; on Blues Styles: An Historical Sketch; and a section (appendix C) Blues Styles: An Annotated Outline.

Mattfeld, Julius. *Variety Music Cavalcade, 1620-1961.* Englewood Cliffs, New Jersey: Prentice-Hall, Inc., 1962.

A chronological check list of music popular in the U. S. from the time of the Pilgrims to 1962. The list includes hymns, secular and sacred songs, choral compositions, instruments and orchestral works. Listings are based on year of publication or date of copyright.

Ostransky, Leroy. *The Anatomy of Jazz.* Seattle: University of Washington, 1960.

The author relates jazz theory to music theory in general and jazz to the history of music in general. Excellent chapters on the definition of jazz, improvization, elements of jazz, style, and swing. A good selected jazz bibliography.

Panassié, Hugues. *The Real Jazz.* Rev. and enl. ed. New York: Barnes, 1960.

The author presents a carefully selected list of jazz LP's in the appendix.

Schuller, Gunther. *The Hisotry of Jazz.* Volume I *Early Jazz:* "Its Roots and Musical Development." New York: Oxford University Press, 1968.

The origins of jazz: its rhythm, form, harmony, melody, timbre, and improvisation. The big bands in New York and the southwest plus the Ellington style. Excellent glossary on jazz. Excellent discography.

Stearns, Marshall Winslow. *The Story of Jazz.* New York: New American Library, 1964, 1958.

Includes an expanded bibliography and a syllabus of 115 lectures on the history of jazz.

Tanner, Paul and Gerow, Maurice. *A Study of Jazz.* Dubuque, Iowa: Wm. C. Brown Company, 1964.

The historical background and development of jazz in the U. S. A reference or guidebook which will provide a variety of experiences suitable for a course of study on jazz. Excellent reference: "Chart of Jazz Eras." Many jazz scores are illustrated and discussed. Examples of areas covered: Blues, Swing, Funky, Third Stream Music, Soul Jazz, et. al.

Ulanov, Barry. *A Handbook of Jazz.* New York: Viking, 1960.
    The instruments of jazz, the elements of jazz, the language of jazz, the place of jazz, plus many other entries on jazz. Good source material on the musicians of jazz. Also a comparative chronology of jazz and other arts in the 20th century (1900—1957).

_____. *A History of Jazz in America.* New York: Viking, 1957.
    Begins with a discussion of what is jazz, follows with the history of jazz in America from its ancestors, the Negro synthesis, to Cool jazz. Contains a good glossary of jazz words and phrases.

X. Musical Instruments, Instrumentation, Orchestration, Conducting.

Baines, Anthony. *Musical Instruments Through the Ages.* ed. Baltimore: Penguin, 1961. Rev. ed., London: Faber and Faber, 1966.
    Begins with a brief section on primitive and folk instruments followed by chapters devoted to the historical development of each instrument or group of instruments, roughly of the last four or five centuries. There are many photographs and sketches of musical instruments and families of instruments. Note the "Glossary of Technical and Acoustic Terms."

_____. *Woodwind Instruments and Their History.* Rev. ed. New York: Norton, 1963.

443

Part I. The Woodwind Today. Fingering charts, diagrams, woodwind acoustics, tonguing and breathing, transposition, and reed-making. Part II. History and development of the woodwinds beginning with the primitive flute to today's flute systems, oboe systems, clarinet systems, and bassoon systems. Note: "Glossary of Terms."

Berlioz, Hector. *Treatise on Instrumentation.* Enl. and rev. by Richard Strauss, including Berlioz' essay on conducting. New York: Kalmus, 1948.

Not only includes a study of the instruments of the orchestra and their relationship in groups and varied uses but discusses plucked instruments (such as guitar and mandolin), the pianoforte, the organ, band instruments, and early instruments (such as the Serpent). Instruments are discussed, ranges given, transpositions given and how they are used, in orchestra and varied ensembles. Many scores are included with instrumentation. There is also a discussion on conducting and a "Glossary of German Terms and Phrases Used in the Full-Score Examples."

Buchner, Alexander. *Musical Instruments Through the Ages.* Translated by Iris Urwin. London: Batchworth Press Limited, 1961.

The development of musical instruments in pictures from prehistoric times to the present, without extensive written text. 323 instruments are shown in large photographs.

Carse, Adam von ahn. *Musical Wind Instruments;* a history of the wind instruments used in European orchestras and wind-bands from the later middle ages up to the present time. London: Macmillan, 1939.

30 plates show 183 instruments. Also included 41 drawings and diagrams and 11 finger-

ing charts. Republication of original 1939 edition by Da Capo Press, 1965.

Goldman, Richard Franko. *The Wind Band, Its Literature and Technique.* Boston: Allyn and Bacon, 1962.

The author discusses: the European origins of the modern band, the history of band music, instrumentation, band arranging and scoring, repertoire, the conductor, plus other areas related to the wind band.

Krueger, Karl. *The Way of the Conductor, His Origins, Purpose and Procedures.* New York: Scribner, 1958.

Includes sections on: the orchestral origins, beginnings of the modern orchestra, 19th century conductors, the conductor's technique, plus general matters related to the conductor, listener, and audience.

Malm, William P. *Japanese Music and Musical Instruments.* Rutland, Vermont: E. Tuttle Co., 1959.

The book covers three main areas: 1. The history of Japanese music. 2. The construction of the instruments of Japan, and 3. The music itself. Also included: a selective annotated bibliography, a list of recommended recordings, an outline of musical notations, many drawings and photographs of instruments, and a guide to Tokyo's world of Japanese music.

Piston, Walter. *Orchestration.* New York: Norton, 1955.

A one year college course in the art of orchestration. A method of study which is divided into three divisions. The first section discusses the instruments and their playing techniques.

The second section is an approach to the analysis of orchestration, and section three explores problems and solutions in orchestration.

Sachs, Curt. *The History of Musical Instruments.* New York: Norton, 1940.
The first part deals with the primitive instruments, the second part with antiquity, part three with the Middle Ages, and part four with the modern occident. Includes illustrations numbering 24 plates and 167 figures. Extensive references are listed by chapter.

Winternitz, Emanuel. *Musical Instruments of the Western World.* Photographs by Lilly Stunzi. London: Thames and Hudson, 1967.
100 examples of musical instruments in large color photographs representing instruments from the late Middle Ages to the present time. Historical and descriptive material is given opposite each photograph.

XI. Theory, Composition, Form, Notation.

Aldrich, Putnam. *Rhythm in Seventeenth Century Italian Monody, with an Anthology of Songs and Dances.* London: J. M. Dent, 1966.
A discussion of: "musical notation in Italy in the Seventeenth Century." Includes a discussion of some notes used at this time such as: Maxima, Longa, Breve, Semibreve, Minima, Semiminima, Croma and Semicroma. Also a discussion of the four tempi, numbers and proprotions and prolations. "The Relation of Tactus to Meter." Includes an excellent anthology of Italian songs and dances with notes on the transcriptions.

Andrews, Herbert Kennedy. *An Introduction to*

the Technique of Palestrina. London: Novello, 1958.

An examination of Palestrina's technique which is based on linear counterpoint. A discussion of the Ecclesiastical modes in polyphony, the 'Nota Cambiata' and Contrapuntal techniques such as fugue and canon. Generally, a discussion of texture, form, and structure. Many musical illustrations are included.

Apel, Willi. *The Notation of Polyphonic Music, 900–1600.* 5th ed. rev. and with commentary. Cambridge: Medieval Academy of America, 1953.

Presents familiar systems of notation such as white mensural notation as well as comprehensive treatment of various notational systems of the 13th century. Many musical examples are used throughout which are photostatic reproductions of original sources. Several transcriptions are available in the appendix.

Arnold, Franck Thomas. *The Art of Accompaniment From a Thorough-bass as Practiced in the XVIIth and XVIIIth Centuries.* London: Holland, 1961. (Dover ed. 1965, 2 vol. a reproduction of the 1st, 1931, edition).

An exhaustive survey of the historical development of the thorough-bass concept including extensive musical excerpts and interpretative material. Discussions center on the character of the figured bass, accompaniment, forbidden progressions, chords, passing notes, discord, resolution, varieties of notation, etc.

Brindle, Reginald Smith. *Serial Composition.* London, New York: Oxford University Press, 1966.

This study in serial composition includes: constructing the series, melody writing, writing

447

in parts, twelve-note harmony, orchestration, the avant garde, improvisation, free atonalism and free twelve-note composition, among others. Exercises are given in melody writing, part writing, twelve-note harmony, orchestration, etc.

Burkhart, Charles. *Anthology for Musical Analysis.* New York: Holt, Rinehart and Winston, 1964.

An anthology of 108 complete musical compositions which are examples of the chief forms and procedures of Western music from the late 17th century through the mid-20th century. Historical groupings: Part I, Baroque compositions; Part II, Classical compositions; Part III, Romantic and Impressionist Compositions, Part IV, Twentieth Century Composition. Instructor's manual is available which has among other things an analytic comment on 20th century pieces.

Dallin, Leon. *Techniques of Twentieth Century Composition.* Dubuque, Iowa: W. C. Brown, 1957, 1964.

A textbook designed to provide some basic knowledge of 20th century techniques used in composition. The techniques are surveyed and illustrated. Many musical examples illustrate the technique under consideration. The comprehensive musical examples are drawn from works of recognized composers. Partial contents: Harmonic structure, Harmonic Progression, Tonality, Imitative Procedures, the Twelve-Tone Technique, Digest of Forms, and much more.

Hanson, Howard. *Harmonic Materials of Modern Music.* Resources of the tempered scale. New York: Appleton-Century-Crofts, 1960.

A text for the composer: A guide to the analysis of contemporary music. The study of the relationship of tones in melody or harmony. The material is classified and put into logical order chiefly by four devices: interval analysis, projection (construction of scales or chords by any logical process of addition and repetition), involution (the "turning upsidedown of the original chord or scale"), and complementary scales (—"the relationship between any series of tones selected from the twelve-tones and the other tones which are omitted from the series").

Hiller, Lejaren Arthur and Isaacson, Leonard Maxwell. *Experimental Music; Composition with an Electronic Computer.* New York: McGraw-Hill, 1959.

Hodeir, André. *The Forms of Music.* Translated from the French by Noël Burch. New York: Walker, 1966.
A survey of musical forms. The definition of each musical form is given, the study of its structure, and a resumé of its history. Forms are given in alphabetical order. Well-known musical examples are used. About 75 musical forms from various historical periods are discussed.

Leichtentritt, Hugo. *Musical Form.* Cambridge: Harvard University, 1959.
The purpose of the book is to show how the great masters have treated the problems of form and the art of construction. Partial contents: construction of musical phrases; song forms; contrapuntal forms; the suite; theme and variations; the rondo; the sonata; vocal forms; forms of unison music; variation form; sonata form; free forms; concerto form; fantasy; et. al.

Leonhardt, Gustav M. *The Art of Fugue.* Bach's

449

last harpsichord work; an argument. The Hague: M. Nijhoff, 1952.

In 1924, Graeser published his arrangement of the Art of Fugue. This text is an argument that Graeser's thesis was based on wrong fundamental ideas.

Lloyd, Llewelyn Southworth. *Intervals, Scales and Temperaments*. New York: St. Martin's, 1963.

Lowinsky, Edward Elias. *Secret Chromatic Art in the Netherlands Motet*. Translated from the German by Carl Buchman. New York: Russell and Russell, 1967.

The technique and symbolism of the secret chromatic art. A chapter on composers, publishers, and texts in relation to insertion of accidentals and to chromaticism. Generally, a discussion of a technique (the secret chromatic art) developed systematically and used in a number of great works.

Morley, Thomas. *A Plain and Easy Introduction to Practical Music*. Edited by R. Alec Harman. New York: Norton, 1953.

First published in 1597, second edition in 1608. The book is in three sections: 1. Rudiments of music (16th century) e.g. ligatures, metres, mensural notation, teaching to sing, 2. arts of counter point and canon (treating of descant), 3. composition. Many musical examples illustrate his points in the text. All musical examples have been transcribed into modern notation. Many works also appear in original notation (usually in facsimile).

Parrish, Carl. *The Notation of Medieval Music*. New York: Norton, 1957, 1959.

The development of notation from the late

9th century to the beginning of the 15th century. From monophonic notation through the Ars Nova. The text is based on a series of facsimiles from important manuscripts which are arranged in a chronological order. Contents: Gregorian Notation; Secular Monophonic Notation, Early Polyphonic Notation, Modal Notation, Franconian Notation, French Ars Nova Notation, Italian Ars Nova Notation, and Special·Notations of the Late Medieval Period.

Perle, George. *Serial Composition and Atonality.* An introduction to the music of Schoenberg, Berg, and Webern. London: Faber and Faber, 1962.

A comprehensive description and critical examination of the procedures used in the atonal and twelve-tone compositions of Schoenberg, Berg, and Webern. Contents: Tonality, Atonality, Dodecaphony, "Free" Atonality, Nondodecaphonic Serial Composition, Motive Functions of the Set, Simultaneity, and Structural Functions of the Set.

Persichetti, Vincent. *Twentieth-Century Harmony.* Creative aspects and practice. New York: Norton, 1961.

Piston, Walter. *Counterpoint.* New York: Norton, 1947.

A textbook for the student who is well grounded in the principles of harmony. Contents: the Melodic Curve, Melodic Rhythm, The Harmonic Basis, Harmonic Rhythm, Two-part Counterpoint, Motive Structure, Three-part Counterpoint, Counterpoint In More than Three Parts, Invertible Counterpoint, Canon in Two Parts, and Other Types of Canon.

————. *Harmony.* 3d ed. New York: Norton, 1962.

A harmony text that presents the common practice of composers of the 18th and 19th centuries. The harmonic materials and the manner in which they were used.

Sachs, Curt. *Rhythm and Tempo. A Study in Music History.* New York: Norton, 1953.

A study of rhythm and tempo from its primitive stages in history through many styles and periods of time. The meaning of rhythm and tempo throughout the history of music of both the East and West.

Sparks, Edgar H. *Cantus Firmus in Mass and Motet, 1420–1520.* Berkeley: University of California, 1963.

In Part I, a discussion of the methods of treating the cantus firmus from c. 1420–1450; Part II, the Mass and motet from c 1450–1485. (Dúfay, Ockeghem, and their comtemporaries); Part III, The Masses and motets of Obrecht and Josquin des Préz.

Stein, Leon. *Anthology of Musical Forms.* Evanston, Ill.: Summy-Birchard, 1962.

Supplementary source of reference material to *Structure and Style* by L. Stein. Part I is correlated with the text of *Structure and Style.* Part II contains additional compositions for analysis.

————. *Structure and Style.* The study and analysis of musical forms. Evanston, Ill.: Summy-Birchard, 1962.

The majority of the works used fall between 1600 and 1900, although one chapter is devoted to forms before 1600 and another chapter to 20th century techniques. *The Anthology of Musical Forms* by Leon Stein is supplementary musical material to be analyzed and parallels the forms discussed in the text.

Tovey, Donald Francis. *A Companion to "The Art of Fugue" (Die Kunst der Fuge) of J. S. Bach.* London: Oxford University, 1960.
 Part I, an analysis of *Die Kunst der Fuge* of J. S. Bach. Part II, an analysis from other points of view.

melody is horizontal, while the harmonic interest is vertical. The opposite style is polyphonic writing where the emphasis for each voice is placed on its horizontal movement. See *Polyphonic, *Monophonic.

Hopak A folk dance of Russia in lively duple meter. Example: Modest Petrovich Mussorgksy (1839-1881), the "Hopak" from his opera *The Fair at Sorochinsk.* See *Gopak.

Hoquet (Fr.) (ō—kā) (hocquet, (Fr.)) See *Hocket.

Hoquetus In the 13th century hockets, the hoquetus is the part above the tenor.

Hora A round dance or folk dance identified with both Rumania and Israel. A title given to a work arranged by Jascha Heifetz: *Hora Staccato for Violin and Piano* by Diniou.

"Horn" Jazz musicians call any wind instrument a horn.

Horn (1) Generally, a wind instrument made of brass, metal, plastic, animal horns, etc. (2) The modern French horn.

Horn, English See *English horn, *Cor anglais.

Hörner (Ger.) (hĕ(r)'—nå r) Horns.

Horn fifths When an interval of a fifth is reached by similar motion it is said to be a hidden fifth or a horn fifth. The term horn fifth is used as this is a typical writing when natural horns are used. See *Hidden fifths.

Horn, French See *French horn.

Hornpipe (1) (pibgorn). An obsolete instrument of English origin, made with an ox horn, reed and bell. (2) An early English dance in moderate triple meter and later written in a lively $\frac{4}{4}$ time which is usually associated with sailors and the sailors jig-like dance. Examples: Henry Purcell (1659-1695), the "Hornpipe" from his opera *Fairy Queen* and the "Hornpipe" from his *Suite No. 7 in D Minor for Harpsichord.*

Hosanna in excelsis (Lat.)(hō—zä'—nä in ĕgs—chĕl'—sēs) Praise or adoration. "Hosanna in excelsis" is included in the "Sanctus" of the Ordinary of the Roman Catholic Mass. In Latin: "Sanctus, Sanctus, Sanctus, Dominus Deus Sabaoth. Pleni sunt coeli et terra gloria tua.

Hocket A hiccuping effect. A technique used in performance of medieval polyphonic music whereby rests were inserted to break up a melody or melodies so that one part would rest as the other part sounds. This would give the effect of alternating fragmented sections of one or more melodies. A single note or groups of notes would be sung or played using different time values and alternated. One melody thus could also serve as harmony or accompaniment. The "hocket" technique is often used in the development of fragments in larger works and is an important device in tone-row compositions. It is also used as a technique in smaller compositions. For instance, in the fourth movement (theme one) of *Quartet in Bb,* Op. 130 "Scherzoso" by Ludwig Van Beethoven (1770-1827) and in his *Quartet in F,* Op. 135, movement one theme one. Other excellent examples of hocket are available in the *Historical Anthology of Music,* Davison and Apel, ed.

Höhe (Ger.) (hĕ(r) '–å) Height. High register.

Höher (Ger.)(hĕ(r) '–å r) Higher.

Hold Pause. Represented by the character ⌒. See *Fermata.

Holdselig (Ger.) (hōld '–zā–lĭk) Most gracious.

Holler (Field hollers or cries) In Negro folk music a song which was sung unaccompanied while working in the field. It had an irregular beat and an elaborate melody line. The holler was a form of communication among the workers and a work song. The characteristics of bending a tone and slurring are used in jazz music.

Holz (Ger.) (hōlts) Wood or lumber.

Holzbläser (Ger.)(hōlts '–blĕ--zå r) Players of woodwind instruments.

Holzblasinstrumente (Ger.)(hōlts'–bläs–ĭ n–shtrōo—mĕn—tå) Woodwind instruments, e.g., clarinet, oboe, flute, etc.

Holzflöte (Ger.) (hōlts '–flĕ(r)--tå) Wood flute.

Homophonic (homophony) Music having one predominant melody with accompaniment. The interest in the

177